Law, Ethics, and the Office of the Jurist

The genealogy of legal office is pieced together here to rediscover the scope and ambition of a role that has been largely lost to conscious self-reflection. Organized around a concern with the inheritance of juristic traditions, institutions, and forms of life, the contributors to this book take up the question of how a jurist might learn to live, or die, with law. The collection invites readers to reconsider fundamental questions: What responsibilities accompany the jurist's role? How do different traditions conceptualize the ethical obligations of legal interpretation? What happens when established norms face modern challenges? By reconstructing the genealogy of legal office across diverse traditions, the contributors recover aspects of juridical identity that have faded from contemporary awareness.

Law, Ethics, and the Office of the Jurist will appeal to legal scholars, practitioners, and students, as well as those in adjacent fields concerned with professional ethics, institutional history, and the evolving relationship between law and society in our complex global landscape.

Peter Goodrich, Professor of Law at Cardozo School of Law and Visiting Professor in Social Science at NYU Abu Dhabi, is an ardent advocate of argute alliterations and the habile silent 'p', as in raspberry and psittacist, ptomaine, psithurism, and rhubarb. He is the author, recently and most compositely, of *Advanced Introduction to Law and Literature* (Edward Elgar), of *Judicial Uses of Images: Vision in Decision* (Oxford University Press), and also co-editor of *Performing Law* (Cambridge University Press).

Shaun McVeigh is Professor of Law at the University of Melbourne School of Law. His current work is on the continuing influence of colonial legal inheritance and lawful existence in the South.

Discourses of Law

The publisher gratefully acknowledges the support of the Jacob Burns Institute for Advanced Legal Studies of the Benjamin N. Cardozo School of Law to the series *Discourses of Law.*

a GlassHouse Book

For information about the series and details of previous and forthcoming titles, see https://www.routledge.com/Discourses-of-Law/book-series/SE1036.

Law, Ethics, and the Office of the Jurist

Edited by Peter Goodrich and Shaun McVeigh

Routledge
Taylor & Francis Group
a GlassHouse Book

Designed Cover Image: Tianai Song

First published 2026
by Routledge
4 Park Square, Milton Park, Abingdon, Oxon OX14 4RN

and by Routledge
605 Third Avenue, New York, NY 10158

a GlassHouse Book

Routledge is an imprint of the Taylor & Francis Group, an informa business

British Library Cataloguing-in-Publication Data
A catalogue record for this book is available from the British Library

Library of Congress Cataloging-in-Publication Data
Names: Goodrich, Peter editor | McVeigh, Shaun editor
Title: Law, ethics, and the office of the jurist /
[edited by] Peter Goodrich and Shaun McVeigh.
Description: Abingdon, Oxon [UK]; New York, NY: Routledge, 2026. |
Series: Discourses of law | Includes bibliographical references
and index.
Identifiers: LCCN 2025040124 (print) | LCCN 2025040125 (ebook) |
ISBN 9781041113904 hardback | ISBN 9781041113911 paperback |
ISBN 9781003659754 ebook
Subjects: LCSH: Practice of law--Moral and ethical aspects | Lawyers |
Law offices | LCGFT: Law materials
Classification: LCC K115 .L38 2026 (print) | LCC K115 (ebook) |
DDC 340.023--dc23/eng/20250902 LC record available at
https://lccn.loc.gov/2025040124LC ebook record available at
https://lccn.loc.gov/2025040125

ISBN: 978-1-041-11390-4 (hbk)
ISBN: 978-1-041-11391-1 (pbk)
ISBN: 978-1-003-65975-4 (ebk)

DOI: 10.4324/9781003659754

Typeset in Sabon
by Deanta Global Publishing Services, Chennai, India

Contents

Contributors

Anthony Carty (PhD, University of Cambridge; LLM, University College London) was formerly Professor of Public Law at the University of Hong Kong and is currently Visiting Professor at Peking University. He is Professor at Nanjing University, Nanjing, China, and is Emeritus Professor Beijing Institute of Technology, Beijing, China. Among his books, he edited, with J Nijman, *Moral Responsibility of Rulers: European and Chinese Origins of a Rule of Law as Justice for World Order* (OUP, 2018).

Gian-Giacomo Fusco is Lecturer in Law at Kent Law School, University of Kent, Canterbury, UK.

Adam Gearey is Professor of Law at Birkbeck College, University of London. His most recent book is *Poverty Law and Legal Activism: Lives That Slide Out of View* (Routledge, 2026).

Ann Genovese is Professor of Law at University of Melbourne Law School. Her recent books include *Feminist Jurisography: Law, History, Writing* (Routledge, 2023) and, as co-editor, *The Court as Archive* (ANU Press, 2019).

Valérie Hayaert is a cultural historian interested in the relationship between law and the visual arts in Europe over a broad time span, from the 13th century to the present day. A researcher steeped in the humanist tradition, she speaks standing up, not sitting down; this is her *modus explicandi*. Erudition is also a useful adjunct, but she may use it as a royal scepter or as a fool's bauble. She survived Gibbet Hill, and perhaps one day she will digest something about law.

Adil Hasan Khan is Postdoctoral Research Fellow at Melbourne Law School, where his research explores different traditions and modalities of legal education. His work seeks to describe and recover repertoires of training in living well with authority, with others, and their laws.

Timothy Peters is Associate Professor of Law at the School of Law and Society, University of the Sunshine Coast, Sippy Down, Queensland, Australia. His work contributes to both the field of cultural legal studies and the critical histories of the corporate form. He is the author of *A Theological Jurisprudence of Speculative Cinema: Superheroes, Science Fictions and Fantasies of Modern Law* (2021, Edinburgh University Press) and co-editor (with Karen Crawley and Thomas Giddens) of *The Routledge Handbook of Cultural Legal Studies* (2024, Routledge). He is currently working on a monograph project entitled *Corporate Office: From Political Theology to Legal Technologies*.

Serene Richards is Lecturer in Law at NYU London and the author of *Biopolitics as a System of Thought*, published by Bloomsbury in the summer of 2024. She writes on political and legal theory and contemporary continental philosophy.

Adam Sitze is the John E. Kirkpatrick 1951 Professor in Law, Jurisprudence and Social Thought at Amherst College, Amherst, Massachusetts. He is author of *The Impossible Machine: A Genealogy of South Africa's Truth and Reconciliation Commission* (University of Michigan Press, 2013), editor of Carlo Galli's *Political Spaces and Global War* (University of Minnesota Press, 2010) and *Janus's Gaze* (Duke University Press, 2015), co-editor of *Biopolitics: A Reader* (Duke University Press, 2013), and co-translator of Adriana Cavarero's *Thou Shalt Not Kill* (Fordham University Press, 2015) and *Inclinations* (Stanford University Press, 2016). His *A Political Theory of Academic Freedom* is forthcoming from MIT Press in 2026.

Alexander Thom is Leverhulme Early Career Fellow in the School of English, University of Leeds. His research focuses on religion, law, and drama in the English Renaissance. In 2023, Palgrave Macmillan published his first book, *Office and Duty in King Lear: Shakespeare's Political Theologies*. His current monograph project focuses on displacement in English drama (1575–1625). Thom received his undergraduate degree from the University of Melbourne and his AHRC-funded doctorate from the Shakespeare Institute, University of Birmingham. He is also a Trustee and the Membership Officer for the British Shakespeare Association.

Katrin Trüstedt is a research associate with the project "Politics of Appearing" and head of the Program Area "History of Theory" at the Leibniz Center for Literary and Cultural Studies (ZfL) in Berlin. Her research lies at the intersection of literature, philosophy, and law. Her latest book, *Stellvertretung* (advocacy, agency, representation, substitution) (Konstanz University Press, 2022), unfolds the notion of speaking and acting for others in theater, theology, law, and literature.

Gary Watt is Professor in the School of Law, University of Warwick. He is a founding co-editor of the journal *Law and Humanities* and General Editor of Bloomsbury's *A Cultural History of Law*. As a National Teaching Fellow and UK "Law Teacher of the Year" (2009), he delivered rhetoric workshops for the Royal Shakespeare Company for many years. His monographs include *Shakespeare and the Law* (Oxford), *Shakespeare's Acts of Will* (Arden Shakespeare), *Equity Stirring* (Hart), and *Dress, Law, and Naked Truth* (Bloomsbury). His book *The Making Sense of Politics, Media, and Law* (Cambridge) arose from a Leverhulme Major Research Fellowship.

Thanos Zartaloudis is known for his interdisciplinary work at the intersections of law, philosophy, and the humanities more generally. He currently works at the University of Kent, where his research focuses on urban planning, the uses of space, and the protection of youth cultures of play, as well as ecological thinking and practices. Zartaloudis is the author of works such as *The Birth of Nomos* (2019) and *Giorgio Agamben: Power, Law and the Uses of Criticism* (2010), which explore the historical and philosophical foundations of legal systems and political thought.

Preface

The office of the preface is to attract, entice and allure in a probative manner. Written afterwards, it comes before both text and law, as forlorn hope or advance guard, but either way, the dice have been thrown, the Rubicon crossed, and the face of the text is now visible, its aspirations to print manifest. In sum and litigation, it is a prelude, a word which has its roots in *prae-ludium*: foreplay, in theatrical terms rehearsal, and so implies the eros of the project, the desire that motivated, the amities that contributed, and the experiences that formed the narrative that follows. It is here an opening moment of entry into the intimate public sphere, an intersection, in which the desiderations of intellection are glimpsed in the acknowledgement of networks, contacts, friendships, and chance others who have contributed across the borders of the affective spaces of relationships and the boundaries of institutional disciplinary proprieties.

The preface to a work on offices provides a glimpse of the form of life, the persona or mask, that the actor takes up as author, or in our case editors and authors, of a collection of essays that proffer a self-reflexive series of responses to the rapidly changing morphologies and ethical roles of the jurist, the lawyer academical, in the contemporary malaise and political vicissitudes of the university circa 2026. The burden of office, the lingering dignity, and task of acting officially within scholarly settings is complicated by the loss of status and in many instances dismissal, the public assertion of the insignificance of the humanist legal scholar, the doctor or professor of critical theories of law based in any of the disciplines, although here primarily in law schools. That sidelining, loss of *dignitas* and official reluctance if not non-recognition, instigates in its turn a becoming vernacular; it generates uncertainty as to the jurist's own commitment to official undertakings, and an accompanying resistance to the mask of institutional position and hierarchical place. Contestation of the value of the humanities, to which carousel of disciplines the work of the jurist properly belongs, has thrown up the question of what remains of their official role in the scholarly, didactic, and practical professional activities of the denizens of the legal academy.

The impetus and velocity of the current project emerged initially from the desire to reflect upon and comprehend the existential, ethical, and political commitments, if any, that the jurist inhabits and relays as their office, as inherited duty and adopted role. The focus was on the persona of the jurist as a mode of living with law and so acknowledging and at times embracing one's own law, the normative structure that is relayed, consciously and unconsciously, by the law professor and pedagogue in practice. It is a question of conduct and, as Ann Genovese and Shaun McVeigh formulate it in their essay in this volume, of constancy, of the durance of the persona of the jurist, its ethical and expository consistency over time and place. Impetus, as Hobbes formulated it, may be equal in quantity and time, to which we add that it draws too from its locale and connections. Thus, Australian jurists acknowledge the land which they inhabit as having a complex history and intersection of laws, indigenous and colonial, that form a network over time and have to play together in the life lived according to the jurist's conception of their own office and its laws. Office as a form of life, as a structure that is inhabited and made one's own, incorporated, is a jurisographic question of appropriateness to time and place: the ethical and existential commitment to a persona and conduct that connects with, and continues to shape the sensibility and law of the location, the *genius loci.* To this I will add, for a contemporary context, the impetus and ethic of anticipation, of looking ahead and bringing to the roles of teacher and scholar a sense of emergency, the critical creative task of sensing and thinking through what will emerge next, the office and law to come.

The institution, space, and obligations of juristic office are currently particularly contested. Critical legal scholarship was in many facets committed to dismantling the hierarchical reasonings and decisional impositions of law in favour of a greater degree of equality. It now seems as if, to a certain extent, they unwittingly demitted their role, not least by avoiding taking responsibility for their own performances, and their practical office in reproducing the very hierarchy and law that they were supposedly but ineffectually endeavouring to deconstruct and displace. There is thus a degree of conflict in the pages that follow, and the utopics of office are juxtaposed with visceral antagonisms, bristles, and fights. Some are extremely specific, as in Tony Carty's assessment of the offices of journal editor and scholarly reviewer in determining the suitability of submissions for publication. Are there definite criteria and incontestable standards that allow for objective evaluation? Does the editor of an international law journal abandon both ethics and office if they ignore the reasoned criticisms of a reviewer and publish the paper anyway? What does that say of the role of scholarship, the community of thought, and the ethics of editing?

The essay on the office of the reviewer prefigures in many ways the more trenchant historical and political analyses of scholarly conscience, tenure, and the struggles and sufferings of scholars who have seen it as their obligation of conscience to resist fascism, to contest arbitrary decisions, to question the corporatization of the university, and to fight all manifestations of tyranny. The common theme, because we have no desire here to displace, but only to excite the reading of the texts, is that academic freedom, in many cases the privilege of tenure, has at several points come unloosed from the office and ethics to which it is supposed to be tenured, and for which it is held. As Adam Sitze suggests in his erudite elaboration of Kantorowicz's essay on tenure, the word in legal parlance derives from the Latin *tenura* and references the holding of a tenement. "Tenementum" is the term for holding a house or land "of another", as an estate for life and in fee or faith of the ultimate possessor, institution or sovereign. The latter aspect of tenure raises the question, discussed by Sitze and by Alexander Thom, of the university as a corporation sole, the legal fiction of a corporate person that absorbs and is absorbed by the officiant. The *hieros* and hierarchy, the law that imbues the scholar's office, suggest that the political theology underpinning the institution has continuing and forceful effects upon what we mean by academic freedom. If, as Cicero argues, and as is taken up by Goodrich and Zartaloudis, all action is subject to its offices, then in modernity the comparable form of life is one in which the subject as office holder is governed by sovereign forms inherited through the displacement of theology into political and institutional investitures, places, and roles.

From whom office is held, the mediate and intermediate inheritances and fealties is the theme of Alexander Thom's tracing of the surprising extent to which the common law conception of office as ministerial role depends upon the historically Catholic concept of performing vicarious duties, as mouthpiece and instrument of greater theological causes. This explains the plethora of fiduciary or faith-based obligations that still suffuse institutional offices and which gain modern expression in Timothy Peters' excoriation of the responsibilities of corporate office holders. He argues for an expansion of the concept of corporate stakeholder, a version of governance that takes account of the social investment of the many and the ecological rights of the earth. In a similar spirit, Adam Gearey addresses what he coins as the law of bearing, the gestural and performative role of the Priest, as Christian minister, in using faith to open access to a new life. A complex metaphor that leads in Gary Watt's entertaining account of homophonia of the jawist, in which consistency of sound or monotony leads in his view to the juristic obligation to listen, to give time and attend, as an interlude to the incessant verballing that lawyers and their texts promulgate in law school, and in the public sphere. The call for opening and openness to minor languages and less sovereign discourse is also the theme of Valérie Hayaert's iconography of images of *Justitia* and of Liberty – *Ecce lex* – and argues for a more creative and forward-looking symbolism of justice. Art can capture hearts and lead the cause. In Gian-Giacomo Fusco's account of Dante's *Inferno*, the same theme emerges, a call for a poetic practice in which the jurist has the office of custodian and curator of the textual means of building worlds.

Cycling between theological and secular, legal and political, further chapters address the different structures and professions that provide the emblems and examples of the role that different offices play in the fabrication of the social. For Serene Richards, it is the relation of habitus to human life that defines the *modus vivendi* of the officiant subject as tied to their institutional home and in constant dialogue with it. As Trüstedt puts it in her coruscating account of Kafka's office, we are always already entangled in our offices and it is our struggle to disentangle, to engage and escape, that defines the literature of the encounter with institutional habitus. What is most apparent is that for Kafka office was an ambivalent reference, the source of his brilliant literary excursions in which his antipathy to his bureau is paradoxically the antagonistic relation, the love affair with all its disappointments, that sparks the comedy and complexity of his work.

We end then with a radical attraction to a juristic office that is arguably dying. What Ann Genovese and Shaun McVeigh argue for is a jurisographic constancy, fidelity over time to the cause of living according to one's own law, the embrace of political faith that is true to family and to an inhabitation of public institutions. Theirs is a subtle homily, one might say *pro officio mea*, which is to say a defence of inscribing in practice and over time the lineaments of one's own embodiment and expression of a singular universal, the unique plurality that is one's law. The freedom of one's role, a creative relation to tenure and tenement, is a version of a Nietzschean choosing of necessity and of creatively experiencing that liberty and liberality that exist within the confines of institutions and collective life. A matter of habitus in the sense of habiliment and habitude, but also in the alternate meaning of haecceity and haptics whereby, in the old legal expression *habitus et reputatus*, we are held to our lawful desire, our unconscious dispositions and to the cloth or for the academic the gown and mortar board that symbolically we wear. *Habitus*, to borrow again from the Latin, references the state of a thing, a constancy, and by extension the deportment and appearance of law that we manifest. Over time that is the expression of our nature, quality, and character, extending into our feeling and disposition, the affective state that draws us away from and then back to the office we inhabit. Where Gearey talks of "a disgrace to the cloth", a minister who ought to be defrocked, removed from office, the more positive connotations relate to what Gary Watt depicts as a synaesthetic sensibility. It is an ethical sensibility that opens office to the bodies that occupy it and to a tradition of epistemic faith and community of thought. For the jurist this is a commitment to dialogue and transmission, the relay of theoretical traditions as manifestations of historical lives that formed the institution and moulded the offices that we contemporary scholars inhabit. Facile though it may seem, painful though it may be to admit, fearsome to view, it means taking up the inherited apparatus of the jurist and committing to methodology, to a genuine sense of law as a liberal science. This requires a focus on knowledge rather than expression of mere opinion, an attachment to reason as opposed to pure assertion, and an affection for coherence in the face of harangues, invectives, and the other rhetorics of exclusion and hate. For the jurist it is a matter of choice and of judgement, a willingness to revise and remediate their historical dialogue and substantive inquiries to the variable forms of their offices, meaning most simply the times, places, technologies, and contexts of the contemporary.

Chapter 1

Professing law

An excursus

Peter Goodrich and Thanos Zartaloudis

In the wake of the global pandemic – an event for which mourning is still necessary and will be for generations to come – the place, parameters and practices of office have become contested in a dual sense. The first interrogation is structural and chorographic or, to coin a phrase, jurisgraphic, a description of legal spaces and persons. The office as a physical space, most usually in a corridor, a community of doors and nameplates of office holders, was an institutional *insignum,* a loaded signifier and habitus. It had to be abandoned, during government-imposed shut down, for a period of years, as having become a locus of potential danger, of contagion, and then of masked return. The theatrical comedy of vacated and then hybrid offices posed neo-materialist and existential questions, an ambivalence perhaps, of locale, corporeality and purpose. The office space that existed in the community of workplaces, in the set of chambers, the firm, the lawyers' collective, the faculty, department, studios, as hubs, meeting places, could no longer be complacently assumed, or hidden behind.

To some extent, corporate identities broke apart or perhaps revealed their concealed essence. The office moved and in moving became mobile, subtle flex, and as analysed in the following collect and collection, fundamentally changed. The office, however, primarily controls change. It demarcates the acts it shall hold as officiations and work, and the acts it shall consider an aggression or an egression, a going out. An eminently religious act and work to mark the place and voice of power (*opificium*, genitive *opis* – power, might) vacant, by definition, for it must guarantee itself by itself. Marked by a door, a portal, an ever-sliding gate (*portcullis*, *porte à coulisse* (mod.Fr.)), looking like a seemingly insignificant ornament to the office space it guards. Yet, revealing itself to be an ever potential and active filtering mechanism (from Latin *colatus* to filter, to strain), the place of the mouth (*mund*, in the old Germanic tongue), the place of a projected act, an *opus mundi*, officiating worlds, a motor of official realization.

DOI: 10.4324/9781003659754-1

In one version of mourning for the stability and recognition of *officium*, the certainties of institutional role and duty, it was as if the analyst's couch had died. A particular symbol, and in the case of the psychoanalytic chaise longue a specific function of recumbency and repose, of laying down the mind to let the unconscious appear in a specific environment, corporeal and dialogic placement, affect and aura, evaporated; a vanishing act. Did it matter that Freud's collection of Egyptian statues, the barrister's shelves of official reports, or the professorial array of jurisprudential texts and stacks of paper, quills, pens and inks, were missing from or displaced in the dialogue? The carefully chosen works of art, the window, the desk, the colour of the wall, all had a function and location in the physical habitus of office and in being left behind became strange when, in altered form and virtual valence, they were returned to in the aftermath of separation. The key point, the opening of the office door, is resident in the ambiguous sense of mattering, such that office and *officium* or conduct are indissolubly connected. The architectural space which pre-exists and survives any particular holder of office brings with it not simply a sense of something more, be it tradition, stability, conscience or critical possibility, but also an existential commitment and connection to collective projects and purposes. Being in the office is integral to the office of being, and so ceiling, walls, colour, carpets, art, effluvia, ledges, shelves and windows are all connected to the parts played by bodies that circulate or recline, stand, sit or pace in the room that takes the shape and role of institutional place, and formal, meaning official and normative habitation. By the same token, ideational presence also has an irreducible physical manifestation, costumes, props, inherited roles. The return to office reminds that the face, visage or vizard, frons or front, is much more than a screen headshot presence, a pixelated look from behind a glass or more likely plastic window. The face is the body, the entire integument, carapace or covering that looms and pulsates, moves and gestures, blushes and flows. If only momentarily, for the return to the office reveals a pixelation behind another pixelation, a picture of the elemental (pix and the first syllable of element linked to denote pixel), the most basic form of matter, faced off.

The ontographic point is that "everybody has to be somewhere" – and that somewhere, meaning passage, moving through, being with, in the sense of exposure and opening to environs, architecture, route and atmosphere are integral to the being, the poor theatre, that enacts and performs any office and in our instance that of the jurist and jurisprudent. The second sense of contestation of office relates precisely to the disinvestment in the abandoned institutional space, the structural and architectural habitus, the norms and presuppositions that carry the quotidian as an epiphenomenon of structures. There is an opportunity and opening to rethink the conduct of office that is occasioned by being out of the office, mobile, transitional and in collision with the hybridity of its novel forms of instantaneity and installation. There are new choices, novel ambulatory and virtual spaces, inside and exterior to the architectures that previously housed law faculties and their congregation of jurists. What Lauren Berlant coined as the intimate public sphere has its counterpart in the inquiry into office as an ambulant form of life, the duties of the office holder no longer so obviously architecturally bound to institutional functions, a degree of individuated responsibility and expanded choice of ethics, practices, and the duties of role playing. As Dorsett and McVeigh have argued, updating the itinerant common law as jurisographic, the common law that the jurist carries and transmits becomes visible and ambulant as conduct and apprehension in the city, a narrative of novel encounters, unforeseen intersections, as also imbibition of new atmospheres, trajectories of the semiotics and dialogics of diasporic lawscapes.[1]

At a structural level, indeed as an infrastructural network of passages, perceptions and performances there is both a literal divestment and institutional dissipation of legal academic officialdom, at the same time that the office holder is catapulted into the world, on camera, zoomnambulating, and is both more visible and potentially vulnerable. Social media accentuate this trend, channeling office ever back into action, turning office into performance of duty and role; its originary element. It becomes, anew, an endogenous conduit of institutional functions and goals, and in being potentially always visible and recorded, it is always in both personal and collective senses accountable. In one connotation, this means that office – in Agamben's associative chain, habit and habitus, costume and place – enters the world and becomes a visible passage through public space, while equally entailing that the eye of the world and the demands of the videosphere also enter the office, face to face.[2] There is no *hors d'office,* nor any outside of the roles with which it mingles and the spaces it occupies. What was classically termed the

1 See, specifically on itinerant office as everyday life, see McVeigh, 'Jurisprudent of London: Arts of Association' (2016) 20 *Law Text Culture* 189; and for development of themes related to office, *persona* and obligation, see McVeigh, 'Afterword: Office and the Conduct of the Minor Jurisprudent' (2015) *UC Irvine Law Rev.* 499; McVeigh, 'Reciprocal Relations: Formations of the Office of Legal Scholar' (2018) 9(2) *Jindal Law Rev.* 231; and 'Obligations of Office', in Daniel Matthews and Scott Veitch (eds), *Law, Obligation and Community* (Abingdon: Routledge, 2018) 234.

2 Giorgio Agamben, *The Highest Poverty: Monastic Rules and Form-of-Life* (Palo Alto: Stanford University Press, 2013) 13–19, on habit, habitus, habiliment, habitation and inhabiting.

dignity – the Roman title of administrative offices being *notitia dignitum*, ensigns of honour – has its place and obligations, while the *persona* of the office holder, their charisma and role, has variable links or degrees of attachment to the entailments and form of life that the lawspace and institutional *officium* relay. Thus, in McVeigh's pioneering work on the topic of itinerancy amongst jurists, it is precisely the jurisprudent on the bus, traversing the city, who must inhabit the role and mobile office of the self-conscious jurist, the critical legal theorist, as that of voyager and spiritualist, a bearer of the local legal form of life, traversing an indexical symbolic history of urban landmarks and events embedded in the chatter of stones, legible in the monumental city; a polis as the archgate of the office-portal, the originary act of guarding the gate through which one enters or leaves the system of acts and works.[3] The jurists' office is their journey, literal and metaphorical, as that which assembles their sense and ethic of the juridical, of the public spaces and signs, the legal histories, normative constraints, facilities, customs and conflicts that are inscribed in the architecture, monuments, symbols and memories of the city as marks of dignity and as material manifestations of an imperfect inheritance and of opaque or yet to be determined prospects.

The office of the jurist – in Watt's eloquent coinage that of the jawist – in the Western tradition, has always been an ambivalent one ranging from servant of the sovereign (*delegatus maiestatis*) to glossatorial custodian of sacred texts, to lowly bureaucrat and filing clerk, to the humanist role that the modern and confused professorial tradition of *Ignoramus*, of "lawyers academical," in the main, inherits.[4] The paradox of the contemporary, often hybrid, office of the (academic) jurist is that it exists to transmit a law that the jurist doubts, and with which

3 See particularly McVeigh, 'Jurisprudent of London', 190.

4 The term is, of course, derived from George Ruggle, *Ignoramus; Comœdia* [1615] (London: Payne, 1788), and in translation, see Tucker (ed.), *A Critical Edition of Ferdinando Parkhurst's Ignoramus, The Academical Lawyer* (Abingdon: Routledge, 2018). The modern profession of jurist, post the expansion of universities and of law schools since the 1960s has been increasingly academic and in the UK qualified more often by a PhD than by entry into or extensive practice in the profession. For an interesting history of the university profession of literature and criticism, that is not without parallels, see John Guillory, *Professing Criticism: Essays on the Organization of Literary Study* (Chicago: Chicago University Press, 2022) "The critics take up their megaphones ... in a micro public sphere of like-minded professors", a surrogate politics outside of their specialism and "[the overstatement of aim is the principal form of professional deformation resulting from uncertainty about the social effects of literary study." (72, 79).

she exists in a tenuous relation. To doubt the law or criticize the norms relayed in pedagogic and scholarly spaces of transmission has only the most indirect of effects, their velitations lacking liturgical impact, word against sword. They have a marginal degree of status but no authority. The jurist necessarily contributes indirectly to the law, has no authority as a source of law and while offering critical accounts of disciplinary and normative social forms does not in any direct way contribute to them. In the classical tradition the philosophical, literary and poetic sources of law – *auctoritas philosophorum et poetarum* – were at best minor sources, eccentric gestures that added style and a certain classical aura of *elegantia iuris* to strictly juridical texts and judgements. Such additions, however, need to be rethought and revived, with and against their past. They were of a stylistic and epigrammatic kind but were not only or simply incidental, merely minor keys of a major register. It is the argument of *Offices of the Jurist* that they occupy an unacknowledged space and potential, existential and political, ethical and administrative, at the frontier of the encounter of law and world, the legal and the social. Such offices form an opportunity, a mantle, dignity and form of life, both academic and juristic, to be taken up and activated as aesthetic and performative forms of ethical and normative activity, inside and outside the juridical institutions and architectural spaces of law's monumental urban presence.

The holy lawyer

If absence of content, other-worldliness, is the key to the spiritual tradition in the West, the holy lawyer, a coinage both Victorian and contemporary, in fact returns to the roots of *officium* which are cenobitic and Christian, forming a conduit, presence and doctrinal architecture of natural and so also ethical law.[5] For Cicero, and then later, for example, for Saint Benedict and the monastic order that carries his reformist name, office meant *regulae vitae*, the ordering of life, both daily routine, decorum, duties, places and roles, as well as emotional states, that were all dictated by the apprehension of divine will through its tellurian delegates. Thus, the hierarchical order gives form to life, and in

5 This essentially religious sense of a self-negating ethics of service or self-sacrifice has roots in Roman law, if not before, but is picked up in the sense of holy life-style in Edward O'Brien, *The Lawyer, His Character and Rule of Holy Life, after the Manner of George Herbert's Country Parson* (1842). For a modern excursion, and my primary source of entry into the idea, see Marett Leiboff, *Towards a Theatrical Jurisprudence* (Abingdon: Routledge, 2020) on the holy actor.

Cicero's opening salvo, "no part of life ... can be without office," meaning that all facets of being and relation are governed by rules of conduct, an ethics and etiquette, manners of speech, places and authority of expression, counsel and discipline. Such is the theology of hierarchy and pre-assignment of social reason and efficacy seeking concordance and communication understood as sharing, holding in common, making general. Office is the medium of the social that later would be termed, by the estimable Barnabe Barnes, "harmonious consent or concordance whose ground in unison consisteth of a medium which is the moderator or navel-string of this musical ... and mystical accord of the numberlesse starres and planets" and dictates the specific "divine centres, or moderators, which I do thus denominate, define, and distribute," namely "Temperance, Prudence, Justice, and Fortitude, shadowed ... in the Treasurer, Counsellor, Judge and Souldier."[6]

The four cardinal virtues, grounded in what Barnes, translating the antique conception of *nomos mousikos*, songs of law, or for Cicero *carmen necessarium*, as rhythms of social existence and interaction, patterns of conduct, inscribes as the hierarchy of the common law, Inns of Court, and sovereign dispensations of office. There was, as Zartaloudis well expounds, a play and interchange between music and law, dance and regimen.[7] The *nomos* of *officii* is far more than simply law, but rather incorporates "customary practices, a way of behaving and a certain sense of ordering or appropriateness [that] pre-exist the legal sense of rule making" (391). The stuff out of which the *officii* are eventually made. As modes of belonging, spaces in a communal hierarchy, the classical Roman tree of offices, as noted, was termed *notitia dignitatum*, the orchestration of notes and signs of dignity, places in social rationality that pre-exist and survive any singular occupant, yet provide the persona, the mask that the ephemeral individual holder of that space will occupy. The building or form doesn't die and so too the office lives on and in many senses is historically precisely what is passed on, an inheritance, precedent and predisposition that has to be spiritually taken up, with ceremonies of investiture, rites of acquisition and stages of taking up the pulpit, podium, lectern or microphone. To be in office, for the jurist, was classically to take on a role as medium and conduit of an ethico-juridical inheritance, a form of life and authorization of role and living function. Barnes talks of "provident circumspection," a weighing of all things in the balance of reason, but the element of providence in the classical functionary role of jurist should not be diminished in that it

6 Barnabe Barnes, *Foure Bookes of Offices* (London: Bishop, 1606) A iii v.
7 Thanos Zartaloudis, *The Birth of Nomos* (Edinburgh: Edinburgh University Press, 2018) ch 10 on 'Nomos Mousikos'.

was explicitly a religious role and the office was that of transmission of the scale, strata and system of laws dressed in the cloths and robes, wigs and gowns of ecclesiastical and royal inheritance. Hence perhaps some of the contemporary jurist's unease in their official status, its (political) theology, the decaying tatters of ceremony and investiture, the marks of a fraying dignity concealing an empty throne, without which no Kingdom has a garden of life.

There was a symbolic status and a certain cenobitic or monastic vocational aura and purpose to the juridical definition and delimitation of the *notitia dignitatum*, formulated by Selden as *Titles of Honor*, defined as the notations of "inner dignity and greatnesse of Spirit" evidenced in virtue – *Nobilitas Christiana* – and in learning. The titles of honour were offices whose juristic content was circumscribed by the "varietie of Lawes" generated by and intermingled with "Morall Philosophie [and] Civil Learning."[8] Citing Cicero, the mark of legal office was most broadly "Mores Instituta & Disciplinas" the institution of morals and disciplines, meaning learning. The purpose of office was to pass on "the rich and most select Stores and Cabinets of Civill Learning" rather than fettering it in "the narrow captivity of some Profession."[9] The juristic office in its widest and arguably classical definition was that of inscribing the variegated institutions of life, and in a phrase revived and coined in contemporary psychoanalytic valences by the late Pierre Legendre, the jurist's task and purpose, their office par excellence was *instituere vitam*, meaning their role was to institute a common life, a genealogy of places and of the administrative roles that marked the form of being in common, the public spaces and formations of discourse, that the subject joins.[10] The jurist holds the keys to the social by means of determining the instituent form of public life, of living together, and the spaces of its promulgation, the mandates of social discourse as effective speech. It is here that Agamben, in parallel to Legendre, draws on the Greek concept of *leitourgia* or liturgy as tying office, in early Christian thought, to the concept of symbolic action, as the necessary link between official discourse and social effect. Doing one's official duty is to engage in a ministerial action that puts the message of the superior, and for the jurist this means the edict or rule of law, into effect.

8 John Selden, *Titles of Honor* (London: Stansby, 1631) Preface 5–6 (n.p.).
9 Selden, *Titles of Honor*, Dedication, 4. (n.p.).
10 A reference that has been much debated in relation to Roman law, but can be found in D.1.3.2., in the translation of the Greek by the Swiss commentator Godofredus. See, *Corpus iuris civilis cum Godofredi et aliorum notis. Postrema editio omnibus prioribus auctior & emendatior* (Amsterdam: Elsevier, 1663) 78.

The office of the jurist is thus vicarious, a ministering of the prior and precedent, the higher and holier, in the role of vicar or delegate of the sovereign whose power, as Hobbes noted, exceeds that of all other earthly beings – *non est potestas super terram quæ comparetur ei.* Duty is carriage, in essence a religious role or service of a message that exceeds the existential being or will of the subject and forms the personage and investment *in officio* that marks the title holder, the office bearer, as competent and authorized to effectuate the message that they carry. The jurist as vicar – vicarious – is a ministerial figure giving effect through promulgation and practice to those institutions and circumscriptions that make up the institution of life, that render society governable. It is through offices that the efficacy of messages circulate and law as ethical practice is transmitted. It is the offices as sliding doors, that mark portals of social life, that secure the symbolic production of certain actions and certain words, forming or shifting the real. These, in Sterne's language, are the opificers of governance, the visible symbols that give effect to what is represented, as pedagogic message and as legal practice.[11] The official is in more negative parlance a functionary, someone who makes the system work by performing its theatrical and liturgical actions, thus ruling and administering, rather than governing in the powerful sense of the *mysterium* or *imperium*, encapsulated in the baroque maxim, *rex regnat sed non gubernat*, that the sovereign rules but does not govern.[12] The titles of honour, the titular designations of dignities, the *officia* of institutional life are the means and life blood of sociality, the spaces of communal existence as recognizable sites of action and dialogue, medium and conduit or introit to collective forms of regulation and social rationality. The office is in this theory the form of life of human being and has neither outside, nor any out of office in administerial argot, or, to coin a phrase, *il n'y a pas de hors bureau.* The negative sense of the functionary, the minister of the law, needs to be appreciated anew then as not a mere virtual environment (a bureau-cracy), but the very environment of the genealogy of virtue as work (*opera*).

Meanwhile, the task of the holy lawyer, the historical figure resurrected by Leiboff in her work on poor theatre and jurisprudence, is that

11 Laurence Sterne, *The Life and Opinions of Tristram Shandy, Gentleman* [1759–1767] (London: Penguin, 1978) 214.

12 For extensive discussion of this maxim see Michel Senellart, *Les Arts de gouverner: Du regimen medieval au concept de gouvernement* (Paris: Seuil, 1995) at 40, referencing Hobbes: "One can now say that the moment has arrived when the King rules but does not govern". And see also Agamben, *The Kingdom and the Glory: For a Theological Genealogy of Economy and Government* (Palo Alto: Stanford University Press, 2011) 68 et seq.

of sympathy and is a revival of a scholarly legal tradition, associated above with Selden, that understands such office as based in but unfettered by positive, black letter law. In legal argot, judge and jurist should always have an eye to equity and to doing justice to those present. Like all rituals and rules, an act shifts and conceals its nature in order to perform itself, without occasionally drawing inevitable attention to its enactment as an act of (human) work. The references to equity and justice are historically citations to canon law, as the antiquaries note, but in modern address, the holy lawyer is holistic rather than institutionally religious or in some doctrinal sense an expression of holiness.[13] There is a sense, of course, in which the figure derives expressly from Christian tradition and practices, and certainly the exposition of the holy life of the lawyer in O'Brien's treatise from 1842 is Anglican in the established sense, and in his chapter on the apposite knowledge for the office and role ethics of a lawyer, the starting point is divine law and justice that "gives to each their own" according to natural and moral precepts. Such law is "universal, perpetual, and binding all persons everywhere," and can be found, we learn, "in the recesses of his own heart, and in the written records, and in the living ministers of God's holy word."[14]

The powers of reason and moral law, drawn from the study of natural law and philosophy, provide an expansive set of authorities and investiture of office which Leiboff picks up in the contemporary resonance of accessing the corporeal roots and sensors of responsiveness and sympathy as modes of just presence and judgement. Focused on the theatre of trial as the exemplum of legal relation, the skills of the actor in embodying the affect of the other come to the fore. The lawyer committed to an ethical role and fiduciary office, whether as judge or as advocate, is defined atmospherically and affectively as one capable of empathic understanding; quite directly one who experiences what takes place as such. Audition, a legal hearing, requires the skills of awareness and of noticing as modes of attentiveness to physical antennae and responses as well as to, or in and through, texts. If the holy lawyer seeks to empty the self in service to a higher law, the gnostic jurist performs a contrary motion: not an emptying out, but a filling up with the immediate, sensory data of the world. The one aspires to transcend the persona through duty, the other to immerse it completely in the materiality of practice.

13 Leiboff, *Theatrical Jurisprudence*, at 125 warning "not to mistake the holy actor with holiness in a religious sense, and the holy lawyer isn't holy in the religious sense either."

14 O'Brien, *The Lawyer*, 65–66.

Gnostic offices – roistering criticism

The archetype of the holy lawyer is in current valence an attempt to advocate for an ethical role and holistic practice of juristic office as an active and affective engagement, a mode of presence and awareness. It is to institute life in the sense of performing and passing on the structures of engagement and the patterns of conduct that best facilitate belonging as mutual recognition and a sense of common being.[15] The jurists' competence, their aptitude for such a holistic and ethical as well as legal role, is not without contestation. The contemporary form of life, the patterns of institution and administration, following in the critical wake of Zarathustra's declaration of the death of God, and the subsequent postmodern hewing away of the grand narratives of social totality, both lead to a lived sense of a certain demission or inauthenticity of the jurist and specifically the dilemma of the critical legal scholar who has to teach a law that propagates hierarchies, divisions and inequalities that they resist. The jurist, to use the broadest of terms for the "lawyer academical" as Ruggle depicts the prolix professors, has never had an entirely independent or unambiguous official role.[16] The concept of the holy lawyer has lengthy roots in the theological history of law's offices, the modes of investiture of members of the Bar, and the ethical role and lifestyle that the institution both taught and imposed. From the obvious historical details of gowns, robes, wigs and other incidents of costume, as well as the architecture of thrones and bars, the concept of religion and law lying down together is pervasive in the tradition, and the Inns of Court were expressly modelled on the nine orders of angels, conceived as represented hierarchically and juridically on earth by the profession. The concept, for our purposes, however, of the holy lawyer is of embodying a role and in critical fashion turning it to profane and tellurian, meaning egalitarian purposes. It is a question of a certain self-sacrifice in the sense of coming to appreciate the emptying of ego that is necessary to play a role, inhabit the other, put on a mask, in a world of masks.

The old texts have a certain sense of what Vico termed the university of the body as a necessary prerequisite to internalising a role and

15 The classical texts tend to speak of law in terms of *constituere vitam*. As to etymology it is only the prefix, the difference between *con* and *in statuere*, that distinguishes the definitions, static and active, constituent and instituent or in the latter sense productive of institutions. See Gratiani *Decretum* 2.1 *lex est constitutio populi* ... and Isidore of Seville, *Etymologiae* V.v. *Ius civile est quod quisque populus vel civitas sibi proprium humana divinaque causa constituit.*

16 James Gordley, *The Jurists: A Critical History* (Oxford: OUP, 2013) at 275 – *ubinam gentium summus*?

playing a part. For Barnes, the desiderata for the office of counsellor, to which jurisdiction the jurist belongs in however minor a sense, includes keeping the body "in health by withdrawing all evil humors and infirmities from the head." He continues to opine, drawing support from Salust, Tacitus, Cicero and Caesar, that the "outward senses properly perform [the] inward Offices" (25). Thus counsellors were expressly eyes, ears, and hands of their sovereign, their office being to embody that part of Leviathan that will benefit most from their performance. To be a part object, a member that works for the whole, conceived as sovereign and total remains a structural part of the office and position, even when translated into the disciplinary context of juristic and academic role. How then does one embody legal knowledge and live according to one's own conception of law? What conduct, conversation, manner of living can a critical legal academic, an oppositional professor, perform and play?[17]

The starting point is gnosis in a profane and positive or secular sense and sensibility. Take gnosis in its uncorrupted historical meaning, inscribed for this occasion, as a cutting loose or dividuation that chooses to apprehend nature, environment and socius, self and other in the most immediate of sensory fashions. The gnostic, and the term is wantonly laden with heresy and anti-Christian sentiments, is simply one whose office is no longer defined by religious institutions, by belief in or denial of a divine entity, by the paltry pair, the bland binary of theism or atheism.[18] The gnostic, lower case g, in this definition is rather to be understood in terms of the immediacy of affect, the laughter of the body, the positivity and materiality of electing the manner, the conduct and carriage of any specific knowledge and institutional inhabitation. The laughter is *jouissance*, the energy of being, the *hylos* as materiality is the driving force of gnosis which is here defined as the desire to know more in a profane rather than religious sense, for human environmental purposes in the Anthropocene, rather than and in preference to the religious quest to believe in what is not. The two are not strictly opposed but are historically and institutionally in conflict, meaning most specifically that *nomos* as manner of living, conduct of an office or form of life is the promise to live according to one's own law. This, to play

17 On the *topos* of *nomos*, see Thanos Zartaloudis, *The Birth of Nomos* (Edinburgh: Edinburgh UP, 2019) xxxviii: "The early *nómos* is, perhaps, in a modern sense, an objective rule or ordering, but it is not separable from the life to which it applies. It is not a form that can be distinguished from the living that it 'commands'."

18 On which history, see Jacques Lacarrière, *The Gnostics* (London: Peter Owen, 1977).

upon etymologies, means not to repeat as in religion – *re-ligare*, and also *re-legere* being of uncertain root – but to invent, to bind as a choice of one's own. What Agamben lengthily traces as the liturgical function of office, the homonymy of "your *officium* and your *effectum*" has to take the profane form of choosing to critically apprehend, to challenge and invent the role anew.[19] The critic's dilemma is that of refusing the untrammelled or unconscious tralatition, transmission of the institution of life, the inherited *nomos*, in favour of youth, critical resistance, and a sense of the irony of office as a challenge to critical authenticity and presence.

Increasingly, the jurist doesn't matter or at least the critical legal scholar is caught between the poles of desiring to have effects and promulgate change, while simultaneously vacating the traditional offices that would make such difference at least marginally possible. The two poles were instituted as codependent. It is that paradox of affectively rejecting the office that constitutes your social *persona* and material role, the deep ambivalence of putting on a mask that does not fit, that shapes the questioning of office and specifically a return to the juristic sense of *nomos* and office, the institution of life, as the critical construction of a manner of acting, a theatrical performance that is both ludic and comedic, as well as tragic. In the latter sense, the comic aspect of an ambivalence towards office is that of appreciating the fragility of the position, the transferability of the places, and the choice of inhabitation that facilitates a conduct becoming, or embodiment of an office and role singularly your own, finding your orthodoxy in a sea of doorways.

Office as personality

For Cicero, and Agamben repeats this at length in his archaeology of duty,

> there is no phase of life, whether public or private, whether in business or in the home, whether one is working alone or dealing with another, can be without its ethical obligations (*vacare officio potest*); on the discharge of such *officia* depends all that is honorable, and on their neglect all that is dishonorable in life.[20]

19 Giorgio Agamben, Opus Dei: *An Archaeology of Duty* (Palo Alto: Stanford UP, 2018).

20 Cicero, *De Officiis* 1.2.4. 6–7, translation modified, usefully discussed in Nicholas Heron, *Liturgical Power: Between Economic and Political Theology* (New York: Fordham UP, 2018) 122–123.

The paradox, then, is not that we are trapped by our *officium*, but that we are constituted by it. To critique the law from within is not to speak from a place outside office, but to consciously reshape the very material – the conduct, the persona, the performance – of which the office is made. The critic's rebellion is not an exit, but a renovation from the inside out. Later in the same work, Cicero, who is writing to his son, borrows from the opening of Justinian's *Institutes*, a title and a verb rather than a noun of considerable import, to assert that the greatest of all virtues is knowledge – *sapientia* – and that such sapience is knowledge of things divine and human – *rerum est divinarum et humanarum scientia*.[21] The coincidence of the definition of law, following on immediately from the opening definition of the virtue of justice, is significant. Thus, for the *Institutes*, legal knowledge is equally of things divine and human, knowledge of the difference between justice and injustice – *iuris prudentia est divinarum atque humanarum rerum notitia, iusti atque iniusti scientia*. What is at issue in both cases is an inculcation of virtue, knowledge of the needs of others, both community and friends. There is a structure to be transmitted not simply of duty but of office understood as an ethics, a habitual appreciation of the role of structures in both history and conduct. As Agamben notes, "*officium* is what renders the life of human beings governable, the virtues are the apparatus that allows one to actualize this governance. The treatment of duties as virtues and of virtues as duties is the most ambiguous legacy that Cicero's work was to transmit to the Christian West."[22] It is in that tension, in the inclusive exclusion marked by the binaries of law and office, structure and ethics, obligation and choice, that the paradox of office as lawful conduct emerges over the *longue durée* of the juridical tradition.

If we are always caught up in *officium* as the apparatus through which the social can be accessed and structured, quotidian life experienced, then our office understood as our virtue rather than as necessary duty should be a chosen necessity. Where the early law of the *Digest*, relayed later by Cicero, addresses the principal purpose of office, it is to give form to life and to generate that which conforms, the subject as instituted. The disputed Latin phrase, *instituere vitam*, references the assignment of social place, the sense of belonging that so challenges the critic as apparent or self-designated outsider. Office, as the modality of instituting life, has no outside but only an exterior of interiority; or, as Cicero formulates it "quibus in omnis partis usus vitae conformari possit" (by means of which the enjoyment of life can be shaped in all its

21 Cicero, *De Officiis* 1.153.1. Birks and Mcleod (trans.), *Justinian's Institutes* (London: Duckworth, 1987) 38 (I.1.).

22 Agamben, *Opus Dei*, 74–81, and at 76.

parts.)[23] To translate *usus* as enjoyment is simply to make the point that conformity or being shaped is the chosen aspect, the freedom through which law is lived and institutions are inhabited. It is a question of how one wears the mask, the *persona* of becoming that invests and institutes in the role to be played as jurist, as critic, and necessarily also as office holder in whatever form, or as the bearer of whatever law, right or freedom.

The question of instituting life, of lawful being, is one of practice, of the precepts of practice as conforming to what is appropriate and in a scholastic sense ethical. This sense of ethics appertains most closely to the effects of office, to the doings of the jurist as actor, performer of their *officia*, or the virtues of their duties. For Agamben, these relate to the *mysterium* or spiritual results of actions, the effectiveness of the liturgy, and the secularized legal version of such in the truth or veridiction of judgements as expressions of rule. For the pedagogue, the critical jurist as theorist, the question is that of how the liturgical effect can become an evaluative challenge to the confines of the official precepts. Effects are disseminated, actions commanded, performances instilled in the comic and common drama of interaction. The theatrical context of hierarchy and performative dimension of office still leave open the critical question of how to challenge the precepts, resist the commands while also inhabiting and passing them on: "[t]he official – like the officiant – is what he has to do and has to do what he is: he is a being of command. The transformation of being into having-to-be, which defines the ethics as much as the ontology and politics of modernity, has its paradigm here."[24] If the person becomes the office and the office becomes the person, the key concept is that of the travel, the shifting movement between the two which is a question that can be *addressed* jurisgraphically and atmospherically, as well as in the more conventional terms of ethics and *leges actiones*, legal actions, but which can only be *understood* as an original double bind that power aims, at all costs, to singularize.

How to be a critical jurist? In one sense, the question is otiose. All thinking, each and every action in the performance of office is critical, evaluates, and is some form uses and thus reflects upon the precepts to which it gives effect. What kind of person is a question of the species of performance, and in the case of the jurist, a matter of the critical pedagogic practice embodied in the enactment of the role. It is first an itinerant role, a matter of office as movement, both transmission and becoming as change. Here, the question is of scope and ambulation. The jurist as jurisographer is one who travels, in literal forms and spaces,

23 *De Officiis*, 1.7.
24 *Opus Dei*, 84.

and in doing so pays attention, notices the lawscape of the city, the juristic history, the architectural and atmospheric precedents of the built environment that can be pieced together in a jurisprudence of the material reality of the juridical as encased in offices. The critical jurist *in perpetuum mobile*, a jurishifter, is one who is noticing, thinking, critically apprehending the legal environment, the signs, atmospherics, institutional affective markers, the pleasure and the pain of living within institutions, a bus, a building, a corridor, a freeway, a park. These are precepts and also interior states, affective and cognitive modes of *dasein*, of being in the world as a jurist, and as the performer of the affective, critical and theatrical pedagogic tasks that inhabiting an office requires.

If noticing comes first, inhabitation, habituation, character as theatrical repetition of institutional commitments follows upon the conscious taking up of positions, the embodiment and critical interiorization of the office as practice, as conduct of life, of embodiment. To inhabit is to become aware as a being *of* signs, atmospheres, contexts and commitments as the necessary assessments and affectively critical relations that constitute engagement with title, office, theoretical disquisition and all of the other itinerant interactions of office hours, faculty meetings, conferences, conversations, appointments, engagements, reviews, references and further pedagogic practices. These not only form the atmosphere and lawscape of the offices but equally the form of life that goes with the bearer as an itinerant holder of office. It is here that one can appreciate the extent of oikonomic governance, the *officia* of the emotions, which Cicero translates in terms of disposition, the rhetorical arrangement and ordering of affective topoi, the distribution of feelings that will both allocate and direct the subject in their conduct, inclusive of their relation to their offices and their others.[25]

There are obvious senses in which dress, costume, deportment, etiquette, accessories, modes of address, as well as architectural and aesthetic environments, constitute the *personae* of the officiant who inhabits an office, and the more pressing question becomes with whom and with what do they engage in such forms. The discourse of theory in the humanities and law is largely hermetic, and our primary audience, such as it is, is primarily ourselves, as in the present instance, the community of scholars, the humanist curriculum, the elders, as Carty points

25 This theme is lengthily explicated, in historical and theoretical valences in Agamben, *The Kingdom and the Glory: For a Theological Genealogy of Economy and Government* (Palo Alto: Stanford UP, 2011) 69–82 of particular importance, as adumbrated above, for the concept of office as manner of living, as practice, is the explication of the baroque maxim, *rex regnat sed non gubernat* – the sovereign rules but does not govern.

out in his essay, who review our work. Such constitutes in symbolic form the jurist's contribution to the mystic body of the state, to the *arcana imperii* or secrets of governance that survive in textual circulations and now also in film and social media. Ultimately though, in our sense from the very start, the jurist as an embodiment of the law aims to indicate the experiment of the critical experience. *Vivitur ingenio*, as the emblem has it, the whetstone of wit languishes on. Then pedagogically, it is students, the young eager for law, in Justinian's phrase, future professionals. Here, the mysteries of the juristic knowledge economy, the apparatus of repetition, mingle or drip down into the proleptic domain of legal practice. It provides a vicarious but second-order or surrogate entry into the realm of professional activities, the reproduction of lawyering being only in an initial and somewhat remote sense the purport of academic training. The primary function is the grooming and dressage of the professoriate itself, and it is doctoral students who are the greater focus of *microcosmographia academica*.[26]

The final, third function of the juristic apparatus of academia and the most worthy engagement is advocacy of inclusion and arguments for social change. These can be and are incorporated indirectly in the *arcana* of theory and in pedagogic practice but materialize most directly in the control function of the juristic regime as a disciplinary institution, in who is admitted, who is promoted, and who is funded. They also materialize in the polemical contributions that find exterior form in the diverse spheres and distinctive demographics of social media, commercial enterprises and popular forums. As it is not the office of the academic jurist to move beyond schola and scholarship, classroom and theoretical disquisition, there is something of a rhetorical ambivalence, a push and pull, fort/da, in such efforts at political manifestation. Picking up and engaging with the political topoi and themes of the times, jurists have played their political role in relation to reformulating laws, providing gateways to other and excluded views and voices, and changing the symbolic and social expressions, with varying degrees of effect, of the viscera and vicissitudes of class, gender, sexuality, race, and environment. The minor and the excluded have, in that loose historical order, had a degree of reception and a modicum of impact. When critical legal studies – albeit momentarily – feminist judgements, #Metoo, critical race theory, transsexualism, environmental crisis leading to earth jurisprudence and wild judgements hit the news, law tends to change. The jurists can here claim to play their minor role.

26 See the immortal F.M. Cornford, *Microcosmographia Academica: Being a Guide for the Young Academic Politician* (Cambridge: Bowes & Bowes Publishers Ltd, 1908).

The outer reaches of office, the liminal encounters and boundary engagements of juristic *personae*, outside of habitual comfort zones, tell us a great deal about the *nomos* and manner of living within the institution, as institutions. At a certain level, and significant in the ambivalence of the jurist as critic, is an element of the absurd, a Sisyphean sense that ivory towers, tenure, the cenobitic history and in some cases environs – what Cusset terms the utopian bubble of the college campus – or in a recent version of voyage round my room, on level 9 of "the" Melbourne Law School: "The view from up here, looking north across the university's historic main campus, is removed, is distant. It is a calming view. We can see the construction machinery digging a new train tunnel beyond the green lawns of University Square ... but we can neither hear nor feel their rumble."[27] A space then of restraint but also of opportunity, of choice and of play. It is the latter, *lex ludens*, jocular jurisprudence, playing with theory that becomes the focus of their post-critical imagining of reparative reading, entanglement and thinking beside, bearing across as opposed to or after the carapace of pervasive suspicion, paranoid critique, and the indolence of depression have been cast aside in favour of the dance of (claims to) thought.

Play of course has its norms and limits but is meant here in an expansive morphological sense that includes work (as in playing with the plough), speed or quickness, clapping which was an original meaning of playing with the hands, and player in its myriad senses of theatrical engagement. Mirth, fun, excitement are dimensions of juristic office and academic freedom that gain sparse attention, for fear perhaps that administration might remove them and impose the humdrum boredom of repetitive tasks, the seriousness of ministerial trivia might strangle imagination and creativity alike. The turn to performance, to the theatrical dimensions and entanglements of the scholarly life, of juristic endeavour, seeks in part to revive the sense of play, of fun, of chance and quickness of wit that make for entertainment, the drive and lure that initially generated the lateral move into the groves of academe. Is it the office of the jurist, and appropriate to the *persona* of the law professor, to engage in the theatrical, in the comedic, in an awareness of the corporeal game of performance? *Ius ridens*, a laughing law, to mimic

27 André Dao and Danish Sheikh, 'Translating Dark into Bright: Diary of a Post-Critical Year' (2024) 35 *Law and Critique* 377, at 381. In their engaging terms, this view represents "the carapace of thought" that they seek to break. For Cusset, and worth reading for its digressions on the campus drugs, Derridium and Lacanium, in translation, is *French Theory: How Foucault, Derrida, Deleuze & Co Transformed the Intellectual Life of the United States* (Minneapolis: University of Minnesota Press, 2008).

Aristotle, both pushes against the affective and censorious limit of the serious, and seeks to engage in a different way, with a lighter manner in juridical tasks that inevitably involve imagining, playing, feeling the humour of the case. For the common lawyer in particular the game of casuistry is not only serious, it is also a mixing of the solemn, the absurd, the accidental and the comic. Laughter breaks out, opening up possibilities and expansions, new ways of being in common, where *gravitas*, the weight of seriousness, hems in or drives the subject in upon itself.[28] More importantly, the serious can become comic and the comedic, that minor and ignored genre of comediography, can in turn mutate into the propositional and decisional. The Gods are serious, so Plato elaborates in book 7 of the *Laws*, whereas the human is but the plaything of the divinities and so should perform the noble games, the ethical pastimes of wit, song and dance: "we should live out our lives playing – sacrificing, singing, and dancing," following the poets, exercising wit.[29]

The point is not to digress too far into theories of comic legality or the methodology of satire as critique but rather to return to the insight of theatrical jurisprudence and of performance studies that acting is an essential and critical part of playing an official role. In various senses the critical academic has only theatre, performance at their behest and as their practice. As Guillory points out in his intriguing study of the institution of criticism, the primary function of the critic is publication and maintenance of the credibility of their knowledge, which is overwhelmingly of texts. The literary critic contributes to the culture, but nothing in a self-validating and relatively recent professional status of the university scholar provides any Archimedean point or privileged status for moving or changing the world: "The position of criticism – that is, literary criticism – in the disciplinary system by no means confers upon literary scholars the authority to speak on social and political matters in public venues."[30] By similar token, the institutions that jurists, as academics, as legal critics, inhabit are structurally separated from the sphere of politico-legal action both by the relative autonomy of academic positions and the rubrics of tenure. The jurist writes, their jurisdiction is the text, and their method, for common lawyers, is in large part the logic and critique of casuistry. To produce knowledge is to separate scholarship from opinion, which is both a strategy of attention to the longer term time frame of precedent, and the establishment of a distance from

28 Steven Connor, *Styles of Seriousness* (Palo Alto: Stanford UP, 2023) makes this point well in the first chapter, 'Seriously, Though'.

29 Plato, *Laws*, Book 7, 803; discussed in part in Johan Huizinga, Homo Ludens: *A Study of the Play Element in Culture* (London: Routledge, 1949) 18–19.

30 Guillory, *Professing Criticism*, 46.

the grand motives, prophecy, and surrogate politics of virtue signalling and empty pontification more generally.

The realization that the post-war burgeoning of mass higher education and the emergence of modern law schools, appointment by dint of a doctorate in some aspect of legal studies, does not qualify the jurist in any special way to change the world is a salutary limitation upon pedagogic pronouncement or pontifications upon practice. The office of jurist is that of reflection upon and transmission of legal texts, their cognate practices, and the study of their logical and empirical effects. The *persona* inhabiting such office and jurisdiction requires an authenticity in performing that role but does not exclude travelling out of the office in both disciplinary and theatrical terms. The lawyer as actor, the jurist as pedagogue and scholar, is performing a role, embodying a particular position and *legis actio*, or manner and conduct of professing and, more strongly inhabiting the norm. Self-consciousness in performance, awareness of *genius loci* and atmosphere, embodiment of the part played, an evolving critical awareness of the aesthetic style modelled and transmitted are all parts of imagining and enacting differently. Office can constrain the person, or it can act as a launching pad of self-conscious play, heightened awareness, and the experiment of incorporating and transmitting both system and norms in imaginative fashions and, to have recourse to an overused concept, differently, even if at times wrongly. The jurist translates, bears across, enacts and travels with the legal institution and its professional personnel. Scholarship provides alternatives which include those of playing roles in literal, ludic and transgressive fashions, reminding one of the creativity of law, its shape-shifting, life-giving qualities. The habitus and critical cabin of conduct, their ethical role, is that of staying within the law and, because all is flux, so as to change it. The pandemic, in forcing the office into exile, did not kill it but liberated its spectral form. It revealed that the *officium* of the jurist was always a nomadic construct, a "form-of-life" tethered less to stone and corridor than to conduct and carriage. The mourning for the old, stable office gives way to the melancholic yet creative play of inventing new ones – in the city, on the screen, in the text, and in the heightened, critical performance of the juridical self. The door, that sliding portal, is no longer made of wood but of choice; the key, no longer a metal object, but the decision of how, and as whom, to cross the threshold.

Part I

Histories

Chapter 2

Conscience is the essence of the scholar's office

*Adam Sitze**

Although Ernst Kantorowicz is best known for his 1957 masterpiece *The King's Two Bodies*, it would be a mistake to limit one's consideration of his thought to that work alone. In Germany, where he was born, Kantorowicz initially gained fame as the conservative author of a controversial best-selling 1927 study of Frederick the Second.[1] Increasingly persecuted in Germany because of his Jewish heritage, Kantorowicz finally fled in 1938. Once in the United States, Kantorowicz accepted a position in the History Department at The University of California, Berkeley. It was there that, in the spring of 1940, he seems to have begun reading *Richard II*.[2] It was also there that, in around 1945, he began work on the manuscript that later became *The King's Two Bodies*.

Above all, it was there that, beginning in 1949, he became passionately involved in one of the ugliest conflicts over academic freedom in twentieth-century American history, about which he later would write in a short, strange self-published 1950 pamphlet called *The Fundamental Issue*.

In what follows, I'd like to make a case for the significance of this little text. I believe it's significant both for the study of Kantorowicz's oeuvre and for the study of academic freedom more generally.

I say this not only because Kantorowicz wrote *The Fundamental Issue* during the very same years that he worked on *The King's Two Bodies*, and not only because Kantorowicz took up many of the same problems in both texts (such as the non-dying corporation, the oath, and

* This text was first delivered at Garrick's Temple to Shakespeare, in Hampton, United Kingdom, on June 22, 2019. I thank Richard Wilson for his invitation, and Theo Perez for his editorial and bibliographic assistance. All errors are my responsibility alone.

1 Robert Lerner, *Ernst Kantorowicz: A Life* (Princeton, NJ: Princeton University Press, 2018), 115.

2 Lerner, *Kantorowicz*, 350. Given the prominence of Shakespeare for the George circle, however, it is likely that Kantorowicz encountered Shakespeare prior to his arrival in California.

DOI: 10.4324/9781003659754-3

the concepts of sovereignty, *universitas*, and *dignitas*).[3] I say it above all because *The Fundamental Issue* and *The King's Two Bodies* together form a philosophical and historical knot.

That knot assumes the following form:

On the one hand, the jurisprudential problem at the core of *The King's Two Bodies*—which is to say, the emergence of the legal fiction of quasi-infinite continuity[4]—provides the hermeneutic horizon within which Kantorowicz's arguments in *The Fundamental Issue* become fully intelligible. In particular, as we shall see, the medieval concept of the *Aevum* is the silent presence, the unstated standpoint, that allows and even requires Kantorowicz to formulate his curious defence of academic freedom. *On the other hand*, however, Kantorowicz's elaboration of the jurisprudential problem of continuity in *The King's Two Bodies* would only appear seven years after the publication of *The Fundamental Issue*.

Here then is the knot: Kantoworicz's 1950 defence of academic freedom seems to have preceded the 1957 text that provided that same defence with its jurisprudential basis.[5] Stated differently: Kantorowicz seems to have fully developed the jurisprudential basis for his defence of "the legal right to tenure"[6] only belatedly, indeed only after that defence failed in fact.[7]

In what follows, I'll untie this knot first by reading Kantorowicz's two texts alongside one another, and then by rereading both texts alongside Shakespeare's *Richard II*. The result, I suggest, is an unexpected teaching about the relation of conscience and academic freedom today.

To arrive at this teaching, I'd like to begin by saying a few words about the Berkeley loyalty oath controversy itself. The controversy began at a moment when the American public was beside itself with panic over the spectre of communist spying and subversion. Bowing to the political pressures initially exerted upon the University by the Governor of California, the Regents of the University voted unanimously in March 1949 to require all Berkeley professors to sign an oath of loyalty declaring their opposition to communism, threatening

3 See, on this point, Lerner, *Kantorowicz*, 351. This is also the approach to the interpretation of Kantorowicz favoured by Pierre Legendre.

4 Ernst Kantorowicz, *The King's Two Bodies: A Study in Medieval Political Theology* (Princeton, NJ: Princeton University Press, 1957), 273.

5 Or, as Kantorowicz himself might put it, "practice, as usual, preceded theory" (*King's Two Bodies*, 273).

6 Ernst Kantorowicz, *The Fundamental Issue: Documents and Marginal Notes on the University of California Loyalty Oath* (San Francisco: Parker Printing Co., 1950), 24, 35.

7 Lerner, *Kantorowicz*, 328.

dismissal for those who refused to sign.[8] Kantorowicz had experienced loyalty oaths before. In 1934 he refused to sign an oath declaring his loyalty to the Führer and as a result was dismissed from The University of Frankfurt.[9] In 1947, meanwhile, he devoted a section of his lecture course on "Byzantium" to the use of loyalty oaths to "fascistify" Italian universities.[10] It did not take him much time, therefore, to develop an opinion about the loyalty oath mandated by the Regents. On June 14, 1949, he took a stand against the loyalty oath on the floor of the northern section of the California academic senate, reading out a statement that he later would reprint in *The Fundamental Issue*, and from which *The Fundamental Issue* would take its title.

At the end of his statement, Kantorowicz claimed that those who refused to take the loyalty oath were defending what he called "a superior constitutional principle far beyond and above trivial party lines."[11] He then explained himself in three succinct paragraphs:

> I am not talking about political expediency or academic freedom, nor even about the fact that an oath taken under duress is invalidated at the moment it is taken, but wish to emphasize the true and fundamental issue at stake: professional and human dignity.
>
> There are three professions which are entitled to wear a gown: the judge, the priest, the scholar. This garment stands for its bearer's maturity of mind, his independence of judgment, and his direct responsibility to his conscience and to his God. It signifies the inner sovereignty of those three interrelated professions: they should be

8 Lerner, *Kantorowicz*, 312–313. In a deep sense that would not have been lost on Kantorowicz, it is not incomprehensible why the Regents would suspect members of the university of foreign influence, and in particular communist influence. The medieval *universitas*, not unlike the monastic community from which it was derived and whose habits it shared, was an "*Imperium in Imperio*"—a "State within a State"—composed in large part of itinerant scholars whose first allegiance was to the university itself, and that involved highly regulated ways of life in which membership depended neither on the rule of law nor (crucially) on the ownership of private property. See, on this point, Émile Durkheim, *The Evolution of Educational Thought: Lectures on the Formation and Development of Secondary Education in France*, Trans. Peter Collins (Boston: Routledge & Kegan Paul, 1977), 39, 89.

9 Lerner, *Kantorowicz*, 186.

10 Ernst Kantorowicz, "Lectures for Course, 'Byzantium' (1947)," Ernst Kantorowicz Collection 1908–1982, Box IV, 448–449, online at https://archive.org/details/ernstkantorowicz00reel07/mode/1up (last accessed 29/10/2025). .

11 Kantorowicz, *The Fundamental Issue*, 6.

> the very last to allow themselves to act under duress and to yield to pressure.
>
> It is a shameful and undignified action, it is an affront and a violation of both human sovereignty and professional dignity that the Regents of this University have dared to bully the bearer of this gown into a situation in which—under the pressure of a bewildering economic coercion—he is compelled to give up either his tenure or, together with his freedom of judgment, his human dignity and his responsible sovereignty as a scholar.[12]

In this passage, dignity is both the *centre* of Kantorowicz's text and also its *foundation*. It's the *centre* of the text because Kantorowicz names it as such at the only point in *The Fundamental Issue* where his text's title will appear within the text itself: "the true and fundamental issue at stake," we read, is "professional and human dignity." And it's the *foundation* because it's the basis of the text's argument that the loyalty oath is shameful. Nothing could be more emphatically clear: at four points in three paragraphs, Kantorowicz will speak of dignity or of its opposite.

And yet despite all of this emphasis, or perhaps because of it, dignity can't bear the weight that Kantorowicz places on it. Given the historical conditions under which Kantorowicz spoke of dignity, that's not unsurprising. On December 10, 1948, six months before Kantorowicz's statement in the Berkeley academic senate, *The Universal Declaration of Human Rights* was adopted by the United Nations General Assembly. The Declaration not only positioned dignity as the foundation of the concept of the human being that would be protected by fundamental human rights.[13] It also situated dignity as the foundation of cultural, social, and

12 Kantorowicz, *The Fundamental Issue*, 6.

13 Dignity features most prominently into the Preamble of the Declaration, which recognizes "the inherent dignity and of the equal and inalienable rights of all members of the human family" as "the foundation of freedom, justice and peace in the world." The Preamble also notes that "the peoples of the United Nations have in the Charter reaffirmed their faith in fundamental human rights, in the dignity and worth of the human person and in the equal rights of men and women." Article 1 of the Declaration, meanwhile, states that "[a]ll human beings are born free and equal in dignity and rights" and "are endowed with reason and conscience and should act towards one another in a spirit of brotherhood." See "Universal Declaration of Human Rights," online at https://www.un.org/en/universal-declaration-human-rights/ (last checked June 18, 2019).

economic rights, including the right to work.[14] On the terms of this discourse, dignity is the reason why human beings have rights, and it is also the quality or characteristic of the human being who enjoys rights.

Strange though it may sound, Kantorowicz's text participates in this discourse. In the "Prefatory Note" to *The Fundamental Issue*, for example, he will argue that the oath controversy involved not only "a human principle" but even "*Humanitas* herself."[15] At the conclusion of his text, meanwhile, he will mention "those vested rights of the professor which cannot be easily attacked or ignored by those in power without assailing, at the same time, certain fundamental rights of society."[16] Whatever else it is, therefore, *The Fundamental Issue* is a document that enters into relation in some way with human rights discourse.

Kantorowicz's turn to the new discourse of human dignity, however, also entailed a certain conceptual excess. As if human dignity were not foundational or central enough to defend academic tenure, Kantorowicz will augment it with reference to an additional form of dignity: the fundamental issue, he will argue, is not just human dignity but also professional dignity. The logic of this augmentation is not immediately clear. In particular, it's not clear whether dignity is the same basic essence expressed in two different modes (human and professional), or if professional dignity is a genre of dignity that is altogether different than human dignity.

One is tempted to conclude that professional dignity is qualitatively different than human dignity, for Kantorowicz seems to suggest that it is not embodied in the bare life of all humans, but covers the bodies of only some humans, in the form of the gowns worn by judges, priests, and scholars. And yet Kantorowicz will not say that those gowns signify dignity. He instead will say that they signify something distinct from dignity, something he calls "inner sovereignty." This claim is complicated by the fact that what Kantoworicz at first names as "professional and human dignity" reappears in his statement first as "human sovereignty and professional dignity" and then again as "human dignity and ... responsible sovereignty."

14 Article 23 (3) states that "[e]veryone who works has the right to just and favourable remuneration ensuring for himself and his family an existence worthy of human dignity, and supplemented, if necessary, by other means of social protection." There is similar recourse to dignity in Article 22. See "Universal Declaration of Human Rights," online at https://www.un.org/en/universal-declaration-human-rights/ (last checked June 18, 2019).

15 Kantorowicz, *The Fundamental Issue*, 2. The Declaration, remember, will speak of "fundamental human rights." See n 14 above.

16 Kantorowicz, *The Fundamental Issue*, 33.

At no point in any of these permutations is it clear how or why dignity and sovereignty might be related. What is clear is that Kantorowicz's turn *toward* the language of sovereignty is equally a turn *away from* the language of *The Universal Declaration of Human Rights*, for there is no mention of human sovereignty anywhere in the *Declaration*, and the *Declaration* at no point proposes a relation between dignity and sovereignty. At the same time that Kantorowicz's 1949 statement partakes in the new lexicon of human rights, therefore, it also introduces an intriguing equivocality into that same lexicon.

What we might call the "metonymy" of Kantorowicz's June 1949 statement—the way in which dignity touches and then morphs into a series of cognate concepts, such as sovereignty and the gown—thus seems to be at odds with his declarative emphasis on dignity (which is to say, his attempt to name dignity as the fundamental issue). In Kantorowicz's statement, we might even say, dignity loses the apodictic certainty it possesses, or appears to possess, in *The Declaration*. At the very least, one can see how Kantorowicz's very attempt to take a stand on dignity begins to recoil upon itself, producing the very opposite effect. Far from providing him with a fundamental right, Kantorowicz's turn to dignity instead leaves him with a fundamental issue, which is to say, with a legal concept less stable than unstable, less usable than questionable, less self-evident than in need of further study.[17]

The terms of this problematization of dignity become clearer when we turn to the legal controversy into which *The Fundamental Issue* intervenes. The legal authority for firing tenured Berkeley professors was outlined most forcefully by a Regent named Sidney Ehrman, who was founding partner of a powerful San Francisco law firm. Speaking in a contentious Board of Regents meeting in August 1950, Ehrman argued that professors who teach at The University of California are not "public officers" whose appointment implies "vested rights" to their office, but merely employees of the Regents who work in their offices in the same way that janitors work in university buildings and gardeners work on the grounds of the university.[18] Far from being motivated by a class politics or by egalitarian sentiments—Ehrman was a fervent anti-communist—the point of Ehrman's argument was instead to remove all legal and procedural barriers preventing the Regents from dismissing all tenured professors who refused to obey them.

Much of Kantorowicz's pamphlet proceeds as an extended rebuttal of Ehrman's August 1950 argument. To defend against this attack,

17 For Kantorowicz's own declension of "problematization," see The *King's Two Bodies*, 274.

18 Kantorowicz, *The Fundamental Issue*, 14.

Kantorowicz will explain in detail how the relation of scholars to their office—which is to say, in a Ciceronian sense, to their "duty"[19]—is different from janitors' relation to their buildings or gardeners' relations to their grounds. As a result, many passages of *The Fundamental Issue* will seem to rely on a medieval guild mentality (which in fact Kantorowicz studied as a young scholar[20]), or on modern claims about the division of labour, or indeed on simple elitism. I would even suggest that the first and major part of Kantorowicz's defence of tenure remains structured according to the terms of Ehrman's attack—or, stated a bit more sharply, that Kantorowicz's defence of tenure internalizes the very repression it proposes to resist.[21] However, as I will say later, I don't

19 See, generally, Giorgio Agamben, *Opus Dei: An Archaeology of Duty*, Trans. Adam Kotsko (Stanford: Stanford University Press, 2013).

20 Kantorowicz's 1919 dissertation was on the topic of "The Nature of Muslim Artisan Associations," and analysed the absence of guilds in Islam. See Lerner, *Kantorowicz*, 62–65. This remains a *sub rosa* theme in *The King's Two Bodies*, which closely tracks claims about Averroism in the revival of Roman Law that occurred at The University of Bologna. See, e.g., Kantorowicz, *King's Two Bodies*, 301 n 62.

21 Nowhere so clearly as when he contrasts the indispensability of professors with the dispensability of janitors and gardeners. "A university could exist without gardeners and janitors, who are accessory; it could hardly exist without professors and students, who are essential, actually the only essential part of a university. According to the oldest definitions, which run back to the thirteenth century, 'The University' is the *universitas magistrorum et scholarium*, 'The Body Corporate of Masters and Students.' Teachers and students together are the University regardless of the existence of gardens and buildings, or care-takers of gardens and buildings. One can envisage a university without a single gardener or janitor, without a single secretary, and even—a bewitching mirage—without a single Regent. The constant and essence of a university is always the body of teachers and students" (*The Fundamental Issue*, 16). The dialectical character of these passages needs to underlined. The more explicitly loyal Kantorowicz remains to the concept of the medieval university (as the *universitas magistrorum et scholarium*) the more implicitly aligned he becomes with the arbitrary authority of the modern university: the medieval historian's ability to imagine the university without its "accessories" is the historico-theoretical counterpart to the modern university trustees' discretionary power to fire "mere employees" at will. This passage not only then marks the purest and clearest instance of Kantorowicz's fidelity to the concept of the medieval university; it also marks the point at which his voice most fully merges and becomes indistinguishable from Ehrman's plenary power as trustee (for both agree that in a business corporation "mere employees" can be fired at will [see *The Fundamental Issue*, 18–19]). Here then the concept of the medieval university (modelled on the body corporate) ceases to be

think this strange coincidence of opposites precludes the possibility of a second and minor reading of Kantorowicz's text, one that resists and works through rather than internalizing Ehrman's repression (and is, for this reason, "saner"[22]).

For now, let's examine the way in which Kantorowicz's response to Ehrman extends to include the very core of Kantorowicz's text: his claim that the essence of the scholar's office is conscience. "It is obvious," Kantorowicz states, "that it is his conscience which makes the scholar what he is, and that to act according to his professional conscience is indeed the function of the University professor."[23] Given the equivocality of Kantorowicz's turn to dignity, we should not assume too quickly that we entirely understand what he means by "conscience."[24] Kantorowicz develops this claim in a passage that defies summary, and that I therefore quote at length:

> Through the sheer existence of this conscience, which is undefined and undefinable, the scholar ceases also to be an "employee" of the Regents in any sense whatsoever of business language. It is through his conscience that he acquires vested rights in his office. By this conscience, which is inseparable from his genuine duties as member of the academic body corporate, he is clearly distinguished from gardener and janitor. That almost criminal superficiality of the comparison between janitor and professor breaks down at this point. Trade and profession are not identical. A profession, as the word itself would suggest, is based upon conscience, and not upon working hours as in the case of modern trades, or on Time in general. In this respect the scholar resembles the judge whose duties are not disposed of by sitting in court, or the clergyman whose duties are not exhaustively described by the mention of ritual performances and sermons

non-identical with the practice modern university (modelled on the business corporation), and instead becomes entirely identical with it.

22 On the distinction between the *maior pars* and *sanior pars*, see Kantorowicz, *The Fundamental Issue*, 9.

23 Kantorowicz, *The Fundamental Issue*, 13.

24 Not least because "conscience" is, in addition to dignity, a foundational and central term in The Universal Declaration of Human Rights. It appears first in the Preamble to the Declaration, which notes that "disregard and contempt for human rights have resulted in barbarous acts which have outraged the conscience of mankind[.]" It is also central to Article 1 (cf. note 8 above). In Article 18, meanwhile, it appears in a metonymy with thought and religion: "Everyone has the right to freedom of thought, conscience and religion." See The Universal Declaration of Human Rights, online at https://www.un.org/en/universal-declaration-human-rights/ (last checked June 18, 2019).

> on Sundays. The conscience is actually the essence of the scholars' "office" (*officium*) which he is entrusted with and through which he becomes truly a "public trust."
>
> From whatever angle one may look at the academic profession, it is always, in addition to passion and love, the conscience which makes the scholar a scholar. And it is through the fact that his whole being depends on his conscience that he manifests his connection with the legal profession as well as with the clergy from which, in the high Middle Ages, the academic profession descended and the scholar borrowed his gown.
>
> Unlike the employee, the professor dedicates, in the way of research, even most of his private life to the body corporate of the University of which he is the integral part. His impetus is his conscience. Therefore, if you demoralize that scholarly conscience, that love and passion for research and for teaching, and replace all that in a business fashion by strictly defined working hours, prescribed by the "employer," you have ruined, together with the academic profession, also the University! Only the culpably naïve ignorance on the part of malevolent Regents, not knowing what a scholar's life and being is, could venture to break the backbone of the academic profession—that is, its conscience in order to "save the University,"—nay, to dismiss a scholar for that very conscience whic makes him a scholar.[25]

Crystalline to the point of opacity, this difficult passage is fascinating both because of what it says and also because of what it cannot yet fully say.

Kantorowicz's most direct response to Ehrman's claim—which is, remember, that professors are not public officers and have no vested right in their office—is that conscience is the basis for the scholar's vested rights in his office. To define conscience, however, Kantorowicz will find that he needs to define the body corporate—a massive question that in turn, as we know, could be the topic of an entire book. Instead, almost as a kind of placeholder, Kantorowicz here attempts to activate the Pauline and Lutheran thought dormant in the English word "profession" and in the German word "*Beruf*."[26] On these terms, a profession is a profession of faith, a calling, a vocation. To understand the vested right of modern scholars to their office, it would then follow, one must understand the very idea of a profession as a problem of secularization,

25 Kantorowicz, *The Fundamental Issue*, 19–20.

26 See, on this lineage, Christiane Frey, "χλῆσις/Beruf: Luther, Weber, Agamben," *New German Critique* 105 (Fall 2008), 35–56.

and one must furthermore trace the very idea of "vested rights" to its origins in religious rites and ceremonies. This line of inquiry would in turn allow and even require one to understand the "vested rights" of the academic profession as a residue of the rites and ceremonies of investiture itself. And from this perspective, the scholars' gown would be much more than a mere gown. It would now register itself as the clearest sign not only of scholars' "vested right" to their office but also what he will call their "prerogative rights to and within their institutions[.]"[27] In just the same way that a scholar wears a gown that in turn covers their mortal body, so too does the scholar participate in a body corporate, the *universitas*, that is at once intimately related to that mortal body (touching and expressing it like a garment) and yet also, by virtue of its continuity, completely in excess of that mortal body (inasmuch as the *universitas* is not reducible to any single scholar and indeed outlives all mortal scholars). A scholar who lacks a vested right in their office, on these terms, would be a contradiction in terms. If conscience is the essence of the scholar's office, then a scholar stripped of office—which is to say, without a sense of duty, responsibility, or obligation—would not be a scholar at all. A scholar divested of their right to office may indeed work inside of an office that in turn is located on the grounds of a university. But a scholar of this sort would lack any immanent relation to the body corporate that alone makes scholarship into a profession, and that alone makes a university into a *universitas*.[28] Depriving scholars of their vested rights to office would therefore destroy the very institution the trustees are obliged to preserve.[29]

Many of Kantorowicz's peers, most notably Erwin Panofsky[30], would express admiration for his defence of academic freedom. Nevertheless, this argument in *The Fundamental Issue* was ignored by the most prominent post-war advocates of the American tradition of academic freedom. In 1950, for example, Kantorowicz sent a copy of *The Fundamental*

27 Kantorowicz, *The Fundamental Issue*, 16.

28 Kantorowicz clarifies this point with reference to two constitutive limits. First, he asks, why do professors not form unions? The answer, he says, is because professors together with their students are the *universitas*, in the same way that judges are the court and ministers together with the faithful are the Church. Second, and much more implicitly, how are professors different than nudes hired by casinos to pose in champagne glasses for customers? Here the question answers itself: professors are different than nudes because professors wear gowns. See Kantorowicz, *The Fundamental Issue*, 16, 21, 23.

29 Kantorowicz, *The Fundamental Issue*, 35.

30 Lerner argues that Kantorowicz's stand at Berkeley persuaded Panofsky to support Kantorowicz's candidacy for The Institute of Advanced Study. See Lerner, *Kantorowicz*, 331.

Issue to the pragmatist philosopher Sidney Hook, whose reply oscillated between polite irritation and outright confusion. This sort of reaction continues to this day: *The Fundamental Issue* is consistently avoided by today's leading scholars of American academic freedom.[31] This, however, is not so much a sign of Kantorowicz's irrelevance as it is a symptom of the conceptual poverty of the American tradition of academic freedom, which remains governed by a mix of philosophical pragmatism and German idealism. For a different view, one might consider a note Hannah Arendt jotted down in her *Denktagebuch* in April 1969. There Arendt called the university the "last remnant of the Middle Ages," and wondered if it was an accident that the university and the Catholic Church had both lost their authority at the same moment.[32] Although Arendt does not mention Kantorowicz in her note, that note indicates Kantorowicz's continuing relevance. Far from being reducible to mere nostalgia for the medieval university, *The Fundamental Issue* is an inquiry into what Arendt calls the lost authority of the modern university. It's a study of the modern university that treats the Middle Ages as an analytic standpoint that then, in turn, allows one to comprehend the many ways in which the modern university has become non-identical with its non-modern origins.

This goes above all for the text's claims about dignity. Part of the obscurity of this concept in *The Fundamental Issue* would be remedied seven years later, with the publication of *The King's Two Bodies*. In the concluding chapter of that book, Kantorowicz would take up a set of problems similar to the ones he encountered in his earlier polemical defense of the dignity of the academic profession. In medieval canon law, he now explains, *dignitas* had a meaning very different from the moral or ethical sense it later acquired in modern philosophy or jurisprudence.

Prior to these modern uses, *dignitas* designated the imperishability of an office that may be held, at least for a time, by this or that mortal

31 To take just one among many examples: there is no mention of Kantorowicz in Akeel Bilgrami and Jonathan Cole's *Who's Afraid of Academic Freedom* (New York: Columbia University Press, 2015), an authoritative collection that contains contributions from (among others) Stanley Fish, Judith Butler, Noam Chomsky, John Mearsheimer, Robert Post, Jon Elster. The only scholar to have taken up Kantorowicz's Fundamental Question as a basis to theorize academic freedom in the present is Joshua Barkan. See *Corporate Sovereignty: Law and Government under Capitalism* (Minneapolis: University of Minnesota Press, 2013). The present text is a contribution to the line of inquiry Barkan inaugurates.

32 Hannah Arendt, *Denktagebuch, Zweiter Band*, Ed. Ursula Ludz and Ingeborg Nordmann (München/Berlin/Zürich: Piper, 2016), 710.

being, but that ultimately, and in contrast to that mortal being, was itself immortal. As he put it, dignity referred

> chiefly to the singularity of the royal office, to the sovereignty vested in the king by the people, and resting individually in the king alone ... Since the king's Dignity, together with his prerogative rights, had to be maintained and respected for the sake of the whole realm, the dignity too was of a public, and not merely private, nature. It was as little a private matter as the officium regis, with which it largely coincided.[33]

The relation to *The Fundamental Issue* here should be clear. The word Kantorowicz uses to characterize the relation between king and people in this passage—"vested"—is precisely the same word at the centre of his dispute with Ehrman. The term he uses to designate the royal office—*dignitas*—is precisely the same term he used in 1950 to name "the fundamental issue" at stake in the conflict over the scholar's office. Above all, this passage, even more than its counterparts in *The Fundamental Issue*, suggests why the scholar's office might be considered a "public trust": like the royal office, the scholar's office is not a private affair, but a conceptual relation in which a sovereign people—a body politic that understands itself to be existing in perpetuity[34]—sees a distorted double of its own image reflected back to itself.

All of this, in turn, helps us better understand Kantorowicz's 1949 statement about the "inner sovereignty" of the three professions entitled to wear a gown. (It's worth recalling that the word "regalia" [as in the phrase "academic regalia"] designates "the rights belonging to a monarch or ruler; royal powers or privileges," and also, by extension, "the official decorations or insignia of an order, office, etc., frequently indicating authority" [OED iii].) What in 1949 appears to be an equivocal relation between sovereignty and dignity now therefore seems more deliberate. Those claims now begin to seem like the result of an "equiparation" between the sovereign and the scholar. (Equiparation, as Kantorowicz would argue in a 1961 essay called "The Sovereignty of the Artist," is "the action of placing on equal terms two or more subjects which at first appeared to have nothing to do with each other.")

33 Kantorowciz, *The King's Two Bodies*, 384. Somewhat in contrast to his 1949 Statement, Kantorowicz here explicitly states that "it would be a mistake to assume that the terms Crown and Dignity were coterminous and exchangeable, or simply redundant, even though more often than not, they were lacking precision and were applied thoughtlessly and confusingly" (383).

34 Kantorowicz, *The Fundamental Issue*, 397.

Medieval jurists, as Kantorowicz would show, used equiparation to define the office of the poet with reference to the office of the king.[35]

One thus begins to grasp why it might be necessary to read Kantorowicz's two texts alongside one another. Just as *The Fundamental Issue* opens the inquiry that *The King's Two Bodies* then develops in detail, *The King's Two Bodies* provides the theoretical framework that then explains the defence of academic freedom in *The Fundamental Issue*. Reading the two texts as part of a single palimpsest, in turn, helps clarify what I earlier called "the first and major part" of Kantorowicz's defence of tenure. In his 1957 book, unlike his 1950 pamphlet, Kantorowicz will distinguish Time (understood as the finitude and mutability of terrestrial life) not only from Eternity (understood in terms of God's immutability and infinity), but also from a dimension he will call the "*Aevum*."

Neither the finite nor the infinite, *Aevum* is "a kind of infiniteness and duration which [has] motion and therefore past and future[.]"[36] It's not hard to understand how this experience of time might connect dignity to conscience and both dignity and conscience to scholar's office. In the modern occupations Kantorowicz calls "the trades," which are structured according to the division of labor, working hours at least in principle at some point end and leisure time at some point begins. By contrast, Kantorowicz would seem to imply, the three professions of the gown admit no such distinction. For these professions, the Time of work would seem to be structured differently because work itself would seem to be structured differently. Less a means to an end exterior to itself, and more like a labour of love or a passion one suffers, work that is synonymous with the aeviternal conscience no more allows for the possibility of "time off" than do love or passion themselves.

On these terms, the scholar's work would be doubly distinct from the work of "the trades." On the one hand, the scholar's work would both require and resemble a certain experience of leisure. The Greek word "*scholē*," which gives rise to the English word "scholar," signifies nothing if not a kind of leisure, and the conduct of the scholar, beginning at least with Socrates, is characterized at least in part by the fact that the scholar is exempt or immune from manual labour.[37] And yet, on the other hand, the scholar's work also would be unlike leisure or idleness in a decisive respect, for at no point does this work allow for

35 See Ernst Kantorowicz, "The Sovereignty of the Artist: A Note on Legal Maxims and Renaissance Theories of Art" (1961), *Selected Studies* (New York: J. J. Augustin Pub., 1965), 362, cf. "Kingship Under the Impact of Scientific Jurisprudence" (1961), *Selected Studies*, 154.

36 Kantorowicz, *King's Two Bodies*, 279.

37 Plato, *The Apology of Socrates*, 36d.

the possibility of rest. Even a sabbatical, especially a sabbatical, leaves one only a limited amount of Time to respond to the unsurvivable accumulation of Time that is the library. If the offices of the scholar and the sovereign are both in some way vested by the public with *dignitas*, then the scholar's gown has a clear meaning: it's the emblem of the scholar's second body—the corporate body dedicated to the unending pursuit of truth—and its time is not the scholar's own time, but the time of the *Aevum*.

The fact that Kantorowicz was reading Shakespeare during the years that he wrote *The Fundamental Issue* and *The King's Two Bodies*, however, adds a twist to that conclusion. In *Richard II* but even more so in Henry IV, Parts I and II, the king experiences the crown as a sort of burden: "Uneasy lies the head that wears the crown." In what sense could it be said that a crown makes a head uneasy? Kantorowicz's discussion of the *Aevum* provides one possible answer: the very continuity of the crown—the undying, sempiternal temporality of its *dignitas*—will always already remain in excess of the finitude and mortality of the body of the one who occupies the office it signifies. In just the same way, we might say, the gown should make the scholar uneasy. No finite, mortal body is equal to the task of bearing the perpetuity, the endlessness, of thought itself (which, as Hannah Arendt wrote at the end of her life, "only a god can tolerate forever"[38]). Thought would then seem to exceed the mortal body of the scholar in just the same way that sovereignty would seem to exceed the mortal body of the king. The duties and obligations entailed in the offices of the crown and the gown, we might then say, are uneasy to the exact degree that each indicates an office structured according to the time of the *Aevum*. Each office, we might conclude, imposes endless responsibilities that, by virtue of that temporal excess, weigh upon the mortal body as if possessed of a certain gravity.

This may seem like an extravagant inference, and I confess that it probably is. On the other hand, it can't be an accident that Kantorowicz's "three professions which are entitled to wear a gown"—the judge, the scholar, the priest—correspond precisely to the three professions that Sigmund Freud, writing in the 1937 text that has come to be called his "last will and testament," called "the impossible professions" (law, education, and psychoanalysis).[39] In each case, a certain experience of

38 Hannah Arendt, *The Life of the Mind, Volume 1: Thinking* (New York: Harcourt, Brace and Jovanovich, 1978), 123–124.

39 Sigmund Freud, "Analysis Terminable and Interminable" (1937), in *The Standard Edition of the Complete Psychological Works of Sigmund Freud*, Volume XXIII, Ed. and Trans. James E. Strachey (London: Hogarth Press,

time—what Kantorowicz calls "continuity" and what Freud calls "interminability"—is not accidental but central to the work of the profession itself. And in each case, even permanent tenure of office does not provide enough Time to satisfy a desire hinged to the trace of some impossible Real. (By "impossible Real" I have in mind Justice in the case of the judge, Truth in the case of the scholar, and God/the Unconscious in the case of the priest or psychoanalyst.[40]) Each of these professions, we might say, is structured around fidelity to an event (Justice, Truth, God/the Unconscious) that is in each case initially productive of shocking wonder (or what the Greeks called *thaumazein*), that in each case gradually becomes (as Lacan might say) extimately "mine," and that is in each case enjoyable to an excessive, unbearable, and excruciating degree (in just the same way that the experiences of love, passion, and conscience are "enjoyable").

The more one follows this line of thought, however, the more one becomes aware of a limit internal to *The King's Two Bodies*. Despite the fact that Kantorowicz's writings during the years between 1945 and 1957 contain many traces of an equiparation between the scholar and the sovereign, one searches in vain for a substantial discussion of conscience in *The King's Two Bodies*.[41] Why is that so? If conscience is the

1981), 248. The reader may object that a psychoanalyst is not the same as a priest: the psychoanalyst wears no gown. This is a fair point. On the other hand, in a proper analysis the analysand lies on a couch and faces away from the analyst. This is nothing if not a gown-effect: this office arrangement exempts the analysand from the psychic work of forming an image of the analyst's mortal body. On the couch as in the confessional, the negation of gaze and eye redoubles the power of voice and ear. It is not for nothing that, in 1926, Freud suggested that the phrase "*Seelsorger*" ("secular pastoral worker") "might well serve as a general formula describing the function which the analyst, whether he is a doctor or a layman, has to perform in his relation to the public." Freud then went on to discuss the homologies that link the analyst to the priest. Under conditions of secularization, the office of the psychoanalyst inherits certain functions of the priest. See Sigmund Freud, "The Question of Lay Analysis," in *The Standard Edition of the Complete Psychological Works of Sigmund Freud*, Volume XX, Ed. and Trans. James E. Strachey (London: Hogarth Press, 1981), 255–256.

40 I also have in mind the sections of Martin Heidegger's *Being and Time* in which the call of conscience is understood in terms of the possibility of one's own impossibility.

41 Kantorowicz does mention conscience in a footnote, and what follows is largely an explication of the logic implicit in this citation. In a discussion of the "dual personality" of popes and bishops, Kantorowicz will note that the problem of the duplex persona already had emerged for twelfth-century jurists "in connection with the problem of conscience in court; that is, the

essence of the scholar's office (as Kantorowicz writes in 1950), and if the scholar's office is in certain respects homologous to the royal office (as we realize by juxtaposing Kantorowicz's 1950 and 1957 texts), wouldn't it follow that conscience is in some way constitutive of the royal office as well?

But if it is, why then might it be absent from the book that otherwise investigates the vicissitudes of royal office with such evident care?

This question comes into greater focus once we turn from Kantorowicz's published works to his unpublished lectures, and in particular to Kantorowicz's discussions of Shakespeare in those lectures. There we find that Kantorowicz will turn to Shakespeare not only to understand the various "planes of life" that intersect and collide in the experience of papal office, but also to clarify the way in which it is the office of the poet to speak as the "conscience" of their world and age.[42] This, however, only deepens the question, for although Kantorowicz will refer to "planes" in his reading of *Richard II* in *The King's Two Bodies*,[43] his book will contain no similar reference to "conscience."

Here we learn much by reading over Kantorowicz's shoulder as he in turn reads *Richard II*. In one of the passages of the deposition scene that Kantorowicz leaves in silence, Richard commands or tempts Henry Bolingbroke to "seize" the crown: "Here, cousin, seize the crown."[44] Richard's use of the word "seize" has at least two senses. On the one hand, Richard is commanding or inviting Henry "to grasp" the crown, and thus to become his lawful successor. On the other hand, he is commanding or tempting Henry to "appropriate" or "take" the crown, and

---

question whether a judge was to try a case exclusively on the ground of the evidence produced in court or also on the ground of private knowledge he may have happened to obtain" (395, n 275). Stated differently, the only mention of "conscience" in The King's Two Bodies emerges in response to the question of how the two persona of the judge relate to one another.

42 On poets, see Ernst Kantorowicz, "Lectures for Course, 'Renaissance' (1945–8)," Ernst Kantorowicz Collection 1908–1982, Box V, 366, online at https://archive.org/details/ernstkantorowicz00reel09 (last accessed June 18, 2019). See also King's Two Bodies, 307 n 81. On planes, see Ernst Kantorowicz, "English Constitutional History (1949)," Ernst Kantorowicz Collection 1908–1982, Box V, 6–7, online at https://archive.org/details/ernstkantorowicz00reel08 (last accessed June 18, 2019). Kantorowicz also will discuss Shakespeare's insights into the "planes" of official life in his lectures on the thirteenth and fourteenth century.

43 Kantorowicz, *King's Two Bodies*, 25.

44 William Shakespeare, *King Richard II* 4.1.182.

thus to reveal himself as a usurper.[45] Bolingbroke catches Richard's double meaning and addresses it explicitly: "I thought you had been willing to resign." Richard responds: "My crown I am; but still my griefs are mine:/You may my glories and my state depose,/But not my griefs; still am I king of those ... Your cares set up do not pluck my cares down."[46]

Richard's use of the word "care" here, like his use of the word "seize," has a double meaning. It designates not only a form of "responsibility" or "duty" (or, in short, "office"). It also designates an experience of "grief," "anxiety," and "worry." One therefore may gloss Richard's claim on care in something like the following terms. *By abdicating or losing my hold on royal office, which is to say, on my second body, the king's immortal body—I'm not also thereby giving away the hold that royal office has left on me. I can't give away the grief, anxiety and worry that are incumbent upon the king. Because my loss of my crown obliges me to recognize my own carelessness as king, and because my recognition of that carelessness in turn functions as the mirror image of the care I myself failed to exercise, I now for the first time have a full grasp of the very care I also now for the first time have no authority to discharge or execute. I can't then give away the traces of care that remain in my mortal body. I therefore remain sovereign over my absence of sovereignty, king over my loss of kingship.*

It's not a stretch, I think, to suggest that Richard's play on these two meanings of "care" constitute a relation between *The King's Two Bodies*. Like a piece of fabric from a gown, care would seem to have two planes, comprised of one plane that faces each body. On the immortal and outwardly visible plane, care would seem to register as a form of responsibility or office. In juridical terms, it would seem to correspond to the imperishability of office itself. On the mortal plane, meanwhile, the inward plane that touches the flesh, care would seem to register as a form of grief, anxiety and worry. Here care would seem to be a name for

45 It might also have a third sense, having to do with the "livery of seisen," the ceremony in medieval England that effected the transfer of land from one party to another. I say this because by the time of the deposition scene, Richard already had "farm[ed] our royal realm," profaned the royal desmesne, converting it from a sacred, undivided Edenic garden into divisible units of rentable and fungible property. This would have broken the part of the historical Richard's coronation oath that would have bound him to preserve the integrity and inalienability of England's land (on this see Kantorowicz, *King's Two Bodies*, 167). Before Bolingbroke "seizes" the crown, in other words, Richard himself turns the crown into "seisen," such that the so-called "deposition scene" does not in fact involve the transfer of a crown, but only a "livery of seisen."

46 *King Richard II* 4.1.191–193, 195.

the way that imperishability registers itself in perishable flesh, the way in which an undying duty manifests itself in the body of a mortal being.

Bolingbroke's response to Richard, in any case, implies that he understands at least one of these two meanings of care. "Part of your cares you give me with your crown," he says. But Richard alone, and not Bolingbroke, is capable of grasping the two meanings of "care" at one and the same time, and this is because of the two, only Richard has suffered the splitting of the king's two bodies. Only Richard then is able to grasp the two meanings of care, seizing on them with despondent precision: "My care is loss of care, by old care done;/Your care is gain of care, by new care won:/The cares I give I have, though given away;/They tend the crown, yet still with me they stay."[47]

What these passages seem to show is not only that "care" is the essence of the office that constitutes any second body, but also that "care" remains with the mortal body of the being who once occupied that office.[48] And this, in turn, provides us with the beginnings of an answer to the question of how conscience figures into the office of the king. *If conscience is the essence of the scholar's office, care will have been the essence of conscience as such.*[49] Care, we might even say, will have been the innermost plane of conscience, the mortal being's most

47 *King Richard* II 4.1.180–189.

48 In fact, judging from the very first lines that King Henry speaks in Henry IV, Part 1—"So shaken as we are, so wan with care"—it would seem that he eventually does grasp Richard's play on the two meanings of care, but only belatedly, only after the death of the one with whom he could have shared that word. Indeed, the second meaning of care—anxiety, worry, concern—would seem to return with such a vengeance for King Henry that it accounts for his famous sleeplessness. If the crown is heavy on the head that wears it, it is perhaps because an imperishable duty is an impossible burden for a perishable being: even a mortal being who never sleeps will never be equal to the excessive responsibilities of a regal office that, taken on its own terms, never dies. Henry's belated "incorporation" of this second meaning of care is arguably the only successful instance of the otherwise infelicitous royal succession between Richard II and Henry IV: in contrast to the two bodies of the king, which arguably are not transferred intact between Richard and Henry, the two planes of care are transferred intact: King Henry is riven not only by responsibility and duty but also by worry and grief.

49 In its two planes, "care" would seem to constitute what Arendt, writing late in her life, would call the two-in-one: an experience of conscience, a form of knowing that knows with and by itself. See Arendt, *The Life of the Mind*, 5. Cf. Hannah Arendt, *Love and Saint Augustine* (Chicago: University of Chicago Press, 1996), 28–29 (on *caritas* as a mode of being in which one loses mortality without also achieving immortality).

intimate relation to the tissue of regalia itself, indeed the very activity that knits that tissue into being in the first place.

One then might also wonder whether care is not also the condition of possibility for any equiparation between the king and the scholar. But there is at least one good reason why this conclusion would be premature, and that has to do with the "Garden Scene" of Act 3 Scene 4, where Richard's carelessness is arguably most explicitly thematized, and which to my knowledge presents us with the only gardener to appear in any text by Shakespeare at all.

What, after all, is a gardener? In *Richard II*, the gardener is a figure who cares for land he doesn't own, on which he is merely, in feudal terms, a tenant. And yet the gardener of *Richard II*, together with his two unnamed companions, seems to know how to tend the garden of England better than does *Richard II* himself. Whereas Richard remains fatally uninvolved in the world of that garden, the gardener and his companions intervene in it like executioners, cutting the heads off of the noisome weeds that threaten it.[50] The regimen in which they are engaged, however, involves much more than just the taking of life. They practise the art of pruning, trimming, lopping, and dressing—of "wound[ing] the bark."[51] They actively negate vegetative life, or what Aristotle would call *zoē*, in order to prevent it from overgrowing itself and negating itself in what they call "waste." [52] Whereas Richard merely reigns over the living, banning subjects from England, the gardener and his unnamed companions directly administer the life internal to that garden. Unlike Richard, their botanical knowledge provides them with techniques for guiding and directing life on the basis of its inner reproductive processes and dynamics.[53] Far from ruling over life from a standpoint of timelessness, then, the gardener's relation to the garden is structured by the endlessness internal to various forms of life, which is to say, by a concept of continuity quite different than that of the king's mystical body.[54] A figure of governmentality more than sovereignty—or, if you

50 *King Richard II* 3.4.33–39.
51 *King Richard II* 3.4.58.
52 *King Richard II* 3.4.54, 66.
53 Indicative, perhaps, of what Foucault called the "epistemic precedence" of botany in early modernity. See Michel Foucault, *The Order of Things: An Archaeology of the Human Sciences*, Trans. Alan Sheridan (New York: Vintage Books, 1973), 137.
54 To be precise, the endlessness of vegetative life is a matter of the "immortality of the genera and separate species," which on Kantorowicz's terms marks "a secularization of the angelic *aevum*" (*King's Two Bodies*, 281, cf. 279, 300). The two forms of continuity—angelic, on the one hand, "vivifying," on the

like, economic theology more than political theology[55]—the gardener's relation to the garden is more immanent than transcendent. This extends to his very name: in a tragedy in which the non-identity between names, titles, and estates is central to the drama itself,[56] the name "gardener" is derived from "garden" in precisely the same way that "Adam" is derived from *adameh* (אדמה, Hebrew for "ground" or "earth") and in much the same way that "human" shares a common root with *humus* (Latin for "earth"). In his immanence with that which he governs, the gardener is a figure of caretaking, and the way he tends his garden marks the precise antinomy to Richard's careless reign. The gardener may lack office and vestiture; he may also lack a proper name, a title, and even *dignitas*; he may indeed be, precisely, humble (which is to say, as distinct from

other (277, 284)—are distinct not least by virtue of the place and function of a problem Kantorowicz takes up in his discussion of the Phoenix metaphor: sexual reproduction (394–395). Angels don't have sex and are without sex because sexual reproduction implies finitude and mortal bodies, which in turn angels lack (which explains, in part, the tension internal to the figure of Angelo in *Measure for Measure*).

55 See, generally, Giorgio Agamben, *The Kingdom and the Glory: For a Theological Genealogy of Economy and Government*, Trans. Lorenzo Chiesa (with Matteo Mandarini) (Stanford, CA: Stanford University Press, 2011). The gardener's relation to the garden certainly is not more secular than is Richard's relation to his demesne: not only is the gardener an Adamic figure, as the Queen points out, but Richard himself has profaned his domain by farming it out to pay for his wars in Ireland. See *Richard II* 3.4.72 ("Thou, old Adam's likeness…"). The Gardener's first companion, meanwhile, echoes John of Gaunt's melancholy disquisition on England's Edenic quality. Cf. *Richard II* 3.4.43–47 and 2.1.40–68. The relation between Richard and the gardener is not then a relation of secularization or profanation: both Richard and the gardener speak theological discourses. The difference is that whereas Richard is a figure of political theology (as Kantorowicz shows) the gardener is a figure of economic theology (as Kantorowicz cannot show). That said, it is important to note that *The King's Two Bodies* closely tracks the distinction between *iurisdictio* and *gubernaculum*, which in turn is one among many expressions of the "bipolar machine" Agamben analyses in *The Kingdom and the Glory* (cf. *King's Two Bodies*, 148 n177, 297 n 53). Kantorowicz is therefore not unaware of the conceptual constellation Agamben later will call "economic theology."

56 Marjorie Garber argues that "perhaps the most significant loss of all [in *Richard II*] is the loss of name, the loss of identity, the imagined one-to-one correspondence between the word and that for which it stands" (*Shakespeare After All* [New York: Anchor Books, 2005], 248). The correspondence between the word "garden" and the garden would seem to be the exception to this rule.

Richard the Sun-King, close to the *humus*). But his care for Richard's garden nevertheless exemplifies precisely the form of care Richard lacks in his own rule over England.

Kantorowicz does not comment on the garden scene in *The King's Two Bodies*. And the reason he doesn't comment on it, I believe, is because he cannot comment on it without also departing from the theme that guides his reading of *Richard II*. What the garden scene demonstrates, after all, is the possibility of speaking about the tragical history of *Richard II* without ever speaking of *The King's Two Bodies* at all. As it appears in the discourse of the gardener, for example, the word "crown" refers less to a regal office than to the head of any given tree.[57]

The crown, in this botanical usage, is not separable from the body of the finite living being that bears it. It's not a second body transferable between finite living beings. It's merely the highest point of a finite living being (a tree), and most importantly of all it dies when that living being dies. In this as in other ways, the garden scene is that part of *Richard II* that allows us to summarize the drama of *Richard II* as a whole without also speaking about *The King's Two Bodies*. And yet the garden scene is also what Marjorie Garber calls a "window scene," which is to say, a moment of perception internal to the play that comments trenchantly on the play as a whole.[58] At the same time the garden scene marks the constitutive exterior of the theme of *The King's Two Bodies*, then, it's also positioned as the innermost interior of Shakespeare's *Richard II*.

Earlier, I expressed scepticism about the idea that *The Fundamental Issue* is necessarily and exclusively an elitist text. I also suggested the possibility of a second and minor reading of Kantorowicz's pamphlet, one that works through rather than internalizing Ehrman's attack on the protections of tenure. I'd like to close now by returning to that point. During the same years that he wrote *The Fundamental Issue* and *The King's Two Bodies*, Kantorowicz's studies of *Richard II* provided him with a gardener very different from the gardener cynically

57 *King Richard II* 4.3.63–66 ("Superfluous branches/We lop away that bearing boughs may live./Had he done so, himself had born the crown,/Which waste of idle hours hath quite thrown down.") Note here the botanical register of the verbs "bearing" and "borne." The way in which a tree bears fruit is distinct from the way a king bears the crown: whereas fruit is immanent to the life of the tree, the crown is transferable between kings. Here as elsewhere *zoē* marks an economic theological limit to the political theological theme of the king's two bodies.

58 Garber, *Shakespeare After All*, 245–246.

invoked by Regent Ehrman.[59] Kantorowicz's second gardener—the unnamed gardener of *Richard II*—may have been a gardener about whom Kantorowicz never spoke. He may also have been a gardener about whom Kantorowicz could not speak without also passing beyond the theme of *The King's Two Bodies*. But the gardener's caretaking gives us the conceptual lever we need to begin reversing and displacing Kantorowicz's internalization of Ehrman's distinction between janitors and gardeners, on the one hand, and professors, on the other. If the essence of conscience is care, then it's not impossible to imagine forms of caretaking that would take place outside of the scholar's office, that would not be identical with or reducible to that office, yet that nevertheless would exemplify the conscience that is the essence of that office. And this, in turn, would open up a different sort of dispute with claims of Ehrman's sort. The real issue, on these terms, is not that professor has a conscience and the gardener doesn't. It's that treating both professors and gardeners as mere employees obscures the paradigms of caretaking, and thus too the forms of conscience, that scholars might share with gardeners. This conclusion is perhaps best expressed by Voltaire's Candide, who formulates his imperative that "we must cultivate our garden" [il faut cultivar notre jardin] after listening to Pangloss recall the deaths of over thirty kings, including *Richard II* of England.[60]

In *The Fundamental Issue*, Kantorowicz thinks conscience but without also thinking care. "Teachers and students together are the University," he will argue, "regardless of the existence of gardens and buildings, or care-takers of gardens and buildings."[61] In response to Ehrman's attack, he will equiparate the time of the *universitas* with the time of the sovereign, and not with the care of the gardener. Today, at a moment when universities across the world seem positively overgrown with Ehrmanian discourse, we discover not only the obligation but also the opening to provide a less careless account of caretaking. Perhaps the

59 Garber also notes that the garden scene in *Richard II* foreshadows the inset scenes of later plays, most notably the porter scene in Macbeth (*Shakespeare After All*, 245–246). This is significant because *Richard II* and *Macbeth* are the only two plays by Shakespeare that Kantorowicz discusses in *The King's Two Bodies*. Kantorowicz's study of Shakespeare, in other words, made him familiar not only with a gardener but also with a janitor—if by "janitor" we mean a figure who is responsible for "minding the door" (the English word "janitor" is derived from the Latin *janua*, which means "door") or, in short, a "porter."

60 Voltaire, *Candide*, Third Edition, Ed. Nicholas Cronk (New York: W. W. Norton & Co., 2016), 80–81.

61 Kantorowicz, *The Fundamental Issue*, 16.

problem with running the university as a business corporation rather than a medieval body corporate is not that it reduces professors to the status of janitors and gardeners. Perhaps it's that it leads university leaders to reign without governing, to lay legal claim to the various emblems and titles of the university without also exposing themselves to the care that's the essence of scholarly office. Perhaps the "almost criminal superficiality" of Ehrmanian discourse (to use Kantorowicz's phrase) is that it obliges those who tend to the "quasi-infinite continuity of public institutions"[62] to work on the terms of precarious, temporary contracts that, in turn, render untenable the forms of continuity and regimens of caretaking that allow for the cultivation of many different kinds of gardens. Perhaps, in short, the problem is that those who today are responsible for the future of the university, that last relic of the Middle Ages, can't imagine its past, and therefore feel carefree about leasing it out as if it were a tenement or pelting farm.

62 Kantorowicz, *The King's Two Bodies*, 284.

Chapter 3

Ministerial office in post-Reformation English thought

Alexander Thom

Opus Dei (*lit.* the Work *of* God): the grammar of Giorgio Agamben's title captures the conceit in miniature. This 'technical term', Agamben notes, 'designates the liturgy'—the liturgy itself, in the words of the Second Vatican Council, denoting the 'exercise of the priestly office of Jesus Christ'.[1] This careful reattribution of the work of sacramental observance, from the minister and onto God, is the key premise: 'By His power He is present in the sacraments, so that when a man baptizes it is really Christ Himself who baptizes'.[2] The sense in which the minister is a vicarious conduit within a hierarchy of practices is also evoked by the imagery of cascading power:[3] the liturgy, as Christ's action, is 'the summit' and 'the font from which all her [the Church's] power flows'.[4]

There are two qualifications to these framing observations. As Agamben notes, the use of the terms *opus Dei* and 'liturgy' only takes on prominence in church doctrine with *The Rule of St Benedict* and 'the end of the nineteenth century' respectively.[5] Second, any corporate institution—Agamben goes so far as to say 'every' institution—might rhetorically distinguish acts as their own, though exercised by their

1 Giorgio Agamben, *Opus Dei: An Archaeology of Duty*, trans. Adam Kotsko (Stanford: Stanford University Press, 2013), xi; Vatican Council II, 'Constitution on the Sacred Liturgy – *Sacrosanctum Concilium*', Documents of the Second Vatican Council, 4 December 1963, 1.7, https://www.vatican.va/archive/hist_councils/ii_vatican_council/documents/vat-ii_const_19631204_sacrosanctum-concilium_en.html.

2 Vatican Council II, 'Sacred Liturgy', 1.7.

3 For hierarchy as 'a practice', see Nicholas Heron, *Liturgical Power: Between Economic and Political Theology* (New York: Fordham University Press, 2017), 11.

4 Vatican Council II, 'Sacred Liturgy', 1.10.

5 Agamben, *Opus Dei*, xi.

DOI: 10.4324/9781003659754-4

representatives, in order to validate them.[6] However, the genealogical advance that Agamben's book makes is to sift out the precursors, the evolutions, and deviations that—through this characterisation—elaborated a conception of work that insulates official actions from 'the qualities of the subject who officiates it'.[7] It is this ethical rupture that conjugates vicarious power into a particularly plastic form, which Agamben sees proliferating throughout modernity.[8]

In defining the vicarious character of the sacraments, both the *Sancrosanctum Concilium* and Agamben's *Opus Dei* gesture back to St Augustine and the Baptismal Disputes.[9] As David Gwynn summarises, the Donatist schismatic movement was 'a rigorist party', who argued that 'Sacraments conferred by *traditores*' [*lit.* traitors] 'and even by those who communicated with *traditores* were therefore invalid, whereas the Catholics maintained that the unworthiness of the minister did not affect the validity of sacraments'.[10] In a move still sometimes critiqued as introducing a 'legalistic concept' to grace, Augustine's emphasis on 'validity' distinguishes the formal correctness of the sacramental operation from its 'fruitfulness (or efficacy) and regularity'.[11] As Andrew Louth notes, even if 'unfruitful in that the participants will not receive grace through the sacrament', it 'may still be a real sacrament, conferring membership of the Church (in the case of baptism), holy orders (in the case of ordination), or the real presence of Christ in the eucharist'.[12] In Agamben's words, Augustine affirms 'the validity of baptism conferred by a heretic or by an unworthy minister', thereby 'securing the objective validity of the sacrament and the priestly action beyond *any subjective conditions* that could render them null or ineffective'.[13] In other words, while a variety of other conditions might yet compromise the sacrament, the personal character and spiritual condition of the minister is bracketed as irrelevant.

6 Ibid., 21.
7 Ibid., xii, *cf.* 91.
8 Ibid., xii.
9 Vatican Council II, 'Sacred Liturgy', 21n; Agamben, *Opus Dei*, 21.
10 David Gwynn, 'Donatism', in *The Oxford Dictionary of the Christian Church*, ed. Andrew Louth (Oxford University Press, 2022), https://www.oxfordreference.com/display/10.1093/acref/9780199642465.001.0001/acref-9780199642465-e-2180.
11 Andrew Louth, 'Validity', in *The Oxford Dictionary of the Christian Church*, ed. Andrew Louth (Oxford University Press, 2022), https://www.oxfordreference.com/display/10.1093/acref/9780199642465.001.0001/acref-9780199642465-e-7461.
12 Ibid.
13 Agamben, *Opus Dei*, 21.

To justify this rupture, Augustine produces a memorable exposition. Exploring the baptisms as administered by Christ's disciples, Augustine parses out the distinction between their actions and Christ's power in explicit terms: 'He, and not He: He by power, they by ministry; they performed the service of baptizing, the power of baptizing remained in Christ'.[14] Observing that Judas baptized others—Judas necessarily representing the *traditore* in its strongest possible sense—Augustine arrives at the definitive conclusion: 'those whom Judas baptized, Christ baptized. In like manner, then, they whom a drunkard baptized, those whom a murderer baptized, those whom an adulterer baptized, if it was the baptism of Christ, were baptized by Christ'.[15] No flaw of character, no corrupted subjectivity can—in itself—disqualify the power of the sacrament, provided the ritual is effectively and correctly applied.

Augustine established that the work of God is indifferent to the character of the person performing it. It fell, in large part, to Aquinas to integrate this into the Aristotelian metaphysics that, via Avicenna and Averroes, proliferated within thirteenth-century Catholic theology more broadly.[16] To the four causes examined by Aristotle—material, formal, efficient, and final—Aquinas seemingly adds a fifth: the instrumental cause.[17] The canonical explanation of the causes is the casting of a statue: the bronze is the material cause without which the statue would

14 Augustine, 'Tractates on the Gospel of John', trans. John Gibb, New Advent, 5.18, accessed 16 January 2025, https://www.newadvent.org/fathers/1701005.htm.

15 Ibid.; Agamben, *Opus Dei*, 21.

16 Simon Gaine, 'Thomas Aquinas, St', in *The Oxford Dictionary of the Christian Church*, ed. Andrew Louth (Oxford: Oxford University Press, 2022), https://www.oxfordreference.com/display/10.1093/acref/9780199642465.001.0001/acref-9780199642465-e-7173; Jarred Mercer, 'Avicenna', in *The Oxford Dictionary of the Christian Church*, ed. Andrew Louth (Oxford: Oxford University Press, 2022), https://www.oxfordreference.com/display/10.1093/acref/9780199642465.001.0001/acref-9780199642465-e-628; Lydia Schumacher, 'Averroism', in *The Oxford Dictionary of the Christian Church*, ed. Andrew Louth (Oxford: Oxford University Press, 2022), https://www.oxfordreference.com/display/10.1093/acref/9780199642465.001.0001/acref-9780199642465-e-625; Becket Soule, 'Albertus Magnus, St', in *The Oxford Dictionary of the Christian Church*, ed. Andrew Louth (Oxford: Oxford University Press, 2022), https://www.oxfordreference.com/display/10.1093/acref/9780199642465.001.0001/acref-9780199642465-e-189.

17 Agamben, *Opus Dei*, 52; Heron, *Liturgical Power*, 92–93; Thomas Aquinas, *The Summa Theologiæ of St. Thomas Aquinas*, trans. Fathers of the English Dominican Province, 2nd ed. (New Advent, 1920), III.64, https://www.newadvent.org/summa/.

not exist; the pattern or blueprint is the formal cause; the agency, such as an artisan, is the efficient cause; and the purpose or goal of the sculpture, 'that for the sake of which the result is produced', is the final cause.[18]

As a subcategory beneath the efficient cause, Aquinas would add the tools with which the artisan casts the statue. The instrumental cause itself has its own proper form, but it only acts according to this form insofar as it is moved by another: 'it belongs to an axe to cut asunder by reason of its sharpness, but to make a couch, insofar as it is the instrument of an art'. The axe 'does not accomplish the instrumental action save by exercising its proper action: for it is by cutting that it makes a couch'. The analogy is carried into the sacraments: the minister is an instrument of providential salvation. They obey the proper form of the sacrament and thereby enable a power and an agency that is not their own. They are nothing more than an animate instrument.

To this, Nicholas Heron's *Liturgical Power* (2018) has provided a few crucial elaborations. The minister, in his official capacity, is therefore 'never the author of his own actions'.[19] From this perspective, Heron argues, 'it is not so much the Stoic sage that is reborn in the Christian minister, but [...] Aristotle's household slave'.[20] Aristotle defines the slave as an instrument—though not quite an instrumental cause—and as 'a subordinate agent of action', such that the slave's actions are not their own.[21] Crucially, the virtue that the slave requires, not unlike the indifferent moral standards for a valid ministry, is 'the smallest amount—just enough, as Aristotle explains, to prevent him from failing in his function'.[22] In other words, the ideal minister performs a curious

18 Simon Blackburn, 'Causes: Material, Formal, Efficient, Final', in *The Oxford Dictionary of Philosophy* (Oxford: Oxford University Press, 2008), https://www.oxfordreference.com/display/10.1093/acref/9780199541430.001.0001/acref-9780199541430-e-525. There is a substantial caveat to Simon Blackburn's brief definition of the efficient cause; similarly in Heron, 92–93. As Andrea Falcon rightly observes, Aristotle is working from existing definitions and then refining them. One of his refinements is to shift the efficient cause from the volition of the artisan into the artistry itself, of which the artisan is a conduit. Falcon's observation thereby complicates the commentaries of Agamben and Heron on Aquinas's use of Aristotle. See Andrea Falcon, 'Aristotle on Causality', in *The Stanford Encyclopedia of Philosophy*, ed. Edward N. Zalta and Uri Nodelman, Spring 2023 (Stanford: Metaphysics Research Lab, Stanford University, 2023), https://plato.stanford.edu/archives/spr2023/entries/aristotle-causality/.
19 Heron, *Liturgical Power*, 130.
20 Ibid.
21 Ibid., 100.
22 Ibid., 130.

sacrifice—a self-emptying, kenotic gesture—in which they empty out their moral agency to become an agent of God: an instrument of a higher power.[23]

The value of this doctrine, from a political perspective, is perhaps obvious. The right to dismiss a minister, and their works, is reserved in the hands of the Church that authorises them. As Agamben shows, the Letter of Clement to the Corinthians—two or more centuries earlier than Augustine—had already begun the process of hardening pastoral service into a priesthood of fixed personas: 'It is obvious that in the letter the term *leitourgia*, while also maintaining the originary meaning of a service for the community, acquires the characteristics of a stable and lifelong office, an object of a canon (*kanōn*) and rule (*epinomē*, which the old Latin version of the letter renders as *lex*)'.[24]

Drawing on Rudolf Sohm, Agamben argues that Clement's letter testifies to the transformation of the 'charismatic community' into a 'juridical organisation', in which 'presbyters and bishops have a right to exercise their "liturgy" and that the community cannot remove them from their position'.[25] Clement's epistle was prompted by an attempt of a congregation to dismiss their 'elders' as religious leaders, an action which Clement characterised as infringing on the presbyters' rights.[26] In other words, the emergence of this sacramental metaphysics has a certain utility given an institutional effort to centralise authority in opposition to autonomous religious communities and localised ethical critiques. In Agamben's genealogy, the protective concepts of validity and rights helped concentrate juridical powers, define their distribution, and to produce an institution that was corporate in character, if not yet strictly incorporated.

~

When rehearsing Agamben's genealogy, I have often observed doubt creep over otherwise friendly scholars in the English legal, political, and literary traditions. Their concern has almost invariably been the uncertain fortunes of this foundational Catholic doctrine through the English Reformation. Filling this niche is particularly useful from a juristic perspective, since important foundations to modern Anglo-American law and politics are established in the period between Henry VIII's Act of

23 On the depersonalisation of persons, *cf.* Roberto Esposito, *Persons and Things*, trans. Zakiya Hanafi (Cambridge, MA: Polity Press, 2015).

24 Agamben, *Opus Dei*, 11.

25 Agamben, *Opus Dei*, 9.

26 Ibid., 10.

Supremacy (1534) and the constitutional crises of 1642–51—for example, *Calvin's Case* (1608), *The Case of Sutton's Hospital* (1612), *Slade's Case* (1602) in citizenship, corporation law, and contract law respectively. But in a sense the enquiry entails two rather different questions: first, how does the doctrine fare from a theological perspective? Second, how pertinent is the ministerial paradigm to this formative legal and political culture?

First, religious doctrine. Unhelpfully, the singularity of 'Protestantism' and 'Reformation' evokes a monolithic, uniform change, rather than a diverse, often divided constellation of movements. Alice Hunt offers an overview of the contemporary sacramental debates with characteristic lucidity: 'The 1530s and 1540s had been marked by dissent, debate and compromise over the nature and implications of the spiritual supremacy and the extent of ecclesiastical and doctrinal thought'.[27] There was marked controversy over which sacraments were real, the official position often changing within a few years: 'Where the Ten Articles [1536] recognised only three of the traditional seven sacraments—baptism, the eucharist and penance—the Act of the Six Articles of 1539 reinstated the banished four'.[28]

However, even this fast-moving debate occurred within the constraints of at least one shared assumption. *The Bishops' Book* (1537) indicates the underlying continuity of the paradigm that we have already established—as Hunt puts it, the book defines 'the authority of priests and bishops as the mediators of grace, but not the givers of grace'.[29] The article in question puts it thus:

> the priestes and bysshoppes, all thoughe in the execution of theyr offyce and ministration they do vse and exercyse the power and auctorytie of god commytted vnto theym, and doo supplye and represente his rowme and place: yet they be not the pryncipall, nor the sufficient or efficient causers or gyuers of grace, or of any other spyrytuall gyfte, whiche procedeth, and is gyuen of god.[30]

27 Alice Hunt, *The Drama of Coronation: Medieval Ceremony in Early Modern England* (Cambridge: Cambridge University Press, 2008), 81.

28 Ibid.

29 Ibid., 83.

30 *The Institution of a Christen Man Conteynynge the Exposytion or Interpretation of the Commune Crede [the Bishops' Book]*, EEBO, STC (2nd ed.) / 5164 (London: Thomae Bertheleti, 1537), 42r, https://go.openathens.net/redirector/leeds.ac.uk?url=https://www.proquest.com/eebo/books/institution-christen-man-conteynynge-exposytion/docview/2264207519/sem-2?accountid=14664.

It goes on explicitly to echo the language of Aquinas: 'the sayde priestes or bysshoppes be but onely as *his instruments or officers*, to execute and minister with theyr hands and tongues, the outewarde and corporall thynges, whereby god worketh'.[31] This Henrician text then affirms the moral insulation that Augustine established against the Donatists:

> neyther the merytes and worthynes of the ministers [...] do gyue them theyr auctoritie, strength, or efficacie: neyther yet the malyce or corrupte lyuynge of them [...] can frustrate or take away from the sayde worde or sacraments theyr sayde power, auctoritie, strength, or vertue.[32]

With the accession of Edward VI ten years later (*r.* 1547–53), Thomas Cranmer—then Archbishop of Canterbury—was encouraged to implement far more wide-ranging Protestant reforms than under the previous monarch.[33] Responding in part to the theology of John Calvin and Huldrych Zwingli, rites were conducted in English, priests were permitted to marry, and the most strenuously Protestant position yet was set out for the Church of England—as Dale Hoak catalogues: 'in a revised *Book of Common Prayer*' published in 1552, 'an ordinal (1550), a new catechism, and the Forty-two Articles of Faith (1553)'.[34] Despite the breadth of these new reforms, the old doctrine remained. 'The wickednesse of the Ministres dooeth not take awaie the effectuall operation of Goddes ordinaunces' is the twenty-seventh article.[35]

This thesis—Catholic in origin, as we have established—was necessarily unaffected by the Counter-Reformation initiated by Mary I and shepherded by her chancellor, Bishop Stephen Gardiner. When the

31 Ibid., 42r, my emphasis.

32 Ibid., 42v.

33 Diarmaid MacCulloch, 'Cranmer, Thomas', in *The Oxford Encyclopedia of the Reformation* (Oxford: Oxford University Press, 1996), https://www.oxfordreference.com/display/10.1093/acref/9780195064933.001.0001/acref-9780195064933-e-0377.

34 Dale Hoak, 'Edward VI of England', in *The Oxford Encyclopedia of the Reformation* (Oxford: Oxford University Press, 1996), https://www.oxfordreference.com/display/10.1093/acref/9780195064933.001.0001/acref-9780195064933-e-0454.

35 Church of England, *Articles Agreed on by the Bishoppes, and Other Learned Menne in the Synode at London [Forty-Two Articles]*, EEBO, STC (2nd ed.) / 10034.2 (London: Richardus Craftonus, 1553), img. 9/13, https://go.openathens.net/redirector/leeds.ac.uk?url=https://www.proquest.com/eebo/books/articles-agreed-on-bishoppes-other-learned-menne/docview/2264203865/sem-2?accountid=14664.

pendulum swung back to Anglicanism under Elizabeth I, once again, the dramatic re-negotiation of a Church of England orthodoxy does not prevent the steady continuation of Augustine's and Aquinas's interpretation. Per *The Thirty-nine Articles of Religion* (1571): 'the vnworthynesse of the ministers, which hinder not the effect of the Sacramentes', 'they do not the same in their owne name but in Christes, and do minister by his commission and aucthoritie'.[36] Notably, in the 'commission' of the Elizabethan article—and the Henrician 'instruments or officers'—an analogy is much more explicitly drawn to political and legal office than in Augustine or Aquinas. Priests are like officers of the law, rather than officers being like priests.[37] For a reform movement that drew its authority and security from a political sovereign rather than a Pope, the implicit value of this rhetorical inversion is perhaps obvious.

This is not to say that the priestly paradigm persisted entirely without controversy. Thomas Rogers in *The English Creed* (1585) gives examples of those 'vvho taught that the Sacraments are holie, vvhen theie be administred by holy men, & not els', critiquing, first, Augustine's old opponents, the 'Donatists' and 'Pe[ti]lians',[38] then Rogers's own contemporaries: 'Th'anabaptists' who think 'the seruice of wiked ministers vnprofitable, and not effectual', and in a remarkable twist 'the Papists. For who seeth not that theie tie the graces of God to the worthines of persons' by forbidding people to receive sacraments from married priests.[39]

36 Church of England, *Articles Whereupon It Was Agreed by the Archbishoppes and Bishoppes of Both Prouinces [Thirty-Nine Articles]*, EEBO, STC (2nd ed.) / 10039 (London: Richard Iugge and Iohn Cawood, 1571), 16–17, https://go.openathens.net/redirector/leeds.ac.uk?url=https://www.proquest.com/eebo/books/articles-whereupon-was-agreed-archbishoppes/docview/2240875824/sem-2?accountid=14664.

37 The comparison of magistracy with priesthood was a commonplace of the period. See, for example, Sir Edward Coke's epitaph, in Sir Edward Coke, *The Selected Writings of Sir Edward Coke: In Three Volumes*, ed. Steve Sheppard (Indianapolis: Liberty Fund, 2002), 3:1336–37.

38 *Cf.* Thomas Rogers, *The Faith, Doctrine, and Religion, Professed, & Protected in the Realme of England*, EEBO, STC (2nd ed.) / 21228 (Cambridge: Iohn Legatt, 1607), img. 104, https://go.openathens.net/redirector/leeds.ac.uk?url=https://www.proquest.com/eebo/books/faith-doctrine-religion-professed-protected/docview/2240912984/sem-2?accountid=14664.

39 Thomas Rogers, *The English Creede Consenting Vvith the True, Auncient, Catholique, and Apostolique Church ... The Second Part*, EEBO, STC (2nd ed.) / 21227 (London: Robert Walde-graue for Andrew Maunsel, 1587), img. 26, https://go.openathens.net/redirector/leeds.ac.uk?url=https://www.proquest.com/eebo/books/english-creede-consenting-vvith-true-auncient/docview/2240914020/sem-2?accountid=14664.

Whether it is indicative of an expanding debate or simply a greater forbearance by his publishers, Rogers wrote an even fuller account by 1607—this time also critiquing 'the Apostolikes, or Henricans, who had a fancie that he was no Bishop, which was a wicked man', 'Cyprian, and Origen' who 'were not sound in this point', and, 'adversaries in our time', 'the Anabaptists, the Family of Loue, the disciplinarians (vsually tearmed Puritants); the Sabbatarians; the Brownists; and the Papists'.[40]

Yet, the strength of this opposition is perhaps overstated, at least as far as Rogers's own critique indicates. Apart from the Anabaptists and the Family of Love, the others place conditions on remaining a valid minister, rather than suggesting, as the two more radical sects did, that only the 'regenerate' (reformed, reborn) can 'minister the vpright seruice, or ceremonies of Christ'.[41] In other words, outright opposition to Augustine's sacramental theology fell to the more radical, populist movements, like the Anabaptists—whose name referred to their practice of re-baptizing people, thereby elevating their dissent from Augustinian sacramental validity into a distinct identity.[42] By contrast, the Anglican mainstream upheld the old tradition, even going so far as to invoke it in order to score points against Roman Catholicism concerning other questions of doctrine.

~

It has been observed that the culture of Tudor and Stuart England was much preoccupied with—though never convincingly subdued by—ideas of obedience and service.[43] At the interface of religion and social order, for example, there was a requirement for ministers to preach a 'Homily against Disobedience and Wilful Rebellion'.[44] Likewise, in the routine catechisms of the Elizabethan church, parishioners declared their duty to 'order my selfe lowly and reverently', to 'obey the Quene, and hir minysters' and to accept 'that state of life, unto whiche it shal please

40 Rogers, *The Faith, Doctrine, and Religion*, img. 104.

41 Ibid.

42 The Anabaptists also exhibited a radical rejection of 'magistracy' and 'due processes of law'.

Quentin Skinner, *The Foundations of Modern Political Thought: The Age of Reformation*, vol. 2 (Cambridge: Cambridge University Press, 1978), 193.

43 Christopher Marlow, 'Cultural Materialist Studies', in *The Arden Research Handbook of Contemporary Shakespeare Criticism*, ed. Evelyn Gajowski (London: Arden Shakespeare, 2021), 102.

44 Ibid., 102; Christopher W. Brooks, *Law, Politics and Society in Early Modern England* (Cambridge: Cambridge University Press, 2008), 69.

God to cal me'.[45] In short, an ideological premium was placed upon service, in which the proper performance of one's temporal duties in a godly kingdom was, in effect, service to God also. To this extent, the entanglement of the liturgical paradigm of government with wider societal roles is already remarkably widespread.

Humanist schooling—in particular, rhetoric—further elevated and authorised an ideal of public service: 'Cicero's works, and especially *De officiis*, had become a fundamental part of the curriculum' in Elizabethan schools.[46] (As Heron and Agamben demonstrate, Cicero's systematic and striated interpretation of duties was important for clerics as they extrapolated and consolidated the Augustinian paradigm—a debt which is particularly pronounced in St Ambrose.)[47] The Queen's principal political minister, William Cecil (1520–98), Lord Burghley, was said to carry a copy of Cicero's *De officiis* in his pocket.[48] But it is the Christian liturgical paradigm, in which public service is itself a ministry, that most explicitly inflects his paternal letters. Preparing his son, Robert, for a life in government, Burghley writes that he works: 'for hir service which I esteme the service of God, whose place she holdeth in erth'.[49] Indeed, such devout characterisations only intensify as Burghley enters his terminal illness in 1598. His final surviving letter to his son closes with: 'Serve God by serving of the Quene for all other service is in dede bondage to the Devil'.[50]

The idea of a servant as an animate instrument is also in general circulation. In Thomas Kyd's translation of Torquato Tasso's *The Householder's Philosophy* (1588), they write that the servant is like a hand—'*The instrument of instruments*'—for 'he keepeth all the instruments of household occupied', though 'where they are *Inanima*, things without soule, he is *Animatus*, and diuinelie is enriched'.[51] The argument continues: '*Artificers are Instruments of those things which properly they call workmanship*; but the Seruaunt is *Instrument of the action*, which

45 Brian Cummings, ed., *The Book of Common Prayer: The Texts of 1549, 1559, and 1662* (Oxford: Oxford University Press, 2013), 153.
46 Brooks, *Law, Politics and Society*, 29; for Westminster as a specific example, see Ian Donaldson, *Ben Jonson: A Life* (Oxford: Oxford University Press, 2012), 75.
47 Agamben, *Opus Dei*, 77–82; Heron, *Liturgical Power*, 123–130.
48 Brooks, *Law, Politics and Society*, 59.
49 William Cecil, 'The Letters of Lord Burghley, William Cecil, to His Son Sir Robert Cecil, 1593–1598', *Royal Historical Society Camden Fifth Series* 53 (December 2017): 122–123, https://doi.org/10.1017/S0960116317000069.
50 Ibid., 293.
51 Thomas Kyd, 'The Hovsholders Philosophie', in *The Works of Thomas Kyd*, ed. Frederick S. Boas (Oxford: Clarendon Press, 1901), 267.

also is distinguished from workmanship'.[52] In other words, Tasso and Kyd invoke but disturb the already murky distinctions between efficient causes, subordinate agents, and animate instrumentality. Craftsmen—like Aristotle's bronze-caster—are truly the instruments of their artistry, which is the efficient cause;[53] servants are mediators of someone else's command, someone else's action.

This latter model underpins Sir Francis Bacon's account of the ideal political minister, at least concerning the moral responsibility for official actions. A distinguished, though often frustrated diplomat and jurist,[54] Bacon's essays are at times perceptively critical of a working culture predicated upon alienation. In his essay, 'On Great Place', he argues: 'Men in great place are thrice servants: servants to the sovereign or state; servants of fame; and servants of business [...] It is a strange desire, to seek power and lose liberty; or to seek power over others and to lose power over a man's self'.[55] In the highest positions, men become 'strangers to themselves'.[56] But this is, in large part, simply a description of any difficult and precarious occupation—in which health falls to one side and one's reputation from the mouths of others assumes exaggerated importance.

In terms of ethics, Bacon begins in a promising vein: 'good thoughts' are little better than 'good dreams'; 'Merit and good works are the end of man's motion'.[57] However, though positioned as a *telos*, 'merit and good works' have a strikingly limited scope in his essay. He focuses almost entirely on the skilful and courteous conduct of professional duties: 'In the discharge of thy place set before thee the best examples'.[58] Continuing on, Bacon's concerns reflect pragmatic issues of skill, tone, and consultation—for example, the importance of avoiding the appearance of bribery, not just the fact. In other words, there is almost no engagement with the ethics of one's official acts, only on the conduct

52 Ibid.

53 The efficient cause is often identified in the volition of the agent. For Aristotle's statue analogy, the 'bronze-caster' is routinely termed the efficient cause. See, for example, Blackburn, 'Causes'.

54 Markku Peltonen, 'Bacon, Francis, Viscount St Alban', in *Oxford Dictionary of National Biography* (Oxford: Oxford University Press, 2007), https://doi.org/10.1093/ref:odnb/990.

55 Francis Bacon, *The Major Works*, ed. Brian Vickers, Oxford World's Classics (Oxford: Oxford University Press, 2008), 359.

56 Ibid.

57 Ibid., 360.

58 Ibid.

that frames them.[59] After cautioning people not to wear their authority too openly in social settings, he remarks: 'let it rather be said, "When he sits in place he is another man"', which concisely idealises the ethical severance of ministerial office.[60] As Sir Edward Coke also put it:

> for in the Office and execution of Judgement, he that is a Judge (*Desinet esse Amicus*) ceaseth to be a friend: for in the manner of judgement, no acquaintance, no griefes, no friends, no remembrance of fore-passed present, or hope of future friendship must direct the thoughts of him that is a Judge.[61]

One might object that choosing an essay on high office, I am myself imposing the narrowness that I otherwise impute to Bacon's ethics. However, in 'Of Wisdom for a Man's Self', Bacon once again focuses on service. He argues that referring an order to one's own moral judgment is 'a desperate evil in a servant to a prince, or a citizen in a republic'.[62] The ideal office-holder understands that their 'service' is 'but the accessary' to another's moral action, not their own.[63] For Bacon, adjusting—let alone disobeying—an official act to square it with one's own conscience is a form of corruption equivalent to bribery. Moral satisfaction is, in effect, no different from the satisfaction of any other 'petty ends and envies' that 'crooketh' the servant's conduct from the master's intent'.[64] In other words, Bacon's conception of the official is not as a political or ethical artisan in their own right—like the Stoic sage—but explicitly as Kyd's household servant: an instrument of someone else's action.

However, such instrumentality is not uniformly celebrated in Tudor and Stuart culture—it has an obverse face. In *The Phoenix*, Thomas Middleton's Proditor refers to his 'hired instruments' in a murderous plot (12.15).[65] When Shakespeare's Orsino suspects foul play: 'I partly know the instrument | That screws me from my true place in

59 *Cf.* Hannah Arendt, *Eichmann in Jerusalem: A Report on the Banality of Evil* (London: Penguin Classics, 2006), 50–51, 64–65.
60 Bacon, *The Major Works*, 361.
61 Coke, *Selected Writings*, 2:527.
62 Bacon, *The Major Works*, 386.
63 Ibid.
64 Ibid., 387, 386.
65 All subsequent parenthetical references to Middleton refer to Thomas Middleton, *Thomas Middleton: The Collected Works*, ed. Gary Taylor and John Lavagnino (Oxford: Oxford University Press, 2007) unless otherwise noted.

your favour' (*TN*, 5.1.114–15).[66] Angelo likewise dismisses Isabella and Mariana's complaints against him: 'These poor informal women are no more | But instruments of some more mightier member | That sets them on' (*MM*, 5.1.232–34). Where deployed in either supernatural or more formal contexts, it frequently (though not exclusively) evokes a problematic devotion: 'The instruments of darkness' or 'the ministers and instruments | Of cruel war' (*Mac*, 1.3.119–21; *TC*, Pro.4–5). In other words, one of the prevailing connotations of 'instrument' in literature of the period is as a pejorative: an amoral servant serving a bad cause.

In legal discourse, an 'instrument' is first and foremost a generic term for any 'formal legal document'.[67] For example, Coke's *Reports*: 'any Deed, Charter, or other Instrument'.[68] However, jurists frequently avail themselves of the pejorative connotations for rhetorical purposes also. For example, in discussing treasonous plotters, Coke remarks: 'the Divell (the Pope I should say) might want no instrument for the effecting of murthers, treasons, and rebellions'.[69] Likewise, Bacon critically writes of 'crafty' 'servants and instruments', working to 'put off others cunningly'.[70] Middleton, in *The Nightingale and the Ant*, wittily pairs the two meanings—the legal document and the wily practitioner:

> now I talk of calfskin, 'tis great pity, Lady Nightingale, that the skins of harmless and innocent beasts should be as instruments to work villainy upon, entangling young novices and foolish elder brothers which are caught like woodcocks in the net of the law.
>
> (455–460)

Thus, while a plain sense of 'servants' or 'officials' is often intended, the sinister connotations remain near the surface—even when applied to legal officers. Coke characterises the officials under Richard Empson and Edmund Dudley as 'their instruments', whose 'oppressions and exactions' 'brought infinite treasures to the Kings Cofers'.[71] In 'On Judicature' (1612), Bacon diagnoses 'four bad instruments' in the courts: vexatious

66 All subsequent parenthetical references to Shakespeare refer to William Shakespeare, *The New Oxford Shakespeare: Modern Critical Edition*, ed. Gary Taylor et al. (Oxford: Oxford University Press, 2016) unless otherwise noted.

67 'Instrument, n.', in *OED Online* (Oxford: Oxford University Press), 2.b., accessed 15 February 2025, https://www.oed.com/dictionary/instrument_n.

68 Coke, *Selected Writings*, 1:69.

69 Ibid., 2:539.

70 Bacon, *The Major Works*, 411.

71 Coke, *Selected Writings*, 2:1143.

litigators, jurisdictional zealots, political operators, and the excessively avaricious.[72] In the second and third, Bacon's resentments are legible—against Coke and the Cecils respectively: the former frequently disputing against the prerogative courts, the latter having enjoyed a remarkable political ascendency.[73] While 'bad instruments' plainly denotes officials compromising their duties to their own advantage—the phrase might also imply that they are serving a power other than that they should. Defining and locating that power was precisely the constitutional crisis of the next generation.

The Elizabethan preoccupation with the sovereign in cultural matters has been usefully explored.[74] For all this, Tudor and Stuart England was not an entirely absolutist polity. *The Mirror of Magistrates* (1559) is a typical example of the period's political and legal discourse. The book qualifies its endorsements of monarchy, as Christopher W. Brooks observes—instead celebrating 'the institutions and life of the body politic', such as 'sound administration and the maintenance of law' rather than total prerogative.[75] The model is, as Thomas Norton's translation of John Calvin's *Institutes* (1561) also puts it, the 'temper[ing]' of monarchy by 'common government'.[76] Reviewing treatises of the 1570s and 1580s, Brooks points out such 'mixed-monarchical interpretations of the English constitution [...] would have been both instantly recognised and considered fairly conventional'.[77] In other words, *Mirror* espouses precisely the kind of monarchical republicanism Patrick Collinson influentially proposed, upon which subsequent scholars, like Alice Hunt, Stephen Alford, and Paul Raffield, have perceptively elaborated.[78]

72 Bacon, *The Major Works*, 448.
73 Brooks, *Law, Politics and Society*, 116–118; Pauline Croft, 'Cecil, Robert, First Earl of Salisbury', in *Oxford Dictionary of National Biography* (Oxford: Oxford University Press, 2008), https://doi.org/10.1093/ref:odnb/4980.
74 Roy Strong, *The Cult of Elizabeth: Elizabethan Portraiture and Pageantry* (London: Pimlico, 1999).
75 Brooks, *Law, Politics and Society*, 57.
76 Ibid., 68.
77 Ibid., 81.
78 Patrick Collinson, 'The Monarchical Republic of Queen Elizabeth I', in *Elizabethan Essays* (London and Rio Grande: The Hambledon Press, 1994), 31–57; Alice Hunt, 'The Monarchical Republic of Mary I', *The Historical Journal* 52, no. 3 (2009): 557–572; Stephen Alford, 'Patrick Collinson's Elizabethan Commonwealth', *Reformation* 17, no. 1 (January 2012): 7–27, https://doi.org/10.1558/refm.v17.7; Paul Raffield, 'The Monarchical Republic, Constitutionality, and the Legal Profession', in *The Oxford Handbook of English Law and Literature, 1500–1700*, ed. Lorna Hutson

The culture of this constitution is implicitly ministerial. A religious ideal of service bound the sovereign, the Parliament, and the judiciary to a body of laws and powers: 'the ministers and setters forth of [laws] may right wel be called *Sacerdotes* [priests], that is giuers & teachers of holy things'.[79] The authority of a theocratic administration—a hierarchy, a sacred order—was internalised and practised by a taxonomy of officers, from the sovereign down to the parish beadles. However, an underlying agreement on this sense of instrumental service did not prevent but rather exacerbated the constitutional conflicts of the mid-seventeenth century. On the one hand, as Bacon remarked: 'Let judges also remember, that Salomon's throne was supported by lions on both sides: let them be lions, but yet be lions under the throne; being circumspect that they do not check or oppose any point of sovereignty'.[80] On the other, as Kantorowicz observed, frustrated parliamentarians felt one might dutifully fight the king to protect the Crown.[81]

Such disobedience was already conceivable throughout the sixteenth century, as Quentin Skinner carefully demonstrated in a classic study. The wars of the Reformation altered preconceptions about constitutional resistance to sovereign power.[82] But as Skinner's argument also shows, this slow explosion of a 'duty to resist' was precisely catalysed by the old idea of magistracy as its own form of divine service, albeit relocated onto a continuum with sovereignty rather than entirely derived from it.[83] Such recalibrations never concerned the metaphysics of service *per se*, but merely redefined the efficient cause of whom one becomes an instrument: whether God, the sovereign as God's chief minister, or

(Oxford: Oxford University Press, 2017), 163–179, https://doi.org/10.1093/oxfordhb/9780199660889.013.27.

79 Sir John Fortescue, *A Learned Commendation of the Politique Lawes of England*, trans. Robert Mulcaster, EEBO, STC (2nd ed.) / 11196 (London: Printed by Thomas Wight, and Bonham Norton, 1599), img. 10/136, https://go.openathens.net/redirector/leeds.ac.uk?url=https://www.proquest.com/eebo/books/learned-commendation-politique-lawes-england/docview/2240861576/sem-2?accountid=14664.

80 Bacon, *The Major Works*, 449.

See also Bacon's ideal constitution in *The Advancement of Learning*: 'Kings ruled by their laws as God did by the laws of nature, and ought as rarely to put in use their supreme prerogative as God doth his power of working miracles' (253). *Cf.* Carl Schmitt, *Political Theology*, trans. George Schwab (Cambridge, MA: Massachusetts Institute of Technology Press, 1985), 36–37.

81 Ernst H. Kantorowicz, *The King's Two Bodies: A Study in Medieval Political Theology* (Princeton: Princeton University Press, 2016), 22–23.

82 Skinner, *Reformation*, 2:189–238.

83 Ibid., 2:204–5, 208, 211.

the Crown as the corporate entity of which the sovereign is themselves also an instrument.[84] Ministerial power thereby forms the ideological bedrock—and the source of a contested moral authority—for both sides of the English Revolution.

~

At a late stage in his magnum opus, Kantorowicz cites the Italian jurist, Baldus de Ubaldis (1327–1400), whose phrasing anticipates Bacon's formulation: 'we are aware of the Dignity [office] as the principal, and of the person as the instrumental'.[85] Kantorowicz connects this to the influence of Aquinas's exploration of instrumentality too: 'the bishop could also appear vicariously as an *instrumentum animatum* of the Deity'.[86] While he touches on the sacraments and the economy of salvation, the book remains understandably focused on the implied ontologies and hypostases of such formulations, rather than the ethics. At stake in this comparison is the *corpus mysticum*: official service to a metaphysical body. Among the many species of legal 'fiction' or 'shorthand', the corporation emerged as an effective means for the collective ownership of monastic property.[87] Instructively, Kantorowicz explains the origin of his book with an anecdote on receiving mail from a religious house suffixed with 'Inc.', thereby prompting his investigations into the fiction of incorporation and, from thence, the body politic.[88]

However, the subsequent focus on both 'the body politic' and 'public service'—liturgical power—can occlude how commercial corporations find their premise in the ministerial paradigm too. In *The Case of Sutton's Hospital* (1612), the sacramental logic of Crown servants carried through into the function of the founder, the citizen exercising the law:

84 For a fascinating account of these issues in Royalist literature, see James Loxley, 'Dramatis Personae: Royalism, Theatre and the Political Ontology of the Person in Post-Regicide Writing', in *Royalists and Royalism during the Interregnum*, ed. Jason McElligott and David L. Smith (Manchester: Manchester University Press, 2010), 149–170.

85 Kantorowicz, *King's Two Bodies*, 441–442.

86 Ibid., 443.

87 J. H. Baker, *An Introduction to English Legal History*, 3rd ed. (London: Butterworths, 1990), 213; see also Frederick Pollock and Frederic William Maitland, *The History of English Law Before the Time of Edward I* (Indianapolis: Liberty Fund, 2010), 263–264, 400.

88 Kantorowicz, *King's Two Bodies*, xxxiii, cf. 404.

> And when the common person hath done it and declared it in writing according to his authority, then they are incorporated by the King's Letters Patents, and not by the common person, for he is but an instrument, and the King maketh the Incorporation in such case in the same manner as if all had been comprehended in the Letters Patents themselves.[89]

Coke's description of the corporation echoes almost all the attributes so lavishly discussed regarding the body politic: 'invisible, immortal [...] it is not subject to imbecilities, or death of the natural, body, and divers other cases'.[90] More importantly for our purposes, the artificial person of the corporation not only depends on the liturgical administration of the Crown's power for their founding. They in turn require their own representatives: they formalise their own personas, officers, and administrators.[91]

Agamben asserts that this ministerial model of service has 'exercised an influence so profound—that is, subterranean' on modernity that we can scarcely perceive it.[92] Likewise, Heron identifies 'the seemingly infinite proliferation of offices' as one of the 'defining features' of modernity.[93] Some cases are intuitively understood: the judiciary, the civil service, political ministries, the military—in other words, state officials. However, the most prevalent occurrence of this paradigm is hardly in the service exercised for the state, but rather for those private, oligarchic, and authoritarian entities that populate the registers of the SEC and Companies House. Consequently, it is concerning our mundane service of private metaphysical bodies—corporations, limited companies, limited liability partnerships—wherein Agamben's critique has revelatory potential.

For example, consider fiduciary duties: a legal concept that occupies one of the major overlaps between professional conduct and company law. These duties of fidelity, of faithfulness, are owed 'by trustees to beneficiaries', by 'agents to principals', by 'solicitors to clients', by 'corporate directors and officers to their corporation'.[94] Fiduciary duties

89 Coke, *Selected Writings*, 1:374–75.

90 Coke, *Selected Writings*, 1:371–72.

91 Bishops and abbots were personas and dignities capable of perpetual succession, like kings. *Cf.* Baker, *English Legal History*, 213–214; Kantorowicz, *King's Two Bodies*, 385, 402.

92 Agamben, *Opus Dei*, xii.

93 Heron, *Liturgical Power*, 132.

94 Lionel Smith, 'Fiduciaries', in *The New Oxford Companion to Law*, ed. Peter Cane and Joanne Conaghan (Oxford: Oxford University Press, 2008),

demonstrate a few advantages to the instrumental ideal than Agamben's account perhaps acknowledges—particularly the two 'prophylactic' rules which enforce transparency around conflicts of interest and bar attempts at personal gain without permission.[95] On the other hand, they also work to short-circuit moral objections, squashing dissent in lieu of service. Few are as well-informed about the ongoing climate breakdowns as the directors and attorneys of those corporations most responsible for it.[96] But as faithful agents of the company, a director is prohibited from acting in office to the impairment of the company's 'success', usually understood in narrow commercial terms.[97] So while some may still wrestle with their consciences—many can alleviate their doubts by seeing themselves as dutifully fulfilling their function, as a dutiful cog within a larger machine. Fiduciary duty therefore offers another avenue into the 'cog theory' that Hannah Arendt once observed in Eichmann, for which Agamben has identified a powerful religious heritage.[98]

Augustine's intervention into the nature of a metaphysically specific event—the communication of grace through a sacrament—has metastasised into a remarkably plastic paradigm of power, whether constitutional or corporate, public or private. The concomitant circumscription of ethics into professional conduct is conspicuous in both its ubiquity and its inadequacy. Likewise, the characterisation of servants, lawyers, judges, directors, and ministers as instruments carries a certain normative force, but, as a description, it remains unconvincing. By this I mean that while it may soften the sting of moral compromise, instrumentality requires one to elide the considerable creativity and individual ethos

---

https://www.oxfordreference.com/display/10.1093/acref/9780199290543.001.0001/acref-9780199290543-e-890.

95 Ibid.

96 Benjamin Franta, 'Early Oil Industry Disinformation on Global Warming', *Environmental Politics* 30, no. 4 (7 June 2021): 663–668, https://doi.org/10.1080/09644016.2020.1863703; Benjamin Franta, 'What Big Oil Knew about Climate Change, in Its Own Words', *The Conversation*, 28 October 2021, http://theconversation.com/what-big-oil-knew-about-climate-change-in-its-own-words-170642; this paragraph partly reiterates an argument made in Alexander Thom, *Office and Duty in King Lear: Shakespeare's Political Theologies*, Palgrave Shakespeare Studies (Cham: Palgrave Macmillan, 2023), 247–248.

97 UK Public General Acts, 'Companies Act 2006' (Statute Law Database, 8 December 2017), 10.2.172, https://www.legislation.gov.uk/ukpga/2006/46/section/172.

98 Hannah Arendt, 'Personal Responsibility Under Dictatorship', in *Responsibility and Judgment*, ed. Jerome Kohn (New York: Schocken Books, 2003), 29–32.

routinely involved in such work. Through an ordination that is also a subordination, the governors are, as Heron observes, themselves governed.[99] By doing so, office confers a disempowering power; a responsibility to disavow responsibility. Duty empties ethics and action, offering conduct and operation in their place. In other words, the alienation of labour—which is tellingly pronounced in those sectors devoted to 'services'—was presaged and proliferated by the instrumental operations of grace itself.

99 For more on the 'neutralising' of the traditional distinction between the governors and the governed, see Heron, *Liturgical Power*, 12–13, 84–85, 112, 123, 130, 137.

Chapter 4

Conducting office

Inheriting conduct manuals for jurists in the Islamic legal tradition

Adil Hasan Khan

Introduction

This chapter was completed in the shadow of (yet) another attempt by a colonial project to destroy the tradition(s) of the colonized. It feels the responsibility that this context brings to the task of a jurist heir to redescribe, and thus, inherit a legal tradition. This is a legal tradition that has undergone violent transformations through its encounters with projects of colonial modernity and the contestation of colonial modernity by this tradition's practitioners. Transformation of the tradition(s) of the colonized must be reckoned with by their heirs. They cannot simply be wished away either as symptoms of inexplicable civilizational amnesia or the contingent choices of naïve ancestral figures. Making audible the choices made by ancestral figures in the tradition is an heir's task as they sift through what remains 'living' and what is now perhaps moribund in the present.

It is within this context that I turn to the question of the office(s) of the jurist. Over the past few years there has been a renewed interest in Anglo-American legal circles in examining the question and concept of office, especially pertaining to the offices of public legal administrator and jurist.[1] Notable in much of this literature is a strong proclivity to formulate the connection between office and *authority* in terms of foundations for actions or authorizing grounds (of the former, by the latter). Any concern with the *conduct* of office holders is limited to discerning what underlying grounds of authority are being sought to be invoked or attached through this conduct. The official's conduct, in this version of institutional thinking, is *authorized conduct* that administers

1 See Special Issue of the *University of Toronto Law Journal*, Volume 70, Supplement 2, 2020.

DOI: 10.4324/9781003659754-5

in the name of different pre-given authorities (especially the state).[2] Office gets conceived in terms of power conferral, with a paucity of concern with evaluating the quality of official conduct by these heirs to a Anglo-Utilitarian legal positivist tradition.[3] Simultaneously, *authority* gets rendered into an attribute or justification for an instrumental action separable from ends – as against its formulation as a relationship created and cared for by practical activity.

Rivalling *this* 'turn to office', amidst the continuing reverberations of a populist anti-institutionalism of the past decade, is a Kantian tradition that configures office as deontological duty, entirely abstracted from an institutional form, relations of authority, practical concerns/purposes, and pedagogical repertoires that might enable/train/cultivate the conduct of the inhabitants/occupants of that office. Thus, *Personal Dignitas* is what every 'human' simply has, not character that requires cultivation through training conduct. In this universe of abstracted selves there are no separate classes of officials, and their specific practical activities or role-duties.

This chapter, in its inheritance of the Islamic legal tradition, approaches the question of the offices of the jurist somewhat differently from these rival (and related) concerns with office. It does so by holding the question of office tightly together with a concern with describing both the *quality of* and *training in* the conduct of offices. This is sought to be accomplished by way of reporting on a specific genre of conduct training manuals for the offices of *faqihs/'alims* (jurists),[4] referred to as *Adab Al-Mufti* (i.e. conduct manuals for a jurist or jurisconsult) and *Adab Al-Qadi* (i.e. conduct manuals for a judge) respectively.

However, this reporting on a jurist's 'conduct of conduct' is very much conducted as an heir to this tradition. I.E. one who asks – how can I conduct myself as a jurist today? And one who cannot inherit *sans* attentiveness to the problems posed to the tradition, and its repertoires of practical activities, relations and institutions, by specific colonial modern projects seeking its destruction. Without this work and

2 See Paul Du Gay, *For Public Service*, London and New York: Routledge, 2023, pp. 49–50.

3 See H.L.A. Hart, *The Concept of Law*, New York: Oxford University Press, 1961.

4 In this chapter I use *faqih* (*fuqaha* pl.) and '*alim* (*ulama* pl.) interchangeably for jurists, which specifically includes jurisconsults (*Muftis*) and judges *(Qadis)*. See M. Khaled Masud, 'Adab al-Mufti: The Muslim Uniderstanding of Values, Characteristics, and Role of a Mufti', *in* Barbara Daly Metcalf, *Moral Conduct and Authority: The Place of Adab in South Asia*, Berkeley, Los Angeles, London: University of California Press, 1984, p. 126.

attentiveness, we cannot receive what is 'living' (and 'livable') in this tradition today. Thus, after reporting on pre-colonial *adab* manuals for jurists in the first section of the chapter, the second section describes colonial modern projects to control and displace the 'Islamic legal tradition' through the undertaking of colonial legal reforms aimed at securing secular legal bureaucratization, with a particular focus upon the British colonization of South Asia from the late-18th to the mid-19th century. As I describe it, a key aim of this colonial modern project, variously conducted through textbook translation projects that excised jurist conduct manuals, was to render the Islamic legal tradition inert/dead. This was sought to be achieved by attempting to reduce a 'living tradition' to a timeless 'legal code' *sans* all the practical arts and institutions that some anachronistically and inaccurately describe as 'procedural', but which are more adequately the arts of jurisprudence and the institutions of the offices of jurist. In the third and penultimate section, the chapter describes the *revival* of the 'Islamic legal tradition' in the face of this colonial modern project of destruction through a description of the jurist conduct manuals that were written and imbibed by jurists in this period in British India and Egypt under 'informal' British occupation in the late 19th century. The 'Islamic legal tradition' – with its jurists, their practical jurisprudence and thus the conduct of their offices – remains vital (and available) even today on account of this embodied capacitation to undertake the practical activity of renewal of the tradition in response to projects of destruction.

Medieval and early modern Adab Al-Mufti wa Adab Al-Qadi

In this section I provide a reading of a genre of conduct training manuals for the offices of the jurist, referred to as the *Adab Al-Mufti wa Adab Al-Qadi*, in the medieval and early modern periods across the Indo-Persian and wider Islamicate world.[5] This genre is commonly contained as specific chapters in a general textbook on jurisprudence (*Kitab al-Usul-ul-Fiqh*) that were penned by jurists belonging to one of the five

5 Specifically I have consulted Imam Al-Nawawi, 'The Etiquettes of a *Fatwa*, the *Mufti*, and the One Seeking a *Fawa* (Translation of Chapter of the Introduction to Al-Nawawi's *al-Majmu*)', Mahdi Lock trans., *Islamic Sciences* 11, 2 (2013), pp. 113–159; Makhdum Muhammad Jafar Bobakani, '*Adab al Mufti*' [Chapter in *al-Matana fi maramma al-khazana*]', 1568, Karachi: Ihya al-adab as-Sindi, 1962.

major schools of Islamic jurisprudence (the four *Sunni Madhabs* and one *Shia*).[6]

The *Adab Al Qadi wa Mufti* forms part of a broader literature of ethical literature for office – including *Nasihatnama's* and the so-called 'Mirror for…'.[7] In recent years there has been a lot of work and attention to the related roles of the secretarial or scribal arts (*Munshis*) in the early modern period. Even when it comes to the training of office conduct of the jurist, these conduct manuals formed part of a broader set of literature, including biographies of ancestral jurists and exemplary histories of the jurists of a specific region.[8]

Offices and practical activities

As is invariably the case with conduct literature, office in these conduct manuals is given shape through embedding it in the conduct of specific practical activities. While in the case of the *Qadi* (judge) this activity was the conduct of *qada* (i.e. delivering a decision on a dispute), in the case of the *Mufti* (jurist) it was the conduct of *ifta* (i.e. issuing legal advice/guidance or a *fatwa*).[9] While the latter could be responding to questions of law posed by those Muslims who ascribed to their particular jurisprudential schools (an individual questioner or a *Mustafi*), it is notable how in this period the role of the *Mufti* was tightly bound up with the role of *Qadi*, with a significant bulk of 'his' duties pertaining to responding, as a jurisconsult, to questions posed by *Qadis* for legal brief to guide their decisions.[10] Good evidence for this relationship is also on display in the common practice of twinning the adab chapters of the two legal roles together in different collections.[11]

6 Usually these were the last chapters of these textbooks. See Wael B. Hallaq, *Sharia: Theory, Practice, Transformations*, New Delhi: Cambridge University Press, 2009, pp. 552–555.

7 See Muzaffar Alam and Sanjay Subrahmanyam, 'The Making of a Munshi', *Comparative Studies of South Asia, Africa and the Middle East*, 24, 2 (2004) 61–72.

8 Masud, 'Adab al-Mufti', p. 134.

9 See Muhammad Khalid Masud et al., 'Muftis, Fatwas, and Islamic Legal Interpretation' in Muhammad Khalid Masud et al. eds., *Islamic Legal Interpretation: Muftis and their Fatwas*, Cambridge, MA and London, England: Harvard University Press, 1996.

10 Messick, 'Fatwa, Modern', in Kate Fleet et al., *Encyclopedia of Islam*, 3rd Edition, Brill Online, 2017.

11 Masud, 'Adab al-Mufti', p. 127.

A practical ethics (doing those activities well)

Significantly contained in these conduct manuals was a description of both the offices attached to the figure of the jurist, as well as a description of exemplary conduct for inhabiting or taking up these offices well ('responsibilities and etiquettes')[12] To the ear shaped by colonial modernity, the use of the term 'etiquettes' (*Adab*) brings to mind notions of 'non-state norms' ('social norms') that are somehow ascribed a lesser force of obligation ('mere etiquette') – in a normative universe where we connect the degree of obligation with the severity and source of sanction and enforcement, such that the highest level of obligation is state-decreed and enforced norms – and furthermore, a paradigm within which jurists of a 'legal tradition' are only concerned with the latter ('law properly so called') and not with 'mere etiquette'.[13] However, in this other orientation to normative life, to which these conduct manuals belonged, all these different practices and institutions belonged to a single broader category of the *practical* that invited, created the conditions for, and trained subjects to inhabit specific 'forms of life'. An orientation to practical normativity is an orientation of normative practices away from foundational questions (e.g. what is the source/foundation of an obligation? or, relatedly, why obey or have fidelity towards a norm?) and towards practical questions of 'how to'[14] live well with obligations.[15]

Crucially, in this normative orientation, obligations themselves are inseparable from the practices of cultivating their inhabiting/embodiment – contra another colonial modern orientation, as we will soon see, whereby obligations (as ends) get rendered external/separable to the various arts and institutions of living with them, thus rendering the latter into separable (and myriad) 'means' or 'instruments' to achieve the 'ends' of obedience to norms (that can themselves only be evaluated as per the purportedly separate 'procedural norms' of effectiveness, efficiency, certainty etc.).[16] Rather, obligations are taken up in terms of

12 Lock, 'The Introduction to Al-Nawawi's *Al-Majmu'*, p. 118.

13 Talal Asad, 'Thinking about Law, Morality, and Religion in the Story of Egyptian Modernization', *JISMOR* 1 (2006) 13, p. 19.

14 Pierre Hadot, 'Ancient Philosophy: An Ethic or a Practice' in *The Selected Writings of Pierre Hadot: Philosophy As a Practice*, London and New York: Bloomsbury, 2020, p. 59.

15 This is not a 'West'/ 'Non-West' question, but, as we will see, a colonial modern/rest question, wherein the inheritor of tradition has to fight the urge to 'retrospectively project'. Cf. Foucault, *The Hermeneutics of the Subject*, pp. 318–319.

16 See Adil Hasan Khan, 'Tradition', in Tony Anghie et al. eds, *Research Handbook on Third World Approaches to International Law (TWAIL)*, Edward Elgar, 2025. See Hart, *The Concept of Law*.

their 'livability' – both embodied and relationally, such that 'the force of obligation…is rooted not in rules but in forms of life that obliges what one can or cannot do'.[17]As Asad puts it:

> …practical programs for the cultivation of moral virtues presuppose authoritative models.[18]

Thus, in the case of the early modern *Adab Al-Mufti* genre, the 'rules/offices of conduct' take the form of embodied exemplars describing/narrating the conduct (both as saying and enactment) of ancestral figures performing (*living*) said obligation well and inviting imitation on the part of the reader. This practice of ethical subject formation through encountering embodied exemplars is not limited to examples described within the pages of the conduct manual itself but rather extends to the practices of reading and relating to the text itself,[19] with the significance of practically imbibing the training of these texts through the embodied guidance ('*Talammudh* or apprenticeship')[20] of exemplary teachers being encouraged. As Al-Nawawi notes:

> They have said that you should not take knowledge from someone who has taken it from the insides of books without reading under shaykhs or one proficient shaykh. Whoever hasn't taken knowledge except from books will fall into misreading, and there will be much error and distortion from him.[21]

Together they very much formed a part of what Sherman Jackson, in his commentary on the Adab Al-Qadi written by Shihab al-Din, the 13th-century Maliki (School) jurist of Ayyubid-Mamluk Egypt, memorably referred to as 'the second education of the *Mufti*' – one which trained jurists in 'the art of living' to inhabit their offices well.[22]

17 Talal Asad, 'Thinking about Religion through Wittgenstein', *Critical Times* 3,3 (2020) 403, p. 418.
18 Asad, 'Thinking About Law', p. 18.
19 On the centrality of the understanding and practice of the relationship of the reader/reciter of the 'text' of the Quran within the 'Islamic tradition' as essentially one of practical capacitation 'into practicing a form of life' – as against speculative interpretation – see Asad, 'Thinking About Religion through Wittgenstein', pp. 18–28.
20 Masud, 'Adab Al-Mufti', p. 134.
21 Al-Nanawi, 'The Etiquettes of a Fatwa', p. 46.
22 Sherman Jackson, 'The Second Education of the Mufti: The Second Education of the Mufti: Notes on Shihab Al-Din Al-Qarafi's Tips to the Jurisconsult'. That Jackson made this distinction from an assumed 'first education', which

Thus, the Adab conduct manual shares the same practical ethical universe as the Prophetic *Sunna* – 'the lived tradition of the Prophet that was documented in the *hadith*'.[23] As Asad notes for this period:

> The figure of the Prophet as the paradigm of Islamic virtues has a long and interesting popular history in Egypt – as elsewhere in the Muslim world. It is thus that he appears not only in scholarly collections of *hadith* (sayings and enactments of the Prophet) but also in popular songs, stories and poems. The scholarly and the popular often merge in public recitations...Hadith were therefore more than simply Islamic source-texts for legal and moral rules. They were solemnly recounted and heard. The rules themselves were neither mere texts nor merely thoughts abouts texts – they were *practices* that one tried to master by a process of embodiment.[24]

The embodied figure of the jurist

However, contrasted with the prophetic paradigm of perfection ('the ethical model par excellence')[25] in the case of the *hadith* genre, in these *adab* manuals for jurists 'lesser' embodied exemplars were deployed, namely in the form of the '*Imam*' (or the founder) of one of the five jurisprudential schools within the 'Islamic legal tradition' that the specific conduct manuals author belonged to,[26] as well as the related figure of 'an absolute Mufti'[27] (*Mujtahid*). Crucially, these exemplars were role/status specific – i.e. confined to figures of jurists – and not more general exemplars (e.g., the Prophet (PHUB) as an 'Insan Kamil' (perfect human) or '*Uswa Hasana*' (excellent exemplar), as against exemplars that are only

was presumably abstracted from the practical, to me, points to a failure to grasp how significantly the education of jurists in the 'Islamic legal tradition' was embodied/practical.

23 On the role of Prophetic embodied practice as rendering Quranic rules ('requirements of the revelation') – including credal principles – *practical* in the 'Islamic Legal Tradition' see Ebrahim Moosa, 'Quranic Ethics', *in* Muhammad Abdel Haleem and Mustafa Shah eds., *The Oxford Handbook of Qur'anic Studies*, Oxford, U.K.: Oxford University Press, 2020, pp. 464–471.

24 Asad, 'Thinking About Law', p. 19.

25 Moosa, 'Qur'anic Ethics ', p. 469.

26 Thus, the final section of the *Adab Al-Mufti* included in the 16th-century South Asian fiqh treatise *Al-Matana*, 'ends with a narration of the excellence of Abu Hanifa, the founder of the *Hanfi* school of Islamic law, and his disciples'. See Masud, 'Adab al-Mufti', p. 129.

27 Al-Nanawi, 'The Etiquettes of a Fatwa', p. 125.

'appropriate to their profession').[28] Furthermore, there was an explicit acknowledgement that conducting oneself as (and imitating) a 'lesser' figure of a jurist who merely 'adheres to a certain school of law'[29] (a *Muqqalid*) was not only more common, but also *adequate*.

It is worth briefly dwelling upon this notion of ethical adequateness – as opposed to a notion of ethical perfection or beautiful perfection (*ihsan*). In these conduct manuals, this most clearly comes across in the identification of the ethical capacity for living well with obligations with having 'the fear of responsibility'[30] (the virtue of *taqwa*, i.e. God-consciousness or rectitude), which capacitates the jurist to adequately adhere to their obligations. Thus, the exemplary jurist is one who is *muttaqin* – i.e. a person of *taqwa*, with the associated characteristic of humility and mindfulness of their obligations.[31] As Masud observes:

> All sources discourage the temptation to exhibit one's knowledge or, on the other hand, to conceal one's ignorance. In fact they praised a *mufti's* saying *'lá adri'* ('I do not know'). The *Adab* explains that the answer 'lá adri' was often given by great jurists such as Malik, Shafi'i, Ahmad b. Hanbal, and others. In fact, Shafi'i used to say that one-half of knowledge consisted of saying 'la adri'. 'La adri' does not indicate false modesty; it is an attitude of respect for and humility towards knowledge. This attitude comes from a sense of responsibility for one's duties as a scholar.[32]

Thus, al-Nawawi, for instance, in the opening section of this conduct manual also provides the edification statements from the founding imams of three of the main schools of Sunni jurisprudence (amongst others) to emphasize the significance of 'the fear from Allah' in adhering to 'the burden of responsibility' of issuing a *fatwa*.[33]

28 Talal Asad, *Secular Translations: Nation-State, Modern Self, and Calculative Reason*, New York: Columbia University Press, p. 68.
29 Masud, 'Adab al-Mufti', p. 133.
30 Fazlur Rahman, 'Some Key Ethical Concepts of the Quran', *The Journal of Religious Ethics* 11, 2 (1983) 170, p. 129.
31 Lock, 'The Introduction to al-Nawawi's *al-Majmu*', pp. 120–122; Mufti'. Masud et al., 'Muftis, Fatwas, and Islamic Legal Interpretation', p. 8.
32 Masud, 'Adab al-Mufti', p. 137.
33 Lock, 'The Introduction to al-Nawawi's *al-Majmu*', p. 121.

Form of life

While the fatwa guidance for individuals no doubt provided a form of 'care of the self' through the jurist as embodied exemplar, making available a training through imitation to petitioners to help them live better with the obligations sought guidance for, the practical activities of both the Mufti and the Qadi also included the related responsibility of caring for specific (social) institutions. Often referred to in Fiqh treatises as the five objectives (*Maqasids*) of the *Sharia*, these include the institutions of personal and communal wealth (*Mal*), institutions of knowledge (*Aql*), institutions of health (*nafs*), and institutions of faith (*din*).[34] Care for these social institutions was a part of the offices of the jurist, and was thus also a key part of the practices of the practical that rendered liveable this 'form of life'. This conduct of care for lives lived with others also very much entailed a care for relations lived with others (*mu'amalat*), including those who were not Muslims.

Islamic legal traditions under British colonialism: projects of secular bureaucratization and colonial legal reforms of 'Islamic law'

In this section I describe the enactment of late 18th- and 19th-century projects of secular bureaucratization by British colonial regimes (with a focus on what became British India), through the undertaking of colonial legal reforms of the 'Islamic legal tradition'. I show how the offices of Islamic jurists – both the Mufti and the Qadi – and their conduct training (including the *Adab* literature), were key objects for this 'colonial reform' project which, I argue, sought the 'destruction' of this tradition. As I show, fundamental to this colonial modern law reform was the attempt to render separable so-called legal procedure and substantive law – or more broadly speaking, the realms and ends and means – with the emergence of the rule of the 'colonial state' and the 'separation of powers' within it, with codification of substantive law through various law commissions and its 'application' 'enforcement' through the 'uniform'/'central' (procedural) legal administration machinery, and with the colonial judge as its key figure.

34 See Hallaq, *Sharia*.

Colonial textbook translation project, the Fuqaha and the Adab manuals

The topic of colonial reform of what gets referred to as 'Islamic Law' is vast. Much of the initial critical literature focused on the textbook translation projects undertaken in the late 18th and mid-19th centuries in British India. This translation of select native law texts project initially emerged during the tenure of Warren Hastings as the Governor of Bengal in the late 18th century with the aim of *incorporation* of the governance, diplomatic and legal cultures of the recently colonized South Asians. Such incorporation was deemed to be the most secure way towards ensuring 'the permanency of any foreign domination'.[35] The so-called 'Hastings Plan':

> ...conceived a multi-tiered system that required exclusively British administrators at the top, seconded by a tier of British judges who could consult with local *qadis* and *muftis*...with regard to issues governed by Islamic law. At the lowest rung of judicial administration stood the run-of-the-mill Muslim judges who administered law in the civil courts of Bengal, Madras and Bombay. The Plan also rested on the assumption that local customs and norms could be incorporated int a British institutional structure of justice that was regulated by 'universal' (read: British) jural ideals.[36]

The key component of this project was of translating texts from Arabic and Persian into English. As part of this exercise, Hastings invested in the training of several East India Company (EIC) employees in these languages.[37] One explanation provided by Charles Hamilton, an 18th-century Orientalist, who, along with William Jones, was one of the main administrative scholars leading this project at the outset, was that the idea behind translating these Islamic 'legal texts' by the EIC was 'to bring Indian legal cultures within the reach of its officials'[38] – especially those engaged in legal administration without having any knowledge of these languages. A second justification, not unrelated to this one but emphasizing the law *reform* element of this project, was provided by Jones, who presented the project as a systematizing 'codification'

35 Charles Hamilton, *The Hedaya or Guide: Commentary on the Mussulman Laws*, Lahore: Premier Book House, Reprint 1963, p. iv.
36 Hallaq, *Sharia*, p. 372.
37 Bernard S. Cohn, 'Law and the Colonial State', in Bernard S. Cohn, *Colonialism and its Form of Knowledge: The British in India*, Princeton, New Jersey: Princeton University Press, 1996, p. 61.
38 John Strawson, 'Revisiting Islamic Law: Marginal Notes from Colonial History', *Griffith Law Review* 12, 2 (2003) 362, p. 366.

exercise ('complete digest of...Mussulman law')[39] that sought to respond to 'what was seen as an uncontrolled and corrupted mass of individual juristic opinion', i.e. the purported 'staggering variety of opinion and pliability of Islamic...law' experienced by EIC magistrates in their engagement with Islamic jurists, especially the Muftis as jurist-consults. Self-styling himself as a Tribonian of India (and the Governor General as 'the Justinian of India'), Jones described the texts he proposed to translate and abstract from as being necessary to achieve the goal of developing 'a complete check on the native interpreters of the several codes'. As he put it:

> I would begin with giving them a plan divided into Books, Chapters, and Section, and would order them to collect the most approved texts under each head, with the names of the Authors, and their Works, and with the chapters and verses of them. When this compilation was fairly, and accurately transcribed, I would write the Translation on the opposite pages, and after all inspect the formation of the perfect index. The material would be these; Six or Seven Law Books believed to be divine with a commentary on each of nearly equal authority; these are analogous to our Littleton, and Coke.[40]

Notable aspects of this reformed translation included the several significant excisions made to these texts. This included making a categorical classificatory distinction between obligations of *ibadat* (conduct between the faithful and God) and *muamalat* (conduct between people, both Muslims and non-Muslims), by entirely excluding the chapters pertaining to the former on the basis that they pertained to acts of 'private morality', and not the proper domain of (positive) law.[41] This assumed separability of practices of piety from a concern for social institutions – one which sought to create the space for the colonial authorities to reform the norms pertaining to the latter, while leaving 'protected' the former – erased the connectedness in terms of the practical arts and institutions (including social institutions) that together enabled the subjects of these obligations to live well with these laws as a 'form of life' – with the Islamic jurist, as we have seen, responsible for the care of both. By rendering *muamalat* as pertaining to 'civil relations', this reformed classification enabled a progressive colonial legal reform of the *Sharia* that narrowed its domain, first by excluding it from matters of revenue,

39 Cited in Cohn, 'Law and the Colonial State', p. 69.
40 Cited in Cohn, 'Law and the Colonial State', p. 70.
41 Hamilton, *The Hedaya*, p. lii.

and then from civil disputes where both or even one of the parties was non-Muslim.[42]

For our purposes, another key excision happened to be the erasure of the jurist conduct manuals from these translated 'Justinian digests'.[43]

We will return in more detail to this construction of the 'problem of Islamic law' by Jones essentially in terms of the 'uncertain conduct' of its jurists in the next sub-section. At this point, I want to note that while this multi-layered institutional incorporation of Islamic legal institutions into the EIC legal administration architecture, especially including the continued operation of *Qadi* courts to administer laws of crime (*faujdari*), was progressively abandoned through the course of the 19th century, by contrast, the textbook translation project component reached its culmination and very much contributed to the eventual displacement of Islamic legal institutions and jurists from the colonial legal administration of Islamic law in this period.

The making of "Anglo-Muhammadan law" and the centralization of the colonial legal administration apparatus

By the early 19th century, we witness the emergence of the lineaments of the colonial company *state* (prominently including a centralizing legal bureaucracy and a concomitant bureaucratization of the colonial administration).[44] We begin to discern that both the Qadis and Muftis, and the colonial legal administrative offices of subordinate legal administrators, intermediary translators, and 'native informants', begin to be marginalized through a series of colonial law reform projects.

The colonial law reform case against the participation of Islamic jurists fundamentally sought to problematize the question of their *conduct* – which was essentially framed as being arbitrary and thus a source of destabilizing uncertainty for the system of legal administration. As Hallaq noted, this casting of Islamic jurists 'as unsystematic, inconsistent and mostly arbitrary' was what later provided the basis for the Weberian ur-figure for charismatic authority – the Qadi meting out justice under the Date Palm.[45] Crucial here was the construction of the problem of arbitrariness in a manner that focussed on the conduct of

42 See Asad, 'The Reconfigurations of Law and Ethics'.

43 See Hallaq, *Sharia*.

44 See Nicholas B. Dirks, *The Scandal of Empire: Indian and Creation of Imperial Britain*, Cambridge, MA and London, England: Harvard University Press.

45 Hallaq, *Sharia*, p. 373.

Islamic jurists. In this account, arbitrariness – which purportedly produced the effect of legal administrative uncertainty – was an effect of the Islamic jurist's conduct displacing 'the law' with 'his own person', such that it was 'his' subjective/personal proclivities and discretionary whims that determine what the law is or requires (rather than some 'objective' 'body of law' that 'he' merely administers).

Significantly, those making the case for colonial law reform simultaneously described Islamic law as being 'too rigid'/'theocratic code-like'. As later critical historians of colonial legal administration have noted, this colonial legal reformer construction of 'Islamic Law' was quite unstable, if not altogether contradictory.[46] Focusing on this seeming contradiction in the law reform discourse, however, risks missing that the combined effect of both these critiques of the Islamic legal tradition was to posit a separability of its legal texts and the conduct of its jurists vis-à-vis these texts, or, to use the emergent Benthamite terminology, the substantive and the procedural in law. It was by formulating the problem thus, and within the framing of an emergent positivist normative tradition, that the colonial law reform 'solution' was what came to be referred to as 'Anglo-Muhammadan' law. This was essentially a body of law administered by colonial judges, with mainly scribal and translatory assistance from subordinated Islamic jurists, wherein the colonial legal reformers sought to continue Jones' project to excise Islamic conduct jurisprudence and 'preserve' (invent) an 'immutable divine code'. Essentially, while the 'Muhammadan' bit of this hybrid formation was conceived as the 'substantive code', the 'Anglo' part was the institutional apparatus and the procedural norms that would apply/enforce these norms into the lives of the colonial subjects.[47] As Hussin notes of the 'Anglo'/procedural side of this hybrid formation:

> ...formalization and regularization became priorities in the implementation of laws in novel ways.[48]

Essentially this created the conditions for a centralized legal administration bureaucratic architecture ('the bureaucratization of Islamic law'),[49] wherein it was exclusively hierarchically organized colonial courts who could now administer/apply this body of purportedly 'Islamic law', with

46 See Cohn, 'Law and the Colonial State in India'.

47 See Hallaq, *Sharia*.

48 Iza R. Hussin, *The Politics of Islamic Law: Local Elites, Colonial Authority, and the Making of the Muslim State*, Chicago and London: The University of Chicago, 2016, p. 85.

49 Hussin, *The Politics of Islamic Law*, p. 82.

the colonial state entirely doing away with the laws of crime (*Faujdari*) courts. The offices of the *Mufti* and *Qadi* were *not yet* entirely abolished, but a plurality of institutions associated with the practical activities that rendered 'Islamic Law' liveable were, while creating the space for the extension and expansion of the colonial state. As Kugle observes:

> The balance between Anglo and Muhammadan became steadily tilted in an Anglo direction throughout the nineteenth century reflecting the solidification of a state bureaucracy and establishment of a civil service which administered law…The translation of Islamic jurisprudence into 'Muhammadan law' preserved it in a new legal system, creating a space for a modern state and British sovereignty.[50]

Of significance with this posited separability of the adjectival and the substantive for our story of conduct of office is the adjectival's denuded relationship with obligations, such that the livability of the practical was sought to be displaced by positivist instrumental actions of sanctioning and enforcement of obligations. Here the jurist's conduct became the depersonalized instrument for and object of the external normative will of the state/bureau. The case in point being the Regulation pertaining to Qazi's contained within the so-called Cornwallis Code or the Permanent Settlement of 1793, which included an extensive set of (procedural) duties, *sans* any practical training in 'how to' conduct them well, *a'la* a *adab al Qadi*.[51]

Codification, Muslim personal law and the fall of Anglo-Muhammadan law

In the wake of the anti-colonial insurgency of 1857 (in which Islamic jurists had no small a role to play), it appeared that the hybrid experiment of 'Anglo-Muhammadan law' had been 'an interim colonialist solution'. What followed was a massive British Indian law codification project entailing more extensive displacement of Islamic law from all fields, except for the narrow and newly invented domain of the 'personal' (what came to be referred to as 'Muslim family law'). As Hallaq puts it:

50 Scott Alan Kugle, 'Framed, Blamed and Renamed: The Recasting of Islamic Jurisprudence in Colonial South Asia', *Modern Asian Studies* 35 (2001) 257, p. 259.

51 Julia Stephens, *Governing Islam: Law, Empire, and Secularism in South Asia*, Cambridge: Cambridge University Press, pp. 28–29.

> The 1860s and 1870s witnessed the abolition of slavery, as well as Islamic laws procedure, criminal law and evidence. All these were superseded by British laws enacted by statute. By the end of the century, and with the exception of family law and certain elements of property transactions, all indigenous laws had been supplanted by British law.[52]

Abolition of the offices of the jurist and the streamlining of the colonial judiciary

Alongside this 'domestication' of 'Islamic Law' – including its exclusive application to only Muslim subjects[53] – there was an 'overhaul of the Indian judiciary' whereby 'the process of judicial appeal was streamlined, creating a single system of high courts'.[54] This was accompanied by the formal abolition of the office of *Mufti* as jurisconsult in 1864, whereby it was declared that colonial judges could consult texts/codes of a circumscribed 'Islamic Law' in order to pass judgement on disputes before them without having to consult *Muftis* in any form whatsoever (the soliciting of *fatwas* from *Muftis* by colonial judges has been already formally abolished in 1832).[55] As Hussin notes:

> In 1864, the Muslim advisors in the courts...were no longer a part of the judicial system, and textbooks of Anglo-Muhammadan law and compilations of fatwa...replaced their advice. Indeed, 'the immediate purpose of these translations was to make Islamic law directly accessible to British judges who deeply mistrusted the native maulvis advising them on points of law.' By replacing the multiple and messy opinions of jurists with a brief and translated code of Hanafi law on personal status, the British attempted to limit the discretion of Muslim legal professionals, allow British judges to pronounce on Islamic law using authoritative code, and subject the content of Islamic law to the forms and logics of British judicature.[56]

52 Hallaq, *Sharia*, p. 383.
53 Stephens, *Governing Islam*, p. 50.
54 Stephens, *Governing Islam*, p. 51.
55 Brannon D. Ingram, *Revival From Below: The Deoband Movement and Global Islam*, Oakland, California: University of California Press, 2018, pp. 45–47.
56 Hussin, *The Politics of Islamic Law*, p. 85.

Colonial modern Islamic revivalist Adab Al-Mufti and Adab Al-Qadi in the British empire (British India and Egypt)

In this section, I argue that despite the colonial onslaught and their excision from textbook translations, the *adab al Mufti* genre did not cease to be written and read. Rather, what took place was a transformation within a 'living tradition' which produced a conduct training manual that differently capacitated the conduct of jurists for transformed offices. These 'Islamic revivalist' adab manuals contained training exercises that borrowed (and duly transformed) the *adab* of *Sufi* mystics, while seeking to combine the figures (and offices) of the jurist and the mystic spiritual guide (*Sufi Sheikh*).

The reconfiguration of offices was also accompanied by the *Mufti* – especially in British India, with the abolition of the office of Qadi – no longer taking up the responsibilities of acting as jurisconsults by issuing *fatwas* to assist with adjudication.[57]

Instead, *fatwas* or legal advice were now not only issued by these Muftis almost exclusively to 'lay Muslims', but, via the extensive use of new print media technologies, were deployed on a mass scale and 'at a hitherto unknown level of detail'.[58] These fatwas were compiled, mass printed, and circulated as fatwa collections of different prominent Muftis, with a specific chapter on the *Adab Al-Mufti* contained therein – as against their inclusion in early modern *Usul-ul Fiqh* treatises that had been the focus of the selective colonial textbook translation project.[59]

While by the early 20th century several prominent dar al-iftas ('literally, a house in which fatwas are issued; that is, an institution in which one or more muftis answered questions about Islamic law')[60] had been established all over British India, the most significant of these was formed at the seminary established in the town of Deoband ('Dar al'ulum'), which was itself established in 1867.[61] By 1892 there was the establishment of a *dar al-ifta* within the Deoband seminary dedicated to receiving queries for and transmitting *fatwas* in response to these queries by Deoband *Muftis*, and by 1911 a register to record these questions

57 Ingram, *Revival From Below*, p. 47.
58 Barbara D. Metcalf, 'Two Fatwas on Hajj in British India', in Muhammad Khalid Masud et al. eds., *Islamic Legal Interpretation*, p. 191.
59 Masud, 'Adab al-Mufti'; Ingram, *Revival From Below*, pp. 47–48.
60 Muhammad Khalid Masud, 'Apostasy and Judicial Separation in British India', in Masud et al. eds., *Islamic Legal Interpretation*, p. 193.
61 See Barabara D. Metcalf, *Islamic Revival in British India: Deoband, 1860–1900*, Princeton: Princeton University Press, 1982, pp. 87–137.

and answering *fatwas*.[62] Notably, the seminary at Deoband and the jurists attached to it are the most prominent representatives from British India of what scholars have referred to as 'Islamic Revival'.[63] As I understand it, these are jurists who conceived themselves as engaging in the *ihya* (revival), *islah* (reforming), or *tajdid* (renewal) of the tradition in response to the colonial legal reform projects referred to above, very much from within the tradition, and focusing upon educational transformation.[64] As Samira Hajj observes with regard to a specific revivalist jurist's project – someonewho we will soon encounter in more detail:

> ...Abduh's project of reform was firmly rooted in the Islamic discursive tradition as was not a mere ideological weapon, a ruse, or a reaction to European power. For him, the reform of Islam was necessary to guarantee the survival of the Muslim community in the modern world; it was also the way to effectively ward off European aggression and expansion.[65]

Notable here is that neither of these revivalist seminaries received any support from the colonial state. In fact, not only were these jurists not attached in any way to the colonial state, they were actively averse to having any associations with the colonial legal administration apparatus.[66]

In this section I describe the adab literature for jurists that these revivalists produced both in British India (with the Deoband seminar and movement), and in Egypt (with the seminary at Al-Azhar under the influence of the *Salafiyya* movement).[67] When compared with the early modern practices of the tradition, and specifically the writing of this genre of jurist conduct training, there were certain key continuities and discontinuities that I organize my own redescription around.

62 Metcalf, 'Two Fatwas on Hajj', pp. 190–191.

63 See Metcalf, *Islamic Revival in British India*; Ingram, *Revival From Below*, p. 47.

64 See Ingram, *Revival From Below*, pp. 17–19; Samira Hajj, *Reconfiguring Islamic Tradition: Reform, Rationality, and Modernity*, Stanford: Standford University Press, 2009, pp. 7-9. As Hajj notes, these activities of revival were themselves 'embedded in the Islamic tradition', and not a 'novelty'.

65 Hajj, *Reconfiguring Islamic Tradition*, p. 28.

66 See Francis Robinson, *The 'Ulama of Farangi Mahall and Islamic Culture in South Asia*, Delhi: Permanent Black, 2001, pp. 92–93.

67 On Egypt see Saba Mahmood, *Politics of Piety: The Islamic Revival and the Feminist Subject*, Princeton and Oxford: Princeton University Press, 2005, p. 61; Asad,' Reconfigurations of Law and Ethics', pp. 218–227; Hussein Ali Agrama, *Questioning Secularism: Islam, Sovereignty, and the Rule of Law in Modern Egypt*, Chicago and London: The University of Chicago Press, 2012.

Incorporating Tasawwuf

As far as the latter is concerned, the most notable transformation concerned the above-mentioned incorporation of practices of Sufi or mystical spiritual training (*tasawwuf*) into these conduct training manuals for jurists. This repurposing of Sufi *tasawwuf* – taking place in a context where these jurists were excluded and rivaled by colonial state legal officials – brought about a combination of what were often treated as two distinct offices within the Islamic tradition, that of the Sufi mystic (*Sheikh*), and the jurist (*Mufti* or *Qadi*).[68] Suggesting that this entanglement was deeper than the simple incorporation of both offices into one person, Nizami brings out how this transformative combination transformed the very conduct training of the Mufti, whereby:

> The idea of a jurist as one who is mainly trained in the traditional subjects of Islamic law and other sciences also came to include spiritual training as an essential part of it.[69]

In terms of the question of conduct of offices, a significant feature of reconfiguration was the jurist's assumption of the responsibility of acting as a spiritual guide or teacher (*Sheikh* or *Murshid*). While this was undoubtedly a significant office associated with the figure of the *Sufi Sheikh* in the early modern period, it had been prominently supplemented in that period by the office of saintly intercession by the mystic as 'friend of God' or saint (*aulia/wali*) for a more general populace of devotees (while the spiritual guidance was reserved for more select initiates or *murids*).[70] What is notable in the revivalist reconfigured take-up here is that it is solely the office of the *Sufi* as spiritual guide that gets taken up by the Shiekh-Mufti but in relationship with a *general*, albeit exclusively Muslim, populace as potential subjects for spiritual development and education, and not reserved for select initiates.

68 Commenting upon this detachment of the Mufti from the institutions of the colonial state and its combination with the role of the Sufi Sheikh, Metcalf – the foremost English language commentator on Islamic revivalism under the British Raj – writes: '*The 'ulama as such had no formal role in the British imperial state, but they found wide scope for guiding Muslims in civil and religious matters. They acted both as muftis to determine appropriate legal precedents and as Sufi shaikhs to offer spiritual guidance to chosen disciples*' (Metcalf, p. 138).

69 Moin Ahmad Nizami, 'Connecting Law and Sufism: Religious Discourse in Pre-Modern South Asia' (Paper on File with Author).

70 See Carl Ernst, *The Shambhala Guide to Sufism*, Boston: Shambhala Publications, 1997, pp. 26–31.

There is a lot to unpack in this manifestation of discontinuity. The first point I wish to make pertains to how this reconfiguration of the tradition was one which also transformed the figure and offices of the early modern *Sufi Sheikh* – and was not a case of simple transposition to the figure of the jurist and their offices. *Sufi tasawwuf* (spiritual exercises) were themselves not fixed or ahistorical practices of the self and had been deployed in very different office conduct training repertoires in early modern South Asia. Illuminating here are the descriptions of the deployments of *tasawwuf* in the office conduct training of early modern Mughal administrative officials – including Ministers, diplomats, and Scribes – which report on how these mystical spiritual exercises sought to cultivate 'a man of mystical civility',[71] an exemplary imperial bureaucrat whose:

> ...attunement to esoteric spiritual gnosis (known as ma'rifat in Sufi parlance) gave him the sort of humility that allowed him to do his job with...detachment (bi-ta'allqui) from material gain...These spiritual and secretarial qualities enhanced a leader's ability to handle affairs of state, over and above the mere brute demands of conquest...the notion that all gentlemen and good imperial servants should cultivate this trivium of ideal qualities – selfless ministerial leadership (wizarat), spiritual gnosis (ma'rifat), and mastery of the secretarial arts (munshigiri)...a great leader's true power stems not merely from the sword but also, even especially, from the intellect, and from the sort of humility, self-defence, and spiritual detachment exemplified by great Sufi *shaikhs*...[72]

We see here a historical example of how the practice *tasawwuf* could be detached from any entanglement with the 'Islamic legal tradition' – and in this specific context formed a part of what the historian Muzaffar Alam refers to as the 'Persianate' tradition – such that the virtues of worldly detachment and mystical gnosis were sought through the conduct of a series of exercises which were variously 'Islamic'/'Indic'/'Mongol', and bore no relationship with the cultivation of adherence to the rules/obligations of revelation.[73]

71 Rajeev Kinra, *Writing Self, Writing Empire: Chandra Bhan Brahman and the Cultural World of the Indian-Persian State Secretary*, Oakland, California: University of California Press, 2015, p. 67.

72 Kinra, *Writing Self, Writing Empire*, pp. 67–69.

73 See Muzaffar Alam, *The Languages of Political Islam: India 1200-1800*, London: Hurst & Company, 2004.

It is also notable that this deployment of 'the bureaucratic and the mystical – together as part of the same cultural dynamic'[74] in the early modern Indo-Islamic Mughal tradition points us towards how an ethic of bureaucratic detachment has historically taken several distinct forms when compared to the colonial modern impersonal proceduralism that we encountered in the previous section. Thus, contrary to the Weberian paradigm,[75] the rational impersonal and the charismatic have simply not been the only available modes of administrative practice, especially when we take seriously the practice of administration in the rest of the world. We encounter more evidence of this in the practice of the 19th-century Islamic revivalists, as I will shortly describe, but here I want to highlight how a key difference in the conduct training for office between the Mughal and British colonial modern bureaucracies came down to the use of exemplary officials' past as 'embodied models' for training conduct in the present by the former.[76] Such an attentiveness to the *practical* was missing in the latter, where, as we encountered in the previous section, in place of the embodied exemplar to be emulated, was the bureau's procedure to be followed.

Pertinently, this early modern deployment of Sufi spiritual exercises took place in a context within the tradition wherein the figure of the *Sufi* (as mystic) appeared as a *rival* to the figure of the jurist and their laws. As the foremost authority on early modern Sufi traditions in South Asia, Alam, observes of this 'conflict between Sufi and jurist'[77] in his analysis of a significant early modern text by the Sufi 'Abd al-Rahman Chishti:

> The primary duty of a *salik* (traveller of the Sufi path) was to follow the path of his preceptor (*pir wa shaikh*)...To Chishti, the model for a *salik* is his *pir*, without much regard for schools of jurisprudence (*fiqh*) or dogmatics and scholasticism (*kalam*)...Chishti then elaborates on the content of the Sufi's *mazhab*...Whatever is unseen (*gha'ib*) for others is manifest (*zahir*) to them. The truth is unveiled (*kashf*) to the Sufi when others reach it only through argumentation (*istidlal*). The sufi is always in states and stages of truthfulness (*sidq*) and, inwardly, constantly keeps company with God most high.

74 Kinra, *Writing Self, Writing Empire*, p. 68.

75 See Paul Du Gay, *In Praise of Bureaucracy*, London, Thousand Oaks, New Delhi: Sage Publications, 2000.

76 As Kinra shows, in the case of the Mughal bureaucrats, these embodied exemplars were not limited to Muslims or even Islamic figures, but very much extended to Hindus and Indic figures. See Kinra, *Writing Self, Writing Empire*.

77 Muzaffar Alam, *The Mughals and the Sufis: Islam and Political Imagination in India, 1500-1750*, Albany: State University of New York, 2021, p. 107.

> However, the Sufi's *mazhab* too has an outer dimension, related to proper conduct (*adab*), and this is their law (*shari'a*). Their interaction with God's creatures (*ba-khalq mu'amalat*) has precedence over the quest to fulfil their own desires (*nik amad khalq ra na justan-i murad-i khwud ra*).[78]

In contrast, the context for the revivalist reconciliation of the figures of the *Sufi mystic* and the jurist was that of colonial modernity and its law reform projects. In this problem-space, it was the figure of the colonial judge 'enforcing' Islamic law codes that operated as the rival to the Islamic jurist.[79]

In semi-peripheral jurisdictions not under formal British colonization, prominentlylate 19th-century Egypt, this emergent revivalist entanglement of the figures of the *Sufi* mystic and jurist was extended to the conduct training of the *Qadi* or judge. At play in this context as well was a revivalist response to the problem of the colonial legal reform project that sought to destroy/displace all non-colonial state rival legal administration institutions by seeking to re-establish rival Islamic legal institutions. In this rival project of resistance from within the Islamic legal tradition, the repurposing of Sufi spiritual training for the conduct of different offices of the jurist also played a very significant role.

In the Egyptian context, while on account of colonial projects of state bureaucratization and secularization 'Islamic Law' was also confined to matters of 'administering family law and pious endowments (*awqaf*)',[80] there continued to be so-called *Sharia* courts, with judges who were trained in the famous Islamic seminar at *Al-Azhar* presiding over them and facing ongoing projects of state bureaucratization and secularization.[81] In a seminal essay on the colonial law reform project in 19th-century Egypt, Talal Asad provides an instructive reading of the interventions made by the aforementioned Mohammad Abduh – a key

78 Alam, *The Mughlas and the Sufis*, p. 100 and 104.

79 For an account of a similar reconciliation of the offices of Sufi Saint and jurist in late medieval Morrocco see Kugle, *Rebel Between Spirit and Law: Ahmad Zarruq, Sainhood, and Authority in Islam*, Bloomington and Indianapolis: Indiana University Press, 2006.

80 Asad, 'Reconfigurations of Law and Ethics', p. 211.

81 As Asad notes: '*The bureaucratization of the* sharia *into the modernizing state. The march from premodern chaos to modern order was initiated by Europeans and overseen at first by them and later by Europeanized Egyptians. Law began to disentangle itself from the dictates of religion, becoming thereby both more modern and more secular*' (Asad, 'Reconfigurations of Law and Ethics', pp. 211–212).

figure in Islamic Revivalism in Egypt, who in 1899 was appointed as the Grand Mufti of Egypt and in this capacity, as the rector of *Al-Azhar*. This includes a report prepared by Abduh on the ongoing reforms of Sharia courts by the Egyptian state. While this report, titled *Taqrir islah al-mahakim al-sharriya,* was formally not an *Adab Al-Qadi* text, its focus was very much on the conduct of the jurist, and, as I show below, by incorporating *Sufi* spiritual exercises into the conduct training of jurists, it sought to transform an Islamic legal tradition's response to colonial law reform projects, quite similar to the Islamic Revivalists in British India and their *Adab Al-Mufti* chapters in *Fatwa* collections.

Contrary to the colonial separation of deontological moral and 'sacred law' codes and procedural 'legal means' of colonial state courts that Asad describes in the earlier part of the essay, his reading of Abduh's report on the Sharia Courts in Egypt, especially focusing on the practical support required for the conduct training of judges presiding over these courts rivalling the two sets of secular courts (i.e. the Mixed Tribunal and the National Courts), is most instructive.[82] Thus, for Abduh, the conduct training of a *Qadi* – so that they may inhabit their responsibilities of office well – cannot be merely limited to conducting oneself in a procedurally competent manner, including by displaying an adequate learning of the body of law ('ends') that they are the 'means' for applying. Rather, it required 'certain moral aptitudes and predispositions'.[83] In Abduh's words:

> ...the Islamic *sharia* has intricate details which cannot be taken into account except by someone who has informed himself thoroughly of all its legal provisions, enquired properly into its objectives and arrived at its precise meanings – that is, someone who knows its language as well as its masters do. No man can attain to that state unless he has acquired the *sharia* from its practitioners, and has been brought up according to the true religious tradition...Furthermore, the judge cannot be a preserver of family and domestic organisation merely by learning sharia injunctions. The injunctions must become and authoritative part of himself...[84]

82 See Abduh, *Taqrir*, pp. 217–297. See also Asad, 'Reconfiguration of Law and Ethics', p. 228.

83 Asad, 'Reconfiguration of Law and Ethics', p. 248.

84 Mohammad Abduh, *Taqrir islah al-mahakim al-shar'iyya'*, in Muhammad Imara ed., *Al-A'mal al-kamila lil-iman Muhammad Abduh, Vol 2, Beirut, 1980*, p. 219.

Furthermore, for Abduh, this embodiment of the *Sharia* was achieved through 'combining both sufism and the sharia',[85] which incorporated the Sufi practices of 'ethics and spiritual education'[86] into the conduct training of Qadis, very much mirroring the Deobandi revivalist jurist curriculum.

At Deoband, a similar emphasis of the Islamic revivalists on embodiment, formation of the ethical character, and capacities of the jurist and judge through a training in conduct, and the continued significance of Islamic legal *institutions* to any extant practice of 'Islamic law' – all practical concepts and categories that refuse an easy separability of procedure and substance/means and ends – were formulated as part of contesting the authority of colonial judges to 'apply' Islamic law in disputes before them. Thus, in this formulation, simply possessing 'knowledge' of certain 'rules and principles' of Islamic Law – one that could be gained by consulting an English translation of a *Usul ul Fiqh* textbook, for instance – did not enable the jurist to take up the office of an 'Islamic law' judge well. Rather, this quality of conduct required that the jurist practice *Sufi tasawwuf* in order to embody the *Sharia*,and not simply 'know' the *Sharia*. Very much like for Abduh, a judge meeting the obligations for his office must not merely *learn* the injunctions of Islamic law but make them 'an authoritative part of himself'[87] by 'combining both *sufism* and the *sharia*'.[88]

Reconciliation has a history

It perhaps speaks to our own proclivities and unstated commitments as 'critical scholars' that we would veer in the other direction and read in this attempted reconciliation of the purportedly irreconcilable offices of the Sufi *Sheikh* and *Fuqaha* by the Islamic revivalists evidence of a break in the Islamic legal tradition on account of colonial modernity.[89]

85 Asad, 'Reconfiguration of Law and Ethics', p. 250.
86 Asad, 'Reconfiguration of Law and Ethics', p. 224.
87 Asad, 'Reconfigurations of Law and Ethics', p. 249.
88 See Nizami, 'Connecting Law and Sufism'.
89 This irreconcilability '*Sufi Saints*' with the 'orthodox doctors of law' thesis is one with a strong pedigree within Western Orientalist scholarship on the Islamic tradition. As Asad observes: '*The idea that these contrasts are at once mutually exclusive and fundamental to Islamic thought and practice was taken up and repeated by an older generation of social anthropologists (for example, E.E. Evans-Pritchard, E. Gellner and C. Geertz)*' (Asad, 'Reconfigurations of Law and Ethics', p. 224).

Thus, we find that there existed a resonance from within the tradition itself when it came to the practice of reconciliation – one which the revivalists emphasized while seeking to persuade fellow participants in the tradition to transform the tradition.[90] In the case of Islamic revivalists in Egypt, the inherited exemplar of this revivalist reconciliation was the famous Hanbali jurist, Athari theologian, and Qadari Sufi, Ibn Taymiyyah, who invoked 'carefully delimited interpretation'[91] of the deployment of *Sufi tasawwuf* in order to 'promote obedience to the sharia command'.[92] In the case of the Deobandi revivalists, this exemplary figure of reconciliation from within the tradition was the 12th-century Shafi'i jurist, Ash'ari theologian and Sufi, Imam Al-Ghazzali, and his version of 'sober Sufism'.[93] As Ingram observes:

> ...many Deobandis looked to Abu Hamid al-Ghazali (d. 1111) as the preeminent theorist of Islam at the intersection of law, ethics, and Sufi piety. For Ashraf 'Ali Thanvi (d. 1943) – the most influential Deobandi scholar in the history of the movement...no self-respecting Islamic scholar...was worthy of the name without having studied al-Ghazzali's *Ihya 'ulum al-din*...[94]

90 A notable contrast/rival position – one that can more accurately be described as heterodox and marginal within the tradition – is the emergence of 'Wahabi Islam' in the late 18th-century spaces of the Ottoman Hijaz, which eventually launched an insurgency against Ottoman Rule in the region, with the support of British Imperial agents in the 19th and 20th century. It was the *Wahabis* who advocated the position that not only was *Sufi tassawwuf* not integral to the Islamic tradition, all *Sufi* practices were in fact *shirk* (blasphemous deviance). See Yasir Qadhi, *Understanding Salafism: Seeking the Path of the Pious Predecessors*, London: OneWorld Academic, 2025; Esther Peskes, 'The Wahhabiyya and Sufism in the Eighteenth Century', in Frederick de Jong and Bernd Radtke eds., *Islamic Mystcism Contested: Thirteen Centuries of Controversies and Polemics*, Leiden: E.J. Brill, 1999, 145. In this context, the Orientalist binary of 'orthodox doctors of law' and '*Sufi saints*' can be seen to insidiously operate to render as 'orthodox' (or 'Islam Proper') to the tradition a position (a 'legal supremacist conceptualization') within it that was in fact at best marginal to it. See Shahab Ahmad, *What is Islam?: The Importance of Being Islamic*, Princeton and Oxford: Princeton University Press, 2016. pp. 113–135; Khaled M. Abou El Fadl, *The Authoritative and Authoritarian in Islamic Discourses: A Contemporary Case Study*, Alexandria, VA and Beirut, Lebanon: Al-Saadawi Publications, 2002.

91 Thomas Michel, 'Ibn Taymiyya's *Sharh* on the *Futuh al-Ghayb* of *Abd al-Qadir Jilani*', *Hamdard Islamicus* 4, 2 (1981), p. 5.

92 Asad, 'Reconfigurations of Law and Ethics', pp. 250–251.

93 Ingram, *Revival From Below*, p. 13.

94 Ingram, *Revival From Below*, p. 14.

For both these towering figures of reconciliation from within the Islamic tradition, Sufi *tasawwuf* had always been integral to Islamic practice, thus incorporating these exercises into a hierarchical relationship with the activities of jurisprudence (*fiqh*) and theology (*aqeeda*), whereby the ethical capacities associated with each activity (*Ihsan* or love for divine beauty, *Islam* or submission to the divine command, and *Iman* or faith in divine providence, respectively) were organized as three ascending levels or ranks (*darajaat*).[95] Thus, Sufi *tasawwuf*, in this deployment within the tradition promoted 'a convergence between human willing and the commands of God as expressed in the sharia',[96] and not a rival *Sharia*, as Chishti deployed it in our earlier examples from early modern Mughal India. While my attention here has been on the re-activation of these exemplars from within the tradition by these 19th-century revivalists, it is also worth noting that this orientation towards 'integral Islam' within the tradition was *historically* not simply asserted by medieval jurists or theologians – like Al-Ghazzali and Ibn Taimiyya – but also included *Sufi* saints, such as the 14th-century Moroccan 'juridical saint', *Sheikh* Ahmad Zarruq.[97]

Generality of training

A second salient point under discontinuities pertains to the generality of the (Muslim) subjects now offered the spiritual guidance of these Mufti-Sheikhs. It is worth contextualizing this shift – whereby the primary recipient of their fatwas went from the figure of the Qadi to potentially any 'Muslim' subject living in the British Indian Empire – in a colonial context in which the singular category of 'Indian Muslim' as the *sole*

95 See Ibn Taymiyyah, *Kitab Al-Imam: Book of Faith*, Salman Hassan Al-Ani and Shadia Ahmad Tel trans., Kuala Lumur: Islamic Book Trust, 2009, pp. 18–47; Al-Ghazali, *Ihya 'ulum al-din* – '*The Revival of the Religious Sciences*' (whose 40 chapters/books are organized as ascending from the capacities for submitting to the five obligations of Islam, to the capacities of faith, and finally the capacities for divine love and mystical union). Iman Taymiyyah invokes the famous 'Hadith of Gabriel' (*Hadith Jibreel*) to make his case for this reconciliation (and thus 'delimitation' of *Sufi* practices), as per which Prophet Muhammad (PBUH) arranged each of these three ethical capacities in a ranked order (*darajat*) in response to questions posed by the Archangel Gabriel. Taymiyyah, *Kitab Al-Iman*, p. 20.

96 Asad, 'Reconfigurations of Law and Ethics', p. 250.

97 Kugle has written about the influence of Zarruq upon contemporary Islamic revivalism amongst Sufis in North America, Scott Kugle, *Rebel Between Spirit and Law: Ahmad Zarruq, Sainthood, and Authority in Islam*, pp. 7–26.

subjects of a singular 'Islamic Law'[98] was being produced through the confinement of the 'Islamic legal tradition' that we discussed earlier.[99] As Metcalf puts it:

> Muslim reformers...sought to make the *'ulama* the guardians of Islam, and individuals under their guidance its bastion. For that effort to succeed, the *'ulama* necessarily had to address a far wider range of Muslims than had scripturalists reformers in earlier times. They were able to seek a wide audience because of new methods and techniques of communication that were available to them, as well as to rivals. They were also motivated by a colonial framework that created an arena for 'communities' whose leaders could 'represent' them.[100]

Part of this was a shift away in focus from a concern with offering guidance to those occupying specific statuses attached to political authority (e.g. Qadi themselves), and towards what might be described as a more proto-Muslim public, in which the only qualifying status was that of being 'Muslim'. The 'piety' of this newly emergent 'common' subject (*amm*) was now both site of their spiritual education/guidance and the marker of status mobility.[101] Pertinently, this extended to and was evidenced by the conduct training literature produced by some of these Sheikh-Muftis. A prominent case in point being the conduct training manual for 'Muslim women' written by the famous Deobandi jurist, Ashraf Ali Thanawi, *Bihishti Zewar,* described by its 20th-century English translator as 'one of the century's most influential books'.[102] The point of contrast for these revivalist 'care of the self' texts is the early modern status role specific mirrors that we previously discussed. Given this generalist 'egalitarian' turn, how did these revivalists persist with also writing specific conduct training manuals for the offices of the jurist? How did they manage this tension?

98 Of importance here is the minimization of the significance of the difference amongst the four *Sunni* jurisprudential schools in both these conduct manuals and the fatwas issued by the Deobandi *Muftis*. See Ingram, *Revival From Below*, p. 48.

99 See Stephens, *Governing Islam*; Ingram, *Revival From Below*.

100 Barbara Daly Metcalf, *Perfecting Women: Maulana Ashraf 'Ali Thanawi's Bihishti Zewar*, Berkeley and Los Angeles, California: University of California Press, pp. 7–8.

101 Metcalf, *Perfecting Women*, pp. 25–26.

102 Metcalf, *Perfecting Women*, p. xi.

A perfectionist ethic

In order to better grasp how they resolved this tension, it is worth considering carefully the perfectionism embedded in the practice of *Sufi tasawwuf*. These spiritual exercises are organized around the love of divine beauty and spiritual perfection of conduct and character (and not simply their adequateness, which, as we noted with the medieval and early modern conduct manuals, was given form by the capacity for adequate righteousness/rectitude or *taqwa*).

Again, from within a more *Sharia* entangled *Sufi* tradition of Al-Ghazali amongst others, this potentially syncretic/boundless spiritual perfectionism had been sought to be contained by binding it to an initial basis in cultivating *taqwa*, such that God mindfulness (and thus adherence to the *Sharia*) was conceived as a *necessary albeit preliminary* station in a spiritual journey that went from mindfulness of divine displeasure, to attaining spiritual perfection through divine love.[103] The device developed to enable this reconciliation of the adequate and the perfect was that of *maqamat* or 'stations'. As Tim Winters observes in his Introduction to the *Ihya*, enframed by this device/method:

> ...the spiritual wayfarer passes in turn through the *maqamat* of faith, fear, reverence, obedience, hope, love, passion, and intimacy with God. In this fashion, attitudes which seem to be opposed can be integrated into the spiritual life in the form of stages in a progressive ascent to God. Although the sequence of these 'stations' was not defined with much consistency in classical Sufism, it is generally the case that the *maqam* of fear is ranked below that of hope, above which are conditions of love (*shawq*) and joyful contentment (*rida*) with God's will. Each of these stations engenders a particular attitude to the world, and requires a particular type of spiritual method in order to overcome the receding passional self.[104]

This specific device of a *Sufi* perfectionist ethic that was organized around a simultaneously universal and hierarchical spectrum of spiritual stations – along a path all the way from novice layman to a

103 This also operated as a corrective to the 'intercessionist' element in the *Sufi* tradition by emphasizing the conduct guidance role, and thus was more oriented to the *Sufi* Master's teaching relationship with the initiate (rather than with mystical relationship with the divine).

104 Winters, 'Introduction', pp. xxxvi–xxxvii. For a contemporary Sunni orthodox exposition of this relationship between *taqwa* and *ihsan* see Omer Sulieman, *Allah Loves*, Kube Publishing, 2020.

Sheikh-e-Kaamil (perfect Guide)[105] – allowed the Islamic revivalists to not only bind mysticism to the *Sharia* (contra Chisthi), but also enabled these revivalist Muftis to maintain a distinctiveness of their roles as (Muslim) jurist guides, while also training a more general (potential) community of subjects: i.e. Muslims. Hence the turn to *tasawwuf* by these revivalist Muftis.

This of course connects to the hierarchical reconciliation of jurisprudence, theology, and spiritual exercises underpinning the reconciliation of the *Sharia* and *tasawwuf* by the Islamic revivalists discussed above, and together they enabled the positing of a unitary normative order in which the pinnacle capacity for ethical perfection (*ihsan*) was reserved for the office of the jurist-saint.[106] Only the jurist-spiritual guide had to *embody the law*, as a *Mohsin or Kaamil*. For the general masses (*awamm*), the capacity to *submit* and adhere to the *Sharia* – and thus become a *pious* Muslim – was adequate.

Contra charismatic (authority)

There exists a tendency in some of the historical literature that reads this revivalist practice of cultivating the spiritual character of the jurist as representing a turn, albeit ironic, to a form of charismatic authority in response to the bureaucratic law reform project of colonial modernity and the loss of attachment to civil authority this effected. This line of enquiry is one that is itself organized in positivist law terms such that it renders the attention to modes of conduct that is secondary to the *primary* concern with uncovering grounds/sources of authority purportedly 'underlying' such conduct, whereby different modes of conduct get exclusively evaluated in terms of their (abstracted) validity, legitimacy or effectiveness. This approach reads the revivalist practices within the

105 See Rashid Ahmad Gangohi, *Imdaad al-Suluk*, Lahore: Idarah i-Islamiya, 1984. This perfectionist telos in these revivalist Adab manuals strikingly comes across in how the exemplary Prophetic practice of the activity of issuing fatwa now appeared in the first section of the Deoband Adab Al Mufti (which entirely omits the founding Imams of the jurisprudential schools). See *Fatwa e'Darul Uloom*, Vol. 1, Deoband: Dar al-Ulum Deoband, 1962, p. 67.

106 Thus, Gangoi, in his Adab Manual (titled 'Training for Conduct') describes the virtues of the exemplary jurist-saint as being such that: '*He must be absorbed in the ocean of divine splendour while being free from all mundane defects and fetters, thus having attained the stage of Ihsaan. In other words he worships Allah as if he is in his presence seeing him*' Gangohi, *Imdaad*, (p. 62).

terms of colonial modernity's project and the separation of ends and means, whereby a jurist's conduct of office could only either be as an instrument for the imposition of authority and its obligations. This could either be an external authority – i.e. the colonial state. Or the internal font of (charismatic) authority contained within the jurist – i.e. with 'his' own *conscience* acting as the grounds for obligations.[107]

In a continuation of the tradition, within the terms of these conduct manuals themselves, such trained spiritual conduct was neither approached as being the source of obligations, nor the instrument for their imposition on others, but rather as embodied guides for *how to* live well with these obligations for those seeking/invited to take up this 'form of life'. Authority, for those living with tradition, is itself a form of conduct or an activity that enables the *forming* of that life ('a conduct of conduct', to borrow a phrase), and is not the ground for, nor simply the goal sought to be achieved/acquired by, said conduct. This continuity in the category of the practical,which disrupts the attempts to separate the ends from the means, for me, is the key point of continuity between the revivalist and early modern conduct training manuals for jurists within the Islamic tradition.

Pathways of the practical: from ruined institutions to remaking spirits

With this in mind, we might reframe our reading of these revivalist conduct manuals along more practical lines. Namely, how was the incorporation of spiritual exercises into the conduct manuals for jurists conceived as capacitating the living well with the obligations of the *Sharia*? The conduct manuals themselves suggest that this capacitation worked at the level of the spirit, thus training/remaking the self (*nafs*) to move beyond mindful adherence towards obligations (*nafs e lawwama*), and towards a mystical state of the soul where the obligation became 'second nature', as the desires of the self and the divine will become one (*nafs e Mutma'innah*). Thus, the Deobandi jurist guide Gangoi makes the following case for incorporating *tasawwuf* into the conduct training of a jurist:

> Knowledge of the law ['ilm-i Shari'at] and knowledge of Sufism ['ilm-i tariqat] are the same thing. The law and Sufism are also the same. When someone knows the commands of the Shari'a, he has knowledge of the law. When someone know the essence of the command,

107 Asad, 'Reconfigurations of Law and Ethics', p. 249.

> he has knowledge of Sufism. To perform a duty or necessary deed against the will of the self [nafs] is to act in line with the law. When sincerity [iklhas] and love for the reality of God completely encompass the depths of the heart, that is called Sufism. So long as knowledge and practice are in conflict with one another, Shari'a will dominate. When the conflict dissipates, that is Sufism.[108]

Thus, embodying the 'essence' of the law, through their practice of spiritual exercises, the jurist is not simply the *means* to enforce the law, but rather an exemplary figure who combines means and ends in their conduct as jurists. This embodied jurist takes up the office of spiritually guiding the subjects of *Sharia* to live well with its obligations – and not simply that of declaring what is legal or illegal, permitted or forbidden, and having the same enforced by the state. Thus, the key activity delivering fatwas by a *Mufti* is practised as a technology of spiritual cultivation in the Islamic revivalist tradition. As Agrama observes of the practices of these Islamic revivalist jurists:

> I suggest that the practice of the fatwa be understood as a mode of the care of the self, as a practice by which selves, in the multiplicity of their affairs are maintained and advanced as part of Islamic traditions. In this, the authority of the Mufti is that of a *guide*. We can put it this way: a typical question in the fatwa has the form: 'I don't know my way about.' Muftis are the ones who have the skills to find their way about. Although the relationship between Mufti and questioner is an asymmetrical one, muftis, as guides, share responsibility with questioners they guide...the fatwa is involved in a practice of tarbawayya – ethical cultivation, that is highly attentive not just to questioners particular situations but also their weaknesses, drives, desires, hopes, fears, and sufferings...[109]

If the repertoire of the practical for the medieval and early modern jurist combined institutions and their care with ethical cultivation, here we notice that the 'care of the self' has become the predominant modality for rendering livable obligations.

Further examination along these practical lines allows us to redescribe 'the loss of political authority' narrative in the wake of the colonial reform project into one where a focus on spiritual capacitation appears as a compensation for the active ruination of the various

108 Rashid Ahmad Gangohi, *Fatawa-yi Rashidiyya*, Karachi: Educational Press, 1985, p. 216.

109 Agrama, *Questioning Islam*, p. 180.

infrastructures and institutions (including through the confinement of Islamic Law to the narrow remit of personal law and the withdrawal of patronage from their institutions of education) that had previously enabled selves and others to live well with the obligations of the *Sharia*. In the case of British India, a case in point is the loss of the institution of the courts of the *Qadis*, and how that created practical difficulties for living with a myriad of *Sharia* obligations – such as the obligations towards one's spouse on account of the fact that certain forms of divorce could no longer be obtained with requisite ease.[110]

In other words, in the face of a crisis and contraction of the public institutional infrastructure of an Islamic 'way of life' on account of the projects of colonial modernity, a spiritual deepening of the norm embodying exemplary self of the jurist guide and a generalization of those invited to their training was proposed by the revivalists as a practical support for the continued livability of this life. These revivalist conduct manuals for jurists were a form of spiritual jurisprudence – not a mystical law.

Conclusion

The legal tradition of the colonized responded to the disaster. What we have inherited as conduct training for the offices of Islamic jurists in the

110 Zaman vividly captures the practical vicissitudes this institutional ruination created for the Muftis and their fatwas, and the acute awareness on the part of the part of these jurists of this state of this state of affairs: '*Those issuing these fatwas were clearly aware that the practice of Islamic law had become disfunctional in British India. Without a qadi, even relatively simple matters such as the dissolution of marriage or the determination of the "waiting period" could not be resolved. Even when, in principle, the Hanafi mufti was willing to allow recourse to the Maliki school of law on a particular matter, he would immediately point out that a Muslim judge was still required to decide according to the Maliki position...These muftis sometimes suggested that the person seeking to dissolve an undesirable marriage might have recourse to the principalities outside British India (such as the Muslim-ruled princely state of Bhopal), which still had qadis. Moreover, they pointed out, if the judge were a Muslim even if the appointing authority was itself non-Muslim, the former's decision should be valid; but there could be no recourse without a Muslim judge.*' Muhammad Qasim Zaman, *The Ulema in Contemporary Islam: The Custodians of Change*, Princeton, New Jersey: Princeton University Press, 2002, p. 27.

wake of this 'surpassing disaster'[111] is neither simply an invention, nor a recovery demanding unchanging imitation. As Asad observes:

> ...the changes that have taken place should not be taken – in the way that many Islamists and orientalists have taken them – to imply that the Islamic tradition has therefore been broken. That tradition, like all living traditions, is full of tensions that emerge sharply in particular contexts. It is capable of change and has indeed changed again and again in its history. The idea that 'tradition' always requires unthinking imitation from one generation to the next and that the existence of serious argument about the existence of new questions and answers means that tradition has given way to modernity, is a serious misconception. But how...ethics, law, and religion are related to one another, and to what degrees they can be negotiated, is never a simple question.[112]

The marginal/fringe position within the tradition of what Ahmed has termed a 'legal supremacist' version of the Islamic legal tradition, associated with the *Wahhabi* quest for 'smashing elegance in the name of piety', has since lent itself to the project of modern postcolonial states to attach and administer a detached and code-like *Sharia* as one form of state law.[113] Thus Islamic jurists and judges attached to the State in countries like Egypt and Pakistan conduct themselves more like the colonial judges and *Wahhabi* jurists, than the state rivaling Islamic revivalists associated with the seminaries of Deoband and Al-Azhar in the late 19th century and early 20th century.[114] I make this point not to suggest a postcolonial surpassing but rather to point out how the tradition continues to be under assault in a postcolonial world. For these state *Muftis* and *Qadis*, the conduct manuals described in this chapter are not formative for their office training.

However, as observed by Messick and Caeiro, amongst others, there has been a continued production and circulation of this genre into contemporary times, particularly amongst minority Muslim communities in

111 Jalal Taufic, *The Withdrawal of Tradition Past a Surpassing Disaster*, Beirut: Toufic Jalal, 2009.

112 Asad, 'Thinking about Law', p. 23.

113 El Fadl, *The Authoritative and the Authoritarian.*

114 See Wael B. Hallaq, *The Impossible State: Islam, Politics, and Modernity's Moral Predicament*, New York: Columbia University Press, 2013; Agrama, *Questioning Secularism.*

the imperial West.[115] One can observe a certain similarity in contexts, with the Islamic jurists, much like the 19th-century revivalists, having to spiritually guide and thus practically enable Muslim subjects to live well with their Islamic obligations, without having the ability to care for any significant social institutions. Here too the allure of 'state complicity' remains ubiquitous.[116]

115 See Alexandre Caeiro, 'The Power of European Fatwas: The Minority Fiqh Project and the Making of a Islamic Counterpublic', *International Journal of Middle East Studies* 42, 3 (2010) 435; Messick, 'Fatwa, modern'.

116 Farah El-Sharif provides a insightful account of the 'state complicity' practiced by several prominent Sufi jurists in the West, as evidence of what Colbert-Hicks has aptly described as 'the transformation of Indian Persian "Mysticism" in Liberal Islamic Modernity'. Farah El-Sharif, 'Manufacturing "Islam Lite": Sufism as "Good Islam", Sermons at the Court, Substack, 4 December 2024.

Chapter 5

Dante, law, and the office of the jurist

Gian-Giacomo Fusco

Introduction

Dante Alighieri's familiarity with the law and his use of legal principles in literary works have long been subjects of scholarly investigation.[1] Despite not having formally studied the law, and therefore lacking the '*forma mentis*' of a jurist, he certainly possessed some structured knowledge of the *Corpus Iuris Civilis*, legal sources and literature of his time.[2] As Ernst Kantorowicz famously observed, by holding a central position in the intellectual landscape of his time, 'Dante the political philosopher as well as Dante the poet assimilated to the full the political doctrines of his century'.[3] In addition, his experience as a convict and exile brought him into direct contact with the relentless operation of the medieval legal system and its political implications and limits. Nevertheless, Dante has never offered a 'unified theory or practical doctrine of law'; his understanding of the law's function and essence is influenced by 'current analyses presented by theologians, by the written corpus of Roman

1 See James Williams, *Dante as a Jurist* (Oxford: B. Blackwell, 1906); Filippo Cancelli, 'Diritto romano in Dante', in *Enciclopedia Dantesca* 2 (Roma: Istituto dell'Enciclopedia Italiana, 1970), pp. 472–479; Justin Steinberg, *Dante and the Limits of the Law* (Chicago and London: The University of Chicago Press, 2013); Daniela Bianchini Jesurum, *Dante Giurista? Sondaggi nella Divina Commedia* (Torino: Giappichelli, 2014); Claudia di Fonzo, *Dante e la Tradizione Giuridica* (Roma: Carocci, 2016); Giuseppe Franco Ferrari (eds.), *Dante Alighieri e il Diritto Pubblico* (Torino: Giappichelli, 2022); Marco Galdi, *Dante tra Diritto e Letteratura* (Salerno: Francesco D'Amato Editore, 2023).

2 See Diego Quaglioni, 'The Law', in Manuele Gragnolati, Elena Lombardi, and Francesca Southerden (eds.), *The Oxford Handbook of Dante* (Oxford: Oxford University Press, 2021), pp. 257–269.

3 Ernst H. Kantorowicz, *The King's Two Bodies: A Study in Medieval Political Theology* (Princeton, NJ: Princeton University Press, 1957), p. 451.

DOI: 10.4324/9781003659754-6

law, and by glossators, lawyers, and jurists'[4] of his time. While the questions concerning the ground and form of his legal knowledge, although of historiographical importance, remain still surrounded by uncertainty, what is instead more open to fruitful interpretation is the use Dante made of legal principles and of the jurisprudential tradition in his works (which Hans Kelsen defined as a proper 'philosophy of law'),[5] especially in light of the originality with which he constantly filtered and re-interpreted the ideas and theorems he handled.

As a learned member of Medieval society, for Dante, the law cannot but be an expression of a 'metaphysical order impressed on the whole universe by God', in which human law is 'just' only to the extent it aligns with such a divine ordering.[6] Revealed in the scriptures, God's law is the source from which 'human reason can deduce that natural law to which all human law should conform'.[7] The core of Dante's vision of the law is included in his political and philosophical writings, the *Convivio* and *Monarchia* – works that, as we will see, also provide a sharp critique of the role and duty of jurists and lawyers. Even his poetic masterpiece, the *Divina Comedia*, however, is constellated by legal themes, principles, and personages. Indeed, as Justin Steinberg argues, 'Dante's literary theoretical framework is simultaneously and manifestly a legal one'; he 'imagines the afterlife as a highly regulated administrative body – complete with an elaborate network of local laws, hierarchical jurisdictions, and rationalised punishments and rewards'.[8]

The literary representation of sin, punishments, and virtue in the *Comedia* constitutes an exemplary and highly articulated form of poetic justice,[9] that strategy according to which in works of fiction, punishments and rewards are distributed proportionally to the vices and virtues of the different characters.[10] In Dante's *Inferno* (and *Purgatorio*), poetic justice is commonly defined through the term 'contrapasso', a *hapax legomenon* of the Divine Comedy that commentators identified as the

4 Peter Armour, 'Law', in Richard Lansing (eds.), *The Dante Encyclopaedia* (London and New York: Routledge, 2010), p. 557.

5 Hans Kelsen, *Die Staatslehre des Dante Alighieri* (Wien and Leipzig: Franz Deuticke, 1905), Ch 3.

6 See: Claudia di Fonzo, 'Dante e il'dantismo giuridico' del Trecento', *TENZONE* 19 (2018), pp. 79–108; Diego Quaglioni, 'The Law'.

7 Armour, 'Law', p. 577.

8 Justin Steinberg, *Dante and the Limits of the Law* (Chicago and London: The University of Chicago Press, 2013), p. 2.

9 The notion of poetic justice has been coined by Thomas Rhymer in his *The Tragedies of the Last Age* (London: Richard Baldwin, 1692).

10 See M.H. Abrams and Geoffrey Harpham, *A Glossary of Literary Terms* (USA: CENGAGE Learning, 2012), pp. 299–300.

general rule for the allocation of punishments based on a symbolic relation with the sins committed. The multitude of characters he encounters are indeed destined to suffer a form of eternal punishment that is directly connected to their guilt. To the extent that the lustful ('the carnal sinner, who subjects their reason to their lust' [*Inf.* 5. 38-39]), overwhelmed by their sexual desire, are unable to control their bodies and souls, they are perpetually thrown in a violent storm. Elsewhere, the heretics (that is, those 'who make the soul die with the body' [*Inf.* 10. 15]) are condemned to spend their afterlives in their graves, until the judgment day when the tombs will be closed forever, and the souls with their earthly bodies sealed inside. Dante's poetic justice in the Inferno seems to be ingrained in an image of the justice of a vindictive and inflexible God[11] for whom the punishments are a 'brutal literalisation of their respective sin' insofar as the damned are tormented by a transfigured (allegorical) manifestation of their own sins.[12]

As perhaps with any form of poetic justice, Dante's poem is an incursion into what separates and connects guilt and punishment: the original, artificial, and therefore fictitious, linguistic/poetic experience of weighing the breaking of the law and deciding on the relative consequences, underpinning all forms of law-making process. One of the hurdles that the history of legal thought constantly clashes against is the ontological heterogeneity of norm and sanction, guilt, and punishment (*ought* and *is*), which places the legislator (and the judge) always in the uneasy position of establishing the appropriate criterion to accommodate irreconcilable terms into a more adequate, just, and equitable form (what we are accustomed to calling [legal] justice). Historically, a sense (perhaps properly a principle) of proportionality has guided the formulation of sanctions. Far from being a purely objective parameter, the proportionality of punishment (despite the innumerable examples and formulations) reveals itself to be constantly tied to historical/cultural/ideological coordinates, which makes the naturalness with which we usually consider the existence of sanctions disappear against the brute reality of mere conventionality. The establishment of punishment has always involved discourses and truths about what it means to be a human, the social world and the instruments to maintain and restore integrity after its violation. Ultimately, to the extent that the practice of law-making is an art (the *ars iuris*), in Dante's words *arte di bene*

11 And indeed, he does not hesitate in speaking about divine justice as *divina vendetta* (*Inf.* XI, 90).

12 Justin Steinberg, 'More than an Eye for an Eye: Dante's Sovereign Justice', in Giulia Gaimari and Catherine Keen (eds.), *Ethics, Politics and Justice in Dante* (London: UCL Press, 2019), p. 80.

e di equitade (art of good and equitable [*Cv.* IV IX 8]), the establishment of norms and sanctions is ultimately a *poietic* (that is 'productive' and 'poetic') activity: a specific *technē* whose orientation towards justice requires necessarily a certain degree of flexibility to make the general utility coincide with what is righteous.

* * *

This chapter pursues a twofold purpose: (i) it will try to bring to the fore how Dante's poetic vision in *Inferno* exposes and confronts the hurdle posed by the *poietic* element that connects guilt and sanction, and (ii) against the backdrop of his ideas on the operation and function of the law and his critique of the legal profession, it will try to show how his work is a valuable source for developing a critique of the office (duty) of the jurist. In what follows, the question will not simply be the identification of specific legal doctrines, principles and themes used by Dante; rather, his oeuvre will be treated as a source of meaning and a critical authority regarding law and justice more generally. Indeed, already in the Middle Ages, his poetic vision has been recognised as an authoritative text to engage with political and legal problems, to the extent that Dante's interpreters speak of a 'juridical dantism'.[13]

While the exploration of the legal significance of literature and, vice versa, of the literary dimension of legal texts, is an established field of studies, entering an interpretative relationship with the cultural past always necessitates an extra dose of care and reflection. The risk is either to produce an antiquarian reading,[14] which confines the text firmly in its context, or to modernise it to such an extent that its overall meaning turns out radically transfigured. True is that Dante constantly produced knowledge about questions of a universal nature. Yet it is equally true that too many epistemological breaks separate us from his time. Here, therefore, Dante's works will be treated as part of a continuous, ongoing discussion, one that constituted and continues to constitute the European text[15] and legal imagination. The interpretative endeavour that is here proposed seeks to identify paradigms that might help illuminate what remains unspoken or obscured in legal texts and their dogmatic interpretations: that part of law's existence that constantly escapes ontological consideration. If anything, the fictional/literary word has proven

13 See Claudia di Fonzo, *Dante e la Tradizione Giuridica*, chapter I.I.

14 See Fredric Jameson, *The Political Unconscious. Narrative as a Socially Symbolic Act* (London and New York: Routledge, 2002).

15 On the notion of European Text see Riccardo Baldissone, *Autós: Individuation in the European Text* (London: Rowman & Littlefield, 2020).

especially effective in shedding light on the dark aspects of legal power that formal language hides behind a veil of naturalness.

Two definitions of the law

Dante's insights into the law and his definition of the supposed function of legal regulation must be interpreted in light of his conception of the conflicting relationships between the two universal authorities dominating the political landscape of his time: the Church and the Empire. As long as 'the medieval conflict between the two was principally a conflict of jurisdictions, Dante's legal and juridical arguments concerning temporal power form an integral part of his "political" attitude and thought'.[16] The Pope and the Emperor (the spiritual and temporal powers), the two suns to which Dante refers in Purgatory (*Pur.* XVI, 107), are the highest authorities whose power and purpose are to remove the life of humans from a state of misery and to conduct them to happiness, and whose legitimacy comes directly and independently from God.

Dante's anti-hierocratic stance supposes a clear-cut separation between the competencies of the Church and of political powers; while the former must take care of the spiritual life of souls, mundane justice reaches its highest degree when it is an expression of the will of a subject, the Emperor, who is supreme in unity of command. By settling the question of jurisdiction and competence between spiritual and temporal powers in such a way, Dante resolutely claims that it is up to those who have the power, the Monarchs, the holders of temporal power, and ultimately the Emperor, to legislate in order to make justice reign. In *Convivio* this is expressed with clarity:

> ...justice must be preserved and injustice avoided, and this justice may be lost in two ways (either through not knowing what it is, or through not willing to follow it), written Law was invented in order both to establish it and to administer it. So Augustine says, 'If men had known it (namely justice) and, when known, had observed it, there would have been no need of written Law.' Therefore it is written in the beginning of the Old Digest that 'Written law is the art of well-doing and justice.' The official of whom we are speaking, namely the Emperor, is appointed to formulate, demonstrate, and enforce precisely this Law, and to him we are subject as far as our own activities extend, which have already been described, and no further. For this reason in every art and in every trade the craftsmen and

16 Armour, 'The Law', p. 577.

> apprentices are, and should be, subject to the chief and master of the activities within those arts and trades, outside of which the subjection ceases, because the rule of the master ceases. Thus we might say of the Emperor, if we were to describe his office with an image, that he is the one who rides in the saddle of the human will. (*Cv* IV, ix, 8-10)[17]

For Dante, the divine ordering of the world conjured up two authorities with different jurisdictions, administering two different forms of law: human/positive law (the one established by the temporal powers) and a divine/natural law, which pertains to the spiritual conditions of individuals and is under the care of the Church.

What is interesting to look at, from our point of view, is the use that Dante made of the renowned Roman law definition of the law: *ius est ars boni et aequi*[18] (in Dante's words: 'la ragione scritta è arte di bene e d'equitade'). Placed in the opening lines of the *Digest*, this definition originated from the ancient jurist Ulpian, who derived it from the writings of another esteemed Roman jurist named Celsus. The dictum has been passed down to successive generations of scholars who have interpreted it as one of the few definitions of law present in the Justinian *Corpus*. Such a definition encapsulates the artificial essence of the (Roman) law – the fact that legal norms are the product of artifice – and the aspiration of norms towards justice and equity. In a sense, the success of this definition might also be linked to its efficacy in revealing, against any purified doctrine of law, that the equitable foundations of positively established rules do not represent a mere ambition of the legislator but constitute an essential element of the validity of every law. For Dante, therefore, justice – reached through the just application of the law – is not administered simply through a strict and literal application of the law but is an art: a *ius commune* that includes norms, general principles, and instruments to adapt them to different and varying circumstances. And the office of the emperor, the ultimate legal authority, although it grounds itself as the origin and source of the mundane law, is far from being that of an absolute legislator, since bound and limited to the pursuit of the good and equitable.

In *Monarchia*, Dante offers a more articulated and substantial definition of the law, which has been celebrated for its clarity and efficacy:

17 Dante Alighieri, *Il Convivio (The Banquet)*. Trans. Richard H. Lansing (Garland Library of Medieval Literature, 1990).

18 *Iuri operam daturum prius nosse oportet, unde nomen iuris descendat. est autem a iustitia appellatum: nam, ut eleganter Celsus definit, ius est ars boni et aequi.* (Dig. 1.1.pr).

> whoever has the good of the community as his goal has the achievement of law as his goal. That the one necessarily follows from the other can be shown in this way: the law is a relationship between one individual and another in respect of things and people; when it is respected it preserves human society and when it is violated it destroys it [...] If therefore our definition correctly embraces both the essence and the purpose of the law, and if the goal of any society is the common good of its members, it necessarily follows that the purpose of every law is the common good, and it is impossible that there can be a law which does not aim at the common good. [...] For if laws are not framed for the benefit of those who are subject to the law, they are laws in name only, but in reality they cannot be laws; for laws must bind men together for their mutual benefit. (*Monarchia* II V).

The law here is interpreted as the 'relationship between one individual and another in respect of things and people' (*Ius est realis et personalis hominis ad hominem proportio)*. This definition has been composed a few years after the one offered in the *Convivio* and has as its source and inspiration Aristotle's notion of *dikaion (*the just) as formulated in the *Nichomachean Ethics*. Here, the Stagirite writes that the 'just is a sort of proportion', which involves the fair distribution and allocation of something, and therefore involves 'four terms: the persons for whom it is just are two, and the shares in which its justice consists are two'.[19] Dante's definition of the law replicates Aristotle's discussion so much so that the *ius* is equated to an intersubjective relationship (*proportio hominis ad hominem*) that involves four terms: the two persons and the relative things to be distributed. The value of the things at stake in the relationship is determined by the merit of the persons to whom they will be distributed. But proportionality here is not simply something that pertains to the individuals in their capacity as subjects of the law, but assumes the role of that social element, the conservation and respect of which allows for establishing a peaceful coexistence.[20]

The law for Dante, therefore, has the noble task of regulating and ordering the society of congregated subjects. Temporal power (the lawgiver, the judge, and ultimately the Emperor) in its autonomy has the

19 Aristotle, *Nichomachean Ethics*, ed. by Roger Crisp (Cambridge: Cambridge University Press, 2004), p. 86.

20 See Dario Mantovani, 'La definizione di *Ius* nella *Monarchia* di Dante: una lettura contestuale', in Giuseppe Franco Ferrari (eds.), *Dante Alighieri e il Diritto Pubblico* (Torino: Giappichelli, 2022); Marco Galdi, *Dante tra Diritto e Letteratura* (Salerno: Francesco D'Amato Editore, 2023).

obvious function of guaranteeing this order of civilisation. However, its *protestas* is not absolute, but is somehow constrained by the necessity of pursuing the good, the equitable, and the just (proportion). It is, in other words, bound by the law. Iniquity and the corruption of the social body arise from the non-application or misapplication of the law. The law (the artificial, positive, just law) is the concrete remedy that humans possess to live in an ordered civilisation that intends to replicate the order impressed by God on the cosmos. The law is nothing other than the bond to which society and its rulers must submit to pursue the common good, since, as Dante wrote, 'whoever has the good of the community as his goal has the achievement of law as his goal'.

'let the presumptuous jurists see...'

It is with this notion of the law in mind that Dante advanced a stark criticism of the figure of the jurist. In the *Convivio* he resolutely claimed: 'Nor should we give the name of true philosopher to anyone who is a friend of wisdom for the sake of utility, as are jurists, physicians, and almost all those belonging to religious orders, who study not in order to gain knowledge but to secure financial rewards or high office; and if anyone were to give them what they seek to gain, they would not persevere in their study' (CV, 3.11, 10). Such a staunch opinion is reiterated also in *Monarchia* where he wrote: 'Now let the presumptuous jurists see just how far they are below that watchtower of reason from which the human mind contemplates these principles and let them be silent and be satisfied to give counsel and judgment in accordance with the sense of the law' (Mn, II 9).

Dante carries out his polemics against the 'presumptuous' and greedy jurists who search for riches (avarice and greed) before they desire truth, which is an indispensable prerequisite for achieving justice. These harsh statements do not have a particular target but are directed towards the jurists as a class, in a time when lawyering was becoming a profession. Such a sceptical vision of legal scholars and practitioners was commonplace in the Middle Ages; indeed, literary production of the time provides numerous examples of expressions of mistrust in the category of the jurist, which was often labelled as greed-bag, tongue-renter, and even prostitutes, to satirise and highlight the mercenary nature of their profession.[21]

21 See James A. Brundage, 'The Medieval Advocate's Profession', *Law and History Review* 6, No. 2 (Autumn, 1988); 'Vultures, Whores, and Hypocrites: Images of Lawyers in Medieval Literature', *Roman Legal Tradition* 1 (2002).

But as Loren Valterza suggests, Dante's arguments are more articulated than simple invective and involve substantial ethical considerations based on his specific conception of the law. The condemnation of those jurists approaching the study of the law guided by the desire for material wealth is moved in the context of a 'larger analysis of desire, the accumulation of wealth, and the spiritual hazard to which these will lead'.[22] Indeed, greed is one of the greatest obstacles to reaching individual 'contentedness or perfection':[23] the desire for possession of wealth makes 'a person less complete' and always in need of a greater amount of riches (*Cv* 4.12.5). But in Dante's vision, greed also has a political connotation and seems to oppose the very essence of the law. The desire for material wealth is what 'imperils and destroys cities, territories, and individuals' (*Cv*, 4.12.4), and it is what the law (both Canon and Civil law) intends to limit. For Valterza, Dante here clearly exposes the paradox the jurists, a professional class that at that time came to dominate the bureaucratic edifice of the nascent states, find themselves operating: in studying the law, *ratio scripta*, the art of the good and equitable, they are driven by a desire that the same law is meant to limit, in order to limit the corruption and destruction of the polis.[24]

In both his ethical/political and poetic works, Dante maintains a rather ambivalent view of the law. It is true that he exalted law's function as that of establishing justice and political peace. But at the same time, he did not refrain from criticising jurists, whose longing for wealth stands in ethical contradiction with the very object of their studies. These contrasting ideas are mirrored in the *Comedia*, more specifically in the *Paradiso* where we find for instance, Justinian (*Par*, VI), and Gratian (*Par*, X), the first for his historical role in recovering the tradition of Roman law, the second as the one who 'who served so well in the two courts of law that Heaven finds great joy in having him in' (Par, X, 104-5). Dante exalted Gratian's *Decretum* for its operation of ordering the immense and somehow chaotic normative production of canon law, showing its specific jurisdiction and possible accord with civil law. And what is more, from a political perspective, he affirmed the rigid separation between spiritual and temporal power (without negating the possibility of the pope acting politically), under the influence of the Gelasian dyarchy.[25]

22 Loren Michael Valterza, *Infernal Retainers: Dante and the Juridical Tradition*, PhD Dissertation, Rutgers University, 2011, p. 21.

23 Ibid., p. 22.

24 Ibid., p. 25.

25 Jesurum, *Dante Giurista?* pp. 97–98.

But later, in Canto XII, Dante insists on a critique of jurists when he writes, 'Not like those men who toil for worldly gain, studying Thaddeus and Hostiensis, but for the love of eternal bread'. Here, Hostiensis (the famous canonist and cardinal Enrico da Susa) becomes the symbol of all those jurists who, moved by the desire for wealth and riches, neglected truth and justice in the study of law, bending their knowledge towards obtaining specific political goals. Dante considers Hostiensis as one of those personalities whose works are studied and appreciated in order to acquire power and worldly fame by those who ambitiously aspire within the Church to well-paid dignities.[26] It is worth noting that, although Dante does not engage in direct polemics with his ideas, Hostiensis at that time was a crucial figure in the development of the doctrine of papal *plenitude potestatis*, supporting at the same time the primacy of the office of the Pope over the temporal powers.[27] And given the importance of his political vision in the whole of his oeuvre, Dante's anti-hierocratic stance cannot but play a role in his polemical attitude towards Hostiensis.

The *ars iuris* at work

The criteria for punishing guilt in *Inferno* (and *Purgatorio*) seem to follow a determined albeit not rigid logic that forms a rather coherent framework. Each category of sinners is separated from the others and treated differently according to a correlated penalty. The gravity of the guilt and the corresponding severity of torments increases proportionally to the gradual descending into the infernal abyss; Dante learns directly from the confession of the souls he encounters about their sins and relative punishments. The literary depiction of hell assumes a fundamental theological meaning; to the extent that being in hell represents a well-deserved separation from God and the divine, punishment cannot be something administered by God but must be the direct consequence of the sin itself.[28]

'Contrapasso' is the term with which interpreters have identified the underlying logic of punishment underpinning the narrative of the

26 Raoul Manselli, 'Enrico da Susa', *Enciclopedia Dantesca* 1970, https://www.treccani.it/enciclopedia/enrico-di-susa_%28Enciclopedia-Dantesca%29/.

27 Anthony Cassell, 'Luna Est Ecclesia': Dante and the 'Two Great Lights', *Dante Studies, with the Annual Report of the Dante Society*, no. 119 (2001), p. 4.

28 Teodolinda Barolini, 'Multiculturalismo Medievale e Teologia dell'inferno Dantesco', *Dante: Rivista internazionale di studi su Dante Alighieri* 2 (2005), pp. 11–13.

Inferno. Often identified as a form of retributive justice replicating the logic of the *lex talionis*, the poetic justice of the *contrapasso* (and of the afterlife more generally) upon which Dante structured his poetics has been influenced by theological themes and speculations, but also by other cultural (pagan/philosophical) sources that were available and popular at the time, so much so that it might be viewed as resulting from specific multiculturalism.[29]

It is now accepted by interpreters that Dante wanted the readers to interpret the poetic justice of the *contrapasso* somehow critically.[30] This becomes clear in the place where the term *contrapasso* first appears, that is *Inferno* XXVIII. This canto describes the punishments in the eighth sub-circle or *bolgia of Malebolge*. The souls in this place are condemned as 'sowers of scandal and schism' (*Inf.* XXVIII, 34-35) for their instigation of civil and religious strife. Here the bodies of the sinners are mutilated and split, just as they have in life split the bodies of society and of the Church.

In the canto, the first soul encountered is that of Mohammed, whose body is depicted as split from his chin to his anus. According to Dante's medieval sources, Mohammed was originally a Nestorian Christian, who by founding Islam was believed to have distorted Christian teachings and led former believers astray from the true Church. And for leading a section of the faithful away from the flock, he now suffers a corresponding loss in the split in his flesh. Following Mohammed, three characters appear in a circular procession: Piero da Medicina, Curio, and Mosca dei Lamberti. Each of them experiences a form of amputation as punishment for advocating actions that contributed to conflicts. At the end of this grim parade stands Bertran de Born, a Troubadour poet Dante knew and admired. His punishment involves being severed from his own head, symbolising how he contributed to the division between a young prince and his father, King Henry II of England. As a result, Bertran holds his own head in his hands and presents it to Dante and Virgil as they pass by.[31]

This macabre display serves as an epigraphic representation of his infernal sentence:

> "Perch'io parti' così giunte persone,
> partito porto il mio cerebro, lasso!,

29 Ibid.

30 See Giuseppe Mazzotta, *Reading Dante* (New Heaven and London: Yale University Press, 2014); Justin Steinber, 'Dante's Justice? A Reappraisal of the Contrapasso', *L'Alighieri* 44 (2014), pp. 59–74.

31 See Steinber, 'Dante's Justice? A Reappraisal of the Contrapasso'.

dal suo principio ch'è in questo troncone.
Così s'osserva in me lo contrapasso"

Because I divided persons so joined,
I carry my brain separated from its source
Which is in this trunk.
In this way you observe in me the law of counter-suffering
(Contrapasso).

(Inf. XXVIII, 139–42)

This episode is important in the economy of the development of the *Divine Comedy* for two reasons: it is the first and only moment in which the term *contrapasso* is named, and it is also the first occasion in which an infernal character seems to question the fairness of the punishment he is suffering. Bertran de Born, in fact, before exposing his own punishment, tells Dante:

"Or vedi la pena molesta,
tu che, spirando, vai veggendo i morti
vedi s'alcuna è grande come questa"

Now see my wretched punishment
You who go still breathing to view the dead:
see if any other is great as this.

(Inf. XXVIII, 130–32)

Bertran de Born is the first personage in hell who seems to openly complain that the punishment inflicted on him is beyond all justice, that no proportionality stands between his guilt and the consequent sanction. The *contrapasso*, which Bertran de Born introduces in the Comedy, has been regarded as the general law governing the symbolism of all the punishments in Dante's afterlife. Commentators have questioned such a position, especially considering that such a notion appears very late in *Inferno* and that it seems to be immediately put into question as a reliable form of justice, by Bertran de Born's lamentation.

Dante took the term contrapasso from the Latin *contrapassum* – the translation of the Greek *antipeponthos* that denotes a counter (reciprocal) suffering for any illicit action. In the Middle Ages, such a term became a synonym for *lex talionis* (eye for an eye). In all likelihood, Dante was aware of the discussions and critique of retributive justice and the contrapasso that authors such as Thomas Aquinas developed by engaging with Aristotle. While it has certainly been acknowledged as a legitimate form of doing justice, the contrapasso explicitly involves some evident limitations. For specific offences, such as murder, the strict quantitative (or arithmetical) retribution would produce the death penalty. But there are other crimes, like perjury, kidnapping, rape, and theft, in which striking back in the same way produces some sort of ethical conundrum. Moreover, there are cases in which the status of the person – their office – results in the contrapasso not being harsh enough. For instance, in all those offences in which the victim is a ruler or a governing figure – the cases which Aquinas, following Aristotle, discussed – it is not simply the body of the person that is violated, but also his office (or in the case of the sovereign, the body politic as a whole). In these cases, a further supplement of punishment is required to achieve a more perfect retributive justice: 'If a clown were to slap the king, it's not enough for the king to slap the clown back, because there is also the violation of the office involved, which can never quite be restored simply by having the king slap the clown back'.[32] As Justin Steinberg puts it, the whole point of Canto XXVIII is that the sowers of discord 'for exactly the types of "public" crimes for which the contrapassum [...] is an inadequate response. These souls have harmed not only private individuals but also corporate bodies, both secular and religious'.[33]

Interpreting the *contrapasso* (as a form of *lex talionis*) as the general law governing punishments in the *Comedia*, therefore, is questionable, since it is far from being a reliable rule for justice applicable to all cases. Rather than encompassing a general and generalisable rule for justice, the contrapasso in a sense opens up to the very rational irreconcilability of guilt and punishment, of the impossibility of expressing fairly how the latter can and should fit the former. And this is somehow expressed at the opening of *Inferno* XXVIII, when using an ineffability, *topos* writes:

> "Chi poria mai pur con parole sciolte
> dicer del sangue e de le piaghe a pieno
> ch'i' ora vidi, per narrar più volte?
> Ogne lingua per certo verria meno
> per lo nostro sermone e per la mente
> c'hanno a tanto comprender poco seno".
>
> Even in words not bounded by rhyme's law
> Through many repetitions of the tale,
> How could the blood and wounds that I now saw
> Be fully told? Every tongue would surely fail, because our

32 Mazzotta, *Reading Dante*, p. 100.
33 Steinberg, 'Dante's Justice? A Reappraisal of the Contrapasso', p. 70.

Language and our memory have little capacity to
Comprehend on such a scale.

(Inf. XXVIII, 1–6)

Dante here asserts that his vision of bleeding gaping wounds cannot be comprehended and expressed by standard poetic conventions. Moreover, memory and language themselves lack the 'capacity' to encompass fully the forms of punishments he saw.[34] Here Dante is stating the impossibility of finding through language the right metaphor, the exact correspondence between a reality and its representation. As Giuseppe Mazzotta suggests, with this canto Dante is telling the reader how arbitrary his own judgments are. He recognises that the way in which punishments and crimes are related is never quite reliable. His judgment is ultimately arbitrary, and the poetic justice of the *contrapasso* is just a touchstone to guide his artistic discretion.[35]

Eye for an eye

The principle of the contrapasso has been arguably derived from the biblical law of retaliation – an eye for an eye, which crudely prescribes that anyone who inflicts an injury shall receive the same in return. Indeed, contrapasso throughout time has been made into a synonym for *lex talionis*. However, as Lino Pertile claimed, the ways in which such a principle works 'in the narrative are as many as the sins, if not as many as the sinners, to which it is applied'.[36] To make the eye for an eye the general norm common to Dante's many and varied forms of punishment might appear, to a certain extent, misleading. While some commentators sustained the similarity of the *contrapasso* to biblical retaliation,[37] others, on the contrary, recognised the irreducibility of Dante's poetic to the tit-for-tat justice of the talion.[38] Of course, both positions are legitimate ones. It is undeniable that when the term contrapasso appeared in literature, it did so as a form of retributive justice. At the same time, Dante's

34 Mazzotta, *Reading Dante*, p. 97.

35 Ibid., p. 100.

36 Lino Pertile, 'Introduction to Inferno', in *The Cambridge Companion to Dante*, Rachel Jacoff (eds.) (New York: Cambridge University Press, 2007), p. 79.

37 For a review of this position see Peter Armour, 'Dante's Contrapasso: Context and Texts', *Italian Studies* 55, no. 1 (2000), pp. 1–20.

38 See Mazzotta, *Reading Dante*; Steinberg, 'Dante's Justice? A Reappraisal of the Contrapasso'.

contrapasso, as a form of justice, is much more articulated than merely getting the same in return.

What has perhaps vitiated and put the different interpretations of the contrapasso on a false track is a common misinterpretation of the principle of the talion and of retribution. In general, retributive justice does not have a good reputation. Hans Kelsen, for instance, claimed that the principle of retribution represents 'the fundamental principle which determines primitive man's behaviour towards nature and towards his own and other social groups'.[39] Until recently, the principle of the lex talionis was regarded as belonging to an early stage of legal development, whereas our modern laws are considered significantly distinct and more humane. By envisaging justice as a form of vengeance, the primitive concept of retribution was considered barbaric compared to the more civilised form of punishment, like monetary sanctions and imprisonment. Such a conception of the talion is generally based on a literal interpretation of the eye for an eye, with the logical consequence of making retributive justice simply a brutal and overly punitive form of public revenge.

However, as Gunther Plaut claimed 'few passages in the Torah have been so thoroughly misunderstood as the one which states that injuries to life and limb are to be met with punishments that reflect the seriousness of the crime': the eye for an eye principle 'which appears to lay down the principle of literal retribution (or talion) – was not at all formulated for such a purpose'.[40] Appearing in Exodus (21:23-25) the talionic law 'life for life, eye for eye, tooth for tooth, hand for hand, foot for foot, burn for burn, wound for wound, stripe for stripe' more than its literal sense, served the purpose of putting a limit on the potential excesses of punishments and revenge, in the general interest of the community. This law set the principle for exacting retribution, 'and this, in turn, was transformed into compensation scaled to the degree of the injury: the value of one eye for the loss of an eye; the value of a limb for its loss, and so forth'.[41] The biblical *lex talionis*, thus, should be read figuratively as expressing a general principle of limitation or criterion of proportionality: the punishment should fit the crime. Even in the Law of Hammurabi and the Roman Law of Twelve Tables, the *talion* seems to serve as a principle slightly different from the literal meaning of its formulation. In the Twelve Tables, for instance, the *lex talionis* seems

39 H. Kelsen, *Society and Nature. A Sociological Enquiry* (Chicago: The University of Chicago Press, 1943), p. 49.

40 Gunther Plaut, *The Torah: A Modern Commentary* (New York: Union of American Hebrew Congregations, 1981), p. 571.

41 Ibid.

to provide an alternative when in a dispute other forms of pacification failed: as we read in the formulation assigned to Table VIII: *si membrum rupsit, ni cum eo pacit, talio esto* – If he destroys a limb, unless he compensates him or makes peace, let there be retaliation.[42]

For jurisprudence, the *lex talionis* has long been a disturbing presence: something archaic that does not belong to our modern scale of values, which at the same time seems to expose formal elements of the present state of the law that is 'what counts as an appropriate punishment'.[43] Finding the more appropriate sanction, however, is far from an easy activity. This is well summarised by H. L. Hart in his discussion of the principle of retribution. As he points out, the notion that 'what the criminal has done should be done to him ... the killer should be killed, the violent assailant should be flogged'[44] represents a crude form of proportionality or fittingness. He goes on, however, to argue that 'this idea is incapable of generalization without absurdity ... Theft cannot be punished by theft, defamation by defamation, forgery by forgery, adultery by adultery'.[45] To make the idea of appropriateness or proportionality the principle of retribution involves a viable principle which Hart refined by including another criterion, 'wickedness', to establish a generalisable relationship between crime and punishment with equally uncertain results:

> the suffering imposed by the punishment should be in some sense equal to or proportionate to the wickedness of the crime. But in what sense? How to measure either wickedness or suffering in the absence of units of either? ... there is no natural relationship to be discerned between wickedness and punishment of a certain degree or kind, so that we can say the latter naturally 'fits' the former.[46]

At stake in the principle of the *lex talionis*, thus, is on the one hand the question of the appropriateness of the punishment, and on the other hand the ontological-radical difference between crime/guilt and the necessary (legal) consequence. The idea of retribution exposes in this way the unnatural and artificial relationship that connects and separates crime and punishment, facts and norms. 'The talion', as William Ian

42 William Ian Miller, *Eye for an Eye* (Cambridge: Cambridge University Press, 2006), p. 47.
43 Jeremy Waldron, 'Lex Talionis', *Arizona Law Review* 34 (1992), pp. 25–51.
44 H. L. A. Hart, *Punishment and Responsibility* (Oxford: Oxford University Press, 1968), p. 161.
45 Ibid.
46 Ibid., pp. 161–162.

Miller rightly claims, 'is about measuring':[47] 'how to measure value and then how to find an appropriate means of payment once value had been determined'.[48] But this necessarily involves the mastering of a technique, of an art, of establishing the exact measure, rather than the determination of a natural relationship between two terms.

Defining Dante's contrapasso as an instance of retributive justice, or as a synonym of *lex talionis*, is not in itself incorrect, as long as the principle of an eye for an eye is not taken in its literal sense. As we have seen above, for Dante, the relationship between guilt and punishment is never based on a purely objective criterion or quantification. The poetic justice of the contrapasso is a poetic expedient to represent vividly a principle of justice whose ultimate definition remains between the boundaries of the poetic practice itself. Dante seems to suggest that the indication of punishments is always linked to an inscrutable evaluation of the legislator'. There is no rule establishing the ultimate relationship between guilt and punishment; what connects the two is an ineffable linguistic practice. Justine Steinberg, in this regard, argues that for Dante: 'fitting the punishment to the crime is, after all, an art. As an art, it must be flexible enough to adapt to the excess of divine justice, whether this excess is expressed as gratuitous redemption or interminable punishment'.[49]

What office for the jurist?

As we have seen, Dante expressed his disdain for those jurists who study the law in pursuit of riches and prestige. At the time he was developing his polemics, jurists and legal practitioners had gained growing influence in both the administration of power and the intellectual life of medieval European society. For this reason, he exposed the impact of greed not only on individuals but on society as a whole. Greed, the relentless drive to accumulate wealth and status, is, for Dante, fundamentally opposed to the essence of the law, as, in his view, the law is meant to curb and restrain all those passions (and behaviour), which he saw as a source of corruption of the social fabric. Dante condemned the materialistic motivations of jurists on both philosophical and political grounds, contrasting the pursuit of wealth with the pursuit of truth, which is essential to justice. He insists that true philosophers must seek truth in autonomy without ulterior motives. By coveting material compensation, jurists disqualify themselves as seekers of truth and become adversaries of genuine

47 Miller, *Eye for an Eye*, p. xii.
48 Ibid., p. 25.
49 Justin Steinberg, 'Dante's Justice? A reappraisal of the contrapasso', 75.

justice. Dante's first explicit reference to jurists as a professional group coincides with this critique, underscoring their deviation from the ideals of the authentic research of justice.

We might distinguish in Dante the true study of law, which is placed in the service of law itself – that is, in function, justice and social equality (as in *Monarchia* the goal of the law is the good of the community: whoever has the good of the community as his goal has the achievement of law as his goal) – from an improper study of law: one in which the professional jurist pursues personal prestige and wealth. We might say that the office of the jurist (their duty) is studying the law for the sake of seeking the truth of the law – that is mastering the art of the good and equitable, and of the right allocation of things and rights between individuals, for the sake of maintaining the common good and justice. An art, as Dante has exposed with a plethora of examples in the *Comedia,* does not have rigid and fixed criteria but always involves an autonomous exercise of conscience in the form of decisions, exceptions, and flexibility in linking what is wrong with righteous/equitable consequences.

In a time like the one we are living in, when the legal form seems to have lost its aura of sacredness, becoming a dominion of bureaucratic and often idiotic rationalisations, when legal scholars learn to abandon the word justice from their lexicon early on in their career, Dante's conception of the law and the role of jurists seems utopian and anachronistic. After the demise of (classic) Natural law, legal regulation, far from being a divinely sourced instrument for producing peace and justice, has become a self-legitimising tool to create a reality that is becoming increasingly incomprehensible. However, what can be retained from Dante's inquiry into law and justice is his exposition of the poetic dimension of the artificial linkage of the statements of norms and their legal consequences, so well exposed through all those metaphorical illustrations of sin and punishments that make the *Comedia* the fundamental text that we all know about.

The contiguity of the *ars iuris* with poetics – and consequently of the offices of the jurist and that of the poet – is at the core of Kantorowicz's short piece titled: 'The Sovereignty of the Artist: A Note on Legal Maxims and Renaissance Theories of Art'.[50] Here Kantorowicz traced the theological-philosophical discourses that led to the emergence, in the Renaissance, of the idea of the artistic endeavour – that of the poets and artists in general – as akin to that of an omnipotent sovereign God-like creator. As he noted, such an image originated in the Middle

50 Ernst Kantorowicz, 'The Sovereignty of the Artist: A Note on Legal Maxims and Renaissance Theories of Art', in *De Artibus Opuscula XL: Essays in Honor of Erwin Panofsky*, ed. Millard Meiss (New York, 1961), pp. 267–279.

Ages through the mutual equiparation (placing on equal terms two or more subjects which at first appeared to have nothing to do with each other) of the figure of the (sovereign) legislator and the poet (artist).[51] As Kantorowicz claims, the arrogation of an absolute power 'was true of the offices of the spiritual and secular powers, and it became true for the offices of the poet, and by transference, of painter and artist at large'.[52] But if for the sovereign such a fullness of power springs by its perpetual office (*ex officio*) the poet is sovereign through its spirited creativity (*ex ingegno*).

Kantorowicz's core argument is that jurisprudence served as a channel through which the core principles underlying the very ideas of artistic practice and sovereign power in the Middle Ages and early modernity were transmitted. Chief among these principles are the theological-political concept of the sovereign office as holding a *plenitudo potestatis* (fullness of power) and the Aristotelian concept of art as the imitation of nature (mimesis). In an interesting passage, which is worth quoting at length, Kantorowicz exposes the proximity of the office of the poet and that of the jurist in this way:

> While harking back to early Roman jurists of the first and second centuries, Justinian's *Institutes* and *Digest* reproduced, and medieval jurists therefore began to interpret, the essence of the Aristotelian maxim [that 'art imitates nature']. To be sure, in the legal jargon the famous principle did not refer to visual arts or artistic vocation at all, but referred to art only in a very special sense, far removed from painting and sculpture. It was quoted for a rather prosaic and sober purpose, that is, to clarify a certain point of the law of adoption. "It is the opinion that a younger person cannot adopt an older one; for adoption imitates nature, and it would be monstrous if the son were older than the father." That is to say. Jurisprudence, commonly defined as an art (*ius est ars boni et aequi*), "imitated nature" just as every other art was supposed to do, and imitated it, in the case of adoption, by means of an artistic fiction: though blood relationship did not necessarily exist, an older person was yet entitled

51 Such an analogy, Kantorowicz noted, could be traced back to Dante's *Paradiso* (I 28-33) where we could find a praise of Apollo's laurel 'of which in his days so rarely frond was gathered for the triumph of either a Caesar or a poet'. The poet here appears to Dante at the same 'level' as the emperor, 'since only "the highest political and the highest intellectual principates" could be decorated at all with the laurel'. See: 'The Sovereignty of the Artist', pp. 276–277.

52 Ibid. 269.

> to recognize a younger one legally as his son, and a younger one, an older one as his father [...] Fiction, in that whole context, had not the slightest derogatory meaning. It was as little derogatory as Petrarch's definition of the "office of the poet," which was said to "disclose and glorify the truth of things woven, as it were, into a decorous cloud of fiction." Fiction was rather something artfully "created" by the art of the jurist; it was an achievement to his credit because fiction made manifest certain legal consequences, which had been hidden before or which by nature did not exist. For by fiction the jurist could create (so to say, from nothing) a legal person, *persona ficta*—a corporation, for example—and endow it with a truth and a life of its own; or he could interpret an existing body, such as the *corpus mysticum* of the Church, in the sense of a fictitious person, and gain a heuristic element by means of which he might arrive at new insights into administration, property rights, and other conditions. In that sense fiction was a lie as little as poetry was a lie [...] Therefore Aquinas could say that fiction, far from being a lie, might on the contrary be *figura veritatis*, because, ran his argument, otherwise all that had been said by wise and holy men or even by the Lord Himself would be held to be mendacious.[53]

Here, Kantorowicz suggests, with his characteristic idiosyncratic style, that both the *ars* of jurist and the poet (their *officia*) are intimately connected with the mastering of the capacity to create fictions by means of language (legal and poetic), whose truth and reality are not to be questioned. For the poet, fiction defines the particular way artistic practice relates to reality and enables knowledge of it. In law, by contrast, the function of legal fictions is what elevates legal practice to an art. As Yan Thomas argued, with the fiction 'we are in the presence of the mystery most radically alien to the common sense' that allows us to think 'the technique of law, its way of doing things, the *ars iuris*'.[54]

Fictions in law are a crack open over the essential facts that legal objects can have a real effect on the world as long as they are not facts. What most defines the nature of law is its capacity to produce a reality that is distinct from, yet effective within, the factual world. Legal objects, the very world that law helps to create, are not entities whose reality must be doubted. It is indeed very difficult to deny the existence of obligations, binding relations, and subjectivities generated by the language of law. A fact, event, or thing only enters the legal world once it is translated into legal language. As the old adage goes: *quod non est in*

53 Ibid., pp. 269–270.
54 Yan Thomas, *Les Opération du Droit* (Paris: Gallimard, 2011), p. 135.

actis, non est in mundo – what is not in the (legal) records does not exist in the world.

Legal science, at its core, is a discourse concerned with the relationship between law and reality, and law's capacity to create virtual facts out of it. Jurists, therefore, do not work directly with a reality, but with constructs and models of it, which at times diverge significantly from the reality they are meant to regulate. The *officium* of the jurist is to serve as custodian, interpreter, and master of this representational power: to oversee the virtues, vices, and excesses of law's capacity to performatively shape the world through its artificial and fictional language. Unlike other legal actors – such as the judge, bound to the dictates of the law whether they like it or not, or the lawyer, bound to the interests of the client – jurists, particularly in their scholarly role, hold both the privilege and the responsibility of engaging with the law autonomously, guided by their own conscience[55] and judgment.

55 On the role of conscience and the office of the scholar/jurist, see Adam Sitze's contribution to this volume 'Conscience is ... the Essence of the Scholar's 'Office'.

Chapter 6

Office as aesthetic protocol

Valérie Hayaert

In 12th–15th-century Europe, the higher calling ascribed to the class of clerical writers (the *notarii*) was defined by the Latin doublet *officium* and *ministerium*, two words that are parasynonyms. Giorgio Agamben[1] has highlighted what, in the liturgical tradition from antiquity to the late Middle Ages, makes the officer–the officiant–an agent rather than an actor, and shows how this officer is thereby determined and defined by his action. In this respect, his office can be defined in terms of function, whichconsists in acting on someone's behalf and assuming responsibility for their actions: "The term 'function,'" he writes, "denotes the vicarious nature of office."[2]

This vicarious position takes place in a space where function can only become fully visible within a simplified and idealized social hierarchy. The difficulty of writing about the concept of "office" therefore stems primarily from the very wide range of meanings covered by the word itself. In Cicero's treatise, which does not offer any definition of *officium*, the term refers to a "duty in a given situation": office designates what is appropriate and proper to do in a specific context and circumstance, particularly given the social status of the agent in question. I will therefore start from Giorgio Agamben's conclusion that "officium is what makes an individual behave consistently: like a prostitute if she is a prostitute, like a scoundrel if he is a scoundrel, but also like a consul if he is a consul and, later, like a bishop if he is a bishop." More broadly, it is what makes life governable (*De Officiis* I,11–12) by giving every aspect of life a model to which it can conform.

Saint Ambrose, widely regarded as one of the "Fathers" of the Catholic Church, in his work *De Officiis ministrorum*, or *The Duties*

1 Giorgio Agamben, *Opus Dei: archéologie de l'office*, trad. de l'ital. M. Rueff, Paris, Le Seuil, 2012, pp. 110–111.
2 Giorgio Agamben, ibid., p. 112.

DOI: 10.4324/9781003659754-7

of the Clergy, subsequently adopted Donatus' fictitious etymology of the word office, *officium ab efficiendo*, and the concept of office thus became linked to the effective performance of an action. Later, canon law of the Catholic Church transformed the concept into a duty (*munus, exercitium, onus*) that conferred honour (*honor, dignitas*). In examining how the concept of *officium* applies to judicial symbolism, it is striking to note how this concept–which presupposes a zone of indistinctness between the agent, their dignity, their duty to act in a given situation, and the result of their action–is articulated through reference to aesthetics. These remarks about the genealogy of the concept of "officium" demonstrate the relationship between a moral obligation (which serves a community interest rather than a personal interest), the fulfilment of the obligation by carrying out a task or function, and finally, the specific type of subjective participation in the exercise of this function itself. The moral meaning of the term *officium* implies two elements: an axiology, or the valorization of a social norm associated with specific values, and a movement of internalization, or an inner acceptance of the rule that passes through the moral awareness of the task to be performed. A distinction is therefore made between fulfilling a *moral duty* (*officium*) and the notion of *ministerium*, a compulsory obligation to execute orders imposed within a hierarchical structure–in short, a *social duty*. To prevent the *officium* as a moral duty from being reduced to a purely theatrical reality, what Guillaume Durand calls in his *Speculum Judiciale*[3] the *solemne* or *nobile* office (noble office) must be combined with the *deserviens* office, i.e. the office of service to the action undertaken.[4]

3 Guillaume Durand, *Speculum judiciale*, Lyon, Philippe Tinghi, 1578, *De Officium omnium Iudicum rubrica*, pp. 63–65. Bishop of Mende (France) in the XIIIth century, Guillaume Durand also wrote *Rationale divinorum officiorum*, a treatise about religious offices. See especially Chapter II "What is office. Of its institution and its parts, in which the bishop underlines the paronomasis *Officium/Efficium* : « I. Selon Saint Isidore, l'office est un acte propre et proportionné aux personnes, aux mœurs des villes, ou à la profession que l'on a embrassée ; car autre est la règle des moines, autre celle des chanoines, autre celle des ermites, et ainsi du reste. Office, d'après Saint Jérôme dans les livres des Offices, vient de *efficiendo*, en faisant, en agissant, comme si l'on disait : efficium, d'efficio, efficis, en changeant une lettre en une autre, pour la grâce de l'expression (efficere officium; à chacun, en effet, il convient de remplir son office. » *Rationale ou Manuel des Divins Offices de Guillaume Durand*, trad. Charles Barthélemy, vol 3, Paris, Louis Vivès, 1854, p. 8.

4 Charles Lefebvre, 'L'*officium judicis* d'après les canonistes du Moyen-Âge' (The *officium judicis* according to medieval canonists), *L'année canonique*, 2, 1953, pp. 115–124; Paul Ourliac, 'L'office du juge en droit canonique classique' (The office of the judge in classical canon law), in *Mélanges offerts à*

The office as a whole is therefore twofold, but requires a form that can reconcile these two aspects. Artistic representation enables us to play with the notion of office and its criticism, with theological justification challenged by concrete practice, because images of the office are meant to instill these principles in the real human subjects that occupy them. Images of offices are envisaged, materially and anthropologically, as representations of the self, confronted with the idealized specular image of a better self. Likewise, images can rehabilitate the images of corrupted judges by casting them as *martyres* bearing festering sores and the pain of the punishment inflicted.

This articulation is quite clear in one of the components of the *officium judicis* most commonly cited by medieval authors: "The judge cannot accept any of these gifts (*munera, xenia, dona*) which Scripture teaches blind the eyes of the wise and pervert the eyes of the just." In the Tour Baudet in Geneva, in the room where the government of Geneva has sat without interruption since 1488, the city's aldermen felt that the office of the judge should be represented, in front of the thrones where they sat and performed their office, by a fresco depicting the Judges with maimed hands between David and Moses. Facing the bloody stumps of these judges sitting mutilated, Moses makes a gesture to accompany the biblical words inscribed in his phylactery: "Thou shalt take no gift, for a gift blindeth the wise and perverteth the words of the righteous" (Exodus XXIII, 8). This figurative example is particularly striking, escalating the topos taken from Plutarch (*De Iside et Osiride*, X) and relayed by Alciato (*In Senatum Boni Principis*) into a truly nightmarish vision. But above all,such visualizations of the ethic of *officium judicis* allow viewers to interpret the concrete, striking, even shocking image, according to several variables. This is the case in the following text, which summarizes the prohibition on gifts underlying the Theban court. After recalling the passage from Exodus, the jurist adds:

> All kinds of gifts. Not only gifts of the hand, those that involve the transfer of a physical object and make corruption tangible. But also gifts of complacency (*obsequium*), which consist in the exchange of services, small or large, and enslave justice by involving it in the game of influences and clienteles. But also gifts of the tongue, which come only from words of promise and seduction, but also obliterate

Pierre Hébraud, Toulouse, 1981, pp. 625–644; Boris Bernabé, 'Naissance d'une éthique judiciaire à travers la théorie de la récusation des juges (XIIIe-XIVe s.)' (The emergence of judicial ethics through the theory of judicial recusal (13th-14th centuries)), in *Les Justices d'Eglise*. Toulouse, ed. Privat, 2007, pp. 343–372 (Cahiers de Fanjeaux, 42).

> judgement. And finally, gifts of blood, those which every man receives at birth because of family ties and which incline him to favour his own kin.[5]

These issues are also informed by the notion of the office of the artist as central to the new regime of visibility at the dawn of the early modern age. Judges who sit in front of or beneath these images are directly summoned by them in their offices by means of an image. In his famous article, *The Sovereignty of the Artist*, Ernst Hartwig Kantorowicz evidences the profound link between artistic theories and legal techniques of analogy. He thus analyzes the transmission of the concept of office with regard to the poet, and how the concept of *officium* allows for a complete transfer of authority:

> Every *officium*, however, in order to assert itself, demanded or was in need of some kind of quasi-theological justification and exaltation. This arrogation of a *plenitudo potestatis* was true of the offices of the spiritual and secular powers, and it became true for the offices of poet and, by transference, of painter and artist at large.[6]

This chapter will argue that the analogical tool of equiparation may also apply at the margin of texts and in visual culture. In evidencing the "cascading of capacities" within three examples of what is to be seen–what is demonstrated *ad oculos*–this contribution aims to look at how visual equiparation operates as a powerful visual protocol and *officium*.

The concept of the office of the Judge, which combines public role or function, judicial ethics, and an often spiritually-grounded moral conscience, is often analyzed purely textually, based on ancient and modern definitions of the word, without reference to imagery. However, the questions of reverence and of authority implied by the notion of *officium*, inherited from liturgy and ceremonial power, also require us to consider how this notion governs judicial aesthetics and the putative office of the artist. This is why I propose a definition of the concept of *officium* based

5 Robert Jacob, 'Les fondements symboliques de la responsabilité des juges. L'héritage de la culture judiciaire médiévale' (The symbolic foundations of judicial responsibility. The legacy of medieval judicial culture), in *Juger les juges. Histoire de la Justice*, 12, 2000, 11.

6 E. H. Kantorowicz, 'The Sovereignty of the Artist. A note on legal maxims and Renaissance theories of Art', in *De Artibus opuscula XL: Essays in Honor of Erwin Panofsky*, Millard Meiss (ed.), 2 vol., New York, New York University Press, 1961, I, pp. 267–279 at 279.

on a visual axiom of the mirror,[7] rather than on a purely theoretical or textual definition. In doing so, I will present three examples. The first examines the value of minor deities in Roman ritual, whose sole role is to be invoked: the *indigitamenta*. The second will look at how, in a 14th-century manuscript in the "mirror for princes" genre, this concept was depicted in a particularly novel manner that questioned the hierarchy of offices and their decorum. The final study brings us closer to the present day through an examination of Victor Hugo's *Justitia* and the visual implications of this subversive print at a pivotal moment in the history of representations of Justice in France and Europe.

Officium *and* indigitamenta

The Latin meanings of the word *officium* are richly versatile. In Latin, the word refers to a "function," the "duties of a function," "assistance," "service," but also "duty" and "moral obligation." From the 8th century onwards, the word came to refer to liturgical offices in Christian Latin. The Latin meaning of the word *officium* was converted to the Christian liturgical context, and then incorporated into law, government administration, and finally coming in English to mean "a place where public or private affairs are conducted." It is worth remembering in this context that Roman theology is above all a theology of action and of liturgical effects–or, in the doctrinal maxim, *id efficit quod figurat*. As religious historian Hermann Usener published in 1890, there existed in Roman and Greek religion a type of deity that pontiffs and Latinists call "indigitamenta": deities whose function is purely and simply to be invoked. During the performance of a ritual, the major gods' power is deferred, and small functional gods are worshipped more directly: the *Sondergötter*, as Usener called them. According to John Scheid,[8] these are "divinities of service," and the process of diffraction of a main deity that governs a particular activity was not necessarily required of the celebrants. John Scheid gives the following example: at the beginning of the year, the Roman consuls made prayers broadly for the salvation of the Roman state. These prayers were formulated and acquitted at the Capitol and were addressed to the protective triad of the Roman state: Jupiter, Juno, and Minerva. However, to express the desired outcome

7 Carolin Behrmann, 'The Mirror Axiom: Legal Iconology and The Lure of Reflection', in *The Art of Law. Ius Gentium: Comparative Perspectives on Law and Justice*, S. Huygebaert, G. Martyn, V. Paumen, E. Bousmar, and X. Rousseaux (eds.), vol 66. Springer, Cham, 2018.

8 John Scheid, « Les Dieux des Romains », in *Sans le Latin*, dir. Cécilia Suzzoni & Hubert Aupetit, Essai, Mille et une nuits, Fayard, 2012, pp. 329–351.

of the wish, they summoned an additional deity: *Salus public populi Romani Quiritum*, or Public Safety of the Roman people of the Quirites. Sometimes the deity intervened directly, receiving the homage of mortals alone, and sometimes, on the contrary, it withdrew to make way for a whole array of servant gods. The ways in which Roman deities are reduced to their functional characteristics may seem trivial, but the invocation of *indigitamenta* in matters of love may seem completely superfluous.

When the early modern lawyer Barnabé Brisson attempted to recover the ancient meaning of *Jugum matrimonii*,[9] he looked mainly to ancient satiric verses (Plautus, Horace) where the yoke is used in a metaphorical sense. According to him, the word *jugum* means "nothing else than being yoked together in marriage, drawn from the metaphor of oxen, which are said to be yoked, when they undergo the same yoke." The footnote adds, "although the rite here is not so certain, it is not improbable that many old symbols were used in weddings." He further adds that the foolish pagans assigned a particular god's name to each act, an apparently ridiculous belief reported by Saint Augustine. Brisson clearly enjoys quoting Saint Augustine,[10] who poured scorn on the deities of the marriage bed, not least by listing all the trivial gods that oversaw the Roman wedding and its consummation through sexual intercourse.

In his rebuttal of the pagan author Varron, Augustine makes the involvement of the divine look absurd:

> That the god *Jugatinus* yokes couples in marriage may be tolerable. But then the bride has to be led home and the god *Domiducus* (from *domus*: home and *ducere* to lead) is called in too. And to welcome the bride home, there's the god *Domitius*. To see that she stays with her husband, then the goddess *Manturna* (from *manere*: to stay) is thrown in as well. Do we need more? Once some decent privacy has been arranged, just let the urge of flesh and blood do the rest. Why is the bedroom packed with a crowd of deities, when even the bride's attendants withdraw? Then because of the timidity of any novice, the goddess *Virginiensis* (*virgo* means virgin) turns up, and father god *Subigus* (from *subigere* to tame), comes in, the Goddess *Pertunda* (*pertundere* means penetrate) and Venus and Priapus. What is this? If a man need help from the gods would not one god or one goddess be enough? If *Subigus* is there to make her give in to her husband, once

9 Barnabé Brisson (1530–1591), *Opera minora varii argumenti*, p. 314.

10 Augustine, *City of God*, VI, 9, 3 offers a list of *indigitamenta*, functional deities, poking fun at their alleged power to influence sexual intercourse.

she has been overpowered, then what exactly is the role of *Pertunda* here? Let the husband himself do something…

Philippe de Mézières, Le Songe du Viel Pelerin*: an early Gynecocratia (1389)?*

A medieval philosopher and statesman, Philippe de Mézières (1327–1405) is an author, despite later renouncing all earthly honours for himself. Advisor to several kings, Chancellor of Cyprus for forty-five years, founder of a knightly order for which he laid down every practical detail, Mézières retired at the end of his life to a community of hardworking monks who lived an austere life in preparation for the Last Judgment. Separated forever from the world, these monks abhorred all distinctions and ecclesiastical offices.

However, in a "mirror of princes" work written in 1389, *Le Songe du Vieil Pelerin,*[11] Philippe de Mézières–author, influential statesman, Chancellor and ardent supporter of the Crusades[12]–describes in an allegorical tale the need for reform in the Kingdom of France, which in turn requires a complete overhaul of the justice system. The author introduces an old pilgrim, alias *Ardent Désir* (a reference to his zeal to deliver the Holy Land), whose mission is to remind the young King Charles VI (who began to reign personally in 1388) that the royal office is based on a profound truth: to prove himself worthy of this heavy task, he must recognize that his faults weigh four times more heavily than those of his subjects, for "when the mirror is stained, those who look at it will never recognize their own stains."[13] If the young king is to fulfil his duty, he

11 Originally written in Middle French, see Philippe de Mézières, *Songe du Viel Pelerin*, a critical edition by Joël Blanchard, 2 vols., Textes littéraires français, Droz, 2015. J. Quillet, « Figures allégoriques du Songe du Vieil Pèlerin de Philippe de Mézières », *L'Art des confins : mélanges offerts à Maurice de Gandillac*, éd. A. Cazenave, J. F. Lyotard, Paris, 1985, pp. 479–492. Joël Blanchard, « Discours de la réformation et utopie à la fin du Moyen-Âge : le Songe du Vieil Pèlerin de Philippe de Mézières (1389) », *Studi Francesi*, 96, 1989, pp. 397–403; Joël Blanchard, « Les hiérarchies de l'honneur. Avatars d'une grille conceptuelle à la fin du Moyen Âge: Mézières et le Pseudo-Denys », *Revue Historique*, 648, 2008/4, pp. 789–817. Philippe Maupeu, *Pèlerins de la Vie humaine : autobiographie et allégorie narrative, de Guillaume de Digulleville à Octavien de Saint-Gelais*, Paris, 2009. See also *Philippe de Mézières and His Age, Piety and Politics in the Fourteenth Century.*

12 Alphonse Dupront, *Le mythe de croisade*, Paris, 1997, 4 volumes.

13 « Si le miroir est souillé, ceux qui regardent le miroir ne pourront jamais prendre conscience de leurs souillures », in Philippe de Mézières, *Le Songe*

must himself become the shining mirror of all Christendom, to illuminate the whole world.

Just as Moses climbed Mount Sinai to receive the Ten Commandments from God on two tablets, Charles VI in *Le Songe* climbs the "mountain of virtues" (which, at the most literal level, should be understood as the Petit Parquet of the Parliament of Paris) to receive the teachings intended for him, which are engraved there by the finger of God.

Joël Blanchard, undoubtedly the greatest expert on this text, has demonstrated that it is much more than a simple allegorical treatise;the author skillfully adapts the cosmological and unitary hierarchies inherited from Pseudo-Dionysius to the social stratifications of his time. The play of images that reveals the dignity and complexity of the offices culminates when the author proposes the royal chessboard, a checkerboard of 64 squares that comprehensively and effectively incorporates all possible types of political action by the Prince (Figure 6.1).

Book III of *Le Songe* is entirely devoted to the world of justice and its abuses by lawyers,[14] who are described as "political idiots." This book is based entirely on the allegory of the chessboard and its 64 squares, which allows for a comprehensive treatment of all issues relating to social justice. The author's moral and religious activism leads him to reinvent the forms of allegorical expression in use at the time. *Le Songe* is not a mirror like any other, beginning with the image of the chessboard divided into four parts with four corners. The four virtues that adorn the four corners of the chessboard (Truth, Peace, Mercy, and Justice) define the field of royal action. Mézières thus offers a theory of the royal office's effectiveness conceived as thedirect application of these Virtues in the social justice of the time. Several squares on the chessboard detail very directly invoke the idea of offices as hierarchical ("divine office," "ecclesiastical office"); two squares include the then-much-debated question of "promotion to office"; two others deal with the "functioning of justice"; while one square is devoted to the office's liturgy ("office of the dead"). The chessboard is marked in the centre by a cross, which, serving as its nerve centre, articulates all the virtues that legitimize the granting of rewards and positions based on merit and

du Vieil Pèlerin, Paris, BNF, Arsenal, ms. 2683, book III, chap. XII, ff. 56v, col. G.-58r, col. G. translation by Joël Blanchard, *Songe du Vieux Pèlerin*, Paris, 2008, p. 594. Gisela Naegle, 'Resveillier ceulx qui dorment en pechié: Philippe de Mézières et la tradition des miroirs du prince', *Le Moyen Age*, CXVI(3), 2010, pp. 625–643. https://doi.org/10.3917/rma.163.0625.

14 Jacques Krynen, « Un exemple de critique médiévale des juristes professionnels: Philippe de Mézières et les gens du Parlement de Paris », *Histoire du droit social, Hommage à Jean Imbert*, Paris, 1989, pp. 333–344.

Philippe de Mézières : l'Échiquier et la Croix

Figure 6.1 The Chessboard (Joël Blanchard's drawing).

talent. This symbolism of the chessboard for thinking about the distribution of offices is simultaneouslyrandom, dynamic, and closed.

The illuminations in this manuscript deserve special attention because, as Mezières himself highlights, it was because of the "reverence and authority of his office that the emperor was always dressed in purple."[15] The ornaments, clothing, and colours take on heightened symbolic meaning. Two images in particular engage the allegorical office of virtues, as they appear in the illuminated manuscript of the *Songe du vieil Pèlerin* (Dream of the Old Pilgrim) preserved in the Austrian

15 « Lequel pour reverence et auctorité de son office estoit vestu toujours de pourpre ». fol. 480,1, Ms 9200-9201 Bibliothèque nationale de France.

National Library.[16] These two images, which echo each other, are striking in their allegorical refinement, shifting the question of the office of the good judge to that of the offices of the virtues. Under the aegis of the feminine *virtus*,[17] the traditional understanding of the office of the judge, viewed in terms of the centrality of the mirror of the Prince, is rethought.

These two images depict an imaginary court, where feminine virtues embody a form of effective matriarchy gynocracy, in place of a parliamentary session. What will become of the great doctors *in utroque jure*, asks a lawyer, if the examination and judgment of cases are entrusted to simple, lay people? If the jurisprudence of the holy emperors and the decretals of the holy popes are discarded in favour of a new law devised in four days? These matriarchal utopias highlight what Jean Gerson[18] calls the "pure negative utility" of the supposed "benefit" of the legal sciences: in reality, nothing more than an accident resulting from sin (Figure 6.2).

Under the aegis of Truth, Justice, and Mercy, the allegorical trinity, the miniature depicts (that is, makes present with particular *enargeia*) a utopian session of Parliament in a barrel-vaulted room with walls covered in blue fleur-de-lys hangings. This dreamlike image is one of desire, in which women, usually excluded from the judicial enclosure, play a leading role. They are less women than archetypes, their blond hair, round eyes, long braids, and rosy cheeks highlighting their finery and attributes. In the background are three thrones occupied by Justice,

16 Philippe de Mézières, *Le songe du vieil pèlerin*, Mss Cod. 2551, Paris, XVe century, circa 1470. http://data.onb.ac.at/rec/AC13950362, fol. 155. See O. Pächt and D. Thoss, *Die illuminierten Handschriften und Inkunabeln der Österreichischen Nationalbibliothek*, Französische Schule, 2 vol. Vienna, 1974, t. I, p. 89 ill. 158–159. This manuscript contains three miniatures (200 x 193 mm). The two figures reproduced here are at fol. 73 and fol. 130. According to Joël Blanchard (edn quoted), this book belonged to Tanguy du Châtel, who died in 1477, as indicated by a mention fol. 234: "ce livre est a miser Tanguy du Chastel, vicomte de la Beliere et seigneur de Chastelon) and also to Jeanne Raguenel de Malestroit. Artist: Maître François le Barbier père, illuminator. Commanditaire: Jacques d'Armagnac, duc de Nemours (+ 1477).

17 Philippe Contamine, « La place des femmes dans les deux premières règles (1367-1368 et 1384) de l'ordre de la chevalerie de la Passion de Jésus-Christ de Philippe de Mézières, Au cloître dans le monde, femmes, hommes et sociétés (IXe-XVe siècles), éd. P. Henriet et Anne-Marie Legras, Paris, 2000, pp. 79–88.

18 A. Combes, *Jean Gerson, commentateur dyonisien : pour l'histoire des courants doctrinaux à l'université de Paris à la fin du XIVe siècle*, 2nde édition, Études de philosophie médiévale, 30, Paris, 1973.

Figure 6.2 First illumination (fol. 155) Songe du Viel Pelerin.

Truth, and Mercy. A fourth throne is reserved for Peace, perpendicular to the other three; this central position recalls the king's throne in contemporary representations of the *Lit de Justice*, in which the king always sits in the middle. The artist thus suggests that Peace, whose attributes are an olive branch in her left arm and a basket containing the fruits of Peace in her right hand, is in fact the result of the alliance of the three other virtues. At the feet of these virtues, kneeling in a posture of prayer or meditation, are what I would call the *virtues of service*, which are their obligatory counterparts: *Power*, *Discretion*, *Humility*, *Righteousness*, *Devotion*, *Dilectio*, and *Sisterhood* (Sororité). With their eyes downcast, they ensure the transition between the world above (the trinity of virtues seated) and the world of judicial *actio*, the arena itself, below. On the checkerboard where the joust, the judicial combat, takes place, a virtue stands upright: *Boldness* (*Hardiesse*), who allows herself to criticize, is in dispute with the Parliament's lawyer. Against the right-hand wall are two much more modest thrones: one, decorated with fleurs-de-lis, is occupied by King Charles VI, assisted by *Humility* and *Patience;* a white falcon with a golden beak and talons is perched upon his left fist, which *Patience* is about to seize. On the other throne sits the king's brother, Duke Louis of Orleans, holding a black falcon with white wings on his left fist.

Between the two princes stands a small winged deer with a royal crown around its neck. On either side of the hall, advisors sit on benches that end at the front of the stage, at a fence decorated with sculptures: this is the floor. This fence opens in the middle, allowing the winged "old pilgrim" to enter the hall accompanied by *Bonne Espérance and Volonté* (*Good Hope* and *Will*), his sister, who accompanies him, winged like him. The old pilgrim looks at her, not at the scene around him, and protects her with his right foot, which blocks access to the enclosure of the floor. In contrast to a parliamentary session,in which the floor is usually guarded by gendarmes, i.e. armed warriors, here the two winged figures form a couple apart, united by the emphatic gesture of their raised thumb and index finger (Figure 6.3).

The second image, also in the Parliament room, depicts the court of the Queens of Paradise. It is presented as a utopian representation of a court composed mainly of queens. Apart from the figures of the two kings and the allegory of *Ardent Désir* in the centre, all male presence has evaporated. *Ardent Désir* no longer wears his hat; he kneels before the King, still accompanied by *Bonne Espérance* and *Volonté* (*Good Hope* and *Will)*, offering his work to King Charles VI, who carries a chessboard[19] and the tablets of the law. Behind the king stand *Prudence, Diligence, Patience*, and *Humility*. Attached to the throne and the royal office is a phylactery bearing the inscription: "the divine teachings of the Queens of Paradise." What this phylactery announces very concretely is that the King will owe his salvation, as a monarch by divine right, only to the exercise of justice inspired by the Virtues. The moral

19 J. M. Mehl, « Le roi et l'échiquier. Approche du mythe oral à la fin du Moyen-Âge », *Revue d'histoire et de philosophie religieuses*, 1978, pp. 145–161.

Figure 6.3 Second Illumination (fol.--) Songe du Viel Pelerin.

responsibility incumbent upon the King, seated on his throne of justice, is expressed metaphorically by the curious alliance of the chessboard and the tablets of the law. He is both a new Moses, holding in his right hand the laws transmitted directly by the finger of God, but also wears a chess set on his breastplate, which makes him subject to the randomness of his earthly life and the necessary calculations he must make in order to reign. What is extraordinary is that the chessboard serves as both the floor of the Chamber[20]–the physical place where Parliament sits, where pleas, arguments, and counterarguments are made and unmade–and also an attribute worn across the chest by the king himself. Instead of the codes he would carry like a cabinet in his chest, the king wears a game board that asserts both his function as the ultimate judicial authority and the fact that he too puts his life on the line (and therefore possibly in check) if he does not judge in strict accordance with the court of the Queens of All Virtues.

If Justice is indeed the queen of all virtues (*Regina virtutum*), here she is multiplied by all the vicarious divinities that lend her effectiveness, if in a slightly theatrical and staged fashion. As a mirror of the virtues, the royal office presents itself as a horizontal assembly of Queens where the virtues themselves become figures of desire. Here, the king's throne is quite modest, supplanted by the imposing trinity of the three allegorical queens. In the foreground, around thirty servants of the allegorical queens are arranged in an assembly: *Humility, Righteousness, Patience, Harmony, Pleasure, Security, Gentle Thought, Loyalty*, and *Strength* in the first row, then in the second row, *Poverty, Meekness, Right Interiority, Good Will, Debonairness, Good Faith, Temperance*, and *Repentance*, whose long braids sway in emulation. While the small door leading to the enclosure of the parquet remains open, *Diligence* and *Prudence* stand at the opening that leads to the outside world;through a gap on the left, we can see an urban square and a motley crowd of men, surmounted by a statue of the royal effigy on a column.

On the chessboard of attributes and their suggestive manifestations, two curious sets of details suggest strange transformations. First, *Truth*, enthroned, is dressed in a cloak that features either peepholes or small ocellated mirrors. She now shares with *Justice* the attribute of the scales of justice. *Truth*, a new Argus with a hundred eyes, is also a figure of virtue. *Charity* now wears the halo (in the previous illumination, *Truth* was haloed), and finally, *Wisdom* is cast as a Christ-like figure wearing the crown of thorns. The second detail is the simple empty cushion between the thrones of *Wisdom* and *Mercy*. Although the ceremony depicted in the illumination suggests that this cushion may be soon occupied by one of the allegories, its emptiness serves as a type of void and emblem of the negativity of desire (Figure 6.4).

20 L. de Carbonnières, *La procédure devant la chambre criminelle du Parlement de Paris au XIVe siècle*, Paris, 2004.

Figure 6.4 Victor Hugo, *Justitia* (1857).

Victor Hugo's Justitia (1857): The rainbows of black shadows

While the two 14th-century illuminations rely on an iconological relationship between images and words, a counter-motif can materially envision sacred horror that lies beyond any illustration: a spectre, a mist of the abyss, a testimony to the martyrdom of those who saw differently. Beyond the iconography of the judge in office, daunting, nightmarish images can also act as a memento falliri: "remember that you are fallible." When night falls and blurs all contours, when the air itself is heavy with tragedy, Victor Hugo paints a vision, a testimony that truly captures the infinite meaning of the office of good judgement. The drawing, bearing the Latin inscription *Justitia*, is an exemplary testimony to the sense of infinity in human consciousness, apprehending the world itself as the realm of evil. A mutilated head, mouth wide open, eyes bulging, presents a face that no longer bears any resemblance to a victory over human nature achieved through the power of representation. In ancient times, when office and royal dignity relied upon effigies based on resemblance by contact, the concept of office (whether ecclesiastical, royal, or judicial) was based on a form of action; here instead, we enter the abrupt psyche of a tormented mind. Victor Hugo's drawing bears the inscription "Justitia" in large red capital Roman letters. The feminine allegory has disappeared.

"Justitia" has long been seen as a counterpart to "Ecce Lex," as Victor Hugo gave them the same frame and hung both in Hauteville House. It was therefore seen as part of Hugo's tireless fight against the death penalty. However, "Justitia" literally illustrates the end of the poem "La Révolution," which was published in *Les Quatre Vents de l'Esprit*. Written between October and Christmas of 1857, the poem reveals the identity of this fantastical head, both screaming and silent, fluttering in front of the posts of the guillotine.

In the last section of the poem, *L'Arrivée* (The Arrival), the equestrian statues of Henry IV, Louis XIII, and Louis XIV arrive at the Place de la Concorde. Instead of finding the statue of Louis XV that had previously given the square its name, the statues discover the scaffold of Louis XVI:

> Au lieu de la statue, au point même où leurs yeux/Cherchaient le Bien-Aimé triomphal et joyeux, / Apparaissaient, hideux et debout dans le vide,/ Deux poteaux noirs portant un triangle livide ; / Le triangle pendait, nu, dans la profondeur ;/ Plus bas on distinguait une vague rondeur,/ Espèce de lucarne ouverte sur de l'ombre ; / Deux nuages traçaient au fond des cieux ce nombre- Quatrevingt-treize-chiffre on ne sait d'où venu/ … C'était on ne sait quel échafaud inconnu./ … L'échafaud, immobile et monstrueux, semblait/ Communiquer avec

> la tombe universelle./ Une pourpre, semblable à celle qui ruisselle/ Et qui fume le long du mur des abattoirs,/ Filtrait de telle sorte entre les pavés noirs/ Qu'elle écrivait ce mot mystérieux : Justice.

The violence of this vision lies primarily in the destruction of the Office of the supreme judge, the King by divine right; with his effigy dismembered and his head guillotined, the very dignity of the ceremonial Office is eliminated. On a symbolic level, representing Justitia by a specific negation of this centuries-old iconological tradition is to question anew the metaphysical dimension of the office of judgment. Thus, Victor Hugo's "Justitia" can be read as a fantastical figure of a secularized Last Judgment. Moreover, as Maurice Agulhon noted in 1979, France occupies a special position:

> Our revolutions of the 19th century succeeded in abolishing the monarchy, so with the Republic we had a State without a monarch, and therefore a State *without a living effigy*, and therefore a State forced to represent itself by giving itself the head of an allegory.[21]

Here, representation does not take the form of illumination, but rather a fascination with the darkness of night. As soon as we approach Victor Hugo's work, the judge's role takes on the dark colours of vertigo in the darkness. "Ink, that darkness from which light emerges" is his way of expressing torment, the pain inflicted by the agony of judging, the tormented mind like a storm inside a skull ("Tempête sous un crâne"). Everything always comes from storm and chaos. One of the key phrases in *Promontoire du Songe* is "The man who does not meditate lives in blindness, the man who meditates lives in darkness: we have only the choice of darkness." While the classic representation of the God of Judgment Day depicts him on a rainbow, Hugo is the seer who sees beyond. In his collection *Choses vues*, he paid attention to others; the world expands with the attention we give it. It is within ourselves that we must look outward. At Hauteville House, Hugo had mirrors installed in the glass roof he had built on the top floor. There he confronted the infinity of light.

As Nietzsche reminds us in the *Genealogy of Morals*, the alibi which we call justice functions by a mnemotechnics of pain: the permanent

21 Maurice Agulhon, 'Propos sur l'allégorie politique (en réponse à Eric Hobsbawm)', *Actes de la recherche en sciences sociales*, 28, 1979, pp. 27–32. *Les fonctions de l'art* [special issue]. In response to Eric Hobsbawn, 'Sexes, symboles, vêtement et socialisme', *Actes de la recherche en sciences sociales*, 23, 1978, pp. 2–18.

inscription and etching of the body in order to produce "man" as a responsible subject. Victor Hugo's powerful depiction of Justitia is a fierce criticism of its traditional representation. The inspiration from which all institutions derive, and of which they are a projection, calls for another language.

Emilios Christodoulidis has argued that the key to this necessary transcendence of the "words of law" is the concept of attention, underpins justice; this resonates too with Simone Weil's powerful statement that "human attention alone legitimately exercises the judicial function."[22]

Extreme attention, "which constitutes the creative faculty in human beings," is an essentially religious phenomenon that requires us to look at others and the world with a "certain gaze … attentive, where the soul empties itself of all its own content in order to receive within itself the being it is looking at as it is, in all its truth."[23]

Just as Hugo's drawing contrasts suffering humanity with the guillotine, our new machines act as screens, both literally and figuratively, to any exchange of gazes–starting with that between mother and child, the primary attention essential to hominization, which inspired so many masterpieces of Renaissance art. In the highest form of attention, on the contrary, the self "steps back from the object it pursues," reproducing the creative gesture of God, which was an original movement of withdrawal. This gesture is also that which constitutes the self-awareness of bearing office, which bases the rule of its being on its own self-limitation.

22 Simone Weil, *Carnets de Londres*, dans *Œuvres complètes*, t. VI, vol. 4, Cahiers (juillet 1942-juillet1943) éd. Marie-Antoinette Fourneyron, F. de Lussy et Jean Riaud, Paris, Gallimard, coll. NRF, 2006, p. 380.

Voir aussi Florence de Lussy, « Simone Weil. L'attention comme exercice spirituel : « Boire la lumière », Sorgue, n°6, novembre 2006, pp. 13–21.

23 Simone Weil, « Réflexions sur le bon usage des études scolaires », dans *Attente de Dieu* (1942), préface de Christiane Rancé, Paris, Albin Michel, coll. « Espaces libres », 2016, p. 106.

Part 2

Aesthetics and politics

Chapter 7

Precarious procurators

Kafka's writing scenes and the vicariousness of office

Katrin Trüstedt

"The term *function*," writes Giorgio Agamben in his *Genealogy of Office*, "names the constitutive vicariousness of office."[1] To function in terms of office in this sense means, as Agamben quotes Gasparri, "to act as if one were another, in the capacity of someone's *alter ego*, either an individual person or a community. To have a function means not only to be competent to carry out acts for which others carry the responsibility for the agent, but to act declaratively, openly as such."[2] In the following I read two scenes from Kafka with and against this function: a writing scene in the office from the *Trial*, and a scene from *The Metamorphosis*, where the office comes into the home.

Offices play a crucial role in Kafka, on various levels; the strange architecture of the various offices of the lawyers and court officials in the Trial, that Benjamin among others describes;[3] the competing institutions with their various equally strange offices (the bank, the church, the court) and the duties that go along with each of them, and that constitute the protagonist in contradicting and problematic ways. In contrast to the German Bildungsroman like Goethe's *Wilhelm Meister*, where the protagonist encounters the call for duty and office, struggles with it, attempts to free himself from it, and somehow grows through that encounter, Kafka's novels reverse the perspective: the protagonist is always already entangled in and constituted by an office.[4] The myth that Franz Kafka hated his office job and wanted to free himself to be a writer

1 Giorgio Agamben, *Opus Dei: An Archaeology of Duty* (Stanford: Stanford University Press, 2013), p. 85.
2 Agamben, *Opus Dei*, pp. 85–86.
3 Walter Benjamin, "Franz Kafka: Zur zehnten Wiederkehr seines Todestages," in *Benjamin über Kafka: Texte, Briefzeugnisse, Aufzeichnungen*, ed. H. Schweppenhäuser (Frankfurt am Main: Suhrkamp, 1981).
4 Cf. Rüdiger Campe, "Kafkas Institutionenroman: 'Der Prozeß', 'Das Schloß'," in *Gesetz. Ironie. Festschrift für Manfred Schneider*, eds. R. Campe and M.

DOI: 10.4324/9781003659754-9

is largely contradicted by his writings themselves, whose brilliance lies precisely in the entanglement of life and office, or literature and office – two modes of existence that replace one another again and again. The complex interconnection of the two procedures, which evade, get in each other's way, overlap, condition, and prevent each other, is reminiscent of Kafka's own "double-entry bookkeeping," of which Friedrich Kittler writes that it "enters one and the same file processes into bureaucratic anonymity during the day and into literary manuscripts at night."[5]

The hypothesis that I want to trace in my reading of the two scenes is that, on the one hand, Kafka reveals and radicalizes Agamben's notion of the office, particularly in the office of the procurator, where the split and the dependence between self and office is doubled. On the other hand, exactly by deepening this paradoxical split, Kafka also undermines it. The playful and comedic quality of these scenes seems to hint at other uses of office.[6]

Life entering office: Kafka's trial

In *The Trial*, the prominent function of the various offices is exactly that of speaking for another that Agamben describes. The most prominent office characters are the priest and the advocate, both speaking for the institution, but also, of course, in that function for K. His, Josef K.'s, office in his bank, on the other hand, comes under threat with his other office – that of the trial. In the process, K. evolves from a rather passive object of arrest to taking over the function from his own lawyer – acting in place of the one whose office it is to act for him. The first Scene is from the chapter "The Lawyer · The Factory-Owner · The Painter":

Niehaus (Heidelberg: Synchron Wissenschaftsverlag der Autoren, 2004), pp. 197–208.

5 Cf. Friedrich Kittler, *Aufschreibesysteme 1800/1900* (München: Fink, 2003), p. 438, my translation.

6 Agamben would perhaps call this a profanation of office: "If 'to consecrate' (sacrare) was the term that indicated the removal of things from the sphere of human law," Agamben writes in Profanation, "'to profane' meant, conversely, to return them to the free use of men. Use here, accordingly, does not appear as something natural: rather, one arrives at it only by means of profanation." "The passage from the sacred to the profane can, in fact, also come about by means of an entirely inappropriate use (or, rather, reuse) of the sacred: namely, play. It is well known that the spheres of play and the sacred are closely connected. Most of the games with which we are familiar derive from ancient sacred ceremonies, from divinatory practices and rituals that once belonged, broadly speaking, to the religious sphere." Giorgio Agamben, *Profanations* (Cambridge: Mit Press, 2007)

> One winter's morning – outside snow was falling in the murky light – K. was in his office, feeling extremely tired already despite the early hour. In order to prevent himself from at least being disturbed by the clerks, he'd told the messenger not to let any of them in, because he was occupied with an important piece of work. But instead of working, he spun round in his chair, slowly rearranged objects on his desk, and then, without realizing it, left the whole of his arm stretched out across the desktop and sat there, motionless, his head bowed. He couldn't get the trial out of his mind any more. Several times already he'd wondered whether it might not be a good idea to draw up a written statement and submit it to the court. His intention was to present a brief account of his life, explaining for every event that was in any way important why he'd acted as he had, whether he now looked on his course of action with approval or disapproval, and the reasons he could adduce for either conclusion. The advantages of submitting such a statement in his defence, as against simply being defended by the lawyer, who was open to criticism on other counts anyway, were indubitable.[7]

Of course, this attempt at something like a Bildungsroman of his life – exactly what this novel is not, what is, from the perspective of the Bildungsroman, is omitted, fails. It fails in multiple ways:

> Even though K. was confident of his ability to carry all this out, the difficulty of drawing up the submission was immense. ... He remembered how, one afternoon when he had been snowed under with work, he had suddenly pushed everything to one side and taken out his writing-pad to rough out a possible line of thought for such a submission, which he might then put at the disposal of the sluggish lawyer; at that very moment the door to the managerial suite had opened and the deputy manager had emerged, laughing loudly. It had been very embarrassing for K., even though the deputy manager had not been laughing at his submission, but at a joke he had just heard, a joke which, in order to be explained, needed a drawing, which the deputy manager, bending over K.'s desk and taking K.'s pencil out of his hand, proceeded to draw on the writingpad K. had intended to use for his submission. ... [N]ow, at a time when K. needed to concentrate wholly on his work, when, as he was still climbing the ladder and already represented a threat to the deputy manager, every hour passed with the utmost swiftness, and when, as a young man,

7 Franz Kafka, *The Trial*, trans. by Willa and Edwin Muir; rev. by E. M. Butler (New York: Schocken Books, 1995), p. 80; 91.

> he wanted to enjoy the short evenings and nights, now he had to start drawing up this submission. Once more his reflections had ended in lamentation. Almost automatically, simply to put an end to it, his finger felt for the button of the electric bell in the outer office.[8]

The failure of this office writing scene is twofold. There is the conflict between two contradicting and rivaling offices – his office within the bank, and that of acting as his own lawyer – and the crux of taking over the function from his own lawyer: acting in place of the one whose office it is to act for him. This crux – speaking for himself as speaking for another – is at the heart of the crux of the function of any office. It necessarily but, it is also only in this function that a potentiality of a life outside or beyond any office emerges (as potentiality).

What we find here are particular scenes of office writing involving tables, pens, paper, gestures, as we can also find them in Kafka's so-called *Office Writings*. In his office, Kafka was often signing texts written by others, and having his own writings signed by his supervisor, Marschner. We also find the many scenes of his practices of writing something to avoid writing something else, writing to his fiancé about not wanting to work (and yet thus negatively writing about the work he is trying to avoid), or keeping busy inhabiting his office only in order to avoid being replaced by another, like the deputy manager.

In the writing scenes of *The Trial*, what is, as a praxis, supposed to produce meaning, is instead fail. And yet, precisely by acting out the paradoxical structure of office – acting for another and yet being constituted by that office – a space seems to open up: a space of potentiality, while it is a scene of failure with regard to the product of the writing scene, as a literary writing scene it opens up other possibilities.[9]

Office entering life: Kafka's metamorphosis

The second scene from *The Metamorphosis* is not about the (im-)possibility of life entering the office, but rather of the office entering a life. Agamben writes with regard to the office of the priest: the "circular relation between being and praxis, by which the priest's being defines his praxis and his praxis, in turn, defines his being. In *officium* ontology

8 Kafka, *The Trial*, p. 91.

9 Cf. Rüdiger Campe, "Kafkas Institutionenroman: 'Der Prozeß', 'Das Schloß'," in *Gesetz. Ironie. Festschrift für Manfred Schneider*, eds. R. Campe and M. Niehaus (Heidelberg: Synchron Wissenschaftsverlag der Autoren, 2004), pp. 197–208.

and praxis become undecidable: the priest has to be what he is and is what he has to be."

Gregor Samsa is summoned by "the office" to appear and explain himself as the person he is expected to be: as the office worker and breadwinner for the family. When the front doorbell rings, Gregor expects "someone from the office," a thought that paralyzes him. Given that expectation, the non-appearance of a monstrous vermin seems like an instance of falling short of this expectation, or even as a radical negation of it. One might ask whether a failure to meet the expectations of office is enough to make one appear as a monstrous vermin (ungeheures Ungeziefer). What appears in this distinctive form of non-appearance cannot be just a certain personality or characteristic that is not expected or not called for at this point; it is a more radical other of the expected person – the remainder of the un-person or im-person that is the correlate of any subjectivation.[10]

The call for an appearance comes from the Prokurist. The oscillating mode of being called to appear, attempting, hesitating, and failing to appear involves not only a dual constellation – Gregor facing another, calling him – but a more complex scenario indebted to an older, Roman procedural tradition (we know Kafka studied Roman law as part of his law school curriculum):[11] namely that which is encapsulated in the juridical genre of rhetoric where an orator, patron, or *procurator* speaks for another (the client) against an accusing or antagonistic party, and in front of a third party that is addressed in order to judge.[12]

So, when the front doorbell rings, Gregor expects "someone from the office," a thought that paralyzes him – Gregor said to himself:

> "They're not going to answer," captivated by some senseless hope. But then, of course, the maid went to the door as usual with her firm

10 Cf. Niklas Luhmann, "Die Form 'Person'," in Luhmann, *Soziologische Aufklärung. Bd. 6. Die Soziologie und der Mensch* (Opladen: Westdeutscher Verlag, 1995), pp. 142–154, here p. 148: "Anderes bleibt auf der unmarkierten Seite, weil man nicht erwartet, daß dies zum Gegenstand von Kommunikation wird. Daher ist das, was zur Unperson gehört, ebenso unbestimmt wie die Unmasche beim Stricken oder das Unloch beim Billard."

11 See Peter-André Alt, *Franz Kafka: Der ewige Sohn. Eine Biographie* (München: Beck, 2008), p. 128.

12 See Rüdiger Campe, "An Outline for a Critical History of Fürsprache: Synegoria and Advocacy," *DVjs* 82 (2008), pp. 355–381; Rüdiger Campe, "Kafkas Fürsprache," in *Kafkas Institutionen*, eds. Arne Höcker and Oliver Simons (Bielefeld: transcript, 2007), pp. 189–212.

> stride and opened up. Gregor only had to hear the visitor's first word of greeting to know who it was—*the procurist himself*.[13]

The *Prokurist* in Kafka's story is referred to not by his name, but by his function – which is to speak and act for another. The Latin *procuratio* designates an agent taking care (*cura*) of some task for (*pro*) another. A "*Prokurist*" is someone, "whose functions include both representation and execution, both speaking for the company and carrying out its policies. ... In accordance with Austrian business practice, the Prokurist is the agent who has been delegated 'full power of attorney' (*Prokura*), the *pleinpouvoir* or *Vollmacht*, to inspect the case on the firm's behalf," as John Hamilton has developed at greater length.[14]

> [D]id the procurist himself have to come, and did the whole innocent family have to be shown in this way that the *investigation of this suspicious affair* could be entrusted only to the intellect of the manager? And more as a result of the excitement produced in Gregor by these thoughts than as a result of any real decision, he swung himself out of bed with all his might.[15]

The situation of the *Prokurist* speaking for the company and acting as Gregor's adversary in front of the family leads to the final scene of

13 Kafka, *Die Verwandlung*, p. 30, my emphasis; Kafka, *The Metamorphosis*, p. 7. The German original reads: "'Sie öffnen nicht,' sagte sich Gregor, befangen in irgendeiner unsinnigen Hoffnung. Aber dann ging natürlich wie immer das Dienstmädchen festen Schrittes zur Tür und öffnete. Gregor brauchte nur das erste Grußwort des Besuchers zu hören und wußte schon, wer es war—*der Prokurist selbst.*"

14 John Hamilton, "Procuratores: On the Limits of Caring for Another," *Telos* 170 (2015), pp. 7–22. It is in the presence of this *Prokurist*, reduced to his function of speaking not for himself but for an other, that Gregor loses the ability to speak for himself. Moreover, the *Prokurist* speaks primarily not for another person with a genuine voice of his/her own, but for "the company." Gregor claims that the *Prokurist* himself (again: *Prokurist* selbst) has a better understanding of the organization than the boss. See also Doreen Densky, "Proxies in Kafka: *Koncipist* FK and *Prokurist* Joseph K.," in *Kafka for the Twenty-First Century*, eds. Stanley Corngold and Ruth Gross (Rochester, NY: Camden House, 2011), pp. 120–135.

15 Kafka, *Die Verwandlung*, p. 31, my emphasis; Kafka, *The Metamorphosis*, p. 8. The German original reads: "[M]ußte da der Prokurist selbst kommen, und mußte dadurch der ganzen unschuldigen Familie gezeigt werden, daß die *Untersuchung dieser verdächtigen Angelegenheit* nur dem Verstand des Prokuristen anvertraut werden konnte? Und mehr infolge der Erregung, in welche Gregor durch diese Überlegungen versetzt wurde, als infolge eines richtigen Entschlusses, schwang er sich mit aller Macht aus dem Bett."

(non-)appearance as vermin. The office of the *procurator* needs to be inhabited by someone who is fully invested in this role – who *cares* and *takes care* – but at the same time never coincides with this office nor the office (institution) it represents, as the procurator cares and takes care precisely *for another* (*pro cura*), as Agamben's notion of the function of office suggests, but also, as I mentioned, of the *oikonomia* of power and glory, and his elaboration of the theological paradigm of *potestas vicaria*, where every instance of power is represented by another.

To come back to my opening quotation from Agamben: if the term *function* names the constitutive vicariousness of office, then, as he continues, the analogy with the paradigm of instrumental cause in Aquinas, in which God acts by means of the one who exercises the priestly function, is obvious. Agamben has unfolded a "vicarious economy" also in his *The Kingdom and the Glory* by re-reading the church fathers:

> The intra-Trinitarian relation between the Father and the Son can be considered to be the theological paradigm of every *potestas vicaria*, in which every act of the vicar is considered to be a manifestation of the will of the one who is represented by him. And yet, as we have seen, the an-archic character of the Son, who is not founded ontologically in the Father, is essential to the Trinitarian economy. That is, the Trinitarian economy is the expression of an anarchic power and being that circulates among the three persons according to an essentially vicarious paradigm.[16]

Such a "vicarious economy" that Agamben here depicts seems to be grounded on a primordial "source" of power (namely, God who employs representation to manifest himself and rule). But by introducing this representative, the vicarious economy at the same time already opens itself up to an anarchic and circular element in which the source might seem to be actually grounded on its representation. Kafka seems to reinforce and radicalize this shift and foregrounds the anarchic element. What distinguishes Kafka's praxis of speaking for another in the following scene is that it never stabilizes.

It is in the moment that the *Prokurist* addresses Gregor "himself," that the constellation shifts. His mother – until then part of the "innocent" third party in front of whom the *Prokurist* speaks for the company vis-à-vis Gregor – now steps in and in turn speaks "for Gregor" in his place, defending him as "his *Prokurist*," so to speak, against an

16 Giorgio Agamben, *The Kingdom and the Glory: For a Theological Genealogy of Economy and Government* (Meridian: Crossing Aesthetics, 2011), pp. 495–496.

assumed accusation by the company, and thereby giving an account of him in a third-person narration. "'He's not well,' said the mother to the procurist."[17] The mother makes a claim on Gregor's behalf that Gregor himself – despite the numerous speculations about travel-sickness[18] – had denied in those exact same terms: that he is "quite well" (*Gregor fühlte sich tatsächlich ganz wohl*), thereby showing that she regards herself to be in a better position to speak for him than he himself could. The silenced conflict between these statements – quite well vs. not well – ("*Gregor fühlte sich tatsächlich ganz wohl*" and "*ihm ist nicht wohl*") suggests that she at the same time blocks him by speaking in his place.

While the *Prokurist* speaks for the office – "someone from the office" – in his address to Gregor, he turns the constellation yet again when he claims to speak for the parents first and foremost and for his company only in the second place: "I am speaking here in the name of your parents and of your employer and ask you in all seriousness for an immediate, clear explanation [*augenblickliche, deutliche Erklärung*]."[19] Claiming to speak not in his own, but in the mother's name in his demand for an explanation – who just gave him such an explanation: that Gregor is not well – the *Prokurist*, ironically just like the mother with regard to Gregor, assumes himself to be able to speak in a more convincing way for her than the mother herself. In a final, yet crucial twist, the *Prokurist* suggests himself as a potential procurator for Gregor vis-à-vis the company's boss, but only by way of denying his willingness to actualize such a potential *procuratio*:

> The head of the firm did suggest to me this morning a possible explanation for your tardiness—it concerned the cash payments recently entrusted to you—but really, I practically gave my word of honor that this explanation could not be right. But now, seeing your incomprehensible obstinacy, I am about to lose even the slightest desire to

17 Kafka, *Die Verwandlung*, p. 32, my translation. The German original reads: "'Ihm ist nicht wohl,' sagte die Mutter zum Prokuristen."

18 Cf. John Zilcosky, "'Samsa war Reisender': Trains, Trauma, and the Unreadable Body," in *Kafka for the Twenty-First Century*, eds. Stanley Corngold and Ruth Gross (Rochester, NY: Camden House, 2011), pp. 179–206.

19 Kafka, *Die Verwandlung*, p. 33; Kafka, *The Metamorphosis*, p. 9. The German original reads: "Ich spreche hier im Namen Ihrer Eltern und Ihres Chefs und bitte Sie ganz ernsthaft um eine augenblickliche, deutliche Erklärung."

> *stick up for you in any way at all* [verliere ganz und gar jede Lust, *mich auch nur im geringsten für Sie einzusetzen*.][20]

"*Mich* für *Sie* einsetzen" means "taking your side," "sticking up for you," but also "taking your place" (setting *me* in for *you*, positing me instead of you). This declaration by the *Prokurist* seems to be a threat of a double bind: the threat of the *Prokurist* to take his place or part, just as much as the threat to not take his place or part. This double bind seems to be inherent in the practice of *procuratio* as speaking or acting on behalf of another and stepping into another's place (in German: *Stellvertretung*).[21]

The narrative procedures that prepare the protagonist's appearance underpin the scene with a juridical setting, as it were: a court proceeding with the instances of the prosecution, the defense, and the judging instance before which the case is brought and defended. With the procurator, a Roman legal tradition is also evoked, which inwardly connects the rhetorical question of representation with that of juridical appearance before the law. In this tradition, it is incumbent upon an orator, patron, or even *Procuratio* to present rhetorically the one cited before the court, that is, to speak for his client, against the opposing party (the prosecution), and before the judging authority. *Procuratio* in this sense designates an instance that bears care (cura) for another (pro), as John Hamilton has also pointed out with regard to Austrian law in Kafka's time: "[A] Prokurist [is someone] whose functions include both representation and execution, both speaking for the company and carrying out its policies. [T]he Prokurist is the agent who has been delegated 'full power of attorney' (Prokura), the *pleinpouvoir* or *Vollmacht*, to inspect the case on the firm's behalf."[22]

The non-appearance of the subject as a "monstrous vermin" ultimately also has political implications. Questions about textual and literary form also point to further interrogations of the political-legal status of the protagonist. Appearing in the double negative as "monstrous

20 Kafka, *Die Verwandlung*, p. 34, my emphasis; Kafka, *The Metamorphosis*, p. 9. The German original reads: "Der Chef deutete mir zwar heute früh eine mögliche Erklärung für Ihre Versäumnisse an …, aber ich legte wahrhaftig fast mein Ehrenwort dafür ein, daß diese Erklärung nicht zutreffen könne. Nun aber sehe ich hier Ihren unbegreiflichen Starrsinn und verliere ganz und gar jede Lust, *mich auch nur im geringsten für Sie einzusetzen*."

21 Cf. Trüstedt, *Katrin: Stellvertretung*. Zur Szene der Person (Konstanz: Konstanz University Press, 2022).

22 John Hamilton, "Procuratores: On the Limits of Caring for Another," *Telos* 170 (2015), pp. 7–22.

vermin" not only contrasts with the (supposed) expectations of others, but also, at least if we take it literally, is in tension with becoming recognizable as an actor with the legal status of a person. The cultural history of the term "vermin" points to two important connotations. As Stanley Corngold notes, the noun "vermin" in Middle High German meant an "unclean animal not suited for sacrifice." Sander L. Gilman traces in detail the anti-Semitic connotations of the word "vermin" as it was common in turn-of-the-century Prague. Thus, in German and Austrian anti-Semitic publications, Jews/Jewesses were referred to as rats, mice, insects, and, indeed, "vermin" – in the whole, "vermin of mankind." In the context of the Dreyfus Affair, in which Kafka took a keen interest, "the Jew" was described as "a stinking and dangerous animal, a plague, a centipede, a microbe, a mite, a cancer, an ugly spider and synagogue louse. [...] 'Long live the sabre that will rid us of the vermin.'" Kafka himself writes to Jesenská: "Is it not the natural thing to go away from where one is so hated (Zionism or popular feeling is not at all necessary for this)? The heroism of staying after all is that of cockroaches, which cannot be eradicated from the bathroom either."

The "monstrous vermin" into which Gregory is said to have transformed himself thus appears as produced by a logic of the state of exception in which he is deprived of the status of personhood in the full sense. When Simon Ryan points out that Kafka did not want to see the vermin imagined as a particular kind of insect, but must have thought of it as "a generic species of vermin, a hybrid thing, a true mongrel," he makes clear that the transformation is not thought of as a transformation into a positive being of a different kind, the assumption of a different particular status, but rather, as it were, as a withdrawal of personhood that produces an unbeing.

Instead of a description of his actual appearance, we see the image of Gregor in the picture hanging on the wall. It depicts Gregor in his former shape, which is characterized as "carefree" ("*sorglos*") and which displays Gregor as someone. As his attempt to appear has just failed, the picture shows him as a proxy, namely a lieutenant: "Right opposite Gregor on the wall hung a photograph of himself in military service, as a lieutenant, hand on sword, a carefree smile on his face, inviting respect for his uniform and military bearing."[23] *Lieu-tenant* – a participle of *lieu tenir* – in French means place holding. Gregor's appearance is not being described, only the reactions to it; in place of his appearance, we only

23 Kafka, *Die Verwandlung*, p. 39.

find the description of this picture of Gregor as a place holder,[24] itself holding and blocking the central omission of his appearance.

The possibility of stepping out, which is emphasized by the many openings, is "opposed" by the image of Gregor, which is shown instead of his failing appearance (holding place) – his "sight" is just not described as the sight of this image is described. Thus, the very desire that Gregor himself should appear – directly, actually, and precisely not by proxy – seems to provoke the enormity that constitutes this scene and blows up the proceedings. Thus it seems that Gregor Samsa – as well as, in a different way, Josef K. in the *Proceß* – is called upon to appear, and to do so, as Derrida calls it, through an "appearance, in the legal sense."[25] In the narrative *The Metamorphosis*, such a place, a situation is evoked – "that which is necessary for such an event, 'appearing before the law,' to take place."[26] It is perhaps evident here that not only is law permeated by literature, but literature is also permeated by law. Thus, narrative procedures can rest on juridical procedures, when narrative not only necessarily occurs by proxy, but also takes place in response to being called upon, as a kind of defense. But Gregor Samsa as "monstrous vermin" exposes himself to the inherent desire of the procedure for the appearance of the subject and at the same time eludes it, when the various roles constantly change places and rearrange themselves, in what Benjamin called "experimental arrangements": "Kafka's entire work constitutes a code of gestures which surely had no definite symbolic meaning for the author from the outset, rather the author tried to address such a meaning in ever-changing contexts and experimental

24 This scene could be read as a "Vexierbild" in Rainer Nägele's sense; see Nägele, "Vexierbilder des Andern: Kafkas Identitäten," in Nägele, *Literarische Vexierbilder. Drei Versuche zu einer Figur* (Eggingen: Isele, 2002), pp. 9–29; On the importance of this picture, see also Ryan, "Franz Kafka's Die Verwandlung," p. 5: "As Gilman's evidence for the cultural significance of Jewishness in relation to fitness for military service will suggest, a direct link may be made between the suggestion of loss when Gregor catches sight of his portrait and his experience, only a few moments before struggling to open the door to the living room, of the loss of his normal human voice." Hartmut Binder calls Gregor in the picture a "Stellvertreter der Staatsmacht" and a borrowed authority (see Hartmut Binder, *Kafkas "Verwandlung." Entstehung, Deutung, Wirkung* (Frankfurt am Main, Basel: Stroemfeld Verlag, 2004), pp. 449–450).

25 Jacques Derrida, "Before the Law," in *Acts of Literature*, ed. Derek Attridge (New York/London: Routledge, 1992), pp. 181–220, here: p. 191.

26 Ibid.

arrangements [*Versuchsanordnungen*]."[27] When who is a procurator for whom goes in circles in ever-changing constellations, the sense of the vicarious function of the office is both hyperbolically carried to an excess, and thereby at the same time subverted, highlighting the anarchic element of any office function and opening it up for yet another possible use, be it, at night, that of writing literature itself.

27 Walter Benjamin, "Franz Kafka: Zur zehnten Wiederkehr seines Todestages," in *Benjamin über Kafka: Texte, Briefzeugnisse, Aufzeichnungen*, ed. H. Schweppenhäuser (Frankfurt am Main: Suhrkamp, 1981), p. 18, my translation. The German original reads: "... daß Kafkas ganzes Werk einen Kodex von Gesten darstellt, die keineswegs von Hause aus für den Verfasser eine sichere symbolische Bedeutung haben, vielmehr in immer wieder anderen Zusammenhängen und Versuchsanordnungen um eine solche angegangen werden."

Chapter 8

A disgrace to the collar and divine office

Ministry, poetry and the law of bearing

Adam Gearey

Introit

Serving time in 1968 for his part in the Catonsville protest, Father Philip Berrigan wrote in his prison journal that Eldridge Cleaver's *Soul on Ice* "performed a ministry for me." Cleaver's ministry broke through a feeling of "powerlessness" – the reduction of reality to a "vapid common denominator." Reading Cleaver opened up a sense of renewal (Berrigan, 1968, 106).[1] This is admittedly an unconventional use of the word ministry that goes well beyond ecclesiastical office: and is defined by "service." Berrigan endeavours to articulate "ministry" – office as service – in terms of a breaking through of deadness and paralysis. The fundamental reference point is a profoundly Christian call to new life and the worldly actions that this calling requires. Referring to Daniel Berrigan's engagement with similar experiences, we could hazard that the Berrigans were "defining" a law of bearing.[2] The law of bearing is

1 Whatever this awakening is, it is one experienced by both Cleaver and Berrigan; it is expressed in terms of "captur[ing] something that you never had"--a meaning in life that exceeds one's understanding. The action of ministry is bound up with reading and writing: what one reads, how one acts and with whom one acts. Cleaver's book "performed a ministry" – a forced breaking through of the "tedium" that "destroys the soul" (108). In other expressions, the ministry of Cleaver's text is found in the way it overturns the "institutions of domination" that prevent new life (Berrigan, 1968, 109). The book summons the "energy" to become "a better man" (Berrigan, 1968, 110).

2 Daniel Berrigan was reading Bonhoeffer whilst underground (alongside Cleaver, St John the Cross and others). Most specifically, Daniel Berrigan takes from Bonhoeffer a most peculiar re-working of the term: a derivation of radical ministry. Radical ministry does not depend upon formal office in the church. For Bonhoeffer it is "justified ... by service." One can appreciate how – in the context of the times and read alongside liberation theology – this idea could be linked to service to the poor. Service to the poor could be based

DOI: 10.4324/9781003659754-10

the obligation of a demand to interpret the interruption through which it is announced.[3] If the awakening can be triggered by reading *Soul on Ice*, we have to move away from a sense that the summoning comes from conventional faith sources. How can one live the new life that has inbroken and seized you?

The focus of our engagement will be the actions of the Catonsville 9. The Catonsville 9 were anti-war protestors who were imprisoned for destroying draft files in May 1968. Daniel and Philip Berrigan were amongst the 9. The problematic of bearing will be traced through a series of texts by the Berrigan brothers, William Stringfellow, Anthony Towne and Dorothy Day. These writings are, variously, notes from the underground, prison diaries and theological meditations. From Stringfellow and Towne's *Suspect Tenderness*, we will move to a study of the poems Daniel Berrigan composed on Block Island and Towne's poem *Capernaum;* a dialogue with a text by Dorothy Day on pilgrimage. The key figure in *Block Island* is Stringfellow and Towne's home

---

on the interpretation of a passage of significance to Bonhoeffer: "mind not high things, but condescend to men of low estate" (Romans 12:16). Radical ministry, then, is expressed as a "law of bearing" that exists in "interruption by God" (Bonhoeffer, 1954, 100). How to put these pieces together? Take the etymologies of ministry and office. Ministry can be securely linked to Latin and French terms that are more or less cognate with the idea of office as an ecclesiastical post. However, confronted with the peculiarity of Berrigan's writings, it is necessary to return to the Indo-European *mei- which is the root for a complex of terms that carry the meaning of changing, meeting, but also diminishing. These significations carry the fundamental link between the law of bearing and ministry. Certainly in a Christian sense, the sense of ministry – as that which refers back to Christ – must carry with it the notion of a servant who is much less than the master. The master, as exemplar, is that against which the servant must always measure his/her self – and always fall short. In this strange meeting of the notion of exemplar and of falling short is the notion of a transformation that comes through failure: ongoing transformation must always fall short at the same time as it must measure itself. Definitional of ministry is something exuberant, excessive and completely demanding. These are perhaps the "norms" of radical ministry (Berrigan, Stringfellow and Townes, 1971, 75).

3 Bearing, in this extended sense, is the obligation to witness the powers of darkness that articulate themselves in poverty, violence and war. The law of bearing carries a freight of inter-locked senses. The first one is that of taking up a burden. This connects with an idea of interpretation: of discovering the bearing that one thing has on another. This sense of discovery continues in the notion of finding one's bearings – of following a direction. But one can also be knocked off one's bearing. A bearing carries the risk of being driven by forces that one cannot control.

– Escahton – perched on the cliffs above the ocean. Block Island functions as refuge, dwelling, hiding place, cell and membrane between death and life: a place of retreat, or meditation, of different scales of time and of reckoning. The argument will be that *Block Island* and *Capernaum* provide forms for working through the obligations of the law of bearing;[4] articulations of a "process" of normative reflection. *Block Island* and *Capernaum*, as texts of ministry, perform the law of bearing as an ongoing agon. Bearing, worked through poetically, is inseparable from dwelling with others, taking on personal burdens of death and grief, and inventing the symbols necessary for these traumas to be transfigured – and for life to continue.

Love and napalm

The recipe for homemade napalm was found in an army handbook. Instead of jellying the mixture, the decision was made to use it as a liquid. On May 17, the nine Catonsville activists went into the draft board offices. Whilst one of the nine acted as a lookout, the others removed draft files from cabinets. The nine activists took the files into the car park and burnt them in a wire bin, after which they recited a prayer and waited to be arrested.[5] The trial of the Catonsville 9 was itself a

4 This is perhaps one of the essential – and perhaps forgotten – contexts for contemporary jurisprudence; a line that can be traced through Hart and Finnis to Dworkin and Raz. To what extent does the debate on morality and law come out of the social and political traumas of the late 1960s and early 1970s? Whilst there are no explicit references to Catonsville or the similar protests in the canonical texts of jurisprudence, it would be intriguing to write these back into what passes for the central debates of jurisprudence. It may be that this would re-orientate the subject to the profound and ongoing problematic of poverty, racism and state violence.

5 The anti-war movement gathered pace with the march on Washington in 1965, as a response to the decision to begin bombing North Vietnam. Over the next two years, the war escalated; as did American military casualties and the cost of the war, which by 1967 was over $25 billion dollars a year. Troop numbers were maintained by a draft system which became the target of resistance and protest. Burning draft cards began around 1964, and was prominent in the 1967 march on the Lincoln Memorial and the Pentagon. The police response to anti-war protest also became increasingly brutal. In 1967, Martin Luther King declared his opposition to the war, drawing attention to the disproportionate number of African Americans serving in the armed forces and suffering higher casualty rates. King's opposition also served to stress that the cost of the war impacted heavily on federal aid programmes. Nixon's election in 1968, King's assassination and military losses in the Tet Offence, served to deepen

focal point for protest and the anti-war movement.[6] A month before the Catonsville action, Martin Luther King's assassination had provoked riots in Chicago, Washington and Baltimore. Against this backdrop of simmering racial tensions, the Poor People's March on Washington had drawn attention to the scale of the endemic racism and poverty that existed in the country. President Johnson had suspended anti-poverty initiatives to provide funding for the Tet Offensive in Vietnam. Mounting American casualties, military setbacks and a growing sense that the war could not be won fuelled national opposition to the draft. The summer after the trial of the Catonsville 9 was marked by further violence. In August 1968, the scale and brutality of the police response to anti-war protests in Chicago led to a further high-profile public trial, ongoing national demonstrations and, after the Days of Rage in 1969, the bombing campaign initiated by the Weather Underground – a radical group that emerged from the collapse of the SDS, a national movement coordinating student radicalism.[7]

---

divides in American society and to build further support for the peace movement. The introduction of a draft lottery in 1969 served to further radicalise young people and students. Massive national demonstrations, rioting, the militancy of the Black Panthers and the Weather Underground, who engaged in a campaign of bombing and agitation designed to "bring the war home" served to compromise deep-seated ideologies of American culture and made for a profound dis-identification by significant portions of the national population with the notion that America was a decent, rule of law state.

6 Demonstrations and protests took place throughout the trial. William Stringfellow and Anthony Towne were present, as was James Pike, the controversial Bishop of California. A former lawyer, he worked with the defence, and preached an impromptu sermon to the assembled protesters. He introduced Dorothy Day, who spoke of Roger Allen La Porte, the young Catholic Worker who has immolated himself in 1965 as a protest against the war. The nine defendants were found guilty. They received sentences for between 2 and 3 and a half years for damaging government property. Reneging on an earlier promise to submit to punishment, four of the defendants chose to go underground, including Daniel and Philip Berrigan. William Kunstler's defence proved entirely unsuccessful. Kunstler later wrote a poem about the trial. See William Kunstler, Catonsville-Twenty Five Years Later, in *Hints and Allegations* (New York: Four Walls, Eight Windows, 1994), 36–37.

7 The Catonsville 9 were a very specific and distinct group of Catholic anti-war activists. A number had served as missionaries in Latin America or Africa, where they had witnessed American support for corrupt and violent regimes. Philip Berrigan was a member of the Order of St Joseph, and his brother, Daniel, was a Jesuit priest. They framed their action in terms of a theology that drew on diverse sources, but was directly influenced by liberation theology. Liberation theology took its focus from Pope John Paul II's understanding that

Some days before the action, on his way to Hanoi to negotiate for the release of American POWs, Daniel Berrigan sought to articulate his reasons for burning draft files. Re-purposing the SDS slogan "bring the war home," he went on to write:

> In a time of death, some men and women – the resisters, those who work hardily for social change, those who preach and embrace the unpalatable truth – such men and women overcome death, their lives are bathed in the light of the resurrection, the truth has set them free. (Berrigan, 1971, xix)

Berrigan's text "serves a ministry." The title itself, Night Flight to Hanoi, an allusion to the dark night of the soul, suggests a process of suffering and transformation. How to articulate the symbolic birth of a signification that has to be lived? The key theological notion is bearing witness. In conscience one acts as a Christian, as one has to act. One witnesses one's own acts. Connecting this theme with Berrigan's reading of Bonhoeffer suggests that bearing is an active sense-making that is inseparable from the person who has acted and taken up the burden: the burden of overcoming death in the light of the resurrection. Bearing is difficult. It has political and theological elements.[8] The fundamental

---

the poor of the Brazilian favelas, the landless peasants, the dispossessed of the teeming cities had an intuitive understanding of the Gospel's call for "radical and integral liberation" (Gutiérrez, 1971, xxxviii). Addressing this "irruption of the poor" (xx) meant the Church had to acknowledge a specific and new situation; rooting its theology and its practice in socio economic realities. If, as the Gospel urges, the Church is a Church of the poor, then, a political dimension becomes inseparable from evangelical mission.

8 Daniel Berrigan's "Letter to the Weathermen", written a few days before his final apprehension, can be read as a negotiation of bearing (True 1988). The "Letter to the Weathermen" is an extended meditation on non-violent protest. Whilst it does not cite Barbara Deming's or David Dellinger's noted essays on non-violent revolution, its fundamental argument is similar. Non-violence is holding to a position, a "clinging to" a principle that asserts a counter logic to the cycle of state violence and counter violence (Deming 1968 204-5). Whilst the latter might be "defensive", and necessary, the "resource" for social and political change must be found in "the quality of life within our communities" (Deming 1968 95). Deming's understanding of "moral pressure" is Berrigan's assertion that the revolution will fail if it is associated with the "inhuman treatment of human being" - for what, then, is the difference between "the movement" and "the military" (Deming 1968 95)? This is a coherent position, but it is not as clear cut as it might seem. Violence as "sabotage" is acceptable, and the only guiding principle offered as a means of distinction between sabotage

concern is that the truth of the resurrection has to be *performed*. Baptism is its sacrament. The office that defines an ongoing commitment to bear witness as a Christian. If one assumes that Berrigan's own writing is indeed a task of ministry, how does the summoning to new life inform the ongoing hermeneutic task of articulating a law of bearing?[9]

Daniel Berrigan did not "surrender" himself to justice. Towards the end of his period living underground, he sought refuge with Stringfellow and Towne in their house on Block Island, some 13 miles from the coast of the mainland. On his arrest, Stringfellow and Towne were charged with sheltering a fugitive. The task of making sense of events took them to the "Book of Revelations," "The Acts of the Apostles" and "The Letters of James and Peter I." The three friends had frequently discussed these passages together. This is the interpretative community that counts. Sclerotic interpretations sponsored by the established Church were not relevant points of reference. It was also necessary to avoid the obvious. Nixon was not "our Nero." There are no trite parallels between the position of the Apostolic Church and the fate of the peace movement (Stringfellow and Towne, 1971, 71). However, the problems faced by the Apostolic Church do carry parallels with contemporary events – provided that one can read them in the right way.

---

and slaughter is "[d]o only that which one cannot not do" (Deming 1968 96). Berrigan admits that this principle is difficult to interpret. He asserts his own opposition to violence, whilst retaining the argument that violence as self-defence could be justifiable. How to hold to one's bearings? If the movement is becoming "debased" beyond recognition, then it may be necessary to hold a distance from it, to refuse to go down the path of "street fighting for its own sake" (Dellinger 1970 272) whilst continuing, as far as one can, to find "what we can create" (Dellinger 1970 98) and to offer ongoing dialogue as a means of achieving "rival institutions and ways of life" (Dellinger 1970 273). The metaphor of "poise" comes from Deming rather than Berrigan. She uses the image of "new life" (a theme taken from Fanon rather than the Bible). New life is poised between "assertion" and "restraint" (Dellinger 1970 221). There are parallels with Dellinger. For Dellinger poise, bearing, is a "feeling of [one's] way through" – whilst "disrupting ... the system" (Dellinger 1970 274).

9 Philip Berrigan's prison writings calls this working through a process. Process should not be understood as something limited by those institutions that set present themselves as the authoritative guardians of faith. Berrigan, and many of those involved in radical faith organisations, struggled with this problem of ecclesiastic authority. But "[a]cting without ecclesiastic permission" was never simply a question of rejecting an institution. Berrigan specified that he did what he did as a priest, even if it was for some "a disgrace to the collar and its sublime office (Berrigan, 15). See James Hitchcock "The Evolution of the American Catholic Left." *The American Scholar*, vol. 43, no. 1, 1973, pp. 66–84, at 72 and 84.

Christians, seeking to follow a non-violent path, were caught between a state that claims legitimacy and a revolutionary left whose violent tactics merely repeat the violence of the state (Stringfellow and Towne, 1971, 83). This theme took Stringfellow to the arrest of Peter and James in "Acts," after they had healed the crippled beggar at the gates of the temple (Stringfellow and Towne, 1971, 71–72). The fundamental question that confronts the interpreter is: "what does resurrection from the dead mean if 'proclaiming' it leads to arrest? (Stringfellow and Towne, 1971, 72). There is a strong parallel in "The New Testament" between the treatment that Jesus suffered and that suffered by Peter and James: healing is a political act – an act against the Roman state and its proxies. To be a witness to resurrection is to challenge the authority of the state (Stringfellow and Towne, 1971, 72).[10] "Sentimentalism" that passes for organised religion cannot countenance this reading of "Acts." The resurrection as a "political act" is an "unthinkable thought" (Stringfellow and Towne, 1971, 73). Sentimentalism sees the Roman state as an "aberration," rather than a metaphor and index for the power of the state. All "civil power" shares a "common characteristic." No matter which historical context, Christ would have been treated as a criminal. The state itself is fundamentally a power of violence – a power to punish those who question its authority. This power of sanction makes the state an institutional form of death. The resurrection of the dead is the source of the "moral power" of Christ – the "audacity" of this claim has to be understood. Healing is a "cosmic political act" (Stringfellow and Towne, 1971, 73). Preaching the resurrection confronts the war machine.

Thus, Berrigan's ministry assumes its shape in the "Apostolic tradition" that is an "affront" to the state. One has to "live in the authority over death" that "is" the resurrection (Stringfellow and Towne, 1971, 76). Those who are engaged in the witness of Daniel Berrigan must generate their own terms, their own authorisation of their acts. This is linked with a notion of conviviality. This figures heavily in Stringfellow

10 Stringfellow and Towne's theological approach can be related to a broader theory of the radical rejection of the "imaginary register" that constituted the "substance of ... political identity" (Balibar, 2002, 32). Radical theory and practice has always sought to confront the liberal state with the contradictions and limits: in particular that of a violence that cannot be kept within the law. Thus, the increasingly violent state response to the protests of the SDS and other groups revealed precisely what was at stake: the state would resort to extra judicial violence in order to protect its hegemonic forms of social organisation. Moreover, those who identified with the state would also resort to violence to protect what they perceived to be their own dominance or investment in symbols of belonging and control.

and Towne's legal defence of their actions. Ministry, as something shared convivially between friends, is the exemplification of friendship in Christ. It has a mystic and a physical body. The writing of ministry must respond to the law of bearing that carries its truth. The law of bearing becomes most intense when it moves between mystical and physical body, between the spirit and letter – the process of articulation. Ministry's metaphors must be provisional – a process peculiar to the obligations of bearing. These concerns, considered theologically by Stringfellow, become central to the poems Berrigan published in a sequence entitled *Block Island*.

Block Island

How to engage with the flux of interpretation, the shuttling backwards and forwards of meanings in the text of life?

"I sought a unifying theme, sought without knowing. The little house/ all eyes, saw for me."

The house, Eschaton, is the unifying theme. But this theme comes "unbidden" and outside of "knowing." The knowing that comes is linked to metaphors of seeing and being seen. These are appropriate images for a fugitive, who has sought refuge from justice but is not seeking to hide. He is at Eschaton, where all eyes could see him, and see him in different ways: as a fugitive from the law and as a Christian, seeking refuge and aid from other Christians. Understanding this plurality of roles requires one to rework, go over and find one's bearings. Knowing, it would seem, is being opened to a knowledge, which has its own rhythm, its own coming.

How will you have known?

What Eschaton taught is the theme of a later poem:

> "The house taught us slowly right use.
> I wintered there."
>
> (Berrigan, 1985, 4)

The house is a figure of the chance that Stringfellow and Towne took in sheltering Berrigan. This is more than the act of hospitality, of opening the house; it is a "dwelling" – a dwelling together against the "odd enduring." The "I" passed through – "wintering." The passing through, within the terms of these lines, is part of this process of dwelling, and of working out what one knows in dwelling in a house with others:

> "Signed, sealed, delivered
> my letter to the world

> half blotted by sea wind
> those surrogate tears
> written here, sealed here-
> the skin thin envelope of these walls."
>
> (Berrigan, 1985, 5)

The process, the passing through, the right use is also about writing. Writing that bears witness to the times in which it was written, but which can, like a letter, also be sent to a recipient – an addressee who, in the lines above, is the world. The world is a figure of those anonymous others – the readers of these poems – their addressee. The last image – "these walls" – makes sense as the "walls" of the poem itself. But the wall is "skin thin." The image of skin reappears, as does the precariousness of the house with thin walls. If the house is the poem, then this must be a metaphor of a kind of writing. Writing is precarious because it is "blotted" by emotion, by tears, where tears are strangely related to the sea – an important image to which we will have to return – but, to anticipate the argument, the sea is an "outside": an outside breaking in which exists in a series of inbreakings:

> "House took a chance as Christian dwellings must
> against odds enduring. Weathers opposed
> and defects, through which like soul or air
> the essence leaked of house."
>
> (Berrigan, 1985, 1)

House as membrane – "the essence" of house – between death and life, is thus its position as a boundary between opposing forces. The dwelling therefore makes sense as the way in which one can exist alongside – in and against – these forces; dwelling with the elements, walls as membrane between inside and outside:

> "cliff, sea, keep counsel"
>
> (Berrigan, 1985, 63)

The *Block Island* poems frequently record a movement from conversation, discussion and prayer to solitude. This is also the path from the house to the cliffs and the sea; an extended set of meditations on the very name of the house. Eschaton as end time. Time as a stately flow towards its end. The "grand" end. God's righteous judgement as an "eschatological promise." But, Berrigan also thinks about the time of events – or "[h]istory's rule of thumb. ... Things go as they go" (Berrigan, 1985, 79) in "juggernaut America" (Berrigan, 1985, 86). This is the dizzying sense that events are running out of control. But then there is the time of meditation by the sea, and the time of writing and reading created by the poem itself.

Impersonal history and its scattering of events is interrupted by personal memories, of other houses and other times. Things might have been different. How does a person become what that person "is"? Berrigan describes a memory of the "first house in Ely Minnesota" with "the tin washtub athwart the stoop/ talisman of the poor" – when "Winter night, wolves/ howled the moon up over Moose lake" (Berrigan, 1985, 81). The tension between the image of the tin bath tub and the lonely expanses of wild and indifferent nature gives these lines their dynamism. This moment of realisation, of lying awake, of thinking, is both in time and disconnected – the thinker enters a different kind of time, which has earlier been labelled a "large meantime granted against/ the world's mad count down" (Berrigan, 1985, 32). A meantime is a time that is not quite time; a time that is "granted" or which can be granted by seizing, or trying to seize, a counter-time. It is a time of possibility and transformation – not the "mad count down" to disaster.

With something like grace, these moments can repeat themselves:

> "A porch facing the sea
> September noon, late summer haze receding."
>
> (Berrigan, 1985, 89)

The thinker is taken elsewhere. This might still be the time of personal memory, a kind of self consolidation or recuperation (and something stranger; a kind of erasure of self – the non-self that is present in both the image of the heat haze and the wolves).

> But the events of the world impose themselves. Dwelling is
> "impoten[t]" in the face of death.
> Stringfellow was already ill. But death on Block Island
> occurred entirely
> unexpectedly
> Anthony Towne.
> The sequence of poems hinges on his death.

Towne is a lifeforce: a "great bearded bear of man" who "resolved simply to be" – an exemplary life removed from "urban frenzies/ follies, pride of place." He is "the great bearded image of" himself (Berrigan, 1985, 7). To correspond with one's image is to have an authenticity – a way of living from one's own centre, and teaching without teaching, being exemplary without presenting oneself as an example. Towne's sudden death "Teaches us so." Towne chose a kind of "uselessness" – and in this uselessness Berrigan finds an "image of a useless God." The great bearded bear man is celebrated as something pagan – memorialised here, not by a Christian image, but by the enigmatic image of a henge. A henge is a broken circle, rather than a closed circle, and, as such, is also the metaphor for the form of this short poem. It is a scoring of long and short lines; of imperatives strangely offset or qualified by their position in a clause broken over a line end:

> "I thought
> this deliberately useless man
> is image of a useless God.
> Teach us so. You who die and live
> In the great bearded image of yourself."
>
> (Berrigan, 1985, 7)

The first part of this arrangement of lines uses two inset lines to isolate and stress the second line, which aligns with the two final lines. There is a form of sequence and counter-sequence where the thought of the useless God exists in a kind of counterpoint to the moral lesson of Towne's life. The movement of the lines scores the paradox of the example that defeats exemplarity. The high-sounding phrase focused around "Teach us so" – the dogmatic of the preacher, sits uncomfortably alongside the uselessness of the bear man. The effect of the poem on the page, for this is only the concluding strophe, evokes another pagan, rather than Christian, image, and one that is also evoked by the henge: a cairn of stones. Like the henge, and unlike the Christian gravestone with name and dates, the cairn is a kind of useless monument: a jumble of stones which seemingly memorialises a life without pointing a moral, offering contemplation on the materiality of death.

The poems turn from the cairn to another jumbled structure that reflects the inexplicable inbreaking of death for which Stringfellow "sought no explanation" and in the face of which we "lived on/ uncertain as to why" (Berrigan, 1985, 8). The image of the house returns – now the house as a tomb (perhaps yet another pagan image) where the dead and the living exist alongside each other: "as though the walls dissolved, the dead talked back" (Berrigan, 1985, 8). The reader is returned to the image of the henge – a space that allows comings and goings, movements through; a process. There is little comfort in this image:

> "The little house, buffeted, weathered by life
> Initiated death."

The buffeting of the house evokes the worrying thought that the soul is no more than "air." Wind and the soul are the same substance – "stuff of the world." Within the sequence, there are hints that the pagan imagery suggests a kind of pantheism, a sacredness of the material world, which might not accord with more conventional Christian theology. In the next poem, Berrigan and Stringfellow bury Towne's ashes. Following the "silence" that concludes the "scripture reading," this conceit appears:

> "Hear the rain drum. mean time! mean time! The peaceable
> Echo in nature, of that stilled heart."
>
> (Berrigan, 1985, 9)

Mean time – a meanwhile. The time of burial is an interruption. Towne's spirit must be "exorcised" from the house to allow time to be lived again – so that "Pages/ by grief defaced, grew legible once more" (Berrigan, 1985, 10). The howling storm in which Towne is buried turned the pages of scripture into "illiterate oatmeal" – his death, burial and disappearance allow a proper demarcation between the living and the dead, the grave and the house; a setting in place which is also a turning of pages and a turning of time:

> "Grief turned in time
> In turning time, to temperate mourning."
>
> (Berrigan, 1985, 10)

Time is the time of mourning, a transfiguring of grief, which is also the record of the turning pages of the poems, in which grief is recorded, made "legible" – and something of a balance recovered. Towne does not have a gravestone – rather an ancient anchor is laid across his grave as if a cross.

The anchor provides the fundamental image, the resolution of certain tensions that have animated these poems: anchor and cross, a keeping in place. The place is that of a correct practice, a proper understanding of life and death. Anthony is "anchored above the sea." The trauma of his death must be grasped as the irrelevance of a body reduced to ash – the uselessness of hanging onto something that has gone, except to the extent that it can become a metaphor for resurrection, an echo of Hopkins:

> Anthony, Christ, salvage the shipwrecked world

Perhaps the key word in this line is salvage – something taken from a wreck. The wreck of a ship that has been driven off, or has lost its bearing: the wreck of a world. It takes us to a poem about ruins and wreckage; a poem written as an elegy for Bishop Pike by Anthony Towne. A short text introduces the poem:

> [w]hen he isn't writing about Bishop Pike, Anthony Towne is a poet. For some time he had wanted to write in a poem about Bishop Pike. He also wanted to write a poem about the Holy Land, which he got to know because of Bishop Pike. Events kept getting in his way. Daniel Berrigan and the FBI, for example.
>
> (Stringfellow and Towne, 1976, 421)

Poetry is suspended and necessary. Prose, and the demands of making a set of claims, a defence of a person, comes before the composition of poetry and the desire to engage with this kind of writing that remains in abeyance, awaiting the moment when it can crystallise out: the occasion of Pike's death being the precipitant. Events, though, can also interrupt writing. Not least the arrival of the man who will write the poetic epitaph of the poet who is finding time to write the epitaph of another.

The office of the dead

Capernaum. Ruin: jumble of things – "his own proper city" and cursed place; violence and anti-violence. The siege of Masada; ruins that testify. Arrivals and departures; ascents and descents – bearings. To read *Capernaum* is a little difficult because of all the themes at stake. One thematic line that can be traced through the poem is undoubtedly the idea that communicates with bearing and radical ministry – especially as the return to the Holy Land is a return to source, a chance to take stock: renew. The poem takes its title from the Hebrew names for a town (the Arabic name contains the word for ruins) in which the Gospels record Jesus' ministry.[11] The poem marks its own entrance with a marginal note: *introit*. In ritual terms, this marks the entrance of the priest who is to perform her office and celebrate Mass. The refrain of the poem, "Timor mortis conturbat me," comes from the office of the dead – a prayer cycle for souls in purgatory: for souls bearing their own burdens.

The fourth verse is composed of fragments of a letter that Dorothy Day sent to the incarcerated Berrigan brothers entitled "On Pilgrimage."

11 Luke and Mark's Gospels record the driving out of an unclean spirit, in Capernum. Matthew 8:5 contains an enigmatic reference to In Capernaum as "his own city." The place was chosen by Jesus as the starting point of his own ministry, but, like Zarathustra, he cursed the place for not taking him seriously enough (Matthew 11:23).

Her "love orderly like rage" is a reference to Day's description of her work with the poor, her anger at the conditions in which they find themselves and the dismissive attitude of some of the clergy to the problems that the poor, particularly poor women, suffer. The verse tersely names Day's love as a form of conviviality: "the poor, the drunks, the homeless, offcasts/…/ companied, companioned" (Stringfellow and Towne, 1976, 422). Day's convivial love is expressed in the context of duty and office. The open letter congratulates Daniel and his brother, not only for not renouncing the priesthood, but for seeing their own witness as inseparable from their roles as priests. This contrasts with a priest who visited a man in prison – "one of the seven corporal works of mercy" – and another who showed a less charitable attitude. Day's letter also sums up her understanding of the times through which they are all living:

> I feel that, as in the time of the Desert Fathers, the young are fleeing the cities – wandering over the face of the land, living after a fashion in voluntary poverty and manual labor, seeming to be inactive in the "peace movement."

The evocation of the desert fathers and the sense in which a social movement is slowly growing, bringing people together; the idea of "wandering" and seeking; and the links between the imaginary of the peace movement and the Catholic Workers, perhaps lead Towne to organise an entire verse around this letter about salvaging something from the world.

The pilgrimage that Day recommends and celebrates is not a trip to the Holy Land, but the ongoing work for social transformation through non-violence:

> "I know they are still a part of it – just as Cesar Chavez and the Farm Workers' Movement is also part of it, committed to non-violence, even while they resist, fighting for their lives and their families' lives.

Day's line about wandering, writing and meditation are then quoted directly in the poem, setting up a strong correspondence between a kind of writing, a form of meditation and pilgrimage as movement on a bearing. Perhaps this poem works so well because it does find its own fusion of content and form; the digression, the loss of direction is not distraction, but a way of working through images and metaphors – to find one's bearings by losing them, to shut one's eyes in order to find oneself.

The risks that the poem takes in its versification pay off in the movement from the fourth to the final verse. Day's words are placed against the following line:

"Capernaum. We mediate among the ruins like cows.
the saucer sea of Galilee
holds its breath
The very spot where Jesus preached the word."

The reader has been led through various deserts and ruins to the Sea of Galilee and Christ's "own city" (which he cursed). This "very spot" then is ambiguous: both a historic "site," and a tourist site, where you can ruminate like an animal on something that cannot be easily memorialised, because the word is not simply something written down. It is a direction, a bearing and a way of finding one's bearing by losing the way. The world is paused; it holds its breath. The "spot" where the word was preached is "so green, cool under the trees," not the "sunlight fierce as zealot's daggers"; it is at this point that the image of butterflies and larks occurs, a distant echo of the "monarch butterflies and meadowlarks" with which the poem began (Stringfellow and Towne, 1976, 422).

The poem concludes:

"This is the sundered city where it all began.
the ministry of Jesus
the word that thunders
gently
in the screech of time
We get back in the bus. It is time to depart."
(Stringfellow and Towne, 1976, 422)

The time to depart always comes. We can take our bearings from departures if we can see them for what they are. A process has to work itself out if it is given the time to do so. The page can be turned. New life is always possible. In the poem, Capernuam exists in sequence with a visit to Massala – site of siege and a massacre. An image of violence, war and wreckage:

"Conculcated, some bones, plaits, sandals, a stove
Fragments of a scroll of *Ecclesisates*"

The fragments of the text are not important. They are not what can be salvaged. The "sundered" shipwrecked city is something incompatible with a natural order begins. A paradox announces itself as a curse/blessing – a perverse spirit both of and beyond time, the words of thunder that are not of this world.

Ashes and fire: to be born again

Bored stupid by the sermons of the prison chaplain in Dansbury where he was incarcerated, Berrigan memorised the *Four Quartets.*[12] Catonsville defines a path and a trajectory – it was now and America: the time was "weirdly right." If a church is a gathering of those who act in the name of Christ, Catonsville defines a community of Christians whose action is their witness and ministry against war and poverty. But the ministry assumed by the Berrigans moves beyond these events of political witness. In the Block Island poems and *Capernaum,* a different "inscape" emerges. Texts of ministry have to negotiate griefs that are intensely personal, and as testing for faith as actions against poverty and war. Ministry as service beyond office is a grappling with the demand that throws the minister into the darkness and absurdity of the world to salvage the meaning of faith.

References

Daniel Berrigan, *Night Flight to Hanoi* (1971) (New York: Macmillan).

Daniel Berrigan, *Block Island* (1985) (Greensboro, NC: Unicorn Press).

Daniel Berrigan, "Letter to the Weathermen," in *Daniel Berrigan: Poetry, Drama, Prose, edited by Michael True* (1988) (Maryknoll, New York: Orbis Books).

David T. Dellinger, *Revolutionary Nonviolence: Essays by Dave Dellinger* (1970) (Indianapolis: Bobbs-Merrill).

Étienne Balibar, *Politics and the Other Scene* (2002) (London: Verso).

Gustavo Gutiérrez, *A Theology of Liberation* (1971) (Maryknoll, New York: Orbis Books).

Philip Berrigan, *Prison Journal of a Revolutionary Priest* (1968) (New York: Hope, Reinhart and Winston).

W. Stringfellow and A. Towne, *Suspect Tenderness: The Ethics of the Berrigan Witness* (1971) (New York: Holt, Rinehart and Winston).

W. Stringfellow and A. Towne *The Death and Life of Bishop Pike* (1976) (New York: Doubleday).

12 See https://geezmagazine.org/magazine/article/daniel-berrigan-poetry-incarnate).

Chapter 9

The play of office and institution

Serene Richards

We are accustomed to think of the office as that place of duty and responsibility. 'Back to the office' and 'in person meetings' are by now familiar phrases that fill many with dread, and not without good reason. These slogans are, after all, often accompanied by a dreary commute subject to the whims of industrial action – which is all very well, of course – planned engineering works, overpriced tickets, overcrowded trains, and an underwhelming lunchtime sandwich or soup, where thermal discomfort is all but guaranteed (too hot in the summer and too cold in the winter), where awkward smiles and chats with colleagues are a daily feature in the course of one 'bullshit' job or another, as David Graeber put it.[1] Yet, like many institutions that have fallen into disrepute, 'the office' persists; in films and television, politics and law, education and commerce, as a key institution in the fabric of our societies. This is hardly surprising, however, since it has played an anthropological, and even ontological role throughout the centuries. Giorgio Agamben's *Opus Dei: An Archaeology of Duty* (2013) crafts its genealogy: the office as a notion inseparable from the concept of duty with theological origins. The liturgy is exemplary in this regard, whose function was to fulfil the works of God, where it mattered not whether the one carrying out those functions was a good person or not, believed or not, so long as the functions continued to be carried out – effectiveness itself solely matters. This primacy of effectiveness over the subjective qualities of the person, Agamben writes, was born out of the distinction made by the Church in the encyclical *Mediator Dei* between *opus operatum* and *opus operantis*, where the distinction would express 'the independence of the objective effectiveness and validity of the sacrament from the subject who

1 David Graeber, *Bullshit Jobs: A Theory* (London: Allen Lane, 2018).

DOI: 10.4324/9781003659754-11

concretely administers it.'[2] In practice, this distinction formalises something that is intrinsically familiar to us when we think about institutions and offices of all kinds, which is to say that the subjective qualities of an individual were thought to be distinct from the acts subsequently carried out by that individual, or the functions carried out in the name of the particular institution – though the extent to which this is still the case is unclear, as institutions increasingly expect real alignment between one's public and private use of reason. Liturgical praxis follows this distinction between *opus operatum* and *opus operans*, such that, as Agamben describes, the minister resembles a sort of 'animate instrument' where, since the primary agent is Christ, 'not only is it not necessary that he have faith or love, but even a perverse intention ... Does not take away the validity of the sacrament.'[3]

Therefore, the greater aim of the institution takes precedence over the whims of individual servitors. The novelty of Agamben's genealogy lies in the observation that the inheritance of the paradigm of liturgy in the form of office has important implications for ontology and praxis, and therefore, on the mode of being of the human being. Agamben writes: 'in office or duty, being and praxis, what a human does and what a human is, enter into a zone of indistinction.'[4] Any ethical connection between the subject and their actions is effectively broken, since so-called good intention is no longer relevant; what counts is the function carried out.

The ontology of office

According to Hart and Honoré, the performance of a legal duty is widely understood not to entail an element of voluntariness, which is to say that the performance of a legal duty is not a voluntary or wilful act as such. If this is the case, then on what does it depend? Why would an act that is not 'voluntary' or 'wilful' nevertheless be carried out? It is precisely these questions that motivate Agamben's enquiry into the structure of being in *officium* since the latter in turn mimics ontological presuppositions that come to shape our social and political institutions. In other words, what is at stake concerns being and its own actions and the presupposed separation between potential and act, essence and existence, already present in Aristotle. How can one explain the passage from potential to act? This question already assumes that being must be realised in some way and its 'result' having been put to work in

2 Giorgio Agamben, *Opus Dei: An Archaeology of Duty*, translated by Adam Kotsko (Stanford: Stanford University Press, 2013), 21.
3 Agamben, *Opus Dei*, 22.
4 Agamben, *Opus Dei*, xii.

some way either through will, duty, morality or command.[5] Agamben explains that the concept of will was introduced into ontology, that is, as being consubstantial with being, between the third and fourth centuries, precisely because, at that time, being came to take on an operative sense. So the notion of will came to explain how it was that being could pass from potential to effectiveness.[6] In a similar fashion, the question as to why individuals would act out of duty, even if they did not want to, was answered by way of commandment. That is to say, in other words, the performance of a duty was believed to be in response to an order or commandment. For this reason, Agamben writes that 'the ontology of command and the ontology of operativity are therefore closely bound: as a putting-to-work, the command also presupposes a will ... If being does not exist, but must actualise itself, then in its very essence it is will and command.'[7]

Because of its theological origins, the liturgical paradigm is concerned with morality and therefore with an idea of good and evil. However, in Cicero, this is not necessarily the case. Agamben recalls that Cicero translates the Stoic concept of *kathēkon* (defined as 'what is appropriate, opportune') with *officium*.[8] *De officiis* is understood as what is appropriate to do in a given situation or set of circumstances; in terms of ethics, therefore, it is unconcerned with questions of good or evil.[9] Agamben explains that *officium* is:

> Neither a juridical or moral obligation nor a pure and simple natural necessity: it is the behaviour that is expected among persons who are bound by a relation that is socially codified, but the compulsory nature of which is sufficiently vague and indeterminate that it can be connected [...] even to behaviour that common sense considered self-evidently offensive to decency."[10]

A key aspect of the meaning of *officium*, according to Cicero, is the 'giving form to the use of life [*usum vitae conformare*].'[11] Since, if human beings do not live their lives as animals but rather 'conduct' and 'govern' life, then *officium* forms a key aspect of making life governable – that is,

5 Agamben, *Opus Dei*, 128.
6 Agamben, *Opus Dei*, 128.
7 Agamben, *Opus Dei*, 129.
8 Agamben, *Opus Dei*, 67.
9 Agamben, *Opus Dei*, 67.
10 Agamben, *Opus Dei*, 72.
11 Agamben, *Opus Dei*, 74.

by instituting it.[12] Such that *officium* 'constitutes the human condition itself, and human beings, insofar as they are *membra ... corporis magni* (parts of one great body), are beings of *officium*.[13]

Agamben shows that Cicero's strategy is to define the sphere of *officium* as placed between morality and law – thus inscribing the theory of virtue, which in fact can be thought of as the apparatus that enables the actualisation of governance.[14] It transpires that this concept of *officium* is met with interest by Ambrose, as is shown in the treatise on the ethics of the priests – which, Agamben shows, borrows from Cicero's *De Officiis*.[15] The purpose, Agamben explains, is to bring to the Christian Church the secular philosophical concept of *officium*.[16] For Agamben, 'what is at stake in both cases is, rather, essentially terminological and political. That is to say, in the one case it is a matter of bringing a concept extraneous to politics and morality into those spheres and – under the pretext of a Greek translation – technicising it. In the other case it is a matter of transferring Cicero's *officium* point-by-point into the Church to found on it the praxis of priests.'[17]

Cicero's notion of the *devoir de situation* by way of the translation of *kathēkon* into *officium* – the mode of behaviour appropriate to a given situation – is granted central space in Kantian ethics. Agamben points out that this contemporary understanding is an inheritance of the ontological scission referred to earlier, that of a separation between the human being's subjective wants and desires from the actions that could contradict those, in the name of the office or institution. For Kant, the missing ingredient that functions to tie this scission together is the notion of duty or respect that compels individuals to forgo their own will in favour of another 'general' or institutional will or aim. Kant constructs a moral law or transfers juridical and religious elements into an ethics based on commandment, obedience and judgement. Curiously, perhaps, there is no concept of duty in Spinoza's ethics – why? Essentially, this is because being is simply its manner; there is no presupposed separation between essence and existence, potential and act, being and having-to-be, and therefore no prescription to formulate the transition from one to the other. There is no transcendental value that ascribes duties to be fulfilled in accordance with a specific task or function. It is this latter perspective that this paper is curious to explore, or rather, more precisely,

12 Agamben, *Opus Dei*, 75.
13 Agamben, *Opus Dei*, 75.
14 Agamben, *Opus Dei*, 76.
15 Agamben, *Opus Dei*, 77.
16 Agamben, *Opus Dei*, 77.
17 Agamben, *Opus Dei*, 79.

to examine the tension between both perspectives when characters from different walks of life come into contact with them, since these are not mere abstractions, but rather compose what we could term our realities. We have surely encountered numerous characters who, for one reason or another, are less inclined to fulfil duties, or fulfil them reluctantly, some in jest, some more seriously, and also those who refuse.

The hat makes the man

In *L'opinion et la foule* (1901), in a discussion on the evolution of the conversational, or the modes through which we human beings might communicate, the sociologist Gabriel Tarde notes that skilful conversation has always depended on external factors including new occasions, geographic localities, religious or political ideas, literary works and so on. In a slight digression, Tarde notes that the phenomenon of the court jester is not one that is found everywhere, not in Rome or Athens. In France, the last court jester was named 'Angly,' and served under the reign of Louis XIII. Before him, a curious character named 'Brusquet' led a colourful life that would eventually see him leading a prestigious office.[18] Jean Antoine Lombard (1510–1568), informally known as Brusquet, served as the King's fool during the reign of François I and his successors up to Charles IX. With little to no knowledge of the subject, Brusquet pretended to be a doctor, treating patients at the Anne de Montmorency's camp. It is said that all the patients that he treated were sent to premature deaths.[19] Initially threatened with the severe sentence of death by hanging, his actions so amused Henri II that instead Brusquet was appointed to the office of Paris postmaster, managing the organisation and performing a range of duties. Interestingly, Brusquet is a court jester that did not start out as 'fou' [mad], that is, a jester.[20] Indeed, unlike his predecessors, Brusquet was an adult when he took up the position; he was also wealthy and married with children. As an adept courtier, he is thought to be the first to have 'played' the role of jester precisely to take up the office, to wear the hat appropriate for that particular job, as Max Ernst's *The Hat Makes the Man* (1920) neatly captures (Figure 9.1).[21]

18 Gabriel Tarde, *L'opinion et la foule* (Paris: Puf, 1989), 52.
19 Tarde, *L'opinion et la foule*, 52.
20 Bernard Guenée, 'Fou du roi: Quelle place eurent les fous à la cour de Charles VI ?', *Comptes-rendus des séances de l'année – Académie des inscriptions et belles-lettres*, 146e année, n 2, 2002, 649–666, 660.
21 Max Ernst, *The Hat Makes the Man* (New York: The Museum of Modern Art, 1920).

Figure 9.1 Max Ernst, The Hat Makes the Man (Cologne, 1920). Digital Image, The Museum of Modern Art, New York/Scala, Florence. 2025@Photo Scala, Florence.

Ernst's work is a collage of images of men's hats taken from a sales catalogue, depicting what could be seen to be the hierarchy involved in various office settings; we can imagine each worker would be wearing their own hat fit for the purpose of the job, fit, in other words, for the devoir de situation. As it happens, *The Hat Makes the Man* is said to be inspired by Sigmund Freud's *Jokes and their Relation to the Unconscious* (1905), where the hat is seen to symbolise the repressed desire of the bourgeois man. Elsewhere, in *The Interpretation of Dreams* (1900), Freud writes that the hat is the archetypical symbol of man: 'the hat is really a male genital organ, with its raised middle piece and two downward-hanging side pieces' and eventually suggests that the hat could also stand 'for the female genitals.'[22] A universal apparatus, then, of all shapes and sizes, that both facilitates and invites role-play. It is curious, however, that the office can be seen as a space for 'role'

22 Sigmund Freud, *The Interpretation of Dreams*, translated by A. A. Brill (New York: The Macmillan Company, 1913), 249.

but not of play, while simultaneously requiring a degree of *role-play*, as the notion of affective labour implies. Indeed, affective labour obliges a degree of managing one's emotions to better appeal to a particular workplace culture and, more broadly, that of our consumer societies. As Hardt and Negri write: 'affective labour, then, is labour that produces or manipulates affects such as a feeling of ease, well-being, satisfaction, excitement, or passion. One can recognise affective labour, for example, in the work of legal assistants, flight attendants, and fast-food workers (service with a smile).'[23] This role-play, or play without play, in our consumer societies is reminiscent of what Baudrillard describes as the prevalence of the ludic, which, for him, is play devoid of pathos. As Baudrillard writes:

> It is the ludic which is becoming the dominant tone of our daily habitus, to the extent indeed that everything – objects, goods, relationships, services – is becoming gadget or gimmickry … The ludic activity may give the appearance of being a passion. But it never is. It is consumption … Consumption is combinatorial investment: it is exclusive of passion.[24]

Ludic play is without passion and without pathos – rather, resembling exchange, it is the inputting of elements for a particular result, an exhaustive list of combinations that, through the gadget, is never completed: the software can always be updated, the timeline can be refreshed and managerial language refined.

Office role-play, or ludic play, takes the form of rituals rather than play as such that necessarily contains elements of spontaneity, experimentation, messiness or disruption. This is seen in Carlo Collodi's *Pinocchio* (1883), where, as Agamben writes, when Pinocchio arrives in Playland, a land where nothing but play exists, we see play take over life, interrupting coordinates taken as given.[25] In Playland, one outcome, for instance, is an acceleration of time: 'in the hullabaloo of amusement the hours, the days, and the weeks passed like lightening.'[26] This is in stark contrast to the office environment, with timesheets to track time

23 Michael Hardt and Toni Negri, *Multitude: War and Democracy in the Age of Empire* (London: Penguin Publishing Group, 2005), 108.
24 Jean Baudrillard, *The Consumer Society: Myths and Structures* (London: Sage Publications,1999), 114.
25 Giorgio Agamben, *Infancy and History: Essays on the Destruction of Experience*, translated by Liz Heron (London and New York: Verso, 2007), 75–76.
26 Agamben, *Infancy and History*, 76.

and one's use of time, the fact of trying to pass the time or running out of time to complete tasks. If, as Levi-Strauss writes, rituals structure the calendar, then, for Agamben, it is play that disrupts it: 'though we do not yet know how and why, [play] changes and destroys it.'[27] Benveniste equally observes the potentially destructive character of play. Indeed, for Benveniste, while play can be traced back to an idea of the sacred, particularly in the form of rituals, something in play differs: that with play, the ritual survives, but the meaning behind it, the myth that is attached to rituals, dissolves. There is no necessary meaning or purpose to play as such: 'if the sacred can be defined as the consubstantial unity of myth and ritual, we can say that play exists when only one half of the sacred enactment is fulfilled, translating myth alone into words and ritual alone into actions.'[28] In this way, play, while connected to time, is at the same time a radical break from it, and while connected to ritual can operate without its original, or other, purpose. For Agamben, in play, 'man frees himself from sacred time and "forgets" it in human time.'[29] Indeed, this is unlike the gadget, and ludic play, in that it is not a question of governance – of role-play or *devoir de situation*.

The gadget, or contemporary technological apparatus, has the quality of play in that it is a gamification of relations and affects. Far from being passive objects thought to be wholly directed by the user, they are intermediaries and for this reason are inherently to do with governance. They are mediums and mediators, shaping how the user comes to understand both themselves and others; there is, as Vilém Flusser writes on the idea of the usual object, an intersubjective relationship at play that is *directional*.[30] Indeed, it is the user who, most of all, learns and unlearns or adapts. Similarly, for Agamben, the apparatus in question always implies a process of subjectification because the apparatus produces their subject and in so doing there is governance, where through a series of practices and discourses, an assumption of identity takes place – a role-play. In this way, through the gadget and ludic play, the ontological dimension of the sphere of liturgy reaches its completion: that is, a mode of being where effectiveness coincides with being, since, in ludic play, being is inseparable from its effects – a collapse of complexity resulting from the total enmeshment with the apparatus, its forms, limits, and language.

27 Agamben, *Infancy and History*, 76.
28 Benveniste cited in Agamben, *Infancy and History*, 78.
29 Agamben, *Infancy and History*, 78.
30 See Vilém Flusser, *Petite philosophie du design*, translated by Claude Maillard (Belval: Les éditions circé, 2002).

Role-play

Brusquet was so convincing in his role that it was impossible to tell for certain whether he was a 'buffoon' or a sage, with just as many 'taking him for a sage as for a buffoon.'[31] The example of Brusquet highlights the very real ontological 'splitting' that occurs in the notion of taking up 'office' and the role-play or game that *officium* ensues over the course of its performance.

With Brusquet's adventures, the idea of duty or responsibility for its own sake or in the name of the office or institution does not appear as a sufficient motivator for a job well done; that is, as that which propels individuals into their roles, into a scission between their being on the one hand and the actions demanded or expected by the institution on the other. In other words, commandments, orders or injunctions are simply not enough; sensibilities must be tickled for the radical gesture, the ontological splitting, to take effect. An appeal to the passions is the ungraspable yet essential element. As Legendre writes in *L'Empire de la verité* (1983), the role of fiction, for example, is essential in the reproduction of humanity.[32] Seldom do we encounter obedience for its own sake. Indeed, there must be a love of power, and power's 'grand project,' as Legendre writes, 'consists precisely in making itself loved.'[33] For Legendre, this was made possible by supposing a particular science whose function would be to camouflage this desire. A 'perpetual science of power,' from theologians to legislators of antiquity to advertising creatives, has succeeded in perfecting the proliferation of the love for power, or the love of the censor. This is what proponents of instrumentalism or functionalism tend to miss. The idea that the functionary would simply 'behave' and act as instructed guided only by the notion of duty and appeals to responsibility is a simplification or even a theoretical abstraction. I say abstraction since a key element is missing: the potential for errancy, a certain degree of mischief inscribed in the human being; what Western philosophy has characterised as the irrational passions, all that cannot be perfectly controlled and for this reason has been the subject of control or management under various guises including through the paradigm of *officium* and duty.

31 Guillaume Berthon, 'Triboulet a frères et sœurs: Fou de cour et littérature au tournant des XVe et XVIe siècles', *Babel : Littératures plurielles*, n25, 2012, 97–120.

32 Pierre Legendre, *L'Empire de la verité: Introduction aux espaces dogmatique industriels* (Paris: Fayard, 2001), 41.

33 Pierre Legendre, *L'Amour du Censeur: essai sur l'ordre dogmatique* (Paris: Éditions du Seuil, 1974).

Indeed, I would argue that when an individual 'behaves as they should' and does indeed perform their duties in perfect accordance with the *devoir de situation* that Cicero had envisaged, then a certain discomfort emerges. Take, for instance, the case of the woman who was interned at various asylums from the Salpêtrière to Sainte-Anne during the 1920s. Following a bombing raid in 1915 that left the patient's home completely destroyed but thankfully left her with only superficial injuries, she became afflicted with an unusual illness: walking backwards. Despite receiving a range of treatments from psychiatrists at the various institutions where she was interned, none of them were able to offer an explanation for this affliction nor a cure; why was she walking backwards? Jacques Lacan and Maurice Trénel, having heard of this curious case, began a close observation of the patient and confirmed that there were, indeed, no signs of neurological or organic disease. One day, they discovered that when the patient believed herself to be unobserved by the medical teams of the institution, something unexpected occurred: she would walk perfectly, that is to say, not backwards but forwards, and even to and fro if the occasion necessitated it, as one does.[34] Could it be that the patient, being interned in the asylum, knew that in order to fit into the institution a certain *devoir de situation* would be expected which, in the present circumstances, is an expectation, or obligation, of an illness or affliction? As it happens, according to Lacan, the patient's illness of being able only to walk backwards was actually picked up in the asylum over the course of treatment.[35] Out of duty perhaps, or obligation, the woman takes on the role of patient and wears its hat.

During the same period, this time in Switzerland, following a suicide attempt in 1929, a young Robert Walser found himself interned in an asylum in Herisau where his depression was misdiagnosed as schizophrenia. It is said that he remained in full possession of his faculties though was no longer writing. A visitor, troubled by this, asked him why. Walser replied: 'I'm not here to write, I'm here to be mad.'[36] Walser's genius and lucidity in fully embodying the *devoir de situation* of the context, that is the idea that the asylum is to be populated by the mad, perfectly undermines the coherence of the dual articulation of

34 See Maurice Trénel et Jacques Lacan à la Société de Neurologie de Paris, parue dans la *Revue neurologique de Paris*, 1928, t.1, n2. For more on this fascinating case see Sinan Richards, *Homo Alienatus: Freedom and Psychosis in Lacan and Fanon* (Oxford: Oxford University Press, forthcoming).

35 See Maurice Trénel et Jacques Lacan à la Société de Neurologie de Paris, parue dans la *Revue neurologique de Paris*, 1928, t.1, n2.

36 See the introduction to Walser's *The Assistant* in Robert Walser, *The Assistant*, translated by Susan Bernofsky (London: Penguin, 2008).

being and having-to-be that is presupposed in *officium*. Indeed, there is something troubling in being confronted with the person fully aware of their having-to-be, that is, of their splitting of being – the blunt admission that the apparatus contains within it a certain madness and an alienating function.

If you still need convincing, take for instance the case of Aby Warburg's internment, who, unlike Walser and the lady who walked backwards, appears to be indifferent to the whims and expectations of *officium*, and the *devoir de situation* of the patient's role in the asylum. Warburg sought to continue his work and indeed organised what is today believed to be his most important intervention, his 1923 conference entitled 'The Serpent Ritual.' Unfortunately, his doctors did not take too kindly to his labouring efforts, believing it to be more evidence of his need for care. So disturbed by this lack of understanding, Warburg wrote a letter to the directors of the Bellevue sanatorium in 1924 saying:

> I'd like to take this opportunity to get some clarification on what my doctors think about the symptom of resuming scientific work as a factor in subjective healing. In a recent conversation, Dr Ludwig Binswanger once remarked: 'It's all very well for you to do scientific work, but first think about getting better!'[37]

It would seem then that the refusal to split one's being into being and having-to-be, into how one would ordinarily act and how one is expected to behave in the context of office or institution – no matter what one's role is, whether manager or employee, or doctor or patient – is a cause for alarm and even perhaps a sign of madness. When Bartleby declared 'I would prefer not to,' the response to this has not received the same degree of attention, which is: '"I think, sir, he's a little *luny*," replied Ginger Nut with a grin.'[38]

One could say, then, that taking part in the office or institution involves a certain awareness of the rules of the game, and a willingness to *roleplay* whether that be officer or inmate. So that when this does not take place, as with Bartleby's, 'I would prefer not to,' the only plausible explanation is an appeal to the irrational, that one must be 'a little *luny*.' It's for this reason that Kostas Axelos calls for a new game for the world. For our purposes, this term could be seen to encompass

37 Aby Warburg, *La guérison infinie*, edited by Davide Stimilli, translated by Maël Renouard and Martin Rueff (Paris: Éditions Payot & Rivages, 2020), 189.

38 Herman Melville, *Bartleby, The Scrivener: A Story of Wall-Street* (Brooklyn: Melville House Publishing, 2004), 21.

the dominant ontological structure that encompasses *officium*, and the separation between being and having-to-be, essence and existence, that dominate both our politics and our ethics. Axelos writes that: 'the *world* deploys itself as a *game*. That means that it refuses any sense, any rule that is exterior to itself,' and, paradoxically perhaps, 'the play *of* the world itself is different from all the particular games that are played *in* the world.'[39] In thinking about 'a new game of the world,' perhaps the most difficult of questions concern law, office and institution. There are those who would argue for their abolition, some for their reform, and others arguing in defence of their current forms. All three positions work not just on the basis of a coherent definition or idea of law, institution and office, but also of how these function. The examples discussed so far illustrate precisely the opposite, the ambiguity and fragility that exists in the human being's interaction with them. Obedience is not self-evident; errancy or refusal remain possible. However, one thing that perhaps unites these three divergent positions is the idea of alienation with respect to the office or institution, and the subjects that compose them.

Alienation and the manner of play

For the philosopher Cornelius Castoriadis, the institution exists in a kind of circular relation to the idea of alienation. Inasmuch as while the institution can be alienating, alienation is itself instituted by the institution. For Castoriadis, the reason for this is that institutions tend to replicate and sanction a particular mode of sociality, a particular class structure, thereby presupposing an antagonistic division of society. However, in *The Imaginary Institution of Society* (1975), Castoriadis points out that 'there is an alienation of society, irrespective of class, with regard to its institutions' and 'once an institution is established it seems to become autonomous, the fact that it possesses its own inertia and its own logic, that, in its continuance and in its effects, it outstrips its function, its "ends", and its "reasons for existing."'[40] The danger then, is that rather than having institutions working in the service of society, the opposite ensues where society becomes instead 'in the service of institutions.'[41] This danger is also highlighted by Félix Guattari, who, in analysing group subjectivity finds that at the level of the institution it possesses its own laws that are not necessarily those of the individuals,

39 Kostas Axelos and Stuart Elden, 'Kostas Axelos: Mondialisation without the World', *Radical Philosophy* 130, Mar/Apr 2005, 25–28, 28.

40 Cornelius Castoriadis, *The Imaginary Institution of Society*, translated by Kathleen Blamey (Cambridge: Polity Press, 2005), 110.

41 Castoriadis, *The Imaginary*, 110.

where the individual as such is an object in the economic machine. Who speaks, Guattari asks, when:

> The Finance Minister modifies the discount rate by one percent? ... The Minister, of course, or at least the Ministry! Yet who is the subject of this signifying chain? ... A Minister's words obviously do not refer intimately to the person but to the relationships of production and the contradictions that regulate industrial societies.[42]

And, indeed, Castoriadis reminds us that surpassing these forms of alienation was key to Marx's ideas, particularly concerning the 'leap from the realm of necessity to the realm of freedom.'[43] This, then, presupposes a transformation in the mode of existence of human beings, where it is important to add, the very idea of institution or office must have a continual relation to a mode of life. This is not to say that any antagonism as such will forever be abolished, where desires would exist in complete harmony and perfect coincidence; that is neither possible nor necessarily desirable. The difficulty arises from the fact that the idea of the social is a fragile abstraction, it is 'what is everyone and what is no one ... in which we are wholly immersed yet which we can never apprehend "in person."'[44] For Castoriadis, it is something that can only be presented through the institution and for this reason the institution both exceeds and reduces the social's manifold complexity. The institution 'creates it, maintains it in existence, alters it, destroys it.'[45] There is always an excess in this manoeuvre and for this reason alienation appears as co-constitutive. In this sense, for Castoriadis, alienation as such does not discriminate, institutions 'cannot mystify the rest of society with its ideology without at the same time mystifying itself' and this includes the so-called dominant classes.[46]

Today, the institutions are said to take on a functionalist approach, that is, approaching their role as one of fulfilling functions in service of means and ends; but the world cannot be limited to a series of tasks to be accomplished. This ignores the symbolic relation that, while not being reduced to it, the social and its institutions still operate alongside. Both the problems of alienation and the symbolic are resolved in our

42 Félix Guattari, 'Reflections on Institutional Psychiatry for Philosophers', in *Psychoanalysis and Transversality: Texts and Interviews 1955–1971* (California: Semiotext(e), 2015), 131.
43 Castoriadis, *The Imaginary*, 110.
44 Castoriades, *The Imaginary*, 111.
45 Castoriadis, *The Imaginary*, 112.
46 Castoriadis, *The Imaginary*, 115.

modern societies by the notion of 'representation' or 'identity' which only further inscribes an alienating potential; just as something always exceeds the institution or the social, something always exceeds the representation of the individual by virtue of its singularity. For this reason, I would argue that there is a difference between the idea of institution in its constituent mode (affixed to representation for example) and the idea of institution in relation to its function in the mode of life of the human being. While the former relies upon an ontological splitting between being and having-to-be, the latter operates immanently with respect to the modality of being. In other words, it is where the institution operates as a *habitus* and it is for this reason that it is inseparable from one mode of life or another. Where the word '*gerere*' characterises the paradigm of the office, defined as 'the effectuation of a function,' the word '*manare*' characterises the institution of the mode of life, as the manner of being defined immanently by its mode. The tension between these two ways of seeing the world is captured in the case of *Milirrpum v Nabalco Pty Ltd* [1971], Australia's first indigenous land rights case, where over the course of a dismissive judgement, Justice Blackburn reluctantly concedes that it could not be said that the Yolngu people did not have a system of law and customs. Quite the opposite was the case, a mode of institution precisely as *habitus*, deriving its sense from the mode of life specific to it.

It remains difficult for us to imagine a mode of institution that would operate only so long as a mode of life made it such that it had to exist or operate. Between being and having-to-be, is a vast space traditionally filled by commandments, duties, governance, laws and regulations, to cajole being into its function. It seems that increasingly, the role of the gadget or apparatus in this context cannot be overlooked, precisely in its seduction of a ludic play that for the first time gives an appearance of mutual exchange, immediate reply or satisfaction, resulting in enmeshment and a certain degree of homogeneity and a forgetting of play and the manner of being.

Chapter 10

Calling out homophonia

A word in the ear of a jawist

Gary Watt

"If the judicial role is to speak, then the lawyer's first task must be to learn how to listen".[1] Here Paul W. Khan posits an elegant antithesis that helpfully identifies listening as a necessary corollary to speaking, but the distinction he draws between judge and lawyer risks obscuring the fact that both roles have traditionally been characterised in terms of speech and that the office of the jurist, whether lawyer or judge, is to listen as well as to speak. Traditionally, the judge's role has been to speak justice (to ad-ju(s)-dicate) and the lawyer's role has been to speak for another (to ad-vocate). Corresponding to both speaking roles is the need to perform the contrasting but complimentary role of listening, or, better still "hearing". The judge's role is one of fair hearing (to offer a judicial audience), and the lawyer's role is to attend; first and foremost to the client, but also to fellow lawyers and to the judge.

Peter Goodrich, clocking the significance of hearing as an aspect of the judicial office, emphasises that even the lowliest lawyer must become attuned to the auricular key in which the profession incants the common law's choral history:

> The office of the Judge was *oyer*, to hear, and the role of the lawyer, from the itinerant Justice all the way down to the grand little mootman with scarcely a word of Latin, was to lend an ear to the customs and conversations, the ancient practices and antique patterns that would form the common erudition, frequently of the locality – *de cel Countie* – and more often of that audible nature and auricular *humanitas* from which the judges extracted the *commune ley*.[2]

1 Paul W. Kahn, *Making the Case: The Art of the Judicial Opinion* (New Haven, Yale University Press, 2016), 6.

2 Peter Goodrich, "The Great Dialogue" Introduction to P. Goodrich (ed.), *A Cultural History of Law in The Early Modern Age* (London, Bloomsbury, 2019), 4.

DOI: 10.4324/9781003659754-12

For this notion of a cultural erudition that is common to all branches of the office of jurist, the erudite Goodrich cites a case report by the first of the law reporters, the Tudor judge Sir James Dyer (1510–1582).[3] As Goodrich wrestles with this report of common erudition, he wrests it out of the writing and returns it to being, what it was and still is and is to come: a retelling, a rumour passing from ear to ear, a rapport between jurists, common erudition as communal ear-audition. The aural report is the original, the written is the novice: the *noverint*. As Goodrich writes elsewhere:

> Jurisdiction and specifically that of the jurist ... refers to a spoken law, a mnemonic of maxims, auditory recollections, a tradition of pronouncements, orally aired learned opinions latterly collected in treatises, scholarly texts, judicial decisions, collections of arguments as well as the conversations, opinions and other aural recollections that formed the common knowledge or *communis opinio* of the legally learned.[4]

As we rifle through the law books today, the challenge is to hear in them the report of dead litigants and dead lawyers echoing a living law. The letter of the law must always be wrestled with; never thrown over, but always fiercely resisted by the need to hear that which the script with its visive might and printed permanence suppresses. Benjamin Cardozo lamented the perfunctory way in which, bound by the dubious logic of legal precedent, judges feel obliged to discharge the obligations of their office:

> Judges march at times to pitiless conclusions under the prod of a remorseless logic which is supposed to leave them no alternative. They deplore the sacrificial rite. They perform it, none the less, with averted gaze, convinced as they plunge the knife that they obey the bidding of their office. The victim is offered up to the gods of jurisprudence on the altar of regularity.[5]

3 The case, *Mynours v. Turke* 1 Dy. 65, 66a-66b, is cited in Sir John Doderidge, *The English Lawyer* (London, I. More, 1631), 154.

4 Peter Goodrich, "Law's Labour's Lost" (Review of Alain Supiot, *Homo Juridicus. On the Anthropological Function of Law*) (2009) 72(2) *The Modern Law Review* 296–312, 297.

5 Benjamin N. Cardozo, *The Growth of the Law* (New Haven, Yale University Press, 1924), 66.

How can a judge perform justice when their gaze is averted? Cardozo identified listening as the way towards a more equitable hearing:

> I suspect that many of these sacrifices would have been discovered to be needless if a sounder analysis of the growth of law, a deeper and truer comprehension of its methods, had opened the priestly ears to the call of other voices.[6]

When we read, we hear the play of sounds in our heads.[7] The written word becomes a new thing heard, or to speak more properly, we can say that the innermost ear of the mind hears again a sound that formerly was voiced and now is silently fossilised in the form of the written word. There is inside of us a silent speaker: a noiseless voice. As we see words on the page, they only make sense to us because, despite their silent reception by the eye, the ear of the mind hears them. Something like this occurs when we watch a person silently mouthing a familiar sequence of words, for example, the numbers one to ten. It is the hearing part of our brain that perceives the stimulus. The unfamiliar sight of silent speech defers in our subconscious to the familiar auditory record of words heard.[8] To achieve the auditory feat of hearing sound in silent script, our innermost ear must wrestle with the dominance of the letter as sign. Every homophone prescribes a little ring to wrestle in. The eye distinguishes the jurist from the jawist, but the ear does not. The "oral" sound spoken and the "aural" sound heard are the same to the ear. In homophones, disjunction between the visual sign of the script and its heard or remembered audible sound produces a dynamic tension between perception and persuasion, between eye and ear. This tension becomes in microcosm an exercise in just judgment. The mind sits as judge of a competition between the contrary submissions of visual and acoustic stimuli.

It is just to listen to the common heartbeat of the human under shades of skin colour, signs of gender, and the lines of age. To operate homophonically by sounding out the common note behind the sight of conflicting visual evidence is the very work and art of fair hearing.

6 Ibid.

7 See, for example, Marianne Abramson & Stephen D. Goldinger, "What the Reader's Eye Tells the Mind's Ear: Silent Reading Activates Inner Speech" (1997) 59(7) *Perception & Psychophysics* 1059, and, more generally, Lev S. Vygotsky, *Thought and Language* (Cambridge, MIT Press, 1986).

8 Lawrence D. Rosenblum, *See What I'm Saying: The Extraordinary Powers of Our Five Senses* (New York, W. W. Norton & Company, 2010), 254–256: "Your Brain Hears the Speech You See".

A homophone invites us to hear commonality between one word and another, between one sign and another. To hear the sight of otherness in this way exercises our capacity for hearing the other side of the argument. Homophonia is and should be a productive struggle, one that tugs on the sight lines produced by conflicting evidence until it produces sound judgment; the judge plucks the string held in tension between two sides and when it is justly plucked, the right note issues forth. Occasionally, the law has acknowledged in express terms that justice is to be found not in the letter but in the sound. The 1808 report of the case *R* v. *Samuel Shakespeare* informs us that the defendant was indicted in the name "Shakepear" on a charge of assault.[9] "Shakepear" and "Shakespeare" look the same at first glance, but the eye is easily deceived. Sounded aloud, they are unmistakably distinct, and Mr Shakespeare was therefore able to avoid the indictment by pleading the principle *idem sonans* (same sound). By this doctrine, a person's identity can be presumed known in law despite a misspelling only if the misspelled version is pronounced substantially alike to the name correctly spelled. In the exercise of homophonia, the eye as supervisor of the ear and the ear as superauditor of the eye grapple hand-to-hand, eye-to-eye, ear-to-ear, eye-to-ear, and ear-to-eye. The coined word "ghoti" (dubiously attributed to George Bernard Shaw) shows how playful the tension can be, and how mischievous. It is a homophone of "fish" (pronouncing "gh" as in "cough"; "o" as in "women"; and, "ti" as in "nation"). The technique achieves what might seem impossible, which is to make this jurist almost completely silent. If we pronounce "Gary" with the G in "light", the second A in "romantically" and the first R in "surprise", the sound of the name disappears leaving us with a "Y". It is only that final letter that resists our pitch for perfect silence, and in combination with the surname "Watt" the whole would have been fittingly inquisitorial were not the final "Y" in fact pronounced as "E".

Unless the eye is closed and the ear is stuffed, there is no way to bar admittance to visual and aural stimuli. When judges, having heard an argument, say that they cannot hear it, what they really mean to say is that they cannot attend to it. The truth is that they can hear, and even when they silence a submission pre-emptively before it is sounded, they have the physical capacity to hear. They just will not (and perhaps justly cannot) attend to it. On one occasion, Mr Justice Kekewich interrupted a new QC who was not dressed in proper form: "I can't hear you, Mr. Carson", he said, "But I don't propose to send you home to put on your knee-breeches, as perhaps I should". "I should hope *not*", retorted

9 *R.* v. *Shakespeare* (1808) 10 East 83, 84.

Carson, which elicited a petulant response from the judge: "I warn you I shall tolerate no impertinence". Carson had the last word: "I thought your lordship could not hear me".[10] The same is true of visual stimuli. The eyes of the law are always open. The law sees everything, which is the very reason why the law must fabricate sightlessness by blindfolding itself whenever it wants to bar admittance to unwanted visual stimuli.[11] A visual twin to the auditory anecdote just cited is the following exchange between Mr Justice Croom-Johnson (C-J) and Mr Fearnley-Whittingstall (F-W). C-J: "I cannot see you, Mr Fearnley-Whittingstall."; F-W: "My Lord, I am before you wigged and gowned."; C-J: "I still cannot see you, Mr Fearnley-Whittingstall."; F-W: "My Lord, is it my yellow waistcoat that you cannot see?"; C-J: "Yes, it is."; F-W: "Well, my Lord, you can see me."[12]

The communal and choral erudition or ear-audition of the common law echoes a very ancient association between sound and song and law. Aristotle asked "Why are the nomoi that people sing so called?", and wondered if it is "because before they knew how to write, they sang their laws, so as not to forget them".[13] I have suggested that one aspect of just listening (I mostly mean "just" in the ethical sense) is the conscious act of engaging in the struggle between sound and sight, between tone and note, but Aristotle makes an even bolder claim for the inherent ethics of the heard. He poses this problem: "Why does what is heard, alone of perceptible objects, possess ethical character?".[14] The premise of his question is supported by the observation that "even if a melody is without words, it nonetheless possesses ethical character".[15] For Aristotle, sound is ethical even in the absence of the word; it is ethos independent

10 Based on the account in H. Montgomery Hyde, *Carson* (London, Heinemann, 1953).

11 On "The Paradox of Justitia's Transparent Blindfold", see Valérie Hayaert, "Justice" in P. Goodrich (ed.), *A Cultural History of Law in The Early Modern Age* (London, Bloomsbury, 2019), 28–29. Also, Valérie Hayaert, *Lady Justice: An Anatomy of Allegory* (Edinburgh, Edinburgh University Press, 2023).

12 J. Pugh, *Goodbye for Ever – The Victim of a System* (London, Barry Rose, 1981), 27–28 (reproduced in M. Gilbert (ed.), *The Oxford Book of Legal Anecdotes* (Oxford, Oxford University Press, 1986), 119. For bringing this anecdote (and the one in the previous footnote) to my attention, I am grateful to my colleague John Snape.

13 Aristotle *Problems*, Volume I Books 1–19 by Robert Mayhew (ed and trans) Aristotle Volume XV Loeb Classical Library 316 (Cambridge, MA, Harvard University Press, 2011), book XIX, problem 28.

14 Ibid., book XIX, Problem 27.

15 Ibid.

of logos. Having posed the problem, he posits a possible solution in these terms:

> Is it because (what is heard) alone possesses movement, though not that which the sound moves in us? ... This movement has a likeness (to ethical character) both in the rhythms and in the arrangement of high and low notes, not in their mixture. But consonance has no ethical character. ... these movements are connected with action, and actions are signs of ethical character.[16]

Word play in the context of script and speech is an exercise in pliability. It is a type of movement between the contrary pleadings of sight and sound. How is a jurist to fulfil the vocation inherent in their office if they lack the skill to stretch a word; if they lack the playful spirit that can open an ear to a mouth, and open up a word to a world of potential meanings? A lawyer's task, often against the contracting instinct of the law, is to stretch a text on tenterhooks, to hold at once all poetic possibilities of a word, to draw each strand taut so that it will hold a tone, and to harp on the whole to produce a harmony of opposing parts between opposing parties. A lawyer should be a lyre in other words.

Within the strand or string of each word, the smallest fibre is the letter. Letters, even more than words, present a special challenge to the ear. Letters are seldom heard as free-standing acoustic features of speech. They are almost invariably features of written script and therefore have a peculiarly strong hold on our visual imagination. Letters empower the eye and amplify its dominance over the ear. Presented with a seemingly arbitrary jumble of letters, we are imaginatively predisposed to assemble them into words according to remembered precedents. The operation of the eye and the mind is intuitively anagrammatic. We do not permit letters to remain isolated and independent, but incorporate them into the existing frames and sequences of remembered words; or it may be more accurate to say that remembered words will not let us hold letters in free-floating form. Through the power of sight and remembrance, letters and words conspire against our unprejudiced judgment. As legal cases demand to be built into the body of the Lex, upper-case and lower-case letters compel us to incorporate them into the body of an existing lexicon. The word commands that its letters, the fragmentary members scrabbled before our eyes, should be re-membered as parts of its body. There is little that our minds can do to resist the prejudice that binds us to the precedent of the word. The satirical songster Tim Minchin

16 Ibid.

demonstrates the deceiving power of scattered letters in his song "Prejudice". He may be the preeminent musical letter-smith at work today, having also written "The Alphabet Song" for the musical *Matilda* based on Roald Dahl's eponymous book. Minchin's "Prejudice" can be accessed on YouTube and, first time through, is best appreciated with ears open and eyes closed. The lyric includes the following lines: "In our modern free-spoken society / There is a word that we still hold taboo", "A couple of Gs, an R and an E, an I and an N / Just six little letters all jumbled together". As we listen to the song with eyes closed, we never see the letters in physical or visual form, but we see them in our mind's eye even as they come to us through the ear. We imagine them as image, and we picture them anagrammatically. Our subconscious spells out the whole from the parts. Having heard Minchin's "Prejudice", which presents the letters of a word that should not be spoken, you may conclude that the letter, conceived as a silent scripted element, is a particularly powerful deceiver of the eye, and that the eye distracted by the letter is particularly powerless to see the whole truth. (For the avoidance of YouTube, the whole truth of the red-headed Minchin's "Prejudice" is the word "GINGER".)

The eye is famously unreliable as a witness to "the truth". This is in part because of the deceiving dominance of our sense of sight. Psychological "confirmation bias" predisposes us to the prejudicial expectation that the thing we have been habituated to see through past experience is the thing that we are seeing now. Richard Wiseman, a Professor of Psychology, conducted a nationwide experiment in the United Kingdom in search of practical clues to spotting a liar. First in his list of conclusions is this advice: "Don't look at a liar, just listen":

> It transpired that people were better lie detectors when they just heard the soundtrack or read the transcript. Those who watched it on television struggled to detect the lies. This is because visual cues distract us from what is being said and good liars can control their body language more easily than their voice. So, if you want to spot a liar, don't look at them. Listen to what they say and how they say it. If you want to distinguish fact from fiction then radio, not TV or video, is your friend...[17]

The psychological capacity of sight to deceive the ear is demonstrated dramatically by the "McGurk Effect".[18] The best way to approach it is

17 *The Life Scientific* (BBC Radio 4) 1 October 2019.
18 Rosenblum, "Your Brain Hears the Speech You See", n.7 above.

to watch it performed on video.[19] The McGurk Effect stimulates the eye with the sight of a person silently and repeatedly mouthing one carefully selected syllable (say "va") while the sound of another syllable (say "ba") is simultaneously and repeatedly voiced. Remarkably, the brain hears the syllable that is silently mouthed and cannot hear the syllable that is actually being uttered. It has to be experienced to be believed, and, even then, the psychological effect is so strong that it defies our conscious cognitive effort to overcome it. The McGurk effect demonstrates the dominance of visual stimuli over acoustic stimuli, although curiously the visual stimulus in this case triggers the auditory part of the brain. It might be said that hearing (not the ear) is monarch in the McGurk effect, but that the eye, like a sort of court jester, conjures a visual trick that fools the monarch into perceiving an acoustic stimulus that is not actually present.

In some contexts, one can discipline oneself to counter the bias of the eye. The first lesson for the novice in graphic art wherein accurate (and in that limited sense "true") representation is required is to "draw what you see, not what you think you see". One may be prejudiced to draw a symmetrical human face, but look again – is that face really symmetrical? Is any? Stephen A. Kliment makes the point in his book *Architectural Sketching and Rendering: Techniques for Designers and Artists*:

> You must realize as early as possible that you should draw what you see, not what you think you see. This is all that true drawing really is: training yourself to see accurately and then putting down on paper, without any false representation.[20]

"False representation" – the artist's call to challenge the natural prejudice of the eye might almost become a programme for attuned advocacy and sound judgment in a court of law. Despite the visive etymology of our word "evidence", the unreliability of eye-witnessing is a commonplace tenet of forensic contexts. In many crimes, sight and spectacle are the chief suspects.[21] It was perhaps to counter doubts about eyewitness

19 Many demonstrations are available on YouTube, including one from the BBC programme *Horizon* that features Lawrence D. Rosenblum (ibid.).

20 *Architectural Sketching and Rendering: Techniques for Designers and Artists* (New York, Whitney Library of Design, 1984), 41.

21 The unreliability of eyewitnesses is of special concern in criminal contexts, especially where the death penalty is involved. See, for example, Steven Penrod, "Eyewitness Identification Evidence – How Well Are Witnesses and Police Performing?" (2003) 18 *Crim Just* 36.

accounts that the gospel report of the first witness of Jesus' bodily resurrection was given to the ears and not to the eyes of Mary Magdalene. Her eyes blinded by tears, she recognises Jesus only when she hears His familiar voice.[22] Even doubting Thomas, who would not believe in the resurrection without seeing the evidence, did not feel secure in sight alone, but would only be satisfied if he could physically touch the truth of it: "Except I shall see on his hands the print of the nails, and put my finger into the print of the nails, and thrust my hand into his side, I will not believe".[23] Thomas insisted on proving it in the original etymological sense of probing it. In that episode, Jesus blessed those who do not base their faith upon visual evidence alone.[24] Elsewhere, He exhorts caution in hearing too, with such sayings as "Take heede therefore how yee heare",[25] and "Whoever has ears, let them hear".[26] The latter alludes to a distinction between hearing words spoken and actually attending to what is said; a distinction not dissimilar to the one advanced when a judge refuses to "hear" a submission that he or she has already heard. Cardozo hoped that the judge's "priestly ears" might be opened "to the call of other voices".[27]

It is somewhat ironic that the Thomas episode, with its cautionary critique of faith based on sight, has become a popular subject of hagiographical pictorial art. In the ecclesiastic traditions of the Roman Catholic Church, the sight of the image of Christ, far from being suppressed, has attained parity with, if not primacy over, the sound of His voice. (The dominance of the image may be even greater in the iconographical tradition of the Eastern Orthodox Church.) It was not until the early modern period, and the Puritan movement in Protestantism, that iconoclastic suspicion of the sign replaced Roman Catholic regard and respect for the eye with a new pitch of deference to the ear. In seventeenth-century England, there was a remarkable proliferation of Protestant prescriptive texts on listening.[28] Amongst the myriad tracts

22 John 20: 14-16.

23 John 20:25. On Thomas's touch, see Subha Mukherji, "'O, she's warm': Evidence, Assent, and the Sensory Numinous in Shakespeare and his World" in Robin Macdonald et al (eds.), *Sensing the Sacred in Medieval and Early Modern Culture* (Abingdon, Routledge, 2018), 183–201.

24 John 20:29.

25 Luke 8:18.

26 Matthew 11:15; 13:9.

27 Note 5 above.

28 See Ceri Sullivan, "The Art of Listening in the Seventeenth Century" (2006) 104(1) *Modern Philology* 34–71. See, also, Jennifer Rae McDermott, "'The Melodie of Heaven': Sermonizing the Open Ear in Early Modern England" in

are such diverting titles as *A Jewell for the Eare* (Robert Wilkinson, 1605), *The Difference of Hearers* (William Harrison, 1614), and, a personal favourite, *The Boring of the Eare* (1623) (the title plays on the piercing of the outer ear and piercing to the inner sense of hearing). Referring to the author of that treatise, Abigail Shinn notes that for the clergyman Stephen Egerton, "the ear is the link to the heart".[29] She quotes his opinion that "to hear. . .is to attend with the eare, to receiue with the heart, to conuert in the life and conuersation, else our sinfull soules can never be healed".[30]

The Protestant iconoclastic project has had limited success. The power of the sign still overpowers the quiet sound of the voice within the word. As Paul Ricoeur puts it, "we have not finished doing away with *idols* and we have barely begun to *listen* to symbols".[31] Not that image and sound are the only sensory stimuli, nor sight and hearing the only senses. Matthew Milner observes that "sixteenth-century religion was more than eyes and ears; it was a full, synesthetic experience".[32] Sight and hearing tend to dominate discussion of the senses, and the struggle between them is our main subject here, but it is important always to consider them in the context of what we might call "whole body" or "synesthetic" sensation. Returning to Aristotle, we will recall that, for him, sound – especially of the musical variety – demonstrated ethical character through movement, both in terms of rhythm and in terms of the structural arrangement of musical elements. There is, I would suggest, a strongly spatial and embodied quality to this ethical appreciation of music. Form and movement of sound appeal because they engender in us a sympathetic dancing in the spirit. The instinctive tapping of the toe signals our subconscious assent. Something like this thought might have prompted Aristotle to take an interesting step from the claim that musical sound has ethical character to the suggestion that the movement inherent in music makes it not only ethically good but aesthetically pleasurable. He asks, "Why does everyone enjoy rhythm and melody and in general all concords?". He wonders if it is "because we naturally

---

Weistse de Boer and Christine Göttler (eds.), *Religion and the Senses in Early Modern Europe* (Leiden, Brill, 2012), 177–198.

29 "The senses and the seventeenth-century English conversion narrative" in Macdonald et al, *Sensing the Sacred*, note 21 above, 99–116.

30 Stephen Egerton, *The Boring of the Eare Contayning a Plaine and Profitable Discourse by Way of Dialogue. . .* (London, 1623), A4r.

31 Paul Ricoeur, *Freud and Philosophy: An Essay on Interpretation* (New Haven, Yale University Press, 1970), 27.

32 Matthew Milner, *The Senses and the English Reformation* (Farnham, Ashgate, 2011), 6.

enjoy natural movements?",[33] and concludes that "we enjoy rhythm because it has a recognizable and orderly number and moves us in an orderly fashion; for orderly movement is naturally more akin to us than disorderly movement, and so is more natural".[34]

The observation that ordered movement is more natural to us than disorderly movement and is therefore more pleasant and appealing has the potential to say something about humans' natural attraction to regularity in the form of music and of law.[35] Could the appeal of rhythmic sound and the appeal of regulated social life have something to do with the fact that rhythmic sound and regulated life are in some sense naturally occurring? Even the fact that law (and music) is human-made and in that sense "artificial" need not detract from the possibility that the best-made law (and music) is that which chimes with us as something speaking directly out of nature to our human natures. The point is epitomised in the art of poetry, kindred both to law and music, which by its etymology announces itself as an art of making (*poiesis*).[36] Bernard J. Hibbitts makes the point that: "Early Greek law depended heavily on performances that implicated the ear as much as the eye; it was routinely understood as having intimate ties to oral poetry, and even music".[37] Shakespeare's poetry is exemplary of the intimacy of nature and art. When his characters speak in regular iambic pentameter, their language is in one sense artificial and crafted because the metrical verse conforms to a regular rhythmic form. Yet, despite being formally more artificial than prose, verse appeals to us as being more natural than prose. The metre has musicality and seems to flow mellifluously. It is sweet on the tongue of the speaker and seductive to the ear of the hearer. No one would deny that honey is perfectly natural despite the extreme regularity of the honeycomb and the orderly dance by which the bee in the factory of the hive turns nectar into strange new stuff. Like honey, rhythm in

33 Problem 38.
34 Ibid.
35 See further, Gary Watt, "Law Making Music" (2020) 14:1 *Law and Humanities* 26–56.
36 See, generally, Gary Watt, *The Making Sense of Politics, Media, and Law: Rhetorical Performance as Invention, Creation, Production* (Cambridge, Cambridge University Press, 2023).
37 Bernard J. Hibbitts, "The Metaphor is the Message: Visuality, Aurality and the Reconfiguration of American Legal Discourse" (1995) 8 (22) *International Journal for the Semiotics of Law* 53–86, 58. See, further, P. Murray and P. Wilson, *Music and the Muses: The Culture of Mousike in the Classical Athenian City* (Oxford, Oxford University Press, 2010), and M. P. Mittica, "When the World was Mousiké: On the Origins of the Relationship between Law and Music" (2015) 9(1) *Law and Humanities* 29–54, 53.

music and poetry can be considered natural despite its patently artificial nature. Consider the regular iambic pentameter of Shakespearean blank verse. The five-fold repetition of the di-syllabic foot "da-DUM" is formal, stylistic, and artificial, but it naturally appeals to us. This may be because, with a stressed beat following the unstressed, it echoes the "'lub-DUB'" double beat of the human heart. Not only that, but the repeated double rhythm of the iambic foot echoes the paired steps of human feet as they walk "left-right", "left-right". The heartbeat cannot be called an "action" in the sense that Aristotle employs that idea, but the artificial process by which humans express naturally occurring rhythms in the form of poetic metre can claim to have ethical character and to please because it is mimetically in tune with the embodied metronome of human nature. Where the rhythm is regular it operates like a natural law that feels just and right because it is fundamentally in tune with the pulse of humanity. Appreciated in this way, listening has the potential to become a discipline or exercise in attuning to, of sounding out, a felt sense of justice. As David Levin writes, "development of our capacity for listening exercises and develops our (bodily felt) sense of justice. The primary sense of justice is not seeing, but hearing".[38]

In his *Sylva sylvarum*, Francis Bacon attributes a deeper level of visceral and embodied affect to sound than to sight:

> Harsh sounds, as of … grinding of one Stone against another … make a shivering or horror in the Body, and set the Teeth on edge. The *Cause* is, for that the *Objects* of the *Eare*, doe affect the *Spirits* (immediately) most with *Pleasure* and Offence. We see there is no *Colour* that affecteth the *Eye* much with *Displeasure*. There be *Sights* that are *Horrible*, because they excite the *Memory of Things* that are *Odious* or *Fearefull*; But the same *Things Painted*, doe little affect, by a *Participation* or *Impulsion* of the *Body*, of the *Object*. So it is *Sound* alone that doth immediately and incorporeally affect most.[39]

He is surely picking up on Aristotle's theme of ethical music when he writes that:

> It hath been anciently held, and observed, that the *Sense of Hearing*, and the *Kinds of Musick*, have most Operation upon *Manners*; As

38 *The Listening Self: Personal Growth, Social Change and the Closure of Metaphysics* (Abingdon, Routledge, 1989), 184; cited in Richard Dawson "Listening" in *Justice as Attunement* (Abingdon, Routledge, 2014), 163–169.

39 Francis Bacon, *Sylva Sylvarum: Or a Naturall Historie. In Ten Centuries* (London, John Haviland, for William Lee, 1635), 700.

> to Incourage Men, and make them warlike; To make them Soft and Effeminate; To make them Grave; To make them Light; To make them Gentle and inclined to Pitty.[40]

Aristotle attributed the ethical effect of music to the movement inherent in its rhetorically stirring figures, rhythms, melodies and harmonies. Bacon, similarly, attributes music's effect on ethics or manners (that it makes men "Gentle and inclined to Pitty") to the way in which it strikes us, in other words to the manner in which its movement moves us: "The *Cause* is, for that the *Sense of Hearing* striketh the *Spirits* more immediately, than the other *Senses*".[41]

Thomas Wilson also saw in rhetorical persuasion the hope of "moving pity, and stirryng menne to mercy". Wilson was writing in connection with the rhetorician's art of rousing sympathy or fellow-feeling (what rhetoricians term "pathos"), and his advice was to evoke in the judge a recollection of the judge's own suffering so that the judge will incline to sympathise with the suffering of the lawyer's client – "that by hearing their awne, thei maie the better hearken to others".[42]

Eye is enthroned in the brain (bra-i-n); ear is enthroned in the heart (h-ear-t). This is playful, but there's a point to it. The heart is the seat of our interior sounds; the pounding of the pulse. It is involuntary. It is unwilled. It is the wild nature of sound within us. James Boyd White wrote that 'the heart of law is ... the open hearing'.[43] We might say that hearing our heartbeat is a sort of law within us. It regulates. It drums out a rhythm that we feel and hear constantly; even when, which is most of the time, we are not conscious of it. Iambic pentameter has the same pulse. Lawyers may consider themselves paramount amongst the professions when it comes to precision in the way they work with words, but the truth is that few jurists are aware of how profoundly words are always at work on the lawyer. It is to open jurists up to receive and perceive what they do not see or hear (or otherwise sense) that an interdisciplinary approach is essential. Lawyers, if they are to work in the smithy of English words, should apprentice themselves to the great poets, of whom none is greater than Shakespeare. Consider the following lines from the start of a speech by Bassanio in *The Merchant of Venice*:

40 Ibid, 114.

41 Ibid.

42 Thomas Wilson, *The Arte of Rhetorique* (London, 1553), Page t1r.

43 James Boyd White, *When Words Lose Their Meaning: Constitutions and Reconstitutions of Language, Character, and Community* (Chicago, University of Chicago Press, 1984), 273.

So may the outward shows be least themselves.
The world is still deceived with ornament.
In law, what plea so tainted and corrupt
But, being seasoned with a gracious voice,
Obscures the show of evil? ... (3.2.73–7)

What strikes us first? What strikes us most? Is it the sight of the words? Is it the logical sense of the words? Do the decorative figures drawn by the poet seduce our eyes and deceive our judgment? The argument of the lines is curiously synesthetic, for it uses visual language of "ornament" and "show" to describe the seductive power of sweet-sounding speech. *The Garden of Eloquence*, being the title of Henry Peacham's 1577 manual or treatise of rhetorical style, was written within the same early modern cultural tendency to appreciate rhetorical acoustic effects in terms more usually associated with senses other than sound. To describe rhetorical sound effects as flowers in a garden, or as figures of speech, tells us a great deal about their decorative and ornamental operation, but is curiously coy as to the acoustic or musical methods by which rhetoric operates. In fact, although the early modern rhetoricians attributed rhetorical persuasion to some degree to gesture and dress and to other visible devices, they understood well that the power of rhetoric is nowhere more potent than in its sound effects. Thus George Puttenham, in his essay "Of Ornament" (being the third book of *The Arte of English Poesie*), describes the Gallic Hercules "with a long chayne tyed by one end at his tong, by the other end at the peoples eares, who stood afarre of and seemed to be drawen to him by the force of that chayne fastned to his tong, as who would say, by force of his perswasions".[44] Puttenham might have been inspired by the emblem in Andrea Alciato, *Toutes Les Emblemes* that depicts Hercules drawing listeners on by means of golden chains connecting their ears to his tongue.[45] The legend informs us that "*Eloquence est plus excellente que force*" [eloquence is better than force]. Puttenham, in turn, might have inspired Thomas Dekker whose play *If It Be Not Good, The Diuel Is In It* (1612) contains a prologue in which we learn that the playwright

44 George Puttenham, *The Arte of English Poesie* (1589) (Kent, OH, Kent State University Press, 1971), 154. On this image, see Piyel Haldar, "The Tongue and the Eye: Eloquence and Office in Renaissance Emblems" in P. Goodrich and V. Hayaert (eds.), *Genealogies of Legal Vision* (Abingdon, Routledge, 2015), 152–178, 164.

45 Lyons, Guillaume Rouillé, 1558. The emblem is discussed in Haldar, "The Tongue and the Eye", 152–178, 164.

aspired to be that sort of poet who "Can call the banish'd auditor home, and tie / His ear, with golden chains, to his melody" (Prologue, 177–8).

Consider those lines of Shakespeare again, but this time try reading them aloud. Attend less to the showy consonants that are struck by teeth and plucked by lips and listen more to the jaw and the breath as together they bellow, stretch, and forge the vowels. Make of the vowels an acoustic chain from mouth to ear. Do you notice any repeated pattern in the links? Try voicing the vowels aloud without the consonants.[46] The lines are set out again, next, with one repeated vowel sound amplified by underlining (on paper the visual note is necessary). The syllable that I have selected is the weighty sound of "or"; a phoneme that connects our current concern with law, the oral and the aural. With the marked rhoticity of original Elizabethan pronunciation, "or" would have been "orrr".[47] The sound is grave and profound, and Shakespeare uses it to great effect to sound out hidden depths.

So may the outward shows be least themselves.
The w<u>or</u>ld is still deceived with <u>or</u>nament.
In l<u>aw</u>, what plea so tainted and c<u>or</u>rupt
But, being seasoned with a gracious voice,
Obsc<u>ures</u> the show of evil? .... (3.2.73–7)

Today we would include the "war" in "outward" as a phoneme that rhymes with "or", but in Shakespeare's day that would have more closely rhymed with the modern pronunciation of the word "far".[48] Other vowel sounds are repeated in this one short passage of verse – including the "aye" sound in "may"; the "o" sound in "so"; and the "ee" sound in "least". The latter is particularly impressive. The lines are set out again next, this time with the "ee" phoneme underlined. (The closing words – "in religion" – that make up the final line of the extract have been omitted because they start a new long sentence within which the "ee" sound is not repeated.)

So may the outward shows be l<u>ea</u>st themselves.
The world is still dec<u>ei</u>ved with ornament.

46 This is a standard rehearsal technique in Shakespearean acting. See Patsy Rodenburg, *Speaking Shakespeare* (London, Bloomsbury, 2002), 88. In the same book, the author advises that "listening" is "the first and last thing you must do. You must practice listening, not to your voice, but to the outside world" (69).

47 David Crystal, *The Oxford Dictionary of Original Shakespearean Pronunciation* (Oxford, Oxford University Press, 2016).

48 Crystal, note 43 above.

In law, what plea so tainted and corrupt
But, being seasoned with a gracious voice,
Obscures the show of evil? .... (3.2.73–7)

The "ee" sound appears in line one at beat 8 of 10, in line two at beat 6 of 10, in line three at beat 4 of 10, in line four at beat 2 of 10 and 4 of 10, and in line five at beat 6 of 10. Thus, with a sequence of 8-6-4-2-4-6, it moves through the pentameter like a wave. In the fourth line, the double "ee" at beats 2 and 4 produces a sort of rebound sensation that sets up the "ee" in the final, dramatic word, "evil". The verse has a heart. It has a pulse. It has all those essential qualities that for Aristotle speak of order, music, movement, ethos, and pleasure. Shakespeare has a genius way of fitting sound to sense, and here, in a sermon on the deceiving power of sensual stimuli, a secreted sound slips in under our radar. We are subconsciously seduced by the appeal of Shakespeare's musical verse, and the sweet seasoning we swallow is only revealed, at last, and too late, to have been "evil" all along. The lines are also, of course, addressed specifically to the pleasing and deceiving power of lawyers' pleading in a play that culminates in Portia's deceptive speech about mercy delivered right before she inflicts her merciless revenge on Shylock.

Peter Goodrich, building on the classical view that ideal architecture should combine parts within an organic whole as the human body does (for which the renaissance paradigm is Alberti's *De re aedificatoria*), observes that "The Inns of Court were built in the medieval era of organic architecture and take the shape of an ear, a space of audition".[49] The visible, external ear is curious for it is merely a gateway to the real seat of hearing, which is the inner ear. In this it parallels the law, which through its architectural edifices displays grand external orifices that promise open access to its offices, whereas the real business of hearing takes place (if it takes place at all) within the secreted inner chambers of the edifice.[50] Franz Kafka's fable "Vor dem Gesetz"',[51] set before the door of the law, concludes when the doorkeeper perceives that the man seeking justice "is at the end of his strength and his hearing is failing, so he bellows in his ear: 'No one but you could gain admittance through this door, since this door was intended only for you. I am now going to shut it.'"[52] Even within the inner chamber, where the legal hearing takes place, there is a further barrier to overcome in the judges' capacity

49 Goodrich, "The Great Dialogue", n.2 above, 4.

50 Citing David Evans, "The Theatre of Deferral: The Image of The Law and the Architecture of the Inns of Court" (1999) 10 *Law and Critique* 1–25, 14–15.

51 *Almanach dem Neuer Dichtung* (Leipzig, Kurt Wolff Verlag, 1916).

52 Evans, "Deferral", note 49 above, 24.

to deafen themselves legally to arguments that they have heard physically (the very point we discussed earlier in connection with the judicial statement "I cannot hear that argument"). The so-called "inner ear" is actually just an outer portal to the sensory faculty of the brain, and the brain is subject (in the matter of judgment) to the will of the mind. In connection with the (only somewhat) different context of listening to religious sermons, Federico Visconti makes reference to our *inner*-inner ears as ears 'of the mind' (*aures Mentis*).[53] Our sensory judge – the common sense that presides judicially over the full range of sensory stimuli – has its judgment seat in the innermost chamber of the mind. When it falls to a jurist to make sense of a statute, the challenge is to achieve a sort of meeting of minds. The thing that parliament had in mind when it expressed its will in the words of the statute must encounter judgment seated in the inner chamber of the interpreter's mind. With something like this thought, Edmund Plowden reports the following opinion of Chief Justice Saunders concerning statutory interpretation:

> Car parols, que nesont auter q*ue* le verberation del ayer, ne sont lesstatut, mes solement le Image del estatute, & le vye del estatute rest en les ments del expositors del parols, queur sont les feasors del estatutes.
>
> [Because words, which are nothing other than the verberation of the air, are not the statute, but only the image of the statute, and the life of the statute resides in the minds of the expositors of words, that is, the makers of the statutes.][54]

"Verberation" – what a wonderful, evocative and resonant word that is. Chief Justice Saunders expresses beautifully the nature of the word (*verbum*) as an acoustic event and the demand that is made upon a judge to sound the depths of the stimulus to find in it the mind of the maker; the demand, in other words, to render a fair hearing.

In terms reminiscent of Aristotle's idea of the "golden mean", the thirteenth-century preacher William Peraldus advanced an idea of virtuous common sense as a way of tempering the excessive influence of individual senses. Richard Newhauser explains that

53 Nicole Bériou et al, *Les Sermons et la Visite Pastorale de Federico Visconti, Archevêque de Pise (1253-1277)* (Rome, École Française de Rome, 2001), 474, 530. Cited in John H. Arnold, "*Problems of Sensory History and The Medieval Laity*" in Macdonald "*Sensing the Sacred*", note 21 above, 19–38, 24.

54 Holger Schott Syme, "The Look of Speech" (2007) 2(2) *Textual Cultures* 34–60, 43. The reference is to Plowden 1578 (STC 20041), signature Xii^{r}.

> The emphasis in Peraldus's examination lies not on padlocking the gateways to sensation, but on guiding the senses to reach a harmonious midpoint between excess and a harmful avoidance of sensory pleasure. As he further explains by appealing to auditory perception, disproportionate and unrelieved rigour in matters of the senses must be avoided if the pleasantness of virtue is to be achieved: "It is the same with the strings of a harp: if they are tightened too little, they make a grating noise; if too much, they break; but if [done] moderately, they give a sweet sound".[55]

The office of the jurist calls for a critical synesthetic, and this requires, not least, the practical common sense to be watchful, to hear, and to hold a balance between the excessive urgings of both sight and sound.

55 Richard Newhauser, "*Virtus regens animam*: William Peraldus on Guiding the Pleasures of the Senses" in MacDonald et al, "*Sensing the Sacred*" note 21 above, 39–59, 43.

Chapter 11

The office of reviewer

Anthony Carty

The reviewing of legal writing has now overtaken the exercise of legal writing itself. There appears to be no doubt that blind peer review is a totally reliable indicator of the creditworthiness of a written work. One recently used model lists the criteria, which are mostly formal and logical, concerned with consistency and clarity. However, there are certain evaluative, subjective elements. The article should be 'a valuable contribution to the relevant research field', and must 'make a real contribution to the field of study'. One must ask, 'is the language sufficient for publication in an academic law journal?' And especially, 'is it a solid academic manuscript; aware of recent scholarship ... showing detailed knowledge of primary sources and demonstrating mastery of the subject?' Finally, worth mentioning is the question of whether the work is in any way offensive or libelous. Much of these criteria alert one to the institutionalization and professionalization (read bureaucratization?) of knowledge, but much is purely evaluative; literally, is the work valuable or, alternatively, offensive in any way?

Blind or confidential review also plays a major role in promotion and tenure assessment, itself now, at least in the UK, strongly influenced by the even more institutionally powerful process of central research assessment. For promotion to professor one is asked to assess whether the work is A World Leading, B Internationally Excellent, C Internationally Recognized, D Does not meet the above criteria. Capitals are used for all words in the first three categories. There is further elaboration of these criteria in a document known as Promotion Benchmarks and Criteria (Academic). Here the criteria become more involved. They range from Assistant Professor grade 8 to Associate Professor grade 9, Professor Band 1, grade 10, to Professor Band 2, grade 10 to Professor Band 3, grade 10. Every grade requires some work, i.e. academic output, which is recognized as world class. However, at the full professor range, the work must also be world leading and world changing, providing leadership within and/or beyond the academy. Finally, at the top, one should

DOI: 10.4324/9781003659754-13

show an outstanding contribution to world leading and world changing research, including successful management of significant research programs. While these criteria are taken at random from a particular English university one may suppose that they are standard for every single academic possessing a university chair in the UK. They are one and all quite simply world leading and world changing; not merely once in a lifetime but on every occasion they crawl up the ladder from different levels within grade 10. This means a country with a population of just under 68 million has literally thousands of academics who all have a world leading and world changing impact upon the world population of just under 7.6 billion people. (Of course as one will see later with explanations of REF criteria, the word 'world' is probably being used metaphorically). As it turned out the candidate under review produced the required four large pieces all of which consistently argued that every issue of public policy was entirely a matter of opinion. Good research required the closest and most exhaustive collection of all opinions from all persons and groups, however different and distinct, after which it was the task of the public lawyer to ensure that Democratic instruments were found to guarantee that every opinion was equally heard and given maximum effect. There was no place for qualitative evaluation of anything. The reviewer could only respond that this was unobjectionable, without adding that he thought he had been consulted because he had been rather liberal in expressing plenty of qualitative views on issues covered by the candidate. Obviously, such qualification of the reviewer's views would not have helped the candidate.

So, it might appear that those who enjoy the role of academic reviewer in Britain, which is also typical at least of all Anglo-American universities, possess a simply stupendous status, overseeing a constant and astronomical scale of world leading and world changing academic activity, all of which is immensely valuable, completely inoffensive, logical, consistent and shows clear mastery of the subject, including all of its primary sources. The status of the reviewer has never been higher and is rising exponentially with every day that he/she recognizes new material. Of course, his/her standing is secret, but he/she knows of his/her weight with those who 'count', and even if that may not be exactly known, vague hints can be dropped and rumor will circulate fast.

Alasdair Macintyre is the standard authority on the problematic of professionalization of 'thinking' (Three Rival Versions of Moral Inquiry 1990). What he writes concerns primarily moral philosophy, but it is applicable to all of the social and human sciences. Philosophy in the 17th and 18th centuries was mainly outside the university, but in the course of the 18th and 19th centuries it became almost exclusively restricted to universities in Scotland, France and Germany and now most fully in the culturally dominant United States (Macintyre 158). This trend came to be rooted in a nominalist individualism, which separated the person from community and any sense of objective good, while taking the primary issue to be the upholding of moral duty against selfish interest. This moral science was assumed to be a separate branch of knowledge which a consensus of reasonable people could systematize from widely held views into a body as a set of rules which everyone could follow (ibid 177). These assumptions were the foundation for the volumes of the 9th edition of the *Encyclopedia Britannica* of the 1880s (ibid 32).

Macintyre takes a contemporary example of how this confident universalism actually works in practice in *The Cambridge History of Later Medieval Philosophy* of 1982, one more imitation of the *Cambridge Modern History* 'conceived by that exemplar of the Encyclopedic mind, Lord Acton' (ibid 160). The editors, in line with the modern demands of analytical philosophy, decided that the late medieval was primarily distinctive in the field of logic, so that the rest could be left aside (ibid 161). The assumption of the 9th edition remains that organized institutional inquiry could proceed as if there is an overall coherence to the academic project and a belief that every rationally defensible standpoint can engage with every other. Whatever the extent of incommensurability in theory, in so-called advanced societies 'the universal translatability of texts from any and every culture into the language of teacher and student is taken for granted' (ibid 171).

Focusing by way of example on the work of Henry Sidgwick (1906), a key figure in the 9th edition of the *Encyclopedia Britannica*, Macintyre earmarks his assumption that one can invoke the consensus of experts who will be able to reach an unconstrained agreement. In Sidgwick's view, what distinguished theology from the natural sciences was that the former relies upon forced religious tests, while the latter can reach an unconstrained consensus. He does not explain how this is reached. Instead, he reverses the order as a matter of belief. The belief is 'that consensus without either formal or informal tests is always a mark of rationality' (ibid 188). In fact, this consensus merely supposes a high degree of social and moral homogeneity which, in Macintyre's view, 'has rarely, if ever, been the case in later modern societies' (ibid). The fundamental feature of 'rule observance in such societies is "One *ought to* do such and such ... except in such and such a case"' (ibid). The correct formulation of the moral rule is in practice a matter of arbitrary individual preference as there are no criteria for determining what weight to give to particular matters that could affect the public good or happiness, since the latter is a matter of its significance to the individual, whose preferences will vary (ibid 187).

Macintyre's argument is obvious and yet distinctive because he applies it consequently to the whole field of academic, institutionalized intellectual inquiry and especially in the area of 'normative' matters such as morality. He himself provides a simple historical explanation. In classical thinking, the objective good was a matter of the place of persons in the hierarchy of community and the cosmos, whereas the essence of modernity is the autonomy of the individual and the inevitable freedom to differ which this has to entail (ibid 191–194). Macintyre is coming from Thomist-Aristotelian thought in making this argument and reinforces it with a Nietzschean genealogical critique of the exercise of autonomy as merely ideological rationalization (ibid 194).

Finally, this brings one to the 'office of the reviewer', apparently so augustly expounded in the above indicated 'criteria'. It is a most stringent necessity that his/her role ought to be diminished or diminishing all the time, because of the intellectual 'modernist' confusion with which he/she exercises her role. As each person learns to follow Kant's maxim of maturity in autonomy of thought – obliterating authority and tradition – we are invited each to go our separate ways. This is hardly itself a matter for comment. However, in the context of the ever more radicalized institutionalization of 'thinking', authority is being reasserted with consequences that are extremely serious for both individual 'careers' and the public expenditure of and public dependence upon education.

Indeed, 'liberal, modern thought' still assumes the impartiality and good faith of reviewers, since it is an axiom of modernity that people are naturally reasonable, once released from authority and tradition. Yet the reviewing process takes place in secret and is itself, notoriously, not reviewable. Given that what is at stake in reviewing is a very significant allocation of resources, one might have expected it to be obvious that what is in play is competition. Now there are available very dark interpretations of the nature of competition, such as that represented by Dany-Robert Dufour (*La Cite Perverse: Liberalisme et pornographie* 2009). From what is most likely an anti-modernist perspective – he prefers Augustine to Pascal, the latter already weakening in self-restraint – he prefers the Marquis de Sade to Adam Smith to understand the nature of competition in modern society. Far from complementing one another's resources in a win-win exchange, people prefer to dominate, consume and destroy one another, hence the exponential expansion of the economy and constantly increasing monopolization (Dufour, 165–185).

It is worth noting that at the very beginning of the struggle of Modernity with the Classical world, Jonathan Swift composed *The Battle of the Books*, which battle he supposed to be motivated by the same malice that governs all other human activity (1697). While some interpretations of his short text claim that he remains neutral in the battle, it appears that his description of the two sides suggests otherwise. Pride, lust and avarice are the grounds for literary, as for any other quarrels. The mark of the 'Modern' – speaking of the spider – is his pride in his autonomy, described by Swift as 'much of a nature and substance with a spider's poison; which however, they pretend to spit wholly out of themselves...' of which '...the materials be nothing but dirt, spun out of your own entrails (the guts of modern brains...)' (Jonathan Swift, Major Works, Oxford World Classics 2003, 10). In contrast, 'As for us the Ancients, we are content, with the bee, to pretend to nothing of our own beyond our wings and our voice, that is to say, our flights and our language ... For the rest ... ranging through every corner of nature ... instead of dirt and poison, we have rather chose to fill our hives with honey and wax, thus furnishing mankind with the two noblest of things, which are sweetness and light' (ibid). In contrast, what the Moderns boast to spit wholly out of themselves (as spiders) '...is improved by the same arts, by feeding upon the insects and vermin of the age' (ibid).

In what follows, two articles will be considered, in both of which the author has a vested or personal interest. The first concerns Neil Duxbury's article 'Post-Modern Jurisprudence and its Discontent', a review article published in the *Oxford Journal of Legal Studies* in vol. 11 no. 4 (Winter 1991), directed at my own edited volume: Anthony Carty, editor, *Post-Modern Law, Enlightenment, Revolution and the Death of Man* (Edinburgh University Press 1990). The passion of the opinions expressed in the review indicate that the reviewer considers the author (myself) irresponsible, and possibly even dangerous, at least to myself. The purpose of my commentary is to suggest that contemporary legal culture is too fragmented between the 'Modern' and the 'Post-Modern' for any reasonable commentary across the divide to be forthcoming. I will endeavor to show this by indicating, in my own case, that is, with respect to the introductory chapter and the chapter on Rousseau, Durkheim and Baudrillard, what the intellectual content was that the reviewer was effectively excluding from 'respectable' academic debate by publishing his diatribe in a supposedly reputable, learned legal journal: effectively an anathematization. This would hardly matter except for the ranking of the journal, which the wider academic legal community will suppose has standards of evaluation that should have consequences for the academic progression of at least junior legal scholars.

Duxbury begins by saying that a colleague of the reviewer (in Manchester University Law Faculty), on seeing the book, asked whether it was intended as a joke. Duxbury responds that it was not a joke but that particularly the editor wrote that post=modern jurisprudence delighted in parody and derision as an accompaniment of disillusion, all expressions of a *fin de siecle* atmosphere (589). These are not misquotations, but the assumption is clear that no 'reasonable' person could possibly hold such views. The Britain that has evolved from the premierships of Tony Blair to Boris Johnson remains as stable as the Rock of Gibraltar. There are no seeds of dementia lurking among the students in the corridors of Manchester and other British Law Faculties.

Parliaments will not be illegally – but good-humoredly – prorogued, nor international treaties torn up 'in derision'. The rule of law preached by Duxbury (his primary academic interest being the quality of judicial practice) and his humorless colleague will possibly have, with Duxbury himself, shaped the generation of 1990/2 that comes to govern us in the generation of 2020/2.

If one reflects more upon Boris Johnson's Britain, Duxbury may well retort that it is the post-modernists who have created the contradiction and chaos, rather than it being post-modernism which exposes in the 'silliness' of rationality the irrationalism which had been overlooked (590). At this point, Duxbury feels alarmed that the 'rationalist', having been deconstructed into an 'irrationalist', finds that 'irrationality' now stands for 'Enlightenment'. Therefore, the 'rationalist' is not confident enough to assert conclusively 'that post-modernism is a philosophy of nihilism' (590). This strategy of argument is, in Duxbury's eyes, not at all funny, but instead a form of trickery by the post-modernist. However, his reaction may be only because Duxbury is choosing (which Jonathan Swift considers the usual practice) to turn what he could have seen as a history of ideas into a personality clash between the 'mischievous' Mr. Post-modernist and the 'civilized' Mr. Rationalist.

Duxbury correctly identifies a key concern of mine as being whether law needs to have a foundation beyond itself. The key debate is around the social contract of Jean Jacques Rousseau. Here, the mischievous Mr. Post-modernist 'smacks of anti-intellectualism' (591), and indeed, reminds Duxbury of 'Thurman Arnold, and, in particular, of the fact that, by debunking legal symbols as the intellectually comforting devices of jurisprudential discourse, Arnold developed a brand of anti-intellectualism and nihilism which took him down a highly dubious political path' (592). This speculation about the future intellectual itinerary of mischievous Mr. Post-modern provides the latter with an opportunity not merely to try to unravel what civilized Mr. Rationalist is saying about his views but also to mention something of the 'dubious paths' he later followed – which might otherwise have been regarded as a defensive and irrelevant indulgence.

Duxbury says that my project is to show that while Enlightenment jurisprudence has sought to construct foundations to avoid the truth of irrationalism, the truth is that the only foundation of law is nothingness. There is no quotation for this assertion. It is Duxbury's take on the argument that a self-referential argument cannot provide a foundation. Duxbury correctly quotes me as asking 'how can something be the source of itself? ... (W)hy should the founding fathers give a law onto themselves?' (591). He recognizes that what I am doing is using the idea of nihilism as a heuristic device to reassert the ontological question, 'Why anything at all?' (591). Yet instead of making any reference to the chapter of the book in which I develop at length my own argument on this issue (Chapter 4, 'Post-Modernism in the Theory and Sociology of Law, or Rousseau and Durkheim as Read by Baudrillard'), Duxbury insinuates that my mystification with what Kelsen was trying to achieve with his Pure Theory of Law is what leads to his concern that I could go down the same pathway as the 'wretched' Thurman Arnold.

I have no idea who Arnold is, though Duxbury, a frequent author in the *Oxford Journal of Legal Studies,* has written something there. A brief look at Wikipedia suggests he was a vigorous enforcer of antitrust law who was removed from his post by Roosevelt in 1943 when the latter needed the unqualified support of corporate America in the arms race against Germany. Duxbury's references to my chapter are derisory quotes of a few words and phrases about ennui in jurisprudential debate and the need to 'quake' a dead discourse (589). The argument I developed through a very close reading of Rousseau's primary texts and through consideration of extensive English and French academic commentary was that Rousseau constructed a concept of the General Will of the People which deified the People in the place of the Christian idea of God. Durkheim continued in the same pathway with his idolization of Society as an objective being with its own internal logic and laws. Again, I draw on basic texts and multiple academic commentaries in English and French. I conclude with Baudrillard's contemporary deconstruction of these collective idols of People and Society in many of his works, but most clearly in his short essay *In the Shadow of the Silent Majorities.* All of this scholarship is erased by the spiderish rhetoric of Duxbury. Baudrillard's argument smacks of Old Testament Sodom and Gomorrah, visions that the success of advanced capitalist consumer society has reduced all human aspirations to the satisfaction of material desires, anxieties and whims. The public space is a matter entirely of a marketing style management of these desires, etc., reducing or raising (depending on one's view) all public law and human rights discourse to an indistinguishable media management exercise of these desires (see especially Jean Baudrillard *La Transparence du Mal* Galilee, 1990, and for a textbook version of much the same see Carty, *Philosophy of International Law,* 2017, 2nd edition, Edinburgh, 17–29).

I go on in subsequent scholarship to argue that the contractarian tradition in Anglo-American political philosophy, as it feeds into constitutional and international law theory, has led to a void of identity in the foreign and defense policies of Anglo-American societies (above all the US, the UK and Australia). I rely on the former Regius Chair of Moral Theology in Oxford, Oliver O'Donovan, for the linking argument that this void in the foundation of these political societies is what makes them among the most unstable and dangerous in present world society (see Carty, *Philosophy of International Law*, especially 71–72).

Eventually, curiosity got the better of me, and I decided to seek out Duxbury's 'exposure' of the 'dark fate' which befell Arnold. This meant reading 'Some Radicalism about Realism?: Thurman Arnold and the Politics of Modern Jurisprudence' (OJLS, 1990, vol. 10, 11). Again, it is difficult to analyze this article in terms of concepts because the idea of 'concept' is or seems alien to Duxbury. The world he inhabits is one of attitudes, preferences and, above all, social standing. His is an 'In-Out' or 'Upstairs-Downstairs' world. This world is described assiduously by Stefan Collini (obviously a person of foreign origin, however remote that origin) in his *Absent Minds, Intellectuals in Britain* (OUP, 2006). Collini explains A J Ayer's debunking of pontiffs who chase after concepts – which point to 'deep meaning', such as Hegel – and journeymen such as himself who realize that nothing has any meaning and there are no answers, just as, indeed, there are no questions (at 394–395).

Instead, we have agreeable and disagreeable would-be 'intellectuals' – in fact, 'chaps' or 'colleagues'. Definitely, Arnold is a most disagreeable person. Duxbury introduces Arnold (at 19) as 'a rather staid and unimaginative law professor who had recently arrived from a relatively minor university'. His 'vocational restlessness' was attributable to his having 'the attention span of a two year old', a gossipy quote which is characteristic of Duxbury's treatment of Arnold, indicating how others found him as disagreeable as did Duxbury (ibid, at 19). Arnold in 1933 was a 'New Dealer' who believed law was too close to capital interests and out of touch with humanitarian needs. However, Arnold was someone who made 'tweedy avowals' of revolutionary views, and again quoting gossip, Duxbury says all Arnold offers is a 'fancy coating for things as they are'. Indeed, in Duxbury's view, Arnold could be compared to F.D.R. himself, Arnold being a theoretical equivalent of the latter's 'opportunistic virtuosity' (at 25). F.D.R. went out to award his kindred spirit, Arnold, with the task of struggling against American trusts or cartels. Duxbury comments that, despite the energy put into his work, Arnold proved ultimately unsuccessful (at 34), because it was no longer convenient for F.D.R. to have an effective cartel policy when winning capitalists for war production. Arnold appears again in the struggle against the anti-communist McCarthy by defending people pro bono to a value estimated at \$2.5 million in one case alone, and yet Duxbury has to comment, again quoting others, that Arnold would defend anyone, regardless, 'including Klu Kluxers, fascists and communists' (at 36–37). The problem for Duxbury is that this did not prevent Arnold from insisting that law had no metaphysical foundation. It was a mere symbol manipulated by elites to confuse the 'masses'. Arnold did not realize, according to Duxbury, that individuals and peoples require satisfaction of their real and not just symbolic needs. In short, Arnold, in stressing the primacy of political symbolics, was ignoring reality (at 37).

It is of course the main thrust of my argument that at present academics, like everyone else, cannot be expected to understand one another. I do not understand Duxbury, although I do tend to categorize him among Ayer's chosen English journeymen, who have a robust loathing of 'pontiffs', an anti-Roman Catholic as well as anti-foreign tag which goes back to the Henrician reformation. Duxbury uses the tag against both myself and Arnold – a much more distinguished and apparently constructive and well-meaning person – branding us as nihilists. Of course, it is too much to expect of the journeyman Duxbury that he offer any definition of this word, as if it were a concept. Meanings found through ordinary language use herald, in any case, the sovereignty of gossip, which is the quintessence of ordinary language.

However, one can gather from Duxbury's long diatribes that he does not like people who say 'things do not work', that law is ideology, manipulated by elites, and at one point there is even a glimpse of what he means by 'nihilist'. It is someone who 'makes difficulties', someone who, having pointed out problems, does not offer solutions, someone who seems to get satisfaction out of 'pointing out difficulties and then not offering solutions'. In fact, Duxbury sees in Arnold something of the bugbear of his own contemporary Critical Legal Studies colleagues, especially Peter Goodrich, mentioned at the beginning of the review of my book. Critical legal scholars 'have a discernibly nihilistic strand of thinking – not far removed from Arnold's own ... (called) trashing or demystification ... the exposing of faults and contradictions ... without any attempt to provide solutions' (at 39).

One might as well call any doctor who demonstrates that his patient has an incurable illness a nihilist. A Spanish Roman Catholic philosopher, Miguel de Unamuno, argues in his signature work, *Tragic Sense of Life* (1921, Dover Trans., 1954) that the most serious and unavoidable issue facing all of us is the certainty of our complete extinction. We are all heading for certain towards absolutely nothing. Of course, he has no remedy, but he does suggest in his concluding chapter that no world view deserves to be considered credible unless it is obviously ridiculous. That is why he ends his book with a chapter entitled 'Don Quixote in the Contemporary European Tragic-Comedy'.

The second case study is of a review process, in which the author participated, concerning the contribution which Lacanian psychoanalysis can make to a radical rethinking of international law, in the words of the abstract (Maria Aristodemou, 'A Constant Craving for Fresh Brains and a Taste for Decaffeinated Neighbours' in *The European Journal of International Law* vol. 25, no. 1 [2014] 35–58 at 35). Imagining international law (and its lawyers) as a neurotic in search of fresh brains, the discipline needs to recognize the 'extimate' that the human hides in herself. Otherwise, international law will continue to crave 'fresh brains'.

The style of rhetoric is heavy with metaphors. Without having anything precise to say about international law or its practitioners, the author declares it to be 'neurotic' and appoints herself as its analyst, obviously a position of superiority, her subject already designated as her patient. Additionally, she announces that she is going to take Lacan's part in an internal feud within especially Viennese psychoanalysis in which the 'enemy' (the extimate?) is ego psychology (36). The assumption of the 'search for fresh brains' is that there is someone somewhere who is perfect and has all the answers (37). Finally, the author declares her aim is to criticize inter or multi-disciplinarity by international lawyers, who look to other disciplines such as history, politics, literature and even psychoanalysis to compensate for the weaknesses of their own discipline (37).

As a blind peer reviewer of this text, I requested evidence of what she meant, and the author added to a second draft as 'being in this vein' one article by myself and a book of mine of which she politely says amounts to 'an important rethinking of the philosophical foundations of international law beyond doctrine and practice' (37). There is no further mention of these pieces, but it may be noted the article was a book review of Gary Simpson, who was the author's host for the guest lecture, the basis of her article, who does receive some attention in the article. The author's aim, following Lacan, is to convince international lawyers that there is no purpose to be gained in going beyond international law to make up its deficiencies because the other disciplines will suffer the same deficiencies. This is precisely the point I make myself in my abovementioned chapter on Rousseau and Durkheim as read by Baudrillard, and it is partially the point I make in the article which the author cites as being 'in this vein', viz 'Visions of the Past of International Society: Law, History or Politics' (69, *MLR* [2006] 644). There I argue that Simpson's wish to provide legitimacy to the status of Great Powers over other states and especially over 'outlaw' states (a book written in the shadow of the coming 2003 invasion of Iraq by the 'Coalition of the Willing') was based upon an incomplete understanding of the historical analogies extracted in a political science mode from European diplomatic history of the early 19th century. She praises Simpson on several occasions for agreeing with her insight. On the first occasion, it is when he recognizes something 'neurotic' about international criminal law 'completing' human rights law and rendering it 'whole' (a rhetorical reference to his book *Law, War and Crime*, 2007). While this is not a case of interdisciplinarity but of 'completion' within the same discipline, the aim of the present author's argument (against publication of the article in its present form) was to demonstrate that it does not engage sufficiently seriously with international law scholarship to say anything of significance to the profession.

There is a direct connection between the superficiality of the author's engagement with international law and her choice of Lacan as its psychoanalyst. Lacan is one who leads the would-be patient 'to commit murder against himself ... the goal of the analysis in effect is to devastate, de-subjectify, and shutter the subject' (39). In this context, she quotes with approval Simpson's general aim, to suggest that the distinction between 'show trials' and actual war crimes trials is so difficult to draw as to cause the international lawyer 'anxiety', presumably because of the 'extimate' hovering in its shadow (41). The article does not alert the lay reader that this is a highly contestable view due to the range of options in psychoanalytical theory, and that the author is not arguing the merit of this theory. She has explicitly chosen it because she thinks it conforms to her own metaphysical theory that the supposed 'death of God' is what international lawyers are yearning to compensate. Her general ambition, here applied to international law, is an atheistic jurisprudence (38). The project, linking Lacan with atheism, may be coherent, but there is no way – perhaps short of composing an encyclopedia – of demonstrating that the argument has any objective or otherwise professional force. One comes back to MacIntyre's fundamental objection to the very idea of an intellectual discipline. For this reason, some mention will be made of psychoanalysts whose perspective is different from Lacan's, in particular, Victor Frankl. Here, in an article about international law, it still has to be to stressed that her engagement with this discipline remains very general. The author cites both Martti Koskenniemi and Gerry Simpson in these vague and adulatory words: 'Gerry Simpson has rightly and aptly described law as a displaced politics, while Martti Koskenniemi has written of the flight to legality as a flight against and away from politics' (40). Her comment is that both still need to acknowledge 'the extimate', that is they still need thorough shuttering, a word whose precise meaning in the present context escapes the present author.

There follows a long discussion of the analyst Kris and his patient, and embedded in it is a statement that international law began, presumably in European history, as a system whose founding fathers based its origin on divine law. God performed the functions of total knowledge, total ownership (of territory) etc. It is the subsequent death of God which finds its expression in the anxiety and emptiness of international lawyers. It might appear to be a pedantic digression, but Hugo Grotius is famous for saying his *Law of War and Peace* was based on the hypothesis that there was no God (Preliminary Discourse, XI), and Alberico Gentili exclaimed that the science of the Law of Nations required the silencing of theologians. The Britannica credits him as the first person in Europe to banish Roman Catholic theology and canon law in favor of secular law. The author/analyst is not listening to her 'neurotic' patient, since she knows, from her metaphysical system, where the 'neurosis' lies.

And the particular analyst, the Lacanian, has a pre-determined very dark presupposition of what she is going to find, as she explains to the 'neurotic' patient where her ills lie. After an extensive discussion of Kant's legal and political theory, she concludes that the capacity for the imperative of practical reason is also the capacity for the *inhuman* (her italics). The inhuman, the undead, is the excessive dimension of the human. Whether it is a matter of considering the individual as a subject or the state (of interest to international law), the 'irrational excess' which it is supposed one has left out (with the categorical imperative or the social contract) '...is always bound to return and shatter [not shutter? this author's comment] the patient's equilibrium' (53). This metaphysic of evil provides the backdrop for the author's very general argument against the worth of public international law having rules against this or that. Rules cannot save us from radical evil, whether as individuals or states. Rules are apparently symbolic in Lacan's terms and, as such, they cannot escape the pathological (53). As a reviewer of this rhetoric, I objected in vain that if the author does not pin down her rhetoric onto individual international lawyers or states, they will escape her quite effortlessly.

The author finishes her 'explanation' of Lacanian psychoanalysis with a run through notions of human rights and humanity, concluding with Kierkegaard that the only good neighbor is a dead neighbor. The reason is the envious hatred that each of us feels for the distinctive spirit of 'jouissance' of the other (54–56). This is the entry into the conclusion, a plea for an atheist international law. We finally learn, in the conclusion, that the extimate, a word not in my Google dictionary, and until now not defined at all, is actually Freud's more recognizable 'death wish', for Lacan is a Freudian (57). The aggressive instinct (Freud) is a derivative of the death instinct. Whether it exists or not, it is unridable, '...and, above all, unlegislatable' (57). According to Slavoj Žižek, it is the 'indivisible remainder' which is oblivious to rules and interventions (57). To get to, once again, the extimate, we have to experience anxiety. Here the extimate is not safely hidden by law (the symbolic) or politics (the imaginary), so that it erupts in all its obscene and violent underside (57–58). The abuse of power forms the obscene underside of all exercise of power that God was so good at concealing, but that now, with the death of God, it is our highest ethical demand to assume this 'gap' in all its ugliness (58).

And this is atheistic jurisprudence of international law, according to the *European Journal of International Law*. I was informed as a reviewer that the editor in chief considered my opinion of the article 'no longer required', and I found out that another reviewer considered the piece to be a very sound exposition of psychoanalysis. The author herself, as her article clearly indicates, knows nothing much about international law, although she does describe herself in her article as 'we international lawyers'. There is nothing before or since on her website about international law that I could find while visiting it in September 2020. I was given the option at the time to comment on the article, but instead considered it better not to engage further with this journal. I have not been asked since then to review any articles.

At the time it was the author's superficial grasp of the discipline of international law that worried me, as did the indifference of the journal's editor in chief to this fact. However, subsequent interest in psychoanalysis, driven by the ever-deteriorating condition of international society and its mental health, has led me to look a little more into the field of psychoanalysis. Now I think it might also have been possible for the author to have taken a broader view of the work of Lacan and considered his *Speech and Language in Psychoanalysis*, translated with notes and commentary by Anthony Wilden (John Hopkins University Press, 1968, 1991). This, for me, subjectively speaking, abstruse work points in the direction of a close psychoanalytical reading of a sizable range of international law texts, as being the very least that the author should have offered for publication in a leading, blind peer-reviewed international law journal.

However, at a more fundamental level, the reader of an international law journal, presented with one view of psychoanalysis – and then only one part of that analyst's thinking – might reasonably expect to be warned that the field is entirely contested among its practitioners and that no objective measure is likely to be accepted that could determine how one view of the field was sound while any opposing view was not. In *Man's Search for Ultimate Meaning*, Victor Frankl (first published 1979, this edition with Kindle, 2011) offers a deliberately alternative approach, especially in chapter 8: 'New Research in Logotherapy Circa 1975' (83 et seq kindle edition). It is proposed here to present the bare bones of his perspective, his struggle against the reductionism of Freudianism in favor of the vision that Man has a conscience and can choose freely to follow it. He says that most motivation theories borrow from biology the idea that Man is basically concerned with satisfying drives and instincts to alleviate inner tensions caused by these, so as to achieve an inner equilibrium called 'homeostasis'. Frankl opposes this vision, arguing that human existence is always directed to 'self-transcendence', to someone or something beyond the self. The origin of neurosis is a frustration of the will to meaning, according to innumerable 'Logo-tests' conducted by Frankl's psychology 'allies'. He bases his work on countless psychological tests at numerous leading American universities. Frankl's attitude to his subject, in contrast to the mean and cynical attitude attributed to Lacan, is what he calls 'crabbing', a concept he takes from airplane flight instruction with respect to crosswinds against which diversionary flight direction is necessary. 'But isn't it the same with man? Doesn't he, too, wind up at some point that is lower than his destination unless he is seen on a level that includes his aspirations? ... Well if I take man as he is I will make him worse if I take him as he ought to be, I make him become what he might be ... The will to power and the will to pleasure are substitutes for a frustrated will to meaning' (87). Frankl supports this thesis with a very lighthearted reference to a scientific study that people visiting the Vienna Prater proved statistically to be more frustrated in their will to meaning than the average population of Vienna (87).

Frankl goes on to make a long list of 'reductionist strategisms' whereby psychoanalysts aim to demoralize their patients and drive them eventually to suicide (96 et seq). For instance, he cites a case study of Peace Corps volunteers being systematically professionally denigrated by psychologists hired to vet them (96–97). Frankl's comment is that the only thing the 'unmasking psychologist' unmasks is his own 'hidden motive', 'his unconscious need to debase and depreciate the humaneness of man' (97). The fundamental reason Frankl offers for this projection of debasement by the psychoanalyst on his would-be 'patient' is that he functions with a closed system concept. For instance, a mechanistic concept of aggression rests upon a motivational theory that 'depicts man as a being to whom the world ultimately serves as a mere tool for the reduction of the tensions aroused and created by libidinal or aggressive impulses ... However ... man is actually a being who is reaching out for meanings to fulfill and other human beings to encounter' (102–103). After describing innumerable field studies, Frankl concludes with a major attack on the whole so-called discipline and practice of psychotherapy. It is responsible for a neuroticization of humanity. 'Now it is my contention that the *deneuroticization of humanity* requires a *rehumanization of psychotherapy*' (104, Frankl).

After completing my 'fresh brains' review of Maria's article, I was alerted by the editor to the existence of podcasts between Jo Weiler and Maria Aristodemou subsequent to the publication of her article. These podcasts are, in my view, hugely informative for my own argument, but rather than trying to modify my argument so far – which can legitimately be confined to this written text – I have decided to offer the subsequent reflections I made to the editor. To retain the spontaneity of these reflections, I have put in italics further final reflections, which I think are necessary because of the cryptic character of my first, as I say, spontaneous reflections:

I am grateful for your reminder (the editor's) to listen to the EJIL Podcast. I need to reflect on it. But first thoughts are that atheists and believers have much more in common than either has with agnostics. And Maria nails Jo as an agnostic. Here by 'agnostic' is meant someone who accepts the limited aims his so-called profession appears to him to set and does not feel existentially challenged to ensure that it realizes some absolute goals. Agnostics are ethically immature for her. The 'problem' for Maria is the all-pervasiveness of the 'extimate' in all of us, and as a professional agnostic, Jo is unaware of this. Besides that, Jo throws at her all the arguments that I make in my reader's review, that she fails to carry through her arguments to the detail, or 'nitty gritty' of international law, and so leaves 'the profession' in the dark about how her argument should work out. She agrees with this, except for her perception of the obsessive character of the agnostic. The international lawyer still has a feeling of incompleteness which he resolves with the obsessive creation of new rules, to fill the gaps which Jo says are only there in her imagination. Obviously, this powerful response by Maria shows that she does have a fairly clear idea as to how to complete her argument in a further essay.

Having watched these podcasts (second reply to the editor) two to three times, my further impression is that Jo realizes he has acted hastily in publishing the piece. He thought Maria was a 'qualified' psychoanalyst. *He goes on the make the fateful challenge to her, that she treats Lacan himself uncritically and does not look to other psychoanalysts – a point which is at the heart of my present review, but which I did not mention in my role as anonymous reviewer.* For her part, Maria has to fend off an editor who is not, in the first place, an international lawyer. He has a diploma from the celebrated Hague Academy of International Law (which the latter says it accords for independent study leading to an examination which shows a thorough knowledge of the law) but Jo is still overwhelmingly an EU lawyer, with a huge range of other interests. The background of the two conversationalists shows in their shadow boxing over the question of gaps in international law. Jo does not seem to be familiar with this 'debate', led by Hersch Lauterpacht. Neither is Maria. *The debate is really a spin-off of the conflict between natural lawyers and positivists. The dominant positivist view is that international law is what states have consented to create. To the extent they do not act, there is no legal restriction on their conduct and it is hardly the responsibility of the so-called profession to 'fill the gap'. For the natural law school – which is pretty well moribund, but does have a ghost life in the tendency which Maria traces in her article, 'to go looking for fresh brains' – the international lawyer does have a professional responsibility to overcome him or herself, the huge gaps which exist in the so-called international legal order.*

As I say in my conclusion, none of this would matter if Jo did not have the power to make or break the careers of international law academics, especially ones beginning their career, when publishing in 'top' journals is usually crucial – because of the very high 'ranking' of the EJIL. It is not suggested that Jo does not exercise this disciplinary authority as conscientiously as possible, but there is in fact no intellectual basis at all for such an authority to exist.

Conclusion

It is particularly worth noting that the UK's 'benchmark' of academic standard of excellence is, as already seen 'world leading' or maybe 'world class'. The explanatory notes of the UK's so-called Research Excellence Framework (REF) explain that 'world leading, internationally and nationally' are not meant literally. They are only metaphors. The REF says 'They do not refer to the nature or geographical scope of particular subjects, nor to the locus of research nor its place of dissemination. For example, research which is focused within one part of the UK might be 'of world leading standard'. It seems this qualification is salutary, given that European and indeed Western civilization no longer dominates the world, although it would appear that Martin Weber and the European Peoples Party, and the European Parliament generally, have not yet thrown in the towel.

MacIntyre's rather optimistic argument is that universities should widen their syllabus to include all perspectives on a particular field (TVMI, chapter 10, 'Reconceiving the University as an Institution and the Lecture as a Genre'). This appears to me a hopeless task. There is also the obvious argument of the liberal John Stuart Mill that the truth will emerge through a free and intelligent exchange of views. My argument is more depressing. Academic study of at least the humanities and social sciences has the pretension to be professionalized into disciplines that are supposedly monitored, just as other, in my view, real professions, such as medicine, the military, or the actual practice of law. A further and crucial factor to consider is that education is largely publicly funded in democratic societies and so, supposedly, it is reasonable that political authorities want evidence that the 'people' are receiving 'value for money'. Unfortunately, the case studies offered here do suggest that such a public expectation cannot be satisfied.

If there was no supposed ranking of journals and monitoring of teaching and research, there is virtually nothing described here that should give rise to real concern. Nonsensical arguments can evoke nonsensical responses, and satire can relieve tensions all around. 'Sticks and stones may break our bones, but names will never hurt'. However, it does appear that the increasing complexity of the review processes indicates increasing desperation that society does not have any overall sense of direction in academic affairs. This intellectual, indeed spiritual confusion ought to, and does, leave academic office holders exhausted, desperate as to how to affirm their social standing in a stable way. This shows itself unmistakably in the huge falloff of research activity once the office holders obtain tenure or a 'prestigious academic location' – witness Duxbury's move from Manchester to the LSE in London. If the profession was completely 'privatized', then 'the market' could decide what should continue to survive. I prefer this option from my experience of the work of 'freelance' historians and political theorists or scientists compared to the streamlined academics in the same 'fields'. Roll on REF-EXIT.

Chapter 12

The exercise of corporate office

Timothy Peters

Introduction

The governance structure of the modern corporation—at least in common law countries—is made up of a board of directors who are elected by shareholders and charged with the oversight of the management of the corporation. For large and publicly listed companies, the board of directors will then appoint corporate officers to whom the management of the company is delegated. In dominant accounts, the 'core' issue of corporate governance is about addressing the 'agency costs' that arise from the 'separation of ownership and control' that this form gives rise to—that is, how to ensure the accountability of those who exercise corporate power. Mechanisms of accountability range from the imposition of legal duties (such as the duty to act with due care and diligence, to act in the best interests of the company and to avoid undisclosed conflicts of interest) to the structuring of incentives so as to align the self-interests of corporate directors and officers with those of shareholders. From this perspective, the very feature of corporate governance—specialised management who oversee and run the corporation on behalf of shareholders—produces potential irresponsibility. Whilst positioned as a question of agency cost—how to ensure that corporate agents act not simply in their own self-interest but in the interests of the corporation—this is a direct feature of what I have referred to elsewhere as the 'constitutive vicariousness of corporate power'.[1] That is, the exercise of corporate

1 See further Timothy D. Peters, "Corporate Office, Corporate Irresponsibility and the Constitutive Vicariousness of Corporate Power," in *Evil Corporations: Law, Culpability and Regulation*, ed. Penny Crofts (New York: Routledge, 2024); Steve Kourabas, Nick Sinanis, and Timothy D. Peters, "A Historical Perspective on Corporate Officer Accountability," *The ECGI Blog*, 21 February 2024, https://www.ecgi.global/blog/historical-perspective-corporate-officer-accountability.

DOI: 10.4324/9781003659754-14

power is never on behalf of oneself but always on behalf of another (whether the company, shareholders or other stakeholders).

This chapter seeks to explore this idea not through a focus on agency costs or an understanding of directors and corporate officers as agents of the corporation or shareholders, but through the paradigm of office. It works through the way in which the emergence of the modern board of directors and the granting of corporate power to them arose out of the understanding of the director as a form of office. In this regard, I follow Susan Watson's tracing of the modern duties of corporate directors to the oaths of office that were sworn by the governors and committee-men of the 17th-century imperial trading companies.[2] If this genealogy is accurate, then contemporary corporate officers have their origin in a period where the notion of office was the dominant form of articulating social morality.[3] As Conal Condren notes, the vocabulary of office carried with it both 'a positive register of rights, liberties, duty, rule and service to the office' as well as a 'negative register imputing neglect, oppression, licence and tyranny' in relation to a failure to appropriately carry out the office.[4] This vocabulary was used in the social construction of particular offices or roles and the appropriate *persona* of the individual performing them.[5] Watson's genealogy, which traces the shift from the oath of corporate office in the 17th century to the emergence of duties of corporate directors from the 18th century, provides significant context to contemporary debates over what the purpose or 'best interests' of the corporation are, and the effectiveness of directors' duties as mechanisms of accountability for the exercise of corporate power. This history also reveals that what is at stake is not so much the articulating of the purpose or 'ends' of the corporation, but rather the structure of the corporate form and the (in)effectiveness of corporate office as a mechanism of accountability.

The chapter proceeds first by tracing the genealogy of modern directors' duties to the oaths of office sworn by officeholders of the imperial

2 Susan Watson, *The Making of the Modern Company* (Oxford: Hart, 2022).

3 Conal Condren, *Argument and Authority in Early Modern England: The Presupposition of Oaths and Offices* (Cambridge: Cambridge University Press, 2006).

4 Conal Condren, "The *Persona* of the Philosopher and the Rhetorics of Office in Early Modern England," in *The Philosopher in Early Modern Europe: The Nature of a Contested Identity*, ed. Conal Condren, Stephen Gaukroger, and Ian Hunter (Cambridge: Cambridge University Press, 2006), 67; see also Condren, *Argument and Authority*.

5 See also Shaun McVeigh, "Obligations of Office," in *Law, Obligation, Community*, ed. Daniel Matthews and Scott Veitch (Oxon: Routledge, 2018).

trading companies and the later articulation of the director as a form of office in the seminal case of *Charitable Corporation v Sutton*. Second, it situates contemporary debates over the 'purpose' of the corporation in relation to a 'jurisdictional account' of the board of directors. Finally, it turns from a consideration of the 'duties' of corporate office to a thicker notion of obligation within which corporations are always-already situated.

From oaths of corporate office to directors' duties

The origin of modern duties of corporate directors and officers is generally traced to the 1742 decision of the UK Court of Chancery, *The Charitable Corporation v Sutton*.[6] This case dealt with a company incorporated by royal charter in 1707 for the purpose of lending money to the poor (hence the title 'the charitable corporation'). Under the charter, the management of the corporation's affairs was vested in seven 'committee-men' (who would today be referred to as a board of directors) including Sir Robert Sutton. Over a number of years, a 'fraud' had been perpetuated on the company by a number of its other officers resulting in significant loss. The corporation, at the instigation of its shareholders, brought a civil case against fifty various officers including all seven of its committee-men (directors). Lord Hardwicke held that, in addition to the fraudulent officers, the directors were liable for 'breach of trust' and 'neglect'.

In order to come to this finding, Lord Hardwicke examined the legal status of directors. Having reviewed the nature of the fraud and negligence perpetrated—in part because the various checks and processes that were initially intended to provide accountability for the activities of the corporation were either removed or not followed—he stated that '[i]t will be proper here to consider the employment of a director or committee-man'.[7] He went on to describe the nature of the director as a

6 See, for example, the discussion in L. S. Sealy, "The Director as Trustee," *Cambridge Law Journal* 25, no. 1 (1967) p. 83–103; Richard B. Dyson, "The Director's Liability for Negligence," *Indiana Law Journal* 40, no. 3 (1965) p. 341–376; Rudolph E. Uhlman, "The Legal Status of Corporate Directors," *Boston University Law Review* 19, no. 1 (1939) p.12–31. There are two separate reports of the case that differ in some of the details: *The Charitable Corporation v Sir Robert Sutton and about Fifty Others* (1742) 88 ER 500; *Charitable Corporation v Sutton* (1742) 26 ER 642; 2 Atk 404.

7 88 ER 500 at 503, para [355].

> mixed-office, partly in the nature of a public office, and partly as a private office in trust for other people. It is public, as it rises under a charter, and as the abuse of it tends to affect public credit. But as it does not concern public government, but the negotiation of private property, it is therefore a private office, like the directors of the Bank, South-Sea, and other trading companies, where they are not obliged to qualify by taking the sacrament and oaths as for a public office, but are only intrusted with the property of the aggregated body: so this is in the nature of a private trust for other persons; and in this view the committee-men are responsible to the corporation for breaches of trust, either by commissions or omissions, for acts of malefeasance or nonfeasance; and at the hearing Domat was cited to shew they are responsible for breaches of private trust.[8]

As such, Lord Hardwicke describes the role of director explicitly in the vocabulary of office—one which had been undertaken voluntarily and for which no salary or remuneration was to be received.[9] The 'mixed nature' of this office reflected both the fact that it arose from the charter as a public document on the one hand and because it dealt with private property on the other hand—making it a private office for which the directors were not required to partake of the sacrament or oaths as required under the Corporation Act 1661. On this basis, entrusted with the property of the 'aggregate body', Lord Hardwicke considered the directors to be agents or acting 'in the nature of a private trust for other persons' and therefore 'responsible to the corporation for breaches of trust, either by commissions or omissions, for acts of malfeasance or nonfeasance'.[10]

The use in the reports of the language of 'agent' and 'trust' has been taken as an indication that what was being expressed was an understanding of the role of directors as akin to either or both agents (and thus 'liable for negligent harm to the principal's interests in carrying out their duties') or trustees (and thus 'liable for negligently injuring the

8 88 ER 500 at 503, para [355].

9 Lord Hardwicke noted that the lack of remuneration—despite submissions for the defendants—was not an excuse: 'if one voluntarily accepts a trust, he must execute it with fidelity, integrity and diligence; and where no allowance is annexed to the trust when created, this Court will not make any.' 88 ER 500 at 503-4, para [355].

10 88 ER 500 at 503, para [355]. In the Atkyns report of the case, the committee-men were described 'most properly' as 'agents to those who employ them in this trust, and who empower them to direct and superintend the affairs of the corporation.' See 26 ER 62; 2 Atkyns 400 at 645, para [405].

trust estate').[11] However, despite the range of cases that describe directors as agents or trustees—as well as 20th-century accounts that explicitly describe directors as trustees, representatives or agents[12]—there are analytical problems with such a reading. Directors do not have that key feature of trustees, which is the legal title to property that is vested in the corporation; nor is their ability to exercise corporate power a delegation of shareholders or the corporation as principal, but rather considered an 'original and undelegated' grant.[13] Furthermore, contemporary accounts that read *Charitable Corporation v Sutton* as grounding directors as 'agency' or 'trust' relationships tend to involve an anachronistic 'reading back' of modern notions of agency and trust law into the 18th-century Chancery decision.[14] Such readings function at best as what Justice Geoffrey Nettle has referred to as an 'imperfect analogy' because, for example, the committee-men were not in actuality trustees owning the corporate property in their own name, but rather appointed to manage the affairs of the corporation.[15]

In contrast to seeing directors as akin to agents or trustees and, therefore, looking to import those legal concepts into corporate law, other

11 Dyson, "The Director's Liability for Negligence," 342.

12 Dalia Tsuk Mitchell, "Status Bound: The Twentieth Century Evolution of Directors' Liability," *New York University Journal of Law & Business* 5 (2009) p.63–151.

13 See the discussion, focused on the US context, in Uhlman, "The Legal Status of Corporate Directors"; Sealy, "The Director as Trustee." For a broader tracing of the powers of directors as undelegated, taking into account the UK and New Zealand positions, see: Susan Watson, "The Significance of the Source of the Powers of Boards of Directors in UK Company Law," *Journal of Business Law* (2010); Chris Noonan and Susan Watson, "The Foundations of Corporate Governance in New Zealand: A Post-Contractualist View of the Role of Company Directors," *New Zealand Universities Law Review* 22 (2007).

14 On the 'modernity' of the law of agency, see: Wolfram Müller-Freinenfels, "Legal Relations in the Law of Agency: Power of Agency and Commercial Certainty," *The American Journal of Comparative Law* 13, no. 2 (1964).

15 The Hon Justice Geoffrey Nettle, "The Changing Position and Duties of Company Directors," *Melbourne University Law Review* 41, no. 3 (2018): 31. On some accounts, the description of directors as trustees is positioned as arising out of the late 18th and early 19th century deed of settlement companies that were based on an underlying trust. However, such misses the fact that directors and trustees, whilst at times overlapping, were distinct roles in these companies and therefore *not* to be seen as identical. Furthermore, the earliest cases such as *Charitable Corporation v Sutton* dealt specifically with corporations and not deed of settlement companies. See discussion by Sealy, "The Director as Trustee," 83–86.

accounts see the role of director as *sui generis* and that their fiduciary duties arise from the role directly—in particular, the position of mutual trust and confidence that they inhabit. Such a claim to the *sui generis* status of the director can be linked back to *Charitable Corporation v Sutton* itself. This is because the authority cited in the judgment was not on the law of trusts and trustees, even in nascent form, but rather the English translation of the French jurist Domat's systematic summary of Roman civil and public law. In the context of that text, whilst noting that the level of care and diligence of a director is the same as that of an agent or factor,[16] the obligations of directors are categorised *not* in relation to roles where there is an agreement or covenant that governs the relationship of engagement (such as partnerships and various forms of proxies, mandates and agency relationships) but circumstances where obligations arise from a particular role—including that of tutor, guardian or curator.[17] It is specifically in the categorisation of the latter that directors and administrators of corporate bodies are considered. This gives further grounding to the argument that Lord Hardwicke should be read *not* as substantiating that directors were either agents or trustees, but rather recognises the specific nature of corporate office as an independent category.[18]

This aligns with Susan Watson's argument, in *The Making of the Modern Company*, that the early cases on directors referred not to the form of trust, but the notion of trustworthiness in the exercise of office. For Watson, rather than being the origin of the fiduciary duties of directors, Lord Hardwicke was judicially recognising a much earlier articulation of the obligations of corporate office.[19] These obligations arose from the office which the directors had taken up and which, at this point, still required an oath to be sworn. In the context of the Charitable Corporation, the directors were required to swear that they would 'duly and faithfully perform the trust of a committee man of the Charitable Corporation, to the best of [their] knowledge and judgment for the benefit and advantage of the said corporation, so long as [they]

16 Domat, *The Civil Law in its Natural Order: Together with the Publick Law: Volume I* (Bettenham, 1722), Bk 2, Tit 3, Sect II, I at p 295 'Those who are named by Companies and Corporations, to have the Direction of their Affairs, are obliged to the same Care and Diligence, as Factors or Agents. And they are answerable not only for any Fraud, and gross Negligence, which they may be guilty of, but also for all Faults that are contrary to the Care required of them.'

17 See Domat, *The Civil Law in its Natural Order*, Bk 2, Tit 1-3.

18 88 ER 500 at 503, para [355].

19 Watson, *Making of the Modern Company*, 92–94.

shall continue in the said trust'.[20] Here, the reference to 'trust' is not that of a formal trust as an equitable instrument, but rather the undertaking of office in acting on behalf of the corporate body and its members. For Watson, the location of the obligations of corporate office in modern directors' duties involved a formalisation and juridification of the earlier oaths of office sworn by committee-men and directors.[21] In the earlier imperial trading companies, it was not a legal duty but the oath that was the site of articulating the obligations and responsibility of directors and corporate officers.

For Watson's overarching argument, the development of the governance of the English East India Company is the site of emergence of the 'modern company'. In contrast to accounts that focus on the 19th-century development of mass-incorporation laws as being the consolidation of the modern company as an artificial legal person, economically and legally separate from its shareholders, governed by a board of directors and having perpetual succession, Watson highlights the way each of these features was achieved with the 1657 charter of the East India Company.[22] The 17th century saw a shift in the governance structures of the East India Company that arose from a tension between 'elite' traders who controlled the 'Court of Committees' and tended to govern the Company in their own interests and the 'generality' of smaller investors whose investments were needed to fund the ventures and voyages of the company, but who were not traders themselves. The generality—which Watson highlights is the origin of the contemporary general meeting of shareholders—raised a number of issues with the practices of the Company, including disputing calls for increased capital instalments without appropriate distribution of dividends as well as challenging the tendency for distributions to be made in the form of surplus commodities rather than cash (a practice that benefited the merchants who could sell the commodities but was disadvantageous to small investors). Watson traces the ways these tensions produced a range of governance reforms such as the appointment of auditors and eventually a shift to the new form of double-entry accounting that enabled a clearer

20 Watson, *Making of the Modern Company*, 88. Watson is quoting from *A Short History of the Charitable Corporation* (A Millar, 1732) at p. 21.

21 Watson, *Making of the Modern Company*, 89–90. It is also worth noting that the substantive notion of a legal 'duty' also arose, at least linguistically, later in the 18th and 19th centuries. See: Chris Dent, "The Introduction of Duty into English Law and the Development of the Legal Subject," *Oxford Journal of Legal Studies* 40, no. 1 (2020).

22 Watson, *Making of the Modern Company*, v.

delineation of the value of one's investment.[23] The generality had the power to advocate for these changes, not only because the company required their ongoing investment, but because a system of feudal voting remained in use whereby each member with a certain threshold value of shares would have a single vote (rather than proportional voting that came later).[24]

It is in this context that Watson places the significance of the new form of oath of office that was introduced in 1657. She sees this as part of a settlement between the elite traders and the generality and, in particular, a recognition that the governors and committees were *not* to act simply in their own interests but in the interests of the generality as a whole. The 1657 oath of the governor, deputy-governor and committee-men involved not only swearing 'to be faithfull and true' during the tenure of their office, but also that 'the good estate of the adventurers in this present Stocke you shall favour and affect, and the privileges graunted unto them (to your power) endeavour to maintaine and preserve'.[25] For Watson, this shift is crucial because it recognised the significance of the interests of the generality, in terms of the 'good estate of the adventurers' and that this was something separate from the private interests of each committee-man and individual investors. Watson therefore sees the oath of office as the origin of the modern duty of good faith to act in the best interests of the company.[26] The significance of the shift from oath to duty also highlights a jurisdictional claim not only about in whose interests directors are to manage the affairs of the company, but on what basis such obligations can be enforced.

The jurisdictional claims of corporate office: role morality and corporate purpose

Watson notes that prior to the 16th century, the addition of an oath to a contract or promise invoked the separate ecclesiastical jurisdiction allowing suit for 'perjury or breach of faith' in addition to the action available in the common law court.[27] This jurisdiction subsequently

23 Watson, *Making of the Modern Company*, 55–64.
24 Watson, *Making of the Modern Company*, 55–64.
25 Ethel Bruce Sainsbury, *A Calendar of the Court Minutes etc of the East India Company 1655–1659* (Clarendon Press, 1916), 186–187; Watson, *Making of the Modern Company*, 86.
26 Watson works through a range of oaths sworn by governors, committee-men and directors in the late 17th and early 18th century: Watson, *Making of the Modern Company*, 90–96.
27 Watson, *Making of the Modern Company*, 88.

shifted to the King's Bench, in theory allowing for the running of a parallel suit for breach of oath, though this was rarely if ever independently enforced. However, the oath was still seen as having value as it invoked a moral duty alongside a legal one.[28] For Watson, the connection between the moral and legal duty is key to interpreting the case of the *Charitable Corporation v Sutton*, because it recognises that what is at stake is the trustworthiness of the committee-men or directors, which the oath seeks to bind. The legal significance of the case is that Lord Hardwicke held the committee-men liable for a breach of office arising not only from positive actions taken but for failure to foresee or recognise the frauds being undertaken by the corporate officers. At the same time, Lord Hardwicke distinguished between actions that were a breach of trust and actions that were a neglect.[29] The former related to failures by directors to follow the requirements of the corporation's charter and by-laws, as well as fraudulent signing off on certain pledges and loans. The latter, however, were distinguished in that these were actions conducted *within* the powers of office—including repealing by-laws, appointing certain individuals and putting affairs in their management, issuing notes and bonds and entering into contracts.[30] These actions were held to be a breach of trust not because they had failed to exercise powers granted to them under their office, but rather because of the *way* they had exercised those powers—providing the opportunity for fraud and removing checks that had been in place.

Whereas the oath functioned as a positive attempt to articulate the requirements and expectations of office, *Charitable Corporation v Sutton* is understood as the first case in which directors are held to be liable for a breach of duties as a corporate officer. In contrast to seeing directors as agents of either the shareholders or the corporation, this articulation of office understands directors as a *sui generis* role that exercises the

28 Though Watson also notes that there was much scepticism as to the efficacy of oaths and that the prevailing view was that, at least for many, they could be broken or set aside without a second thought: Watson, *Making of the Modern Company*, 88–89. On the genealogy of the oath not as an invocation of divine punishment for their breach but as an assertion of *fides* or faithfulness, see: Giorgio Agamben, *The Sacrament of Language: An Archaeology of the Oath*, trans. Adam Kotsko (Stanford, CA: Stanford University Press, 2011).

29 See the consideration of the case by Justice Edelman where he distinguishes between liability based on 'manifest breaches of trust and duty' and liability on the basis that they were 'grossly negligent' (referring to the doctrine of '*crassa negligentia*') and noting that the latter was the lowest of standards of liability recognised: *Australian Securities and Investments Commission v Cassimatis (No 8)* (2016) 336 ALR 209 at [416]-[423].

30 88 ER 500 at 502-503, para [353]-[354].

authority and power of the corporation directly.[31] What remains, however, is the question of how to ensure accountability for this exercise of corporate power. This is because, as Lord Hardwicke noted, by necessity 'executive powers' of a corporate body must be 'lodged in a select part of them'.[32] The linking of duty to office is, therefore, a mechanism of corporate accountability. At the same time, however, the structure of office whereby an individual is to act not in their own interests but on behalf of another produces a form of structural irresponsibility, which the attempts to address corporate accountability aim to resolve.[33]

The concerns over corporate accountability function at two levels. At one level, it is about providing a mechanism for ensuring that directors act in the interests of the company and not their own personal interests (or the interests of another). At a second level, however, is the question about whose interests the 'best interests of the company' include. Recent arguments for a broader 'social' purpose of the corporation and the importance of non-shareholder stakeholders emphasise the concerns of the latter,[34] whilst critiques of this approach tend to focus on the former, noting the amount of discretion that directors have in determining what the interests of the corporation are.[35] The tension between the two can be seen in the context of the strong industry statements being made on the importance of delivering value for all corporate stakeholders including customers, employees, suppliers and communities alongside the long-term value for shareholders.[36] Such involves a shift from

31 On the question of the applicability of agency law to directors, see David A. Westbrook, "A Shallow Harbor and a Cold Horizon: The Deceptive Promise of Modern Agency Law for the Theory of the Firm," *Seattle University Law Review* 35 (2012).

32 88 ER 500 at 500, para [350].

33 Peters, "Corporate Office, Corporate Irresponsibility and the Constitutive Vicariousness of Corporate Power."

34 See, for example, Colin Mayer, *Prosperity: Better Business Makes the Greater Good* (Oxford: Oxford University Press, 2018); Beate Sjafell, "Redefining the Corporation for a Sustainable New Economy," *Journal of Law and Society* 45, no. 1 (2018): 42; Jill E. Fisch and Steven Davidoff Solomon, "Should Corporations Have a Purpose?," *Texas Law Review* 99 (2021).

35 Lucian A. Bebchuk and Roberto Tallarita, "The Illusory Promise of Stakeholder Governance," *Cornell Law Review* 106, no. 1 (2020); Ross Grantham, "People, Planet, and Profits: Re-purposing the Company," *Company & Securities Law Journal* 38 (2021).

36 Business Roundtable, "Statement on the Purpose of a Corporation" (*Business Roundtable* 2019) <https://s3.amazonaws.com/brt.org/BRT-StatementonthePurposeofaCorporationwithSignaturesApril2022.pdf> accessed 11 April 2024; Klaus Schwab, "Davos Manifesto 2020: The Universal Purpose of

the traditional focus on shareholder value to take up the arguments for stakeholderism as a more 'responsible' form of capitalism.[37] However, critiques argue that this shift may make directors and other corporate officers *less* accountable because they then have *less* responsibility to shareholders, whilst not substantially increasing incentives, norms or requirements to actually benefit other stakeholders.[38] Those making this critique argue that corporate governance should remain focused on shareholder interests and oversight, whilst stakeholder interests and concerns should be addressed by other legislative interventions.[39]

What this debate oscillates around is the structural irresponsibility of the paradigm of corporate office. As Andrew Johnston and Lorraine Talbot, writing in the UK, have noted, the structural focus on shareholder wealth maximisation with protections and control rights granted to rentier shareholders uninvolved in management generates a *constitutive* irresponsibility at the core of the corporation.[40] In this context, when corporate irresponsibility *is* identified it is articulated in terms of the lack of accountability of directors and officers *to* shareholders (even if those affected are creditors, employees or society more generally).[41] Attempts to resolve this irresponsibility have then promoted remuneration packages that align directors' incentives with those of shareholders and increasing shareholder oversight rights. However, the enhancing of 'the legal powers of shareholders was one of the key drivers of the irresponsible capitalism we witness today'.[42] Lawrence E Mitchell described this in terms of the combination of the corporate social norm of shareholder wealth maximisation with the form of role morality that functions within the corporation.[43] These constraints, he argues, inhibit 'the

a Company in the Fourth Industrial Revolution" (*World Econ Forum*, 9 December 2019) <https://www.weforum.org/agenda/2019/12/davos-manifesto-2020-the-universal-purpose-of-a-company-in-the-fourth-industrial-revolution/> accessed 11 April 2024.

37 For a critique of this move as a form of legitimising corporate power, see: Joel Bakan, *The New Corporation: How "Good" Corporations are Bad for Democracy* (New York: Vintage Books, 2020).

38 Bebchuk and Tallarita, "The Illusory Promise of Stakeholder Governance."

39 Bebchuk and Tallarita, "The Illusory Promise of Stakeholder Governance"; Grantham, "People, Planet, and Profits."

40 Andrew Johnston and Lorraine Talbot, "Why Is Modern Capitalism Irresponsible and What Would Make It More Responsible? A Company Law Perspective," *King's Law Journal* 29, no. 1 (2018).

41 Johnston and Talbot, "Why is Modern Capitalism Irresponsible," 121.

42 Johnston and Talbot, "Why is Modern Capitalism Irresponsible," 121.

43 Lawrence E. Mitchell, *Corporate Irresponsibility: America's Newest Export* (New Haven: Yale University Press, 2001), 66. On the 'norm' of

freedom of the corporation and its directors to act in the manner they think most consistent with the behaviour of a full moral person'.[44] Whilst directors have a large discretion in terms of how they pursue the 'best interests of the corporation', this is only a contingent morality because the freedom they have is only to achieve the ends of the corporation.[45]

For Mitchell, the problem with defining the corporation's purpose as the maximisation of shareholder wealth is that it 'not only gives managers, stockholders, and workers the excuse to behave badly, but also encourages them to do so'.[46] Otherwise upstanding, ordinary and ethical individuals are required, when acting as a director or manager of a corporation, to take on a particular *persona*—that 'of stockholder price maximiser to the exclusion of all others'.[47] Directors are then protected in performing this role and absolved of 'responsibility and accountability for their actions' by being permitted to reduce the 'corporation's costs of production by shifting them outside the corporation onto those most vulnerable, the workers, the environment, the consumers, and the community'.[48] What we see, therefore, is that the construction of the director in terms of office is presented *both* as a form of responsibility—requiring directors to act in the best interests of the company and being accountable to shareholders—and of irresponsibility, because the responsibility of the director is limited *only* to the fulfilment of office and its acceptable norms of behaviour, and these are reduced to the maximisation of shareholder value.

Calls for addressing stakeholder interest, redefining the purpose of the corporation and specifying a broader notion of what the 'best interests of the company' can or should include seek to address this problem by adjusting the *ends* that corporate office is put towards. In doing so, they do not address the underlying nature of the paradigm of office *nor* the framework of corporate governance, which sees corporations managed by directors and corporate officers. As noted above, critiques of stakeholderism—whilst not necessarily disagreeing with the importance of protecting stakeholder interests—highlight the way in which a

shareholder wealth maximisation or shareholder primacy, see Beate Sjåfjell et al., "Shareholder Primacy: The Main Barrier to Sustainable Companies," in *Company Law and Sustainability: Legal Barriers and Opportunities*, ed. Beate Sjafjell and Benjamin J. Richardson (Cambridge: Cambridge University Press, 2015).

44 Mitchell, *Corporate Irresponsibility*, 68.

45 Mitchell, *Corporate Irresponsibility*, 70.

46 Mitchell, *Corporate Irresponsibility*, 97.

47 Mitchell, *Corporate Irresponsibility*, 98.

48 Mitchell, *Corporate Irresponsibility*, 81.

broader notion of the best interests of the company increases the discretion of directors.[49] What this focus on the discretion of directors reflects is, I argue, a jurisdictional claim regarding the corporation and the decisions made by the board of directors. This is because it reflects the broader demarcation between what, in the actions or decisions of directors, is reviewable by the courts and what is not. This is most clearly seen in the context of the common law development of the 'business judgment rule', whereby courts look to whether actions or decisions by directors are taken in 'good faith' but *not* to their substance or whether they produced a successful outcome for the company.[50] This is justified both on the basis that the Court was not qualified to judge on the quality of commercial decisions *and* because of the need to protect the ability for directors to make decisions involving a certain amount of commercial risk and speculation, which will not always 'pay off'.[51] The result is a protection of the jurisdictional domain of directors and the 'business judgments' that they make.[52] A precursor of this can be seen in the report of Lord Hardwick's judgment, where caution was noted in holding directors too liable for events that happen 'because if so, nobody would accept the direction of corporate affairs'.[53] Whilst the need to 'prevent the frauds of dishonest men' was acknowledged, there was also the need to 'not ... make it unsafe or too perilous for honest men to accept offices of trust, by making them liable to losses in the execution of them'.[54]

This jurisdictional demarcation of the discretion or domain of judgment of the board of directors can be placed within a broader history of the governance of corporations by boards or councils. Franklin A Gevurtz traces the form of the board of directors back not only to the imperial trading companies, but to the use of councils as governance

49 Bebchuk and Tallarita, "The Illusory Promise of Stakeholder Governance."

50 See, for example, *Harlowe's Nominees Pty Ltd v Woodside (Lake's Entrance) Oil Co NL* (1968) 121 CLR 483 at 493; *Howard Smith Ltd v Ampol Petroleum Ltd* [1974] AC 821 at 832.

51 For a tracing of the Australian statutory business judgment rule in the context of both the general law developments and contrasting it with the UK and US positions, see: Nettle, "The Changing Position and Duties of Company Directors."

52 It is worth noting that the scope of this jurisdictional domain differs based on jurisdiction and the particular development of both the laws relating to directors' duties as well as statutory interventions around the 'business judgment rule'. For discussion of these developments from an Australian perspective, see: Nettle, "The Changing Position and Duties of Company Directors."

53 88 ER 500 at 504, para [356].

54 88 ER 500 at 504, para [356].

mechanisms operating between a full assembly and appointed or elected officials across a range of different medieval corporations: towns, guilds and church bodies.[55] He argues that the use of a council arose as both a practical mechanism of representation—enabling the provision of consent on behalf of the full assembly without needing all members to be present—as well as providing a mechanism for adjudicating disputes. The early use of councils in the governance of trading corporations (in the form of committees and boards) arose, therefore, out of the prominence of this representative form.[56] The authority of these various councils, from which the board of directors developed, functioned within the plurality of jurisdictions operative in the medieval and early modern periods.[57] Gevurtz, whilst noting that the concerns regarding both effectiveness and accountability of modern boards of directors are potentially a feature of the peculiarity of their jurisdictional genealogy, emphasises the importance of the principles of political legitimacy as part of the reasons for their continued use.[58] The particular problem of the *legitimacy* of corporate power, however, remains in the paradigm of corporate office that endures. This is because, even where a broader social purpose is articulated or provisions allow for the consideration of non-shareholder stakeholders in determining the best interests of the company, it is *directors* who get to determine what those interests are.

Conclusion: from duty to obligation—or, a 'charitable' corporation

Arguments for a broader corporate purpose or the taking up of stakeholder interests, whilst critical of the dominant form of the corporation as engaged in shareholder wealth maximisation, still acknowledge and recognise the economic benefits and efficiencies that the corporation

55 Franklin A. Gevurtz, "The Historical and Political Origins of the Corporate Board of Directors," *Hofstra Law Review* 33, no. 1 (2004).

56 Gevurtz reads this in a democratic trajectory, looking at the take-up of Roman and canon law notions of representation that then became more broadly applied throughout the medieval and early modern period. This, however, is to privilege only one aspect of the modes of authority prominent in the middle ages, with more top-down or authoritarian forms prominently functioning as well. See, for example, Walter Ullmann, "The Papacy and the Faithful," in *Jurisprudence in the Middle Ages* (Variorum Reprints, 1980).

57 Shaunnaugh Dorsett and Shaun McVeigh, *Jurisdiction* (Oxon: Routledge, 2012).

58 Gevurtz, "The Historical and Political Origins of the Corporate Board of Directors," 172–173.

produces.[59] As such, proposals to adjust the purpose of the corporation and to whom the board is responsible tend to sustain the underlying *form* of the corporation. This can be seen, for example, in Mitchell's concern over the way that role morality produces unethical behaviour, but his solution is *not* to address the form of role morality itself, but rather to address the purpose for which it is deployed. In doing so, the underlying structure remains. Furthermore, that structure oscillates between a form of ascending governance of representation (the directors are elected by shareholders and are to represent their interests) and a form of descending governance of authorisation (directors are granted the powers of the corporation and can appoint officers to whom they can delegate their exercise). Whilst the former seeks to articulate corporate directors in a representational fashion, their election by shareholders *excludes* other interests from the domains of corporate authority (in particular employees, but also creditors, customers and other aspects of society). In response, a range of scholars have turned to forms of shared governance that would enable a more representative board, not only 'representing' the interests of various stakeholders, but actually being elected by them (with the prime example being employees).[60]

Whilst I have sympathies with this approach and endorse a turn towards shared governance mechanisms, my focus here is on the particular structure of office that grounds the modern corporation. Both the turns to a broader social purpose and shared governance mechanisms each retain the particular corporate structure, which involves a redefinition of the complexity of the world through the duty of directors to act in the best interests of the company. An effect of the jurisdictional account of corporate office noted above is that the determination of *what* the best interests of the company is remains with the directors—even if they are, at times, required to take into account certain stakeholders in determining this best interest. The solution is not, therefore, simply to change provisions relating to directors' duties and the best interests of the corporation. Such changes are simply an extension of the

59 For a critical discussion, see James D. Nelson, "The Separation of Ownership and Conscience," *The Journal of Corporate Law* 48, no. 3 (2023).

60 See, for example, Johnston and Talbot, "Why Is Modern Capitalism Irresponsible," 129–131. Simon Deakin et al., "Markets, Finance and Corporations: Does Capitalism Have a Future?," in *Rethinking Society for the 21st Century: Report of the International Panel on Social Progress* (Cambridge: Cambridge University Press, 2018); Grant M. Hayden and Matthew T. Bodie, *Reconstructing the Corporation: From Shareholder Primacy to Shared Governance* (Cambridge: Cambridge University Press, 2021).

development of directors' duties as a form of accountability for corporate office. As Lillian Moncrief has argued, these juridical frameworks 'allow companies to match beings and things to their sense of order, and not the other way around'.[61] The taking account of the 'interests' of stakeholders, or the having 'regard' for the 'existences harmed or frustrated by corporate action', involves a redefinition of those interests or concerns in relation to the corporation.[62]

Moncrief seeks a shift in focus from corporate social responsibility to new lines of accountability grounded by a sense of 'corporate social obligation'. The challenge, however, is that corporate networks and formations bring only certain things to the foreground whilst remaining resourced by an immense matrix of beings and things that are in the background, 'set further back from *obligation* than others'.[63] Whilst crises and disasters (Moncrief's focus is the Rana Plaza collapse in 2013) produce an increase in regulation and accountability practices, the benefits accrue only to some existences and not others. For Moncrief this is the 'other side of accountability practices'—'a shrouded space-time or void' into which individuals, entities or impacts fall.[64] This void becomes productive for business in the era of corporate governance and social responsibility, because it 'allows them to take charge of responsiveness, and to manage existences according to their own sense of right and profitability' and 'to do so under the cover of law'.[65] The legal frameworks and institutions of accountability—and the development of directors' duties as a form of accountability for corporate office discussed above—'confer on companies the organisational capacities to navigate open terrain, and to set their acts apart from the world by *limiting* or *bounding* their responsibilities'.[66] The result is that 'some of the voices or bodies, which might discipline corporate actors, fall into juridical voids and struggle with remaining interactive'.[67] The very entities that could hold corporations to their social obligations, within which they are always-already embedded—corporations being unable to exist outside the groundedness of obligation—are excluded.

61 Lilian Moncrieff, "On the Company's Bounded Sense of Social Obligation," in *Law, Obligation and Community*, ed. Daniel Matthews and Scott Veitch, Critical studies in jurisprudence (Abingdon: Routledge, 2018), 88.
62 Moncrieff, "On the Company's Bounded Sense of Social Obligation," 77.
63 Moncrieff, "On the company's bounded sense of social obligation," 76.
64 Moncrieff, "On the company's bounded sense of social obligation," 76.
65 Moncrieff, "On the Company's Bounded Sense of Social Obligation," 86.
66 Moncrieff, "On the Company's Bounded Sense of Social Obligation," 82. Emphasis in original.
67 Moncrieff, "On the Company's Bounded Sense of Social Obligation," 88.

The understanding of the paradigm of corporate office deployed as a mechanism of both accountability and a limit upon accountability discussed in this chapter is one site of this 'bounding' of responsibilities that Moncrief describes. The question, however, is whether there is the ability to make visible not only the corporation's dependence upon the substrata of human and non-human relations, but to think of a form of corporate office that recognises its always-already grounding in social, communal and environmental obligations. One starting point is to take up and extend the argument for the *sui generis* status of corporate directors as a category of corporate office that is not subordinate to the demands of shareholders and of markets. The notion that directors and corporate officers take up a form of public duty or 'mixed office' needs to then be renovated so as to embed the exercise of corporate office within forms of reciprocity and obligation that directors are to participate in. This is less about extending the discretion granted to directors so as to expand the ability to redefine the world in terms of the corporations' interests (at the risk of also expanding their ability to act in their own interests). Rather it is about developing forms of inhabiting and exercising office that enable the redefining of corporate activity as embedded in fundamental obligations to individuals, community and corporate being together in the world.[68] The appropriate comportment of corporate office would then ground its exercise in forms of corporate social obligation rather than the imposition of duty or responsibility.

With this in mind, it is significant that the case cited as the foundation of contemporary directors' duties is one related to shareholders suing directors over loss arising from activities of a 'charitable' nature. The challenge of inhabiting corporate office well is to look at ways of divesting officers of the dominant *persona* of wealth-maximiser without, at the same time, expanding the corporation's appropriation of the desire to do good—to engage in charitable works—for purposes of legitimising greater forms of extraction and exploitation.[69] This requires a challenge to the presupposition of the self-interest of individuals as that which needs to be guarded against by the strictures of office (and addressed either through the imposition of duties *or* through the guiding of self-interest to corporate ends) and a recognition that self-interest is limited

68 Peters, "Corporate Office, Corporate Irresponsibility and the Constitutive Vicariousness of Corporate Power," 158.

69 Bakan, *The New Corporation.*

by the various social obligations within which it is placed. This also requires a deeper rethinking of the paradigm of corporate office than either stakeholderism or shareholder primacy provide. It is from this rethinking that we can consider alternative ways of inhabiting and exercising corporate office.

Chapter 13

Constancy of office

A jurisographic study of jurists and writers in time of conflict (Bobbio and Ginzburg)[1]

Ann Genovese and Shaun McVeigh

We live and work on the lands of Wurundjeri Woi Wurrung people of the Kulin Nation. We acknowledge their Elders past and present, as custodians of country and law. This acknowledgement includes commensurate obligations on us as people who work in a university law school to address the conduct and conditions of relations between laws and peoples, and to care for sources residing in our own inherited traditions that are capable of training ourselves adequately in this task.

Introduction

In this study,[2] we address the long-established topic of virtues in the office of the jurist and writer, to add a contemporary discussion to the forms of humanist education into civil life. Our focus is on how a jurist or writer cultivates their public role in times of conflict, and maintains a considered vigilance about their duties, rights, liberties and privileges when certainties of official (and unofficial) life are challenged. We work through one example, the virtue of constancy. In undertaking this task, we write as jurisographers.

Jurisography is interested in conducts and ethos of role and office in the writings of law and life that we inherit from others; and writing about these resources ourselves, in a manner that draws self-consciously

1 We thank the following for their engagement and assistance with this chapter: Pier Mario Arscone, Shane Chalmers, Peter Goodrich, Jeffrey Minson, Cinzia Pellicciotta, Peter Rush, Karin Van Marle, Valeria Guevara Vasquez, Scott Veitch, Maria Volpe; staff at the Biblioteca Norberto Bobbio, University of Torino; and audiences at Law Literature and Humanities conferences in Brisbane and Hong Kong.

2 Our use of the form 'study' for this chapter draws from Calvino 1997: 305. See also Genovese 2022: 97.

DOI: 10.4324/9781003659754-15

from our own disciplinary training. Jurisography is for us a collaborative exercise that centres on a conduct of relationship; between ourselves and the jurisprudential and humanist traditions to which we belong, and between our scholarly roles and the diverse sources for which we are responsible and write about. Naming how we do our work has been important, to give these activities a public shape. Bringing our own traditions into relationship has enabled us to experiment with techniques of showing how jurisprudence is addressed and accounted for in writing at different times; but to also stage an argument about why it is a public responsibility to write about the jurisprudence that we inherit, and how it belongs to the places we live and work.

In our jurisographic experiments to date, we have clarified how the resources we work with vary according to the projects in which we are engaged, and how they relate to our own inheritances, placements and formations.[3] Our ambition in these different projects has been to show how writing of and in law has ordered lives and experiences. It has also been to show the ways in which such writing offers a training, to us and to those we teach, in how to live a life with law, or conduct your own obligations to law. The study presented in this collection is an exercise, and experiment, in teaching ourselves how to write with closer scrutiny about character, as a topic of humanist virtues. This training is required to take adequate public responsibility as legal scholars for the situation and circumstances of the conducts, and conflicts, between laws, institutions, histories and peoples that we teach, and with which we live.

The presentation of virtues writings in our study, as a contribution to a book on office, are all selected because they are observably inherited from humanist traditions, which we too inherit. Some are also selected because they respond to a shared experience of conflict (in Italy, during the era of fascism and war in the 1940s), and demonstrate fulfilment of different public roles, as jurists and writers, in response to that conflict. Our range of sources can be addressed, for these reasons, as character studies of lives lived with conflict in public and as studies about those whose lives concerned public matters (*res publica*). The conflicts lived with in 2025 for those taking up office as jurists or writers in Australia are, of course, distinct from those faced in 1940s Italy. Yet both relate to 'external' and 'internal' demands of an office – of crises of international and national law or justice, or the demands of the adequate conduct of university life and scholarship. As inheritors of a humanist tradition of virtue writing and conduct, we argue that character studies in and of virtues written for a different time and place to our own remain as

3 Genovese & McVeigh 2015; McVeigh 2016; McVeigh, Genovese & McMillan 2021; Genovese 2022; Genovese & McVeigh 2024.

resources from which we can learn. Our study of the ways in which jurists and writers train themselves, and others, into office is presented here as a question of experience and excellence of conduct in the situations that we too must confront. In this way, our intention is to elucidate the manner and practice of how people of a discipline and institution maintain constancy in office when it is difficult to take responsibility for knowledge, conduct and action.

As a jurisographical study, our mode of organisation and emphasis is important to note. Each part is a differently staged elaboration of constancy as a virtue in the conduct of official lives of jurists and writers. Our focus is on how advice and training in constancy is written within a tradition; how it is addressed and cultivated in examples; and how our own exercises offer training in quality of conduct in the comportment of a public role.

In the first section, we begin with tradition, and place constancy of character in Renaissance humanist scholarship, giving three examples. We address how Justus Lipsius, Michel de Montaigne and Giambattista Vico variously engaged with the constancy of the jurist, scholar and courtier. In the second section, we relocate an inheritance of this tradition to Turin, Northern Italy, in the early twentieth century, to study how it is received and elaborated in a time and place of heightened political conflict. We give a short examination of sources by Vico's intellectual legatee, the historian, politician and philosopher Benedetto Croce, to emphasise his influence on the cultivation of constancy of character by anti-fascist writers and jurists. We then work with two delineations: the writer Natalia Ginzburg and the jurist Norberto Bobbio. Our examples are chosen not only because Bobbio and Ginzburg were subject to Fascist era laws and famously wrote about that experience throughout their lifetimes, in various genres. Importantly, for our account, Bobbio and Ginzburg also offer examples of how a writer and a jurist were educated into active consideration of their relationship and duties to *res publica*, and within a humanist tradition, as part of the same cultural, intellectual and political community.[4] We place details of how Bobbio and Ginzburg lived with conflict in the second section, to draw out their related training into a tradition. We then present details from a

4 We note that our approach infers a particular historiographical training for us, received through various routes, some of which draw from Croce's influence (for example: Curthoys & Docker 2006: 91–93, 103–104, 185–186; White 1987: 28). See also Genovese 2022: 4. This is not the direct subject of this chapter; but for a recent interpretation of placement and relations of thought in historical writing and method, in context of Croce's writing see Manni 2023: 65–66.

study of their writing in the third section, to draw out how they worked technically with that training. Our engagement with Turin is informed in these ways by our own concern with how people of law write about and address the placement and displacement of 'conducts of life';[5] and in the fourth section of this chapter we reflect on our examples as jurisographers. We address the placement, and movement, of Bobbio and Ginzburg's inheritance of humanist virtues, attached to forms of political, juridical and ethical constancy.

By way of conclusion, we return to the acknowledgement in our epigraph, to weigh how placement and displacement is a theme of our study. It applies to our examples, and to our own presentation. Placement and displacement of a tradition (within Italy, and from Italy to Australia) is an acknowledgement of centring what departs and what arrives. The field of law and humanities scholarship, in which we are engaged, has a point of arrival in Australia which is also a displacement of Indigenous law and knowledge. How this is understood within the university and by jurists is a central concern for us. Our study on constancy presented here is a preliminary part of an ongoing project in training ourselves, and others, into writing with and about our inherited resources prudently and adequately, yet without resiling from the difficult task of conducting relations between laws and people. Constancy of character in official (and personal) relations is important to equip ourselves to write with equanimity and truthfulness, especially when invited to do so by (and with) the first jurisprudents and writers of the traditions of the place where we have landed.[6] In the context of this collection our direction, for now, is to pay attention to public inheritance of role and office, of jurists and writers, and accounts of character required when taking up the obligations of those roles. We argue it is a duty to be clear how a person of law inherits virtues associated with *res publica*, and how that is not circumscribed solely by official legal obligations.

Virtues: constancy and a humanist jurisprudence tradition

There is no simple point of departure for establishing the general topics of the virtues or excellences of the scholar and jurist. The histories and disputes hollow out common sources almost as soon as they are put to work as guides to conduct. For many, it will not be a clear point of

5 For example: Hadot 1995; Minson 1993: 16–40; Minson 2014; Genovese 2022: 3–5, 122–136.
6 For example: McMillan et al 2021; Genovese & McKinnon 2025.

acceptance or rejection of 'humanist' thought. For historically inclined Eurocentric scholars, 'humanist' is tied to the Renaissance cultivation of eloquence in the Court and the reception of a newly rediscovered classical inheritance. For others, the 'humanism' to be praised or denounced belongs to the long nineteenth century or the era of twentieth-century human rights. The same will be said of the discourses of the virtues. Our own purpose here is to draw into view a tradition of discourses on 'constancy', into the humanist offices of jurist and writer; and our point of engagement is with late Renaissance and early modern thought. In part, this is because these early modern discourses (and their present inheritance) mark a development of the role of the jurist and scholar in relation to states (taken up by Bobbio), and also form a dispersed humanist discourse of the virtues and conduct in the 'Republic of Letters' (engaged by Ginzburg).[7] In this sense, our own contemporary engagements with constancy in this chapter do not arrive unannounced and unmediated. To draw this out we, like Vico, rely on two humanist formulas: *similtudo temporum* – the linking of past, present and future; and the topic of *theatrum hodiernae vitae* – the setting of the conduct of life in the theatre of contemporary life. These formulas make visible some of the ways in which Norberto Bobbio and Natalia Ginzburg, and we, come to terms with the institutions of state, university, family and the 'Republic of Letters' in the following parts of our study.[8] Our modern ears are more readily tuned to thinking of virtues, even legal virtues, as extra-official. By way of reminder of inheritance, we offer three brief accounts of constancy to emphasise how training into the conduct of office is central to the literatures on the virtues.

Our first example is Justus Lipsius, who lived between 1547 and 1606 in Northern Europe. He is known today as a philologist and jurist who, for our purposes, wrote two handbooks, one on constancy addressing matters of conduct of citizens in times of conflict in 1583 (*De Constantia)*, and the other on politics giving advice to Princes on how to govern (*De Politica*).[9] To do so, Lipsius revived aspects of Stoic

7 Fumaroli 2018: 218–223, 277–278.

8 This point of entry sets aside two more prominent approaches to the 'virtues' in the law disciplines – those that continue the disciplines of university metaphysics that draw on Aristotle, Thomas Aquinas, Immanuel Kant and differently, Giorgio Agamben. Like, Bobbio and Ginzburg our working through 'of constancy' is conducted on a small scale. As a consequence 'constancy' as patience and service to God are left aside.

9 Lipsius 2006; Lipsius 2004. Lipsius also prepared editions on the work of Tacitus and Seneca; commentaries on the Stoic philosophers and Roman civil military life. See generally, Tuck 1993; McCrea 1997.

and Christian virtues. The advice to Princes was not only concerned with the martial virtues of courage, but also with the Stoic-Christian virtues of perseverance and faith (in the benevolence of God), and the Roman virtues of the *vita activa* and public service. From the sixteenth century, and especially in traditions drawn from the writings of Justus Lipsius, 'constancy' was treated as an inflection of Stoic training in *apatheia* – exercises in how to overcome suffering by taking the standpoint 'from above', and *adiaphora* – the practice of disinterested or impartial engagement in public life. Today, Lipsius is remembered as a political thinker of statecraft, for his Tacitan realism that draws constancy into relation with the contingent decision-making required to govern well, and the articulation of accounts of reason of state that are not justified or authorised by higher values. We inherit these as excellences of institutional life and conduct of office more so than attributes of, and training in, character.

The second example is the French aristocratic estate owner, magistrate, and essayist, Michel de Montaigne (1533–1592). While drawing on Lipsius' Stoic account of office and constancy, Montaigne's essays follow a formation of conduct that shapes constancy and inconstancy as action in the world more than as an intellectual disposition directed towards moral perfection. For Montaigne, humanist discussions of living well were not addressed to living the philosophical life of the sage or the Christian life of the saint, but the (good enough) life of the gentleman, soldier and citizen.[10] Constancy and conduct are linked to finding how to fulfil our offices of public life. In his own brief essay, 'On Constancy', for example, Montaigne takes up Lipsius' Stoic concern with constancy in the face of turmoil and personal threat (standing firm in the face of the enemy).[11] Although moderation of wisdom belongs more to a classical tradition and reception, where the Stoic virtues and training are more explicitly treated as spiritual exercises, Montaigne observes that constancy of temperament in the conduct of life belongs to social offices or conduct. In Book II of *The Essays*, Montaigne sets out his discussion of conduct in terms of inconstancy and a plurality of motives as well as constancy. One formulation, sympathetic to Bobbio's understanding of liberalism, formulates constancy in the language of a skeptic whose experience is shaped by the uncertainty of world and action.[12] Constancy of conduct is held in place by an assumption of

10 Screech 1984: xi–xiii, 153–154.

11 De Montaigne 2003: 93–95 (Book 1, Essay 12: 'On constancy').

12 See for example de Montaigne 2003: 365–371 (Book 2, Essay 1: 'On the inconstancy of our actions') and de Montaigne 2003: 730–736 (Book 2, Essay 29: 'On virtue').

uncertainty. However, Montaigne's later essays, especially in Book III, establish a different engagement where the concern with living well becomes something like 'living well with inconstancy'. In the closing sections of the last essay 'Of Experience', inconstancy and constancy are both linked to finding how to fulfil our own offices of life with decorum (or appropriate pleasure) and not simply endurance.[13] Montaigne is of interest here, not only because of his original influence on the essay as a form for writing in the humanist traditions (including for the writers and jurists of Turin), but because like the Torinese examined in our own study in miniature, Montaigne works through the testing and testimony of how to engage judgment in the middle of events required of living a public life.

Our third example is the Neapolitan rhetorician, philologist and jurisprudent Giambattista Vico (1688–1744). Vico's *Universal Laws* and *New Science* have provided models for the genetic elaboration of a philosophy of history, universal natural law established through a philological natural law and a programme of rhetorical education. Where Lipsius directs attention to the conduct of the governor and the citizen, Vico's cultivation of eloquence, knowledge and education draws on the reception of classical education (*paideia*) in the cultivation of human spirit and the world of civic and public affairs. It also becomes a vernacular jurisprudence.

The quality of constancy and the 'constancy of the jurisprudent' is elaborated in Vico's *Introduction to Universal Law (*1720–1722), an early version of his 'new science' and education. In scholastic fashion, constancy for Vico is tied to coherence and the realisation of 'eternal truths'. For Vico, the constancy of the jurisprudent was directed towards the realisation of the universality of natural law understood through philosophy, and the pattern of history understood through philology. In different formulations, both philology and philosophy find expression as aspects of a *sensus communis* – a natural law that arises as the basis of expression of a nation and its shared human activity (religion, marriage and death). The teaching of eloquence, knowledge and virtues enables the work of making true law explicit true.[14]

For Renaissance philologists and jurists such as Justus Lipsius and Giambattista Vico, this training into public life is shaped as a rhetorical training into 'the Memorie of things' and the practice of judgement. Writing trains us into ourselves and our relations with others, as

13 De Montaigne 2003: 1069–1119 (Book 3, Essay 13: 'On experience'). We also note the significance of the translation by Florio (1603) for its introduction of Montaigne to the Anglophone world and its emphasis on decorum.

14 Vico 2000: 299; Lomonaco 2017: 265; Verene 1981: 62–63; Schaeffer 2020.

a philosophical training into natural law, but also as a rhetorical and epistolary character of office and judgement.[15] While the virtues in these accounts were to be tested against experience, experience was held in place by the training into a discourse of the civil virtues of prudence, moderation and courage, and, especially for Vico, the Christian virtues of charity and humility.[16]

Placement and character: training in constancy

Any leap from Renaissance paideia to modern thought is bound to land poorly. Nevertheless, we have posited an inheritance. What we wish to draw through here is a particular example of how constancy, as a virtue of the jurist or writer, arrives directly into a time and place as a matter of humanist education and training in political and cultural activity. The source for this example is the transmission of Vico, and the location and the point of reception is Turin, in Northern Italy, in the first decades of the twentieth century.

Vico's training (humanist, rhetorical, philosophical, philological and jurisprudential) is cited throughout the activities of historian, politician and philosopher Benedetto Croce (1866–1952). Croce is one of a generation of early twentieth-century philosophers and liberals who read Hegel by reviving Vico's humanist education. Italian idealist liberalism, and Croce's promotion of it, emphasised the training in liberal and aristocratic spirit. There is much that can be said about the influence of Croce, particularly for the disciplines of historiography and philosophy of history.[17] It is the more limited (but not unrelated) question of the techniques by which a humanist training could be inherited, into the formal and personal education of jurists and writers in Italy (and Turin) in the twentieth century, that we wish to emphasise here. In turn, we note the ways in which Norberto Bobbio and Natalia Ginzburg stage their inheritance of Croce's thought.

Inheritance of Croce is a recognised topic for contemporary scholarship. In matters of Italian legal education, for example, historian of medieval and modern legal history Luigi Lacchè has considered Vico,

15 Goodrich 2017a; Goodrich 2017b.

16 Lacchè 2017: 268; Scarpato 2019.

17 For disciplines of historiography and philosophy of history, for one example, it is Croce's insistence on an interpretation of history animated by the contingent experience of facts in the conditions of the present that has been widely inherited (and also understood as a counter to Fascism's antihistoricism, a dead rather than living account of the past put to work in 'new futurism'). See for examples: Manni 2023; Ward 1996: 43–85; Körner 2011.

Giandomenico Romagnosi (1761–1835), and Croce as forming a canon that has provided jurists with the 'principles and themes establishing a common lexicon, shared categories and issues'.[18] We note here the way it describes the rhetorical inheritance of jurists in establishing a distinct 'form of life'.

More generally, Croce's writing shaped the reception of classical education of Italian elites, as they turned their attention to the maintenance of an anti-fascist spirit.[19] Philosopher Eugenio Garrin noted in 1974, reflecting on his own experience, that 'in a country where education was synonymous with literary culture, the influence of Croce's aesthetics over all age groups and sectors of the political spectrum was enormous'.[20] David Ward, a leading historian of anti-fascist Italy and its intellectual culture, has given precedence to the influence of this aesthetic training. Croce's elevation of freedom as 'the animating spirit' or moral impulse[21] for culture was influential on the scholars and writers engaged in fascist opposition.[22] For Croce, though not later for Bobbio, this expression of freedom becomes a constancy of will that unites ethics, politics and culture. The struggle for freedom is the key to understanding History as well as a moral principle.[23]

While not a direct point of orientation of resistance, it was Croce's reformulation of Vico's emphasis on the human side of human law, as well as the generative character of language, that gave Croce the means to emphasise the importance of creating newer and more original forms.[24] Such an emphasis informed Croce's characteristic assertion of the political role of culture, accompanied by a technical training into how to conduct oneself in role in a humanist tradition, and its virtues. He endorsed and explained, for example, the political need for forms

18 Lacchè 2017: 268. Lacchè argues a formulation of legal education close to that of Bobbio: 'history, philosophy, and dogmatics taken alone are not sufficient to found a sound legal education and an effective practice as a jurist. Only a balanced mixture can provide a correct solution' (Lacchè 2017: 270).
19 See for example Ward 1996 and Manni 2023: 64–65.
20 Ward 1996: 45, quoting Garin 1974: 4. Croce's *Estetica come scienza dell'espressione e linguistica generale* (1902) was the 'book which brought him national and international recognition' (Ward 1996: 52).
21 Ward 1996: 46, quoting Croce 1932: 8.
22 There are many examples for evidence of this point, cited across the twentieth century. For example see Calogero 1958.
23 Bellamy 1987: 91–98; Bobbio 1995: 137–140. See also Manni 2023: 65, and with reference to Croce's *Manifesto degli Intellettuali Antifascisti* (1925).
24 Ward 1996: 51; and significance of Croce's reanimation of Vico extends beyond Italy through translation by R G Collingwood: Croce 1913. See also Curthoys & Docker 2006: 103–104.

of writing (or 'literary expression') which refused both empty rhetoric and ostentatious 'dress'.[25] Writing in 1936, Croce argued that 'despite the lack of subtlety and urbanity in our present age, the virtue of literary decorum exists and works',[26] as a means for resisting imposed formulations of experience in writing ('specifications')[27] that acted against reason for the individual writer, and against 'indifference' in their social role.[28] This training positioned jurists like Bobbio, and writers like Ginzburg, to address how aesthetic form and language was a 'particular act of spiritual economy'[29] (in Croce's terms), that insisted on constancy of spirit and 'sincerity' (or truthfulness) in craft.[30] For Vico and Croce, their writing in a tradition of humanist virtues was more a case of continuing to work with the old.[31] We agree with Ward's observation, however, that Bobbio, Ginzburg (and many others) took up that training in order to assert their own creative freedom against the conformity of the fascist regime.

The second aspect of the inheritance of humanist tradition of virtues we wish to emphasise returns us to Vico's formulation of *theatrum hodiernae vitae* – the setting of the conduct of life in the theatre of contemporary life. For a generation of scholars, writers and anti-fascist activists, the link Croce asserted in his own work between culture and politics offered a training into culture as a way of life and lived relations, and as activities of humanist writing about those relations and experiences through aesthetics and action.[32]

For Bobbio and Ginzburg, training into culture was also joined to the conduct of everyday life, in their related experiences of shared institutional community in Turin: family, the publishing house, the university.[33] Following our example, although Natalia Ginzburg (by her

25 Croce 1936 in Verdicchio 2017: 12.
26 Croce 1936 in Verdicchio 2017: 15.
27 Croce 1936 in Verdicchio 2017: 10.
28 Croce 1936 in Verdicchio 2017: 10.
29 Croce 1936 in Verdicchio 2017: 10.
30 Croce 1936 in Verdicchio 2017: 13. Natalia Ginzburg's early essay *Dire La Verità* (1933) demonstrates this training. The essay is discussed and quoted by Domenico Scarpa in his preface to the 2015 Italian edition of *Le Piccole Virtù* : Scarpa 2015: xiii.
31 This point is made by many scholars, for a leading example see Ward 1996: 124–156; and Ward 2025.
32 For example, Boyers 2000: 10 (first published in 1992 in Italian journal *Salmagundi* 9: 130–156).
33 There are many sources that describe, and analyse, the lives and political lives of Bobbio and Ginzburg, and their relationships and activities, during this period, not the least of which is Ginzburg 2018. Our general overview

own admission) never felt 'cultured' in a formal sense of completing a university course of study,[34] the life of Ginzburg's family revolved around the Università di Torino, where her father was a celebrated scientist and teacher, and her future husband, the Russian Jewish emigré Leone Ginzburg, joined as a precociously young professor of Russian Language and Literature. Bobbio studied Law also at the Università di Torino (to which he returned as a professor in 1948).[35] Bobbio, and the Levi/Ginzburg families were involved, outside of the university, as writers, poets and scholars whose work collectively informed the Torinese (and Italian and exiled Italian) resistance to Fascism.[36] Later, after the war, members of this group worked from that experience to participate in the formation of the democratic Republic (and to comment openly about the political and intellectual direction of its institutions, constitution and economic recovery).[37] This Torinese milieu, the educated elite, included the writers Cesare Pavese and the journalist publisher Giulio Einaudi (who were also school friends of Leone Ginzburg and Norberto Bobbio).[38] Together, they established the publishing house Einaudi in 1933. (Einaudi, a prestigious and influential house in Italian cultural life, was the first publisher of Pavese, Primo Levi and Carlo Levi, as well as Ginzburg and Bobbio; and both Ginzburg and Bobbio worked there as editors and translators after 1944).[39] They also started and nurtured a range of journals and publications, circulating around the group Giustizia e Libertà,[40] and later the liberal-socialist *Partito d'Azione* (Action Party),[41] including *L'Italia Libera*, where Ginzburg published her early writing.[42]

---

in the terms given in this section is summarised for the most part from autobiographical accounts (including interviews with friends and political and cultural collaborators) translated into English: Bobbio 2002; Ginzburg 2003.

34 Ginzburg 2003: 20. For interpretations of Ginzburg's self-deprecation as technique see Wienstein 2000.

35 Bobbio 2002: 36.

36 Bobbio 2002: 18–64; and Ginzburg 2003: 3–20.

37 Bobbio 2002: 67–80.

38 Bobbio 2002: 18–20; Bellamy et al 2004: 68.

39 Bobbio 2002: 50, 76; Ginzburg 2003: 76–80; Boyers 2000: 14. Luigi Einaudi, Giulio's Father, became the first president of the republic, and was teacher of Bobbio (Bobbio 2002: 20). See Ginzburg 2018: 198–203 for another account of life at Einaudi. See also Ward 2025.

40 Bobbio 2002: 22–28; Ginzburg 2018: 124–140. See also Ward 1996: 124–134; Ward 2000.

41 Bobbio 2002: 65–69; Ginzburg 2003: 45; Ward 2000.

42 Ward 2000. Examples of this writing by Ginzburg are discussed in Section 3.

Croce was in a social relationship with this elite Torinese community over a significant period of the 1920s and 1930s[43] and was a direct reference point for motivating Natalia Ginzburg in her early writing.[44] At the same time, as noted, the reception of Croce's writing and example posed a basic continuity between him and these anti-fascist activists and writers, in both cultural and political spheres. Many were members of the *Partito d'Azione*, as well as writing for its journals, and played a significant role in armed struggle against Germany between 1943 and 1945. Some became involved in formal politics after Rome was liberated in 1944.[45] Croce's liberalism, however, with its accent on spiritual freedom and ethical unification of politics and culture, was by 1944 set against 'collective' and 'mass' politics.[46] The failure of the Action Party, and of liberal-socialism after 1944 formed part of the chastened response that Ginzburg struggled to reconcile in her writing over her lifetime,[47] and that Bobbio developed in his political writings from the 1950s through to the early 1970s. Bobbio's concern, for example, with the rise of political violence, on both left and right, gave his sense of law and culture, and his inheritance of the virtue of constancy in the office of jurist and public figure, a form of 'holding' a middle.[48]

The sense of the transitoriness of institutions and life, in the conflicts of war, or the conflicts in its aftermath, was met by Bobbio and Ginzburg by writing on the details of living in place, a training in maintaining the constancy of everyday relations. To place this gloss is important to our own account and jurisographic activity. It reminds that details matter, and the presentation of details in writing (including in our own account) is not a search for an inaccessible or reducible truth, but the technical work of sustaining an adequacy of everyday relations in the middle of events.

43 Bobbio 2002: 27–28; Chataway 2002: 3; Teresa Chataway (2002) 'Introduction' to Bobbio 2002: 3; Ward 1996: 43–44.
44 Parks 2018: viii. Ginzburg characteristically underplays this influence, while giving it emphasis in Ginzburg 2018: 167–169. See also Footnote 30.
45 Notably, Vittorio Foa, Felice Balbo: See Ginzburg 2003: 47–50, 177–190.
46 Bobbio's judgment on Croce's opposition to mass politics and culture and democracy is harsh: Bobbio 1995: 137–139.
47 Ginzburg 2003: 48–50. See also Ginzburg 2018: 216; Ward 2000; Francese 2009: 157.
48 See for example Bobbio 1990. See also Bobbio 1995; Ward 1996: 47–48. Ward's argument is drawn from Bobbio 1955: 111. The point made here could be extended to other writers and participants of this intellectual community, although our focus is limited to our two examples. See for example: Gordon 2001.

In this section, we have related a number of engagements with the sweep of the humanist discourse of 'constancy' – at least as it might plausibly have arrived in Turin in the 1940s. Following the cue of both Ginzburg and Bobbio, this has been related through the idioms of culture, office, and institutions. The reference to late humanist and early modern Italian and North European humanism and its training in eloquence is a reminder of the inheritance of a tradition. While this inheritance for scholars has often been at the level of training and comportment, it is one that was self-consciously taken up by Croce and transformed again in the work of Ginzburg and Bobbio as part of an erudite and elite intellectual and political culture. In the next section, we follow the training into constancy – or at least its reporting.

Training into constancy: writing (Bobbio and Ginzburg)

We turn now to our short miniature studies of these observations on the virtue of constancy through examples in Bobbio and Ginzburg's work, rather than an encapsulation of their work as a whole. We begin with two brief essays by Ginzburg, taking her theme of maintenance of human relations as a matter of character, tested in conflict and experienced over time: *My Vocation (Il mio mestiere)* (1949) and *The Little Virtues (Le Piccole Virtù)* (1960).[49] Bobbio's work as a jurist has usually been divided into three parts: linguistic philosophy, philosophy of law and jurisprudence. Our focus on Bobbio concerns his scattered writing on character and virtue. The two essays we examine here are taken from writings in the 1940s collected in *Philosophy of Decadentism* and the 1990s collected in *In Praise of Meekness*.[50] In each study in miniature we wish to draw out, as matters of jurisographical presentation, technique, vocation, education and training. Our style of analysis in our study of Bobbio differs however from the one we have taken with Ginzburg. This is because Bobbio's craft and training are often held to be a formal argument within the offices of jurist and philosopher, and as memoire.

49 Ginzburg 1989b; Ginzburg 1989c. See Ginzburg 2003: 84–88 with regard to writing and reception of the essay, noting feedback given by her friend, novelist Elsa Morante as to the title: Morante did not approve. See also Franco 2024 with regard to the politics of the translation of *Family Lexicon*, which was translated with a different title for each of its three English translations.

50 Bobbio 1948; Bobbio 2000.

a) Ginzburg

Ginzburg's writing is intensely personal, but it is not openly factual or biographically accurate or complete. Apart from her novel-memoir *Family Lexicon* (1963), her 'I' is never attached directly to her name.[51] 'Our children', 'our city', 'their toys', 'my vocation': the commonalities of life are intimate and detailed but also shared, a vocabulary to open an experience that is identifiable and common.[52] Her theme and topic in all of her writing (novels, essays, plays) is family. This is because family, for Natalia Ginzburg, was the clearest institutional site for Fascist era falsity, propaganda, forced conformity and production of lies, as well as the site for its resistance.[53] Both experiences required acute, close attention to language. 'Back then', Natalia Ginzburg wrote in 1944, 'our language could not be clear and limpid because sharpness and clarity are attributes of truth, and truth was not allowed. Back then we were all overloaded with words because words were the only thing we had at a time when all possibility of intimate and public well-being was denied us'.[54]

To respond adequately and to guard against a repeat of life experienced under fascism required a technical precision in language, practised over the course of her lifetime. For Ginzburg, this involved constancy in recognising that the formulations of relations between culture and politics, written or expressed, required reformulation as the shape of conflict changed. Some things needed to be silent, given space to hide in plain sight.[55] Her essays and her fiction merge in their forms and become her own sets of exercises in cultivating a public style and voice that stands to the side of a recounting, or an overcoming; to produce a *memoriam* that is lived, and which guards vigilantly against nostalgia or self-pity. Ginzburg's movement between past and present tenses,[56] for example,

51 Ginzburg 2003: 102. See first Italian edition, Ginzburg 1963. We note different titles given in English, over time, including 'The Things We Used to Say': see Ginzburg 2003: 98–99.

52 See for example Ginzburg 1989c, which was first published in 1960. For a specific discussion of details in the work of Ginzburg see West 2000: 5, with reference to Schor 1987.

53 See for one example Ward 1996: 152.

54 Ginzburg 2000a. This first appeared in the Italian journal *L'Italia Libera* 2/198 (11 December 1944) and is included in full as an appendix in Jeannet & Katz 2000c: 233.

55 For a justly famous example, the account of Leone Ginzburg's death, in Ginzburg 1989d: 8.

56 Fontanella 2000: 35–36. See also Scarpa 2015: xxvi for discussion of her use of the *passato remoto*.

are for reminding us, and her, that the mundanity of a time before tragedy is exactly that: mundane, and worth chronicling and detailing for its very ordinariness. It is also carried forward, and to be faced, and constantly addressed and readdressed, for the formation of character, but through allegory, for the reformation of the nation.

The focus by Ginzburg on family, and her own family (although the relation between them is in dialogue)[57] is expressive of her ethos of constancy as character. To write about family is to also write for them; it is often a necessity, in a literal sense, to keep writing to support one's children.[58] At the same time, public writing offers an example to another generation (the activists, writers, politicians of the generation that followed her own, and whose experience of 1926–1944 was not direct). This example includes a caution, and a contradiction. If one's vocation is to write, you keep writing.[59] But you should not assume, or fall into the trap of thinking, that words on the page ever tell the whole story, reasoned and complete. 'To believe that everything could be changed into poetry and words', she wrote, was 'a common error'.[60] There is nothing ornate in Ginzburg's writing as a consequence. There are no excessive adjectives, sentence structures, or falsity about ambition or scale. Dialogue is reported. Little is said and much is not. Writing, however, is necessary: it is practised as such and described.

In her essay 'My Vocation' (1949), for example, Ginzburg explains the purposes and necessity of writing for her, and how she trained herself to do it. The essay is truthful but not real. It is a story, self-deprecating and funny, to the extent that it reveals something of why one must write rather than take up any other tasks ('if I try and speak in public or take up knitting or go on a journey, I suffer').[61] But it is also a self-reflection on taking up an office. She knows what she can and must do, in terms of genre and its limit. 'Let me be clear', she writes, 'I can only write stories'.[62] This is a warning and instruction. The act of writing is to be faced head on, and endured with steadfastness, because it is an obligation. Your writing is not to sustain happiness, create possessions, belonging or worth. You 'cannot hope to console yourself for your grief by writing' or allow yourself to be 'deceived' into thinking that your own writing will soothe or lull you.[63] Writing, as vocation, is without artifice or

57 Ginzburg 1989c: 99.
58 Ginzburg 1989b: 67; Ginzburg 2003: 41; Boyers 2000.
59 Ginzburg 1989b: 68; see also Ginzburg 2018: 217–218.
60 Ward 2000: 49–50, quoting and translating from Ginzburg 1963.
61 Ginzburg 1989b: 53.
62 Ginzburg 1989b: 53.
63 Ginzburg 1989b: 66.

moral hierarchy. It does not involve being adept at moving words around a page, or reviving stock saved phrases and ideas from other writing. Writing also cannot be a diversion; our own writing passes judgement on us. As she notes: 'We must swallow our saliva and our tears and grit our teeth and dry the blood from our wounds'.[64] Such a discipline of writing means only that constancy in the practice of our craft will 'help us get up on to our feet, fix our feet firmly on the ground; [...] help us overcome madness and delirium, fever and despair'.[65] Our sorrow in the aftermath and face of conflict changes us, Ginzburg notes. The forms of words and their techniques – their clarity and directness – must, as noted, also change, as antidote to an imposed optimism of the fascist era.[66] But what does not change are the tools of our crafts as writers (although what sorrow, conflict and trouble we face means we can and must handle them differently). Ginzburg invites herself, and us, to have 'the strength to be interested in others and devote our time to them',[67] to see the world in full dimension, its secrets and shadows, and pay attention by writing about what we know and experience.[68] This is what Ginzburg means by virtues, our '*terrestrial* condition',[69] literal but also metaphoric.

Our exemplification of Ginzburg's writing ends, appropriately enough, with her famous essay *The Little Virtues* (1960).[70] The essay concerns how we train children to find their own vocations, through which they can form generous relations with others and the world (as opposed to accepting with fear or unreflective reason imposed expectations of success and status, which, for Ginzburg, breed dangerous conformity). The essay contains enough detail and anecdote about the actual raising of children in a family that we can assume it is her own, yet is also capacious enough to speak to the experience of any reader. This purpose, however, is also to make comment on Italy itself. The essay makes, for example, an argument against 'easy' 'family egoism'. This is a term Ginzburg used in a 1944 essay 'Our Children' (*I nostri figli*), which in many ways is a visceral rehearsal for the *Little Virtues*, written without distance from immediate need and grief.[71] 'Family egoism', for

64 Ginzburg 1989b: 66.
65 Ginzburg 1989b: 66.
66 Ginzburg 2018: 215–217.
67 Ginzburg 1989b: 65.
68 Ginzburg 1989b: 65 (paraphrased).
69 Ginzburg 1989b: 65.
70 Ginzburg 1989c.
71 Ginzburg 2000b. This first appeared in the Italian journal *L'Italia Libera* 2/198 (31 December 1944) and is included in full as an appendix in Jeannet & Katz 2000c.

Ginzburg, contains attributes of protection and self-preservation that are commonplace but become distorted in times of conflict, scarcity and demagoguery, forcing an inwardness that speaks against relations of human dialogue and experience. 'Family egoism' is produced in circumstances, like living under fascism and invasion, in which '[p]roblems of a practical nature, minute daily worries cloud us; many interests and cares that we once felt acutely now die in us, and strictly private and family thoughts and fears take their place. What will our child eat? What will he play with? How to dress him? What to do to make sure he's always healthy, strong, happy?'[72]

In 1960, Ginzburg's direction is less explicit. This version of the same themes is no longer addressed to the parent of the small child requiring shelter (*I nostri figli* was written at the birth of a fragile democracy in 1944), but to the parent worried about how to best resource their child as they mature, and as they make their own way in relating to others (1960 and *Le piccoli virtú* is 14 years into the new republic). The opening lines are justly famous:

> As far as the education of children is concerned, I think they should be taught not the little virtues but the great ones. Not thrift but generosity and an indifference to money; not caution but courage in a contempt for danger; nor shrewdness but frankness and a love of truth; not a desire for success but a desire to be and to know.[73]

Ginzburg's argument is that the education of children in the little virtues (and, we could suggest, also of scholars, writers and university people)[74] 'arise[s] ... from a defensive instinct; ... the result of reflection and calculation and so we think that they absolutely must be taught'.[75] By contrast, she argues, 'we do not bother to teach the great virtues, though we love them and want our children to have them ... The great virtues well up from an instinct in which reason does not speak, and instinct that seems to be difficult to name ....But one cannot breathe in the great virtues from the surrounding air, and they should be the basis of our relationship with our children, the first foundation of their education'.[76]

72 Ginzburg 2000b: 288.
73 Ginzburg 1989c: 97.
74 See Ginzburg 2003: 170–171 on 'pedagogic vocation', in relation to *The Little Virtues*. See also Fontanella 2000: 33–34. Fontanella reflects on his own personal training from Ginzburg.
75 Ginzburg 1989c: 97.
76 Ginzburg 1989c: 97.

The formation and inheritance of this training cannot be through the exertion of authority over another, telling them what to do, or what to write, as '[a]uthority in us would be a hypocrisy and a sham ... We've looked within ourselves for too long and seen too many things there'. Instead, she argues 'we must invent another kind of relationship'.[77] Perhaps returning to her own formative traditions, that relationship was written and dialogic. 'In dialogue', she notes, 'we show ourselves for what we are, imperfect, in the hope that our children will not resemble us but be stronger and better than us'.[78] The purpose of the essay is then to guard against little virtues, and instead to equip 'our children' to be constant in discovering their own vocation, a great virtue that will be tested in daily practice.[79] For Ginzburg, that demonstration of constancy includes 'being moderate with oneself and generous with others',[80] 'to expect sacrifice and not to expect reward'[81] and to be prepared for the trials and conflicts a person must live with, without false hope, as acts of generosity. '[P]erhaps the one real chance we have of giving them some kind of help in their search for a vocation', she writes, '[is] to have a vocation ourselves, to know it, to love it and serve it passionately; because love of life begets a love of life'.[82]

b) Bobbio

Our sense of Norberto Bobbio's writing on conduct is shaped by his office. His early writing is conducted as a Professor of Law, and then of Political Philosophy; his later writing is often presented as a reflection on his vocation as a teacher. Along with others, we read Bobbio's account of constancy and his division of spheres of ethics and action in law as a cultivation of moderation and middle grounds, as much for its sense of analytical clarity.[83] For our study in miniature, we address two pieces, presented as incidental writing, in which Bobbio considers the virtue of constancy a part of the character required for public life.

The first example, *The Philosophy of Decadentism: A Study in Existentialism* ('Decadentism') was published in Italian in 1946 and in English in 1948. It was drawn from a series of essays written between 1942 and 1944, written in contrast to Bobbio's teaching legal philosophy

77 Ginzburg 1989c: 99.
78 Ginzburg 1989c: 99.
79 'A vocation is man's one true wealth and salvation' (Ginzburg 1989c: 106).
80 Ginzburg 1989c: 102.
81 Ginzburg 1989c: 105.
82 Ginzburg 1989c: 110.
83 Craiutu 2017.

at the University of Camerino and Padua, and his engagement with the work of Thomas Hobbes and the philosophy of personalism.[84] Bobbio's polemic in 'Decadentism' is both diagnostic and judgemental. Existentialism is a diagnosis of the loss of authority in thought and life in the twentieth century. For Bobbio, it was also a symptom of that loss, and inadequate to the task of meeting the challenge it diagnosed. Existentialists, in Bobbio's judgement, whether authentic or not, have been uninterested in cultivating the creativity of imagination and public reason necessary to sustain a life lived in common.[85] The central motif of the crisis of existentialism is its elaboration of a relation to the world, and spiritual training (or 'attitude') of authenticity which cultivates an unbounded individualism (and crisis) of inner and outer experience. This training, at least in Bobbio's presentation, is irrational since it refuses objective form; it is one part a romantic transcendental spiritualism, and one part decisionist action.[86] In terms of political association, existentialism offers in these ways a training, but for Bobbio this training is limited to a realisation of the exception and the singular, and a realisation of the inauthenticity of office and order.[87] Bobbio continued his polemic against left and right irrationalism through the upheavals of the 1960s.[88]

The 'decadentism' of the title of Bobbio's book draws on a polemic established by Croce against the romantic dissolution of politics and culture. In doing so, Bobbio links the writings of existentialism to forms of Baroque mannerism.[89] This assertion combines a disdain for mannerist and decadent presentation of the loss of sovereignty and of relation, both in literature and art. The Baroque, for Bobbio, also forms part of a critique of mannerist philosophical style which represents training in conduct of office as an aspect of a 'will to power'.[90] We note that Bobbio's criticism is accompanied (and compromised) by a reactionary account of decadentism as degenerate behaviour.[91]

84 Bobbio 1993; Sciara 2022.
85 Bobbio 1948: 35.
86 Bobbio 1948: 5; Bobbio also raises the same criticism against the asceticism of Stoic and Epicurean ethics. See Bobbio 2002: 43 for a different judgement of Concetto Marchesi who works on Senecca and Tacitus formed a part of resistance to fascism.
87 See Bobbio 2002: 77 detailing a debate between Jaspers and Lukacs at the European Institute of Culture in Turin in 1946. For a very different account of Karl Jaspers see Arendt 1973.
88 Bobbio 1996.
89 Drake 1982: 79–81.
90 Bobbio 1948: xx; Bull 2013.
91 Bobbio 1948: 54.

Bobbio's critical account of the philosophy of existentialism in the 1940s sits comfortably with forms of personalism (Crocean, Marxist and Christian) that emphasise human relationality in community as the starting point of freedom in both political (civil) and personal life.[92] This emphasis also informed the ethical commitments of the Action Party. As Bobbio argues in *Political Life*, such commitments are better considered as ideologies in resistance, rather than ideologies of resistance.[93] Giuseppe Sciara has noted that after the war and the end of Resistance, Bobbio's liberalism became increasingly influenced by the individualism of Hobbes and the natural rights tradition, as well as the formulation of association in procedures of government and democracy rather than community. But Bobbio's accounts of liberal-socialism and legal order set associative ethical commitments across a number of different registers, for example: the limit of the state in relation to the citizen or person, and the participation of the citizen in the democratic state. Liberal questions of freedom (freedom from state authority as well as freedom to judge and act) are instituted for Bobbio in office and activity. Constancy in this formulation lies with technical forms of institutional life and of liberal democratic government. Bobbio's ethos of moderation, in these ways, joins the constancy of public reason and judgement to the rationality and virtues of prudence, civility, and self-control.

The second source for our study in miniature, the essay 'In Praise of Meekness', might be read as an exercise in establishing the proper modes for Bobbio's ethos of moderation. 'In Praise of Meekness' started as a lecture on the virtues in the late 1980s and was later the eponymous signature essay in a collection on ethics and politics. The essay gives a succinct formulation of Bobbio's understanding of virtue and morality and is framed in terms of reflection on a political and ethical life, more so than a scholarly life.

'In Praise of Meekness' is set in a world where the democratic promise of Italy in 1945 has passed into something more complex, and where the project of a state-centred liberal-socialism no longer sustains public and economic life. It is also a world where the relation between law and legal form, and power and political life, is still beset by violence pitched against the rule of law state. Our point of departure is with the arrangement of topics and the distribution of arguments. 'In Praise of Meekness' is modelled on a form of presentation of argument familiar to Vico – first, a philological study of meaning; second, a study of institutions; and third, a reflection on the appropriateness of conduct for public life. The traditions of the virtues are canvassed before Bobbio sets his accounts of

92 Sciara 2022: 253–254. See also Zolo 1990.
93 Bobbio 2002: 37.

the 'strong' and 'weak' virtues in place.[94] Meekness is a human attribute and the meek are social actors ('Blessed are the meek for they shall inherit the earth'). Etymologically, its cognate terms relate to mitigation rather than mildness, and acknowledgement of this excellence of meekness recognises the power (or ability) to let the 'other be themselves'.[95] The contrast that follows from this recognition is also made clear by Bobbio. The 'strong' virtues (courage, justice, constancy) are those of the powerful and of those who govern (and can exercise power through violence). The 'weak' virtues (humility, modesty, temperance, decency and so on), fully gendered, are attributed to those 'below'. The list of 'weak' virtues might outline the characteristics of the downtrodden, but they are also, for Erasmus (and, differently, Montaigne) the attributes of the Christian prince. On the one side, Bobbio places Machiavellian and Schmittian politics, and whatever counterposes politics in that register, it is not meekness. Yet meekness is not simply the refusal of politics. The meek, says Bobbio, are the opposite of those who seek glory in politics (they are not arrogant, do not overrate the importance of politics and refrain from contest and rivalry). This is not submission so much as a sense of refusal of what is useless about politics in the name of what is important, and incites Bobbio to claim that the meek are 'precursors' to a better world.[96] Like simplicity and charity, the work of the meek is done regardless of its reception or reciprocity. Bobbio's own choice for discussing the virtues is, he says, a reaction to the 'violence' of the world.[97] He concludes by stating that meekness is the 'antithesis of politics' – by which he means 'our' European politics, a politics shaped by a relation between law and power, and understood in terms of 'reason of state'.[98]

'In Praise of Meekness' is a late essay – one whose arrangement draws the reader back both to the state of political reality and the demands of democratic participation. It also struggles with questions of faith, and with lay (non-religious) ethics. If meekness is the tain of the mirror of political virtues, Bobbio is still prepared to hold to the political virtues of humility and patience as central to the prudence of the scholar, and citizens in general, in their participation in public life. Rather than follow this engagement further, we return briefly to Bobbio's characterisation of himself as following a vocation as professor and teacher rather than

94 Bobbio 2000: 23.

95 Bobbio also writes 'A meek person is needed by others to help them defeat evil in themselves' (Bobbio 2000: 24).

96 Bobbio 2000: 31.

97 Bobbio 2000: 34.

98 Bobbio 2000: 35; Bobbio 2001: 74–80.

as a politician.[99] Within the office of scholar and jurist, the virtues are ordered around the 'honour of learned men'.[100] In the essay 'In Praise of Meekness', Bobbio addresses formulations of the virtues of office in terms of prudence and humility, and to these can be added lucidity (and responsibility) in fulfilling the offices of scholar and public actor well. As a public writer, Bobbio's work is noted for its analytical care, and a willingness to work topically to draw history, analysis and politics into relation. It is certainly possible to address constancy in Bobbio's writing in philosophy of law and politics as shaped by disciplinary restraint. In noting Bobbio's inheritance of Croce's concern with politics and culture as a concern of public life and office, it would be better to think of his cultivation of historical, analytical and juridico-political understanding of the present as part of a training into character and judgement, as well as a way of sustaining the analysis of the working of institutions and relations between law and power.[101]

Displacement and reception (Australia)

The inheritance of a tradition, or the continued work on a tradition, can feel reactionary. From our miniature studies, however, we have emphasised how constancy as a virtue, part of the training into a humanist tradition, contributes to comportment in a public role through writing. The consideration of Ginzburg and Bobbio's writing as part of a tradition has been consistently parsed in different disciplinary accounts in Italy.[102] Bobbio and Ginzburg's works (and works about them) outside of Italy and outside of the Italian language, by contrast, have had a varied reception. This is dependent on the politics of translation as much as audience.[103] In the twentieth century, their reception was mainly dependent

99 As Bellamy et al (2004: 69–70) argue: 'Between 1955 and 1970, he also published three collections of his most important essays. These writings had a similar place in Italian academic legal circles as the work of H.L.A. Hart in British universities'.

100 Bobbio 2001: 30.

101 Bobbio 2001: 74–80.

102 We refer here to Italian scholars working in two languages, or translated into English; or those working in English directly about reception in Italy. In addition to sources used throughout this chapter see for examples on Bobbio: Ferrari 2004; Urbinati 2003; Bovero 2005; Chataway 2011; and on Ginzburg: Antonietti 2023; Bassi 2023.

103 We note that which languages, as well as which genre of texts and writing, are translated for Anglophone audiences has an unequal history and an unequal public presence: see for example Schwartz 2024. We also note it is in part dependent on Bobbio and Ginzburg's own relations to dissemination

on a small but important group of scholars, working in translation: cultural and political historians of Italy (in the UK and the US) and Italian Studies scholars (in those jurisdictions, and also in Australia).[104] In the twenty-first century, however, Ginzburg has emerged into fuller view through a renaissance of scholarly interest in world literature and translation studies, and a new general readership for a translated Italian literary canon, particularly of Italian women writers.[105] (This refocusing on Ginzburg is due in no small measure to the success of Ann Goldstein's English translation of Elena Ferrante's *The Neapolitan Quartet*.)[106] In Bobbio's case, there is an observable contemporary interest in his conceptualisation of mediated democratic liberalism, particularly in Latin America, by scholars of philosophy of language in law.[107] Bobbio's contributions to analogical reasoning in law have also more recently been brought into closer conversation with Anglo-British traditions, but in a particular direction (by Italian jurisprudents and philosophers, writing in English).[108] We observe from this brief survey that the humanist tradition we are working within, and comment on in this chapter, is constantly varied and displaced by the situation of writers and their translators, and varied and displaced again according to how, when, where and with whom it arrives somewhere new.

---

of their work, and affinity with other languages. Ginzburg spent some time in England with her second husband but noted later in life 'I never managed to get on with English; and I didn't learn it' (Ginzburg 2003: 92). See also her account of this period in Ginzburg 1989a: 21–22. For her views on translation see Boyers 2000: 13.

104 See sources used in Sections 2 and 3 of this essay, for example: Ward 1996; Jeannet & Katz 2000c. For other iterations, with regard to Ginzburg's work, see Bullock 1991; Amoia 1996: 61–73. We are not the only scholars in Australia to work with Bobbio and Ginzburg, although the reception has until recently been limited by availability to translations and siloed within particular disciplinary traditions. See Chataway (1997; 2011) on Bobbio as a legal scholar; and Davidson (1995; 1998) on Bobbio as a political philosopher. Ginzburg's reception in Australia has been largely in linguistics and Italian studies: see Cicioni & Formica 2006; Castronuovo 2010.

105 See for one example Rousseva & Ziolkowski 2024 where they discuss Calvino's prominence as well as increased interest alongside Ferrante.

106 Ferrante 2012; Ferrante 2013; Ferrante 2014; Ferrante 2015; Ergun et al 2020.

107 See for example two special editions dedicated to Bobbio: Santos 2004 and Salatini & Barreira 2017. Bobbio has 'significant intellectual presence in Brazil in the spheres of legal and political theory' (Lafer 2022).

108 For example, Poggi & Ferraro 2024; Ratti 2024; Manni 2022. See also Cotterrell 2024.

Our own reception of Bobbio and Ginzburg as sources is mediated by our relationships to a politics of translation, to language and to disciplines, and to each of our familial inheritance of the experiences of life under fascism in Northern Italy and of war in Europe. To write together of Bobbio and Ginzburg in Australia in the 2020s, from within a Law school, and for this study, is a different activity again. In this final section, we consider what Bobbio and Ginzburg offer to our own comportment in the offices of the humanist jurisprudent, with an ear for virtues and a sense of training into the virtue of constancy. We make three observations, drawn primarily from translations of Bobbio and Ginzburg's own writing, and select sources in English that place and study that writing independently, or situate their connection to the Torino anti-fascist experience. These sources (already present in our chapter in previous sections) are addressed here jurisographically, to show how a line of humanist tradition in civic commitment is received through writing as an experience of laws lived, and law taught, and to draw out what training we receive from that writing.

Our first observation is temporal. Bobbio and Ginzburg's writings offer a celebrated but not straightforward representation of the Italian experience of fascism, invasion and the Republic that followed in its aftermath. Bobbio and Ginzburg, like many in their orbit, were, and are, famous in Italy for their relationships, and their role in articulating how to live with resistance. This attention given to their work and lives has not always been positive or unmediated. For example, Ginzburg and Bobbio both faced public criticism for words and actions conducted in one time but read and displaced to another. In 1990, Bobbio was critiqued in *La Repubblica*, when a 'splinter from history leapt out of the archive'.[109] Bobbio signed Mussolini's mandated Oath of University allegiance in 1934, despite his well-known anti-fascist position, to maintain his professorship and continue his teaching. This fact attracted retrospective opprobrium, but also a renewed commitment to public education by those who had experienced Italy in a time many could not see by the 1990s or chose to forget.[110] As the philosopher Eugenio Garin wrote in 1992 (in defence of Bobbio):

> [T]hose who decided to stay in Italy [*as Garin also did*] were obliged to accept the consequences of that decision. Even if they were privately opposed to the regime, and even if they took part in clandestine activities aimed at overturning it, they had to maintain an outward

109 Bobbio 2002: 32–33. This quote is from Torinese historian Marco Revelli in *Il Manifesto* (17 June 1992).

110 Bobbio 2002: 30–36.

> appearance that would allow them to continue with their own business … It was not a matter of a heroic attitude, it was an attempt at self-defence; this was the room for manoeuvre left in the difficult daily business of living under a dictatorship. If you didn't opt for exile, you had to operate in a situation that was completely ambivalent. [111]

In Ginzburg's case, she was critiqued by ostiaries of the formal, weighty Italian literary tradition throughout her life (but particularly before she had been awarded the nation's most prestigious literary award, the Strega Prize, for *Family Lexicon* in 1963) because she either detailed relations and life on a small scale – 'the debris of domesticity'[112] – in spare prose, or because she 'restricted her comments on the highly influential, privileged and politicised peer group she lived among to accounts of their foibles'.[113] In either case, Ginzburg's refusal in her writing to moralise or theorise the past for the present, and her commitment in style and language to guard against sentimental public Memoria, was similarly open for negative comment.

Prudence forms part of the training in constancy in our reception of Bobbio and Ginzburg as thought figures and from their writing. We observe from these examples that a formulation of constancy as testimony, required when living a public life in one time, is nevertheless constantly modified when noticed or acted upon by those who follow. Yet Bobbio and Ginzburg also remained constant in their own commitment (or vocation) to write with ethical clarity about the legacies of their aesthetic and political activities, even as they (and their work) moved from a time of fascism and war into republicanism, the *anni di piombo* and life under Berlusconi.[114] The examples also offer a caution against the insertion of literary and juristic texts, taken outside of their time and language, into an attenuated Anglophone world of generalised or laudatory theory, history or critique. We acknowledge that the writings and receptions of Bobbio and Ginzburg's work, as artefacts of high public visibility and value, are contested in time, as well as over time,[115] even

111 Bobbio 2002: 31. Garin is quoted in interview by Nello Ajello in *La Repubblica* (16 June 1992).
112 For example, see Jeannet 2000: 64.
113 Parks 2018: vii–viii, x; and Ginzburg 2003: 98–108 on reception, and changing perceptions of her work after 1963.
114 See for example, Bobbio 2002: 194–199; Jeannet & Katz 2000b; Jeannet & Katz 2000a; and in general, Ginzburg 2003.
115 There are many examples of scholarship making a similar point: for two, see: Garofalo et al 2019 and Ward 1996.

as we draw from them a limited question of lineage of constancy as a virtue, in role and character.

The second observation we make is jurisprudential. We have chosen to place Bobbio and Ginzburg in relation to each other in this chapter, to emphasise relations to a culture, and to experience of laws. Mussolini used law violently to impose manufactured *Italianatà* and manufactured consent to the fascist regime. This point extends both to the aggressive colonial ambitions of the Italian state in Albania and North Africa from 1936, and the infamous race laws of 1938, which sanctioned deportation, confinement, arrest and stripping of national status and protections for Jewish citizens. The development of machinery through law forced compliance and conformity in institutional life, from the civil service to the university, to the press, to the family. For dissidents, the choices open to remain constant to ideals of freedom, justice and democratic participation required compromise and self-preservation in order both to continue to conduct institutional roles, as well as survive in daily life. The functional creation and sustenance of a police state that induced this condition of life and work, and shaped its ethical choices of character and conduct as matters of perseverance and survival, included instruments of surveillance and repression.[116] These were designed to break morale, send opposition underground or into exile, (or to emigrate),[117] and to intimidate and criminalise thought and conduct.[118] Under public security laws passed in the late 1920s and early 1930s, executed under administrative fiat by police, and evidenced by informers, there was little opportunity for what we might understand as judicial review of imposed sanctions. These sanctions included *confine di polizia* (*confino*, or internal exile) through the *ammonizione* (a renewable two year sanction restricting the liberty, movement and occupation of individuals) and the *diffida* (a formal public warning administered to suspects to deter them from dissident 'wrongdoing').[119] Arrest of those whose actions, publications or words continued after a formal warning, or those who simply refused compliance, appeared before a 'special tribunal' with powers of imprisonment.[120]Aspects of forced compliance were also institution specific, for example, the 1931 Fascist Oath of Allegiance for University Professors,[121] which professors were forced to sign, to maintain their roles.

116 See for example, and overview, Cassata 2024; Talbot 2007; Morgan 1999.
117 See for example Baldassar & Pesman 2005; Cresciani 2007.
118 Morgan 1999: 167–169.
119 Morgan 1999: 166.
120 Morgan 1999: 167; Bobbio 2002: 27.
121 Bobbio 2002: 28–36; Giani 2017.

Leone Ginzburg, Natalia Ginzburg's husband, lost his university position in 1934, one of only 13 university professors in Italy who refused to sign the Oath of Allegiance. Bobbio (as noted) did sign, also in 1934, and continued to teach his students and engage in activities, but remained under surveillance and was later arrested.[122] In 1940, under a combination of these laws and the race laws, Natalia and Leone Ginzburg and their three children were removed from their home, lost their property (and Leone his citizenship). They were exiled within their own country (from North to South, Turin to Abruzzo) and subject to police surveillance, political censorship and curtailment. After the Allied invasion and fall of Mussolini, they escaped to Rome, which was subsequently occupied by the Nazis. They went into hiding. Leone Ginzburg was arrested, tortured, and died in prison in Rome in 1944.[123]

Our study gives here the barest details of fascist era laws. Ginzburg and Bobbio's experiences of lives lived under those laws are traumatic personal examples. But because Ginzburg and Bobbio also became the public custodians of their experiences of law through their writing, their stories of time and place are open to be scaled and also read as representative of many undocumented lives. As historian Philip Morgan notes (drawing on his work from the Central Archives of the State):

> 17,000 people [were] sent to *confino* between 1926 and 1943, and about 160,000 appeared in police files over this same period as having received the *ammonizione* or being under special police surveillance and control ... [and to this must be added] the certainly more numerous though unquantifiable cases of those who received the police warning as to their future conduct, the *diffida*.[124]

What becomes important to notice is how shared law *storia* (both stories and histories of Italian life under fascist laws) informed the content of Natalia Ginzburg and Norberto Bobbio's work, as well as its public

122 Bobbio 2002: 31; 33–36.

123 We note that Leone Ginzburg and Natalia Ginzburg were transferred to Rome at different times: Ginzburg 2018: 209–211; Ginzburg 2003: 23, 35–36, 44–45; Ginzburg 1989d: 8. See also Boyers 2000: 18–20, an interview in which Ginzburg discusses the question of her identity as a Jewish person in response to her war time experience, and in context of work by friends, including Primo Levi.

124 Morgan 1999: 167. For a contemporary and widely read account of the machinery and rise of fascism, blending fictional technique with primary sources, see Scurati 2022. See also a review essay relating Scurati to law and jurisprudence scholars working in English: Veitch 2024.

form.[125] What we have drawn through our examples in miniature in the previous sections, and reflect on here, is the more limited question of how these experiences of law also shaped Ginzburg and Bobbio's intellectual and active commitments to a tradition of humanist virtues, and the ways they made constancy, as topic and as studies of character, visible but complex in their writing, over a lifetime.

Our final observation is about writing as a question of training, and comportment when taking up an office. As jurisographers, we aim to make visible patterns of institutional participation with, and inheritance of, the virtue of constancy as expressed in public writing. By examining examples by Bobbio and Ginzburg, we have emphasised that what they argued was required for life in and under the Italian state was also necessary to cultivate and maintain in their writings about it: of law and law teaching (for Bobbio), and of law's experience (for Ginzburg). In each case, they cultivated a constancy in their relationships to institutional life and institutional rebuilding. For both, as noted, they are creators of institutional worlds that opened forms of aesthetic and political production to reflect the changing circumstances in which they lived (at Einaudi for a period, but also over their lives as commentators in major Italian dailies).[126] Both also, albeit in different ways, participated in the engaged life of the intellectual recommended by Croce later in their lives, by acting as officers in the Republic (Bobbio in the Senate,[127] Ginzburg in the Chamber of Deputies).[128] For Bobbio, the forms of institutional work, and by inference and direct evidence, training of others in his lectures, and development of scholarly works of jurisprudence and political philosophy, are at the university, and straightforward institutional duties and placements for us to see and inherit, as university people. For Ginzburg, it was the institution of the family, as subject matter and fable, that mattered for her own commentary on the circumstances of her place and time. The family was indivisible from her expression of constancy and her warnings about its vulnerability. The family as a public institution in these ways relates directly to a world we inhabit and is important to our account. (This is despite the fact that family is an

125 See also personal observation on this point made by the Vittorio Foa (Torinese friend, member of Giustizia and Libertà, and long serving Italian politician) in dialogue with Ginzburg in Ginzburg 2003: 180.

126 Bobbio 2002: 152–160, discussing also public disputes with Craxi, and later Berlusconi; Boyers 2000: 27; Ginzburg 1973; Ginzburg 1990.

127 Bobbio was appointed a Life Senator by President Sandro Pertini in 1984 (Bobbio 2002: 149–152).

128 Ginzburg was elected as an Independent Deputy of the Left, in 1983, and 1987: Jeannet & Katz 2000b: vii; Ginzburg 2003: 50, 177–190.

institution which remains less regarded, or condescended to, as topic and study for those engaged in their university roles.)

Concluding comment

This chapter has been presented as a study of the training into, and discourses of, constancy. Although we have emphasised constancy and the prudence of the offices of the scholar in this exercise, the sources with which we have worked are not silent on justice, courage, temperance, humility and patience. An education or training into a tradition that carries humanist virtues, on the contrary, directs the cultivation of all of these virtues to the proper conduct of the offices of public life (in our iteration, the office of writer and of jurist). The training inherited by Bobbio and Ginzburg, and their Torinese compatriots, drew on sources that emphasised the institutional and collaborative conduct of political, cultural and scholarly life, and helped them realise the constancy of friendship as a political virtue.[129]

Our own obligations to scholarly and institutional offices are not identical, and together they are not identical to those of Norberto Bobbio and Natalia Ginzburg. We are participants in the migration of thought, and this should, we argue, be addressed historiographically and jurisographically. This is a matter of disciplinary conduct: how the conscious placement of jurisprudence (as practical legal wisdom) and justice (as proportional relationship) take their place within humanist traditions. By way of our examples and chosen sources, an inheritance of that tradition, in response to the experience of laws in Italy circa 1940, arrives at a new place – Australia – through forced migration, internment camps and hard labour, as well as through the reception of intellectual resources in universities, publishing houses and, most recently, mass communication (and consumption).

With some licence, then, we have placed our contemporary concerns with the constraints of academic and institutional experiences, and the testing of prudence, into relation with our sources. The practice of presenting our own account of the writings of Bobbio and Ginzburg, and their intellectual inheritance, is part of our own training in the maintenance of constancy of our public roles. This is both technical and ethical. It has involved acknowledging and working with the tension between examples and detail. In our account, it has also involved

129 For examples, see Bobbio 2002: photo plate 18 (no pagination), and 154 where Bobbio notes he wrote an obituary for Natalia Ginzburg); Manni 2022; Ginzburg 2003: 3–38.

training ourselves in how to develop a tone and style that is lucid and disciplined.

In Australia, and Australian law schools, the question of conduct of those who arrive and place themselves, and those who are displaced, is not the same as that confronted by Bobbio and Ginzburg. There can be no assumption of shared offices, or a social bond, available between laws, traditions and peoples in a place that continues to live with colonial conflict. How traditions arrive in such a place, and what they bring and must leave behind, are our resources for an adequate conduct of lawful relations between Indigenous and non-Indigenous knowledges, peoples and laws. From that perspective, one reason for selecting the writing and writers for this study of the virtue of constancy is that they have ethical clarity and an eye for the lived experience of day-to-day life and its relations. They also have a sense of how to find ways to respond to duties of office that cannot be evaded (or worse, sanctified) in times of conflict. This is as true of the offices of writer and jurist as it is of those of advocate and judge.

References

Amoia A 1996 *20th-Century Italian Women Writers: The Feminine Experience* Southern Illinois University Press Carbondale.

Antonietti L 2023 'Reading novels in Einaudi: the case of Natalia Ginzburg. Reading opinions under the scrutiny of Digital Humanities' *Umanistica Digitale* 7/16: 97–123 DOI:10.6092/issn.2532-8816/16821.

Arendt H 1973 'Karl Jaspers: Citizen of the World?' in H Arendt 1973 *Men in Dark Times* Penguin Books Harmondsworth (first published 1955): 84–96.

Baldassar L and Pesman R 2005 *From Paesani to Global Italians: Veneto Migrants in Australia* UWA Publishing Crawley.

Bassi G 2023 *<<Con assoluta sincerità>>: il lavoro editoriale di Natalia Ginzburg (1943–1952)* Firenze University Press Florence.

Bellamy R 1987 *Modern Italian Social Theory: Ideology and Politics from Pareto to the Present* Stanford University Press Stanford.

Bellamy R, Ferrajoli L, Negri T and Zolo D 2004 'The Legacy of Norberto Bobbio: Assessments and Recollections' *Critical Review of International Social and Political Philosophy* 7/3: 67–83 DOI:10.1080/1369823042000269393.

Bobbio N 1948 *The Philosophy of Decadentism: A Study of Existentialism* Trans D Moore Basil Blackwell Oxford.

Bobbio N 1955 *Politica e cultura* Einaudi Turin.

Bobbio N 1990 *Liberalism and Democracy* Trans M Ryle and K Soper Verso London.

Bobbio N 1993 *Thomas Hobbes and the Natural Law Tradition* Trans D Gobetti Chicago University Press Chicago (first published in Italian 1989).

Bobbio N 1995 *Ideological Profile of Twentieth-Century Italy* Trans L G Cochrane Princeton University Press Princeton (first published in Italian 1968).

Bobbio N 1996 *Left and Right: The Significance of a Political Distinction* Trans A Cameron Polity Press Cambridge (first published in Italian 1994).
Bobbio N 2000 *In Praise of Meekness: Essays on Ethnics and Politics* Trans T Chataway Polity Press Cambridge.
Bobbio N 2001 *Old Age and Other Essays* Ed and Trans A Cameron Polity Press Cambridge (first published in Italian 1996).
Bobbio N 2002 *A Political Life* Ed A Papuzzi Trans A Cameron Polity Press Cambridge (first published in Italian 1997).
Bovero M 2005 'Norberto Bobbio (1909–2004): A Short Guide to a Great Work' *Ratio Juris* 18/2: 271–284 DOI:10.1111/j.1467-9337.2005.00298.x.
Boyers P 2000 'An Interview with Natalia Ginzburg' (first published in Italian 1992) in Jeannet et al 2000c: 10–31 DOI:10.3138/9781442677579-006.
Bull M 2013 *Inventing Falsehood, Making Truth: Vico and Neapolitan Painting* Princeton University Press Princeton.
Bullock A 1991*Natalia Ginzburg: Human Relationships in a Changing World* Berg New York.
Calogero G 1958 'Benedetto Croce: Philosopher and Humanist of Modern Italy' *The Atlantic* Boston 1 December <https://www.theatlantic.com/magazine/archive/1958/12/benedetto-croce-philosopher-and-humanist-of-modern-italy/641074/>.
Calvino I 1997 'In Memory of Roland Barthes' in I Calvino 1997 *The Literature Machine: Essays* Trans P Creagh Vintage London (first published in Italian 1980): 300–306.
Calvino I 2016 'Lightness' in I Calvino 2016 *Six Memos for the Next Millennium* Trans G Brock Penguin Classics London (first published in Italian 1988): 3–35.
Cassata F 2024 *Racism and Antisemitism in Fascist Italy: The Politics, Ideology, and Imagery of 'La Difesa della razza'* Trans S Oglethorpe Routledge London (first published in Italian 2008) DOI:10.4324/9781032675701.
Castronuovo N 2010 *Natalia Ginzburg: Jewishness as moral identity* Troubador Publishing Leicester.
Chataway T 1997 'Introduction to Norberto Bobbio' *Thesis Eleven* 48/1: 111—112 DOI:10.1177/0725513697048000007.
Chataway T 2002 'Introduction' in Bobbio 2002: 1–10.
Chataway T 2011 'Norberto Bobbio (1909-2004) and Law: A Centennial Tribute' *Studies in Law, Politics, and Society* 55: 173–202 DOI:10.1108/S1059-4337(2011)0000055010.
Cicioni M and Formica D 2006 'Translating Idiolects: Natalia Ginzburg's "Lessico Famigliare"' *Monash University Linguistics Papers* 5/1: 17–25.
Cotterrell R 2024 'Radical Legal Pluralism in the Shadow of Fascism (Romano)' in R Cotterrell 2024 *Jurispriudence and Socio-Legal Studies* Routledge Abingdon: 130–146.
Craiutu A 2017 *Faces of Moderation: The Art of Balance in an Age of Extremes* University of Pennsylvania Press Philadelphia.
Cresciani G 2007 'Refractory Migrants. Fascist Surveillance on Italians in Australia, 1922–1943' *Italian Historical Society Journal* 15: 9–58.
Croce B 1913 *The Philosophy of Giambattista Vico* Trans R G Collingwood Russell & Russell Clark Edinburgh (first published in Italian 1911).

Croce B 1932 *Storia d'Europa: Nel Secolo Decimonono* Editori Laterza Bari.
Curthoys A and Docker J 2006 *Is History Fiction?* University of New South Wales Press Sydney.
Davidson A 1995 'Dilemma of Liberal Socialism: The Case of Norberto Bobbio' *Australian Journal of Politics & History* 41/1: 47–54 DOI:10.1111/j.1467-8497.1995.tb01335.x.
Davidson A 1998 'Norberto Bobbio, liberal socialism and the problem of language' *Citizenship Studies* 2/2: 223–245 DOI:10.1080/13621029808420680.
De Montaigne M 2003 *The Complete Essays* Trans M A Screech Penguin London (first published 1991).
Drake R 1982 'Decadence, Decadentism and Decadent Romanticism in Italy: Toward a Theory of Décadence' *Journal of Contemporary History* 17/1: 69–92.
Ergun E, Kripper D, Meï S, Russell S J, Rutkowski S, Shread C and Solberg I H 2020 'Women (re)writing authority: A roundtable discussion on feminist translation' in L von Flotow and H Kamal eds 2020 *The Routledge Handbook of Translation, Feminism and Gender* Routledge London: 5–14.
Ferrante E 2012 *My Brilliant Friend* Trans A Goldstein Europa Editions New York.
Ferrante E 2013 *The Story of a New Name* Trans A Goldstein Europa Editions New York.
Ferrante E 2014 *Those Who Leave and Those Who Stay* Trans A Goldstein Europa Editions New York.
Ferrante E 2015 *The Story of the Lost* Child Trans A Goldstein Europa Editions New York.
Ferrari V 2004 'The Firm Subtleties of a Philosopher in "Everlasting Doubt": Remembering Norberto Bobbio' *Journal of Law & Society* 31/4: 578–591 DOI:10.1111/j.1467-6478.2004.00304.x.
Fontanella L 2000 'Natalia Ginzburg between Fiction and Memory: A Reading of *Le voci della sera* and *Lessicio famigliare*' in Jeannet et al 2000c: 32–45 DOI:10.3138/9781442677579-007.
Francese J 2009 'On Justice and Liberty in Natalia Ginzburg's Non-Fictional Writings' *Quaderni d'Italianistica* 30/1: 147–168 DOI:10.33137/q.i.. v30i1.8430.
Franco T 2024 'Publishing Natalia Ginzburg in the Anglophone World' in S M Rousseva and S E Ziolkowski eds 2024 *Natalia Ginzburg's Global Legacies* Palgrave Macmillan Cham: 17–37 DOI:10.1007/978-3-031-49907-4_2.
Fumaroli M 2018 *The Republic of Letters* Trans L Vergnaud Yale University Press New Haven (first published 2015).
Garin E 1974 *Intellettuali Italiani del XX Secolo* Editori Riuniti Rome.
Garofalo P, Leake E and Renga D 2019 *Internal exile in Fascist Italy: History and representations of* confino Manchester University Press Manchester.
Genovese A 2022 *Feminist Jurisography: Law, History, Writing* Routledge London DOI:10.4324/9780429461132.
Genovese A and McKinnon C 2025 'Lawful Relations: archive, agency, consent' in A Aitkin and K McFarlane eds 2025 *Consent, a Reader* Perimeter Editions and the Potter Museum of Art Melbourne (forthcoming).

Genovese A and McVeigh S 2015 'Nineteen eighty three: A jurisographic report on *Commonwealth v Tasmania*' *Griffith Law Review* 24/1: 68–88 DOI:10.1080/10383441.2015.1022891.

Genovese A and McVeigh S 2024 'Jurisography (A Report on Cultural Legal Study, Australia)' in K Crawley, T Giddens and T D Peters eds 2024 *The Routledge Handbook of Cultural Legal Studies* Routledge London: 108–122 DOI:10.4324/9781003467762-9.

Giani S 2017 'The Italian university professors' oath of allegiance to fascism (1931)' University of Amsterdam Amsterdam viewed 25 May 2025 <https://blognostrumuva.wordpress.com/2017/04/11/the-italian-university-professors-oath-of-allegiance-to-fascism-1931/>.

Ginzburg N 1963 *Lessico Famigliare* Einaudi Turin.

Ginzburg N 1973 *Never Must You Ask Me* Trans I Quigly Michael Joseph London (first published in Italian 1970).

Ginzburg N 1989a 'England: Eulogy and Lament' in N Ginzburg 1989 *The Little Virtues* Trans D Davis Arcade Publishing New York (first published in Italian 1962): 21–28.

Ginzburg N 1989b 'My Vocation' in N Ginzburg 1989 *The Little Virtues* Trans D Davis Arcade Publishing New York (first published in Italian 1962): 53–68.

Ginzburg N 1989c 'The Little Virtues' in N Ginzburg 1989 *The Little Virtues* Trans D Davis Arcade Publishing New York (first published in Italian 1962): 97–110.

Ginzburg N 1989d 'Winter in the Abruzzi' in N Ginzburg 1989 *The Little Virtues* Trans D Davis Arcade Publishing New York (first published in Italian 1962): 3–8.

Ginzburg N 1990 *Serena Cruz o la vera giustizia* Einaudi Turin.

Ginzburg N 2000a 'Chiarezza' Trans D Ward (first published in Italian 1944) in Jeannet et al 2000c: 230–233 DOI:10.3138/9781442677579-017.

Ginzburg N 2000b 'I nostri figli' Trans D Ward (first published in Italian 1944) in Jeannet et al 2000c: 226–229 DOI:10.3138/9781442677579-016.

Ginzburg N 2003 *It's Hard to Talk about Yourself* Ed C Garboli and L Ginzburg Trans L Quirke University of Chicago Press Chicago (first published in Italian 1999).

Ginzburg N 2018 *Family Lexicon* Trans J McPhee Daunt Books Publishing London (first published in Italian 1963).

Goodrich P 2017a 'The International Signs Law' in A Orford and F Hoffmann with M Clark eds 2017 *The Oxford Handbook of the Theory of International Law* Oxford University Press Oxford: 365–385 DOI:10.1093/law/9780198701958.003.0019.

Goodrich P 2017b 'Who Are We?: Persona, Office, Suspicion, and Critique' in J Desautels-Stein and C Tomlins eds 2017 *Searching for Contemporary Legal Thought* Cambridge University Press Cambridge: 43–60 DOI:10.1017/9781316584361.003.

Gordon R S C 2001 *Primo Levi's Ordinary Virtues: From Testimony to Ethics* Oxford University Press Oxford.

Hadot P 1995 *Philosophy as a Way of Life: Spiritual Exercises from Socrates to Foucault* Ed A I Davidson Trans M Chase Blackwell Publishing Malden (first published 1981).

Jeannet A M 2000 'Natalia Ginzburg: Making a Story Out of History' in Jeannet et al 2000c: 63–88 DOI:10.3138/9781442677579-009.
Jeannet A M and Katz G 2000a 'Chronology' in Jeannet et al 2000: xi–xiii DOI:10.3138/9781442677579-003.
Jeannet A M and Katz G 2000b 'Editors' Foreword' in Jeannet et al 2000: vii–ix DOI:10.3138/9781442677579-001.
Jeannet A M and Katz G eds 2000c *Natalia Ginzburg: A Voice of the Twentieth Century* University of Toronto Press Toronto DOI:10.3138/9781442677579.
Körner A 2011 'The Experience of Time as Crisis. On Croce's and Benjamin's Concept of History' *Intellectual History Review* 21/2: 151–169.
Lacchè L 2017 'On the Italian Style: The Eclectic Canon and the Relationship of Theory to Practice as Key-Elements of Italian Legal Culture (19th-20th Centuries)' *Journal of Constitutional History* 34/2: 263–280.
Lafer C 2022 'The School of Thought of Norberto Bobbio in Brazil' in M Sellers and S Kirste eds 2023 *Encyclopedia of the Philosophy of Law and Social Philosophy* Springer Dordrecht: 1–5 DOI:10.1007/978-94-007-6730-0_78-4.
Lipsius J 2004 *Politica: Six Books of Politics or Political Instruction* Ed and Trans J Waszink Royal Van Gorcum Assen (first published 1589).
Lipsius J 2006 *On Constancy* Ed J Sellars Trans J Stradling Bristol Phoenix Press Exeter (first published 1584).
Lomonaco F 2017 *Tracing the Path of Giambattista Vico's Universal Right* Mimesis International Milan.
Manni F 2022 'Norberto Bobbio and Benedetto Croce' *Journal of Italian Philosophy* 5: 130–170.
Manni F 2023 'The Absolute Historicism of Benedetto Croce: Its Birth, Meaning, and Fate' *Humanitas* 36/2: 62–84 DOI:10.5840/humanitas202336210.
McCrea A 1997 *Constant Minds: Political Virtue and the Lipsian Paradigm in England, 1584–1650* Eds P Christiansen, C Slights and D R Woolf University of Toronto Press Toronto DOI:10.3138/9781442673281.
McMillan M, Foster D, Genovese A, McVeigh S and Tehan M 2021 'Obligations of Conduct: Public Law – Treaty Advice' *Melbourne University Law Review* 44/2: 602–633.
McVeigh S 2016 'Jurisprudent of London: Arts of Association' *Law Text Culture* 20/1: 189–215 DOI:10.2139/ssrn.3169144.
Minson J 1993 *Questions of Conduct: Sexual Harassment Citizenship Government* Palgrave Macmillan London DOI:10.1007/978-1-349-22882-9.
Minson J 2014 'How to Speak Well of the State: A Rhetoric of Civil Prudence' *UC Irvine Law Review* 4/1: 437–470.
Morgan P 1999 '"The years of consent"? Popular attitudes and forms of resistance to Fascism in Italy, 1925–1940' in T Kirk and A McElligott eds 1999 *Opposing Fascism: Community, Authority and Resistance in Europe* Cambridge University Press Cambridge: 163–179.
Parks T 2018 'Introduction' in Ginzburg 2018: vii–xv.
Poggi F and Ferraro F 2024 'From the ideal legislator to the competent speaker: uncovering the deception in legislative intent' *Jurisprudence* 15/4: 464–481 DOI:10.1080/20403313.2024.2321028.

Ratti G B 2024 'The Oxbridge-Turin Connection: From Peano and Russell to Bobbio and Hart' *Rivista di Storia dell'Università di Torino* 13/2: 103–112 DOI:10.13135/2281-2164/11572.

Rousseva S M and Ziolkowski S E 2024 'Introduction: Global Ginzburg—Reading Natalia Ginzburg in the Twenty-First Century' in S M Rousseva and S E Ziolkowski eds 2024 *Natalia Ginzburg's Global Legacies* Palgrave Macmillan Cham: 1–14 DOI:10.1007/978-3-031-49907-4_1.

Salatini R and Barreira C eds 2017 *Aurora* 10/1.

Santos E ed 2004 *Prisma Jurídico* 3.

Scarpa D 2015 'Le strade di Natalia Ginzburg' in N Ginzburg 2015 *Le Piccole Virtù* Ed D Scarpa Einaudi Turin (first published in Italian 1962): xi–xxxix.

Scarpato G 2019 'Tra giusnaturalismo e storicismo' in M Griffo ed 2019 *Norberto Bobbio: Filosofo del Diritto, Filosofo della Politica, Storico del Pensiero Politico* Licosia Edizioni Ogliastro Cilento: 227–242.

Schaeffer J 2020 *Giambattista Vico on Natural Law: Rhetoric, Religion and Sensus Communis* Routledge New York.

Schor N 1987 *Reading in Detail: Aesthetics and the Feminine* Methuen New York.

Schwartz C 2024 'Born Untranslatable? On the Translation, Reception and Transnational Circulation of Ginzburg's *Family Lexicon*' in S M Rousseva and S E Ziolkowski eds 2024 *Natalia Ginzburg's Global Legacies* Palgrave Macmillan Cham: 65–88 DOI:10.1007/978-3-031-49907-4_4.

Sciara G 2022 'The genesis of Bobbio's liberalism (1939–1955): between classics old and new' *Journal of Political Ideologies* 27/3: 250–269 DOI:10.1080/13569317.2022.2129214.

Screech M A 1984 *Montaigne & Melancholy: The Wisdom of the Essays* Penguin London (first published 1983).

Scurati A 2021 *M: Son of the Century* Trans A M Appel 4th Estate London (first published in Italian 2018).

Talbot G 2007 *Censorship in Fascist Italy, 1922–43: Policies, Procedures and Protagonists* Palgrave Macmillan London DOI:10.1057/9780230222854.

Tuck R 1993 *Philosophy and Government 1572–1651* Cambridge University Press Cambridge DOI:10.1017/CBO9780511558634.

Urbinati N 2003 'Liberalism in the Cold War: Norberto Bobbio and the dialogue with the PCI' *Journal of Modern Italian Studies* 8/4: 578–603 DOI:10.1080/1354571032000147773.

Veitch S 2024 'M – Son of the Century' *International Journal of Law in Context* 20/3: 423–427 DOI:10.1017/S1744552324000053.

Verdicchio M 2017 *A Croce Reader: Aesthetics, Philosophy, History, and Literary Criticism* University of Toronto Press Toronto.

Verene D P 1981 *Vico's Science of Imagination* Cornell University Press London.

Vico G 2000 *Universal Right* Ed and Trans G Pinton and M Diehl Rodopi Amsterdam.

Ward D 1996 *Antifascisms: Cultural Politics in Italy, 1943–46: Benedetto Croce and the Liberals, Carlo Levi and the "Actionists"* Associated University Presses Cranbury.

Ward D 2000 'Natalia Ginzburg's Early Writings in *L'Italia libera*' in Jeannet et al 2000c: 46–62 DOI:10.3138/9781442677579-008.

Ward D 2025 'Carlo Levi and Piero Gobetti' *Forum Italicum* DOI:10.1177/00145858241308279.

West R 2000 'Introduction' in Jeannet et al 2000c: 3–9 DOI:10.3138/9781442677579-005.

White H 1987 *The Content of the Form: Narrative Discourse and Historical Representation* The John Hopkins University Press Baltimore.

Wienstein J 2000 'The Eloquence of Understatement: Natalia Ginzburg's Public Image and Literary Style' in Jeannet et al 2000c: 179–196 DOI:10.3138/9781442677579-014.

Zolo D 1990 'Personalismo' in N Bobbio 1990 *Dizionario di politica* Eds N Bobbio, N Matteucci and G Pasquino Tascabili degli Editori Associati Milan (first published in Italian 1976): 787–788.

Index